Two Treatises of Philo of Alexandria

Number 25

TWO TREATISES OF PHILO OF ALEXANDRIA
A Commentary on De Gigantibus and Quod Deus Sit Immutabilis

David Winston and John Dillon

Two Treatises of Philo of Alexandria

A Commentary on De Gigantibus and Quod Deus Sit Immutabilis

by
David Winston
and
John Dillon

Scholars Press
Chico, California

TWO TREATISES OF PHILO OF ALEXANDRIA

A Commentary on De Gigantibus and Quod Deus Sit Immutabilis

by

David Winston and John Dillon

©1983
Brown University

Publication of this book is made possible in part by a grant from the National Endowment for the Humanities. Published results and interpretations do not necessarily represent the views of the Endowment.

Library of Congress Cataloging in Publication Data

Winston, David, 1927–
   Two treatises of Philo of Alexandria.

  (Brown Judaic studies ; no. 25) (ISSN 0147–927X)
  1. Philo, of Alexandria. De gigantibus. 2. Philo of Alexandria. Quod Deus sit immutabilis. 3. Bible. O.T. Genesis VI, 1–12—Commentaries. 4. Philosophy, Ancient. 5. Philosophy, Jewish. I. Dillon, John M. II. Title. III. Series.
BS1235.P483W56   181'.06   82–786
ISBN 0–89130–563–7   AACR2

Printed in the United States of America

CONTENTS

PREFACE

The present commentary originated in a National Endowment for the Humanities sponsored project (1976-78) entitled:
Philo of Alexandria, An Interdisciplinary Study in the Fusion
and Diffusion of Cultural Traditions. The principal investi-
gators were the undersigned, and the purpose was to attain, by
means of an interdisciplinary team approach, new and more
detailed insights into the immediate sources and true nature of
Philo's work. The pair of treatises *De Gigantibus--Quod Deus*
were chosen for the production of a detailed commentary on a
representative section of the Philonic corpus to serve as a
paradigm for the type of commentary which we felt was needed.
The Greek text was divided into a series of segments, and each
of us wrote a commentary on those segments assigned to him. The
commentary consisted of two parts: (a) general comments on the
segment as a whole, and (b) detailed line-by-line commentary.
We then read and revised each other's work. Each segment upon
completion was mailed out to a team of scholars who reviewed it
in the light of their respective specialties. The following
are the members of the team: D. Gooding, J. Leopold, and
V. Nikiprowetzky. B. Bokser and R. T. Wallis also commented
on a number of segments. As it turned out, Nikiprowetzky wrote
a detailed commentary on our commentary, which required us to
make a thorough revision of the whole. In the light of this,
we have deemed it appropriate to include his name as one of the
authors of the commentary. The introduction is a composite containing components contributed by Thomas Conley, John Dillon,
David Gooding, John Leopold, Valentin Nikiprowetzky, Richard
Wallis, and David Winston. Each author is responsible for his
own contribution to the introduction, and no attempt has been
made by the editors to harmonize the various views expressed.
The enormous diversity of Philo's learning and the intri-
cate problems involved in the comprehension of his thought cannot
properly be appreciated except by the sort of close work on at
least a segment of his text represented by the present commentary.

While the treatment of anything like his whole *oeuvre* with the
detailed care which we have devoted to this portion of it would
be beyond the resources of all but a large team, the present
work, we feel, points the way to such an enterprise. We are
extremely grateful to the National Endowment for the Humanities
for making it possible through their research grant. The findings and conclusions presented here do not necessarily represent
the view of the Endowment. We are also very grateful to Irene
and Dani Winston and Professor John Leopold for helping in the
preparation of the indices.

David Winston
John Dillon

INTRODUCTION

I.   THE FORM OF PHILO'S COMMENTARY

A. *L'Exégèse de Philon d'Alexandrie dans le* De Gigantibus
et le Quod Deus sit Immutabilis

  Pour qui désire étudier l'exégèse de Philon, *De Gigantibus* et *Quod Deus sit Immutabilis* offrent une plate-forme d'observ-
vation particulièrement commode et significative. En effet,
lorsqu'on lit ces deux écrits, on aperçoit dans une lumière
singulièrement vive la plupart des problèmes majeurs qui jalon-
nent cette recherche.

I. *Sur la Structure et sur le titre des deux traités*

  La première question qui se pose comme d'elle-même est
de savoir s'il est seulement légitime de parler ici de *deux
traités*. Le *De Gigantibus* ne se termine ni par une conclusion
en forme ni par un signe de ponctuation fermant.

  Après avoir noté avec "le très saint Moïse" que le
φαῦλος, dépourvu de maison, de cité, instable, est un transfuge
et un déserteur, par contraste avec l'allié très fidèle qu'est
le σπουδαῖος, Philon poursuit par les lignes suivantes: τοσαῦτα
εἰς γε τὸ παρὸν ἀρκούντως περὶ τῶν γιγάντων εἰρηκότες ἐπὶ τὰ
ἀκόλουθα τοῦ λόγου τρεψώμεθα. Ἔστι δὲ ταῦτα·

  "Ayant parlé suffisamment pour l'instant des géants,
tournons-nous vers la suite du texte. Or, la voici: "

  C'est donc peu dire que d'affirmer qu'il n'y a aucune
frontière entre les deux traités. Il faut souligner encore que
le premier d'entre eux ne se suffit pas à lui-même et qu'il
suppose et appelle l'existence du second.[1]

  Une deuxième constatation, peut-être plux surprenante
encore que la première, a trait au titre des deux écrits. Dans
le *De Gigantibus* il n'est parlé proprement des géants que dans
les dix derniers paragraphes d'un texte qui en comporte soixante
sept. Le problème de l'immutabilité divine n'est, dans le *Quod
Deus sit Immutabilis*, discuté qu'aux paragraphes vingt à soixante douze. En d'autres termes, l'auteur ne lui consacre que
cinquante deux paragraphes sur les cent quatre-vingt trois que
compte le traité. Les titres ne correspondent donc que d'une
manière très imparfaite et partielle au contenu respectif des

textes qu'ils désignent. On est tenté d'évoquer à leur propos
les titres des différents livres du Pentateuque hébraïque. Aucun
d'entre eux, on le sait, ne suggère la moindre idée concrète du
texte qu'il annonce. Il n'en est que le mot initial.

En fait, les titres des deux traités qui nous occupent
sont plus significatifs.

L'apparition des Géants constitue le résultat ultime du
procès qui est décrit dans l'ensemble des parties précédentes.
Ils sont nommés au terme d'une sorte de gradation exégétique et
le titre du *De Gigantibus* se trouve de la sorte n'être pas entièrement arbitraire. Quant aux dix neuf premiers paragraphes
du *Quod Deus Sit Immutabilis* qui proposent l'exégèse de la fin
d'un verset dont le début est commenté dans la partie qui termine
le traité précédent, ils constituent une matière intermédiaire
entre les deux écrits. En effet, comme le note Philon lui-même
en *Deus* 2, dans le *De Gigantibus* il était question de l'impossibilité où se trouve le πνεῦμα divin de reposer en permanence sur
une âme qui s'étant liée à la chair, à ses fonctions et à ses
passions, est devenue nombreuse, multiforme et divisée. Après
l'humanité vulgaire et multiple avec laquelle forme contraste
l'unicité du juste Noé, apparait, suscitée par l'union des âmes
incorporelles et des filles, c'est-à-dire des passions, des
hommes, la génération des géants, gens de la terre et ennemis
de Dieu. Le début du *Quod Deus* précise que les géants se manifestent lorsque l'Esprit saint quittant l'âme en livre l'accès
aux compagnons des ténèbres et leur permet en fécondant les
passions, d'engendrer pour eux-mêmes et non pour Dieu.

Après avoir évoqué la fécondité philautique des géants
et lui avoir opposé celle d'Abraham et d'Anne, Philon, conformément à la suite du texte sacré, aborde le commentaire de la
réaction divine au spectacle du mal et se heurte au redoutable
problème de l'anthropopathie que l'Ecriture attribue à la
divinité, et à la question de savoir s'il est légitime de penser
que le démiurge, à la vue du mal dont ils étaient les fauteurs,
s'est repenti d'avoir créé les hommes et a médité de détruire
le genre humain tout entier: ὅτι ἐπὶ τῇ γενέσει τῶν ἀνθρώπων
ὁ δημιουργὸς μετέγνω κατιδὼν τὴν ἀσέβειαν αὐτῶν, ἧς χάριν ἐβου-
λήθη σύμπαν διαφθεῖραι τὸ γένος (*Deus* 21).

Il est donc légitime de considérer que le titre du *Quod
Deus* réfère à la partie du traité qui, aux yeux de Philon, était
exégétiquement la plus difficile, la plus importante et la plus
caractéristique. On pourrait même, dans ces conditions,

soutenir qu'il existe, entre *Deus* 1-19 d'une part et 20-72
d'autre part, le même rapport qu'entre *De Gigantibus* 1-57 et
58-67. Mais la suite du *Quod Deus* semble n'entretenir plus
aucun lien logique avec le thème de l'immutabilité de Dieu. Si
bien, qu'en définitive, la description la plus adéquate du *De
Gigantibus* et du *Quod Deus* serait celle qui les présenterait
comme deux commentaires suivis ou perpétuels des versets de
Genèse VI, 1-4 a pour le premier et de 4 b-12 pour le second,
sans frontière clairement tracée entre eux et sans véritable
unité externe ni interne.

II.   *Le problème de la composition dans De Gigantibus
        et Quod Deus*

        Dès que l'on veut aller plus loin que cette première
impression, on rencontre un problème qui lui est lié et qui constitue l'une des grandes énigmes de l'étude de Philon.[2] En
effet autant que l'oeuvre même et la pensée de Philon, sa façon
d'écrire et de composer a provoqué des jugements abruptement
contradictoires, soit sévères jusqu'au mépris soit favorables
jusqu'à l'enthousiasme. Nous en rappellerons quelques uns par
souci de clarté. Pour E. Herriot, "Philon ne pratique pas l'art
de composer. . . . se soucie peu de la vraie logique, de la
vraie méthode et de la rigueur dans les déductions." "Philon
ne sait pas composer," affirme de son côté J. Martin. W. Bousset
se plaint des perpétuelles répétitions, des longueurs, de la
monotonie de plomb qui font de la lecture de Philon une véritable
torture. G. Trotti déplore "le manque d'ordre et de méthode dans
l'exposition des commentaires . . . du Pentateuque, les longues
et oiseuses digressions, les diverses contradictions et confu-
sions." Völker reproche à l'Alexandrin toute une série de
défauts dans l'art d'écrire--dont une composition capricieuse--,
qui, avec la meilleure volonté, rendent impossible de découvrir
le plan d'un traité de Philon. F. H. Colson au contraire estime
que l'on peut y parvenir. Néanmoins, il souligne, lui aussi,
l'extraordinaire enchevêtrement de la pensée de notre auteur et
il avoue qu'il a constitué les sommaires dont il a fait précéder
chaque traité de Philon dans la Bibliothèque Loeb autant pour
s'y diriger lui-même que pour y guider les pas de son lecteur.
        Avec ces appréciations qui refusent à Philon toute
science de la composition ou qui soulignent la complexité de sa
démarche contraste d'une manière radicale le jugement de L.
Massebieau. Massebieau souligne, en effet, que Philon compose

avec un art consommé.   "Peu d'hommes, écrit-il, . . . ont connu
mieux que lui l'art de composer et ont divisé plus logiquement
leurs ouvrages."   Philon "a eu la passion de l'ordre"; ses oeuvres
"sont remarquables par la clarté et l'harmonie de leur archi-
tecture."

　　　　Qu'en est-il, en fait? Si l'on jette un coup d'oeil sur
le sommaire que les éditions modernes[3] proposent pour nos deux
traités, l'on est très fortement tenté de donner raison aux
auteurs qui jugent d'une façon négative l'art de composer chez
Philon. Il est impossible pour un lecteur qui ne connaîtrait
pas le texte de Philon et chercherait à s'en faire une idée
préalable, d'appréhender une pensée continue, cohérente et
logique dans ces sommaires. L'impression qui domine est celle
d'une poussière de thèmes se succédant d'une manière tout à fait
arbitraire, sans ordre et sans cohésion. Mais la seconde réflexion amène à se demander s'il est équitable d'imputer ces
défauts à Philon et s'il ne serait pas plus juste d'en faire
porter la responsabilité à ses éditeurs. En effet, l'obscurité
de l'analyse et l'atomisation du texte sont le résultat du fait
que l'on a négligé le fil conducteur, la trame véritable, la
forme essentielle et, si l'on nous passe l'expression, la
cellule mère des développements exégétiques philoniens, à savoir
la *quaestio* suivie de sa *solutio*.

　　　　Quelle que soit la situation chronologique des *Questions
sur la Genèse* ou des *Questions sur l'Exode* par rapport au grand
Commentaire sur le Pentateuque de Philon, il ne faut jamais,
lorsque l'on lit ou l'on étudie ce dernier, perdre de vue la
structure de ces précieux recueils.[4] En effet, que les *Quaestiones* aient constitué la forme primitive des traités de Philon
ou, en quelque manière, les "cahiers" et le "journal exégétique"[5] du philosophe, les traités du *Commentaire*, qu'ils appartiennent à sa partie *cosmopoétique*, à sa partie *généalogique* ou
a sa partie *nomothétique*, ne sont essentiellement qu'une suite
de "questions" liées en un discours suivi. La progression du
développement y est produite par le passage d'une "question" a
une "question" nouvelle et non par l'exposé d'une pensée systématique. Négliger cela et tenter une analyse synthétique des
écrits de Philon en s'efforçant d'y retrouver des idées con-
stituées *a priori* c'est se condamner à déboucher sur des sommaires aussi peu satisfaisants que ceux que les trois éditeurs
ont établis pour le *De Gigantibus* et le *Quod Deus Sit Immutabilis*. Le logique reparait au contraire dès que l'on ne se

contente pas de résumer les "idées" de Philon, mais que l'on
isole apories exégétiques auxquelles le texte de Philon prétend
apporter une solution, bref lorsque l'on prend soin de ramener
le texte aux *quaestiones* qu'il met en oeuvre.

III. *Essai d'une analyse du De Gigantibus et du
       Quod Deus sit Immutabilis*

        Nous tenterons de proposer ici une analyse des deux
traités de Philon en mettant en oeuvre la méthode que nous venons
de décrire et que nous préconisons.

        A. *De Gigantibus*

                    Quaestio et Solutio I: §1-§5

§1. *Le Lemme Scripturaire.* Gen 6, 1. καὶ δὴ ἐγένετο, ἡνίκα
ἤρξαντο οἱ ἄνθρωποι πολλοὶ γίνεσθαι ἐπὶ τῆς γῆς, καὶ θυγατέρες
ἐγεννήθησαν αὐτοῖς.
        "Et il arriva que lorsque les hommes commencèrent à
devenir nombreux sur terre et que des filles leur naquirent."

        Quaestio: Ἄξιον οἶμαι διαπορῆσαι, διὰ τί μετὰ τὴν Νῶε καὶ
τῶν υἱῶν αὐτοῦ γένεσιν εἰς πολυανθρωπίαν ἐπιδίδωσι ἡμῶν τὸ γένος.
        "Mérite, à mon avis, d'être considérée comme une diffi-
culté la question de savoir pourquoi après la naissance de Noé
et de ses fils notre espèce s'accroît jusqu'à former une population nombreuse."
        La naissance de Noé et de ses trois fils est mentionnée
en Genèse 5:28, 29, 32. Dans ce dernier verset, il est spécifié
que Noé était âgé de cinq cents ans lorsqu'il engendra Sem, Cham
et Japhet. Philon considère en bloc la naissance de Noé et de
ses fils et il entend le verset de Gen. 6, 1 comme constituant
une suite immédiate de Genèse 5, 32 auquel il se réfère d'une
manière globale, en quelque sorte, comme s'il consignait la
naissance de Noé et de ses fils. L'aporie naît d'une lecture
qui fait de l'accroissement du nombre des hommes une conséquence
immédiate de la naissance du patriarche et de ses fils.

        §1. *Solutio* Ἀλλ' ἴσως οὐ χαλεπὸν ἀποδοῦναι τὴν αἰτίαν.
"Mais peut être n'est-il pas difficile d'en donner la raison."
Philon invoque *un principe logique*: ce qui est *rare* fait
apparaître son opposé fort commun.

§2.   Application de ce principe au domaine humain.   La
rareté des qualités intellectuelles révèle chez les hommes l'abon-
dance des défauts jusqu'ici latents.

§3.   Le terme ἐπεσκιασμένην entraîne la métaphore du
soleil qui, unique, révèle, en les dissipant, *d'innombrables*
ténèbres.   De même la naissance de Noé et de ses fils révèle
décidément le grand nombre des méchants, les contraires s'éclai-
rant mutuellement.

§4.   Après avoir résolu l'aporie de l'accroîssement
soudain des hommes, consécutif à la naissance de Noé et de ses
fils, Philon est tenu de prouver qu'il est bien question dans
le lemme scripturaire d'une opposition entre le juste unique et
la foule des injustes.   Il s'attache donc à commenter désormais
la dernière partie du lemme: θυγατέρες ἐγεννήθησαν αὐτοῖς.   Il
s'agit bien entendu d'engendrements spirituels.   Aucun injuste
n'est capable de faire concevoir à son âme de descendance mâle.
Elle ne donne que les fruits efféminés du vice et des passions.

§5.   La démonstration est donc achevée.   Philon paraphrase la lemme dans le sens de son exégèse. . . . οὗ χάριν
θυγατέρας οἱ ἄνθρωποι οὗτοι γεννῆσαι λέγονται, υἱὸν δὲ οὐδεὶς
αὐτῶν . . . θηλυτόκος ἡ κατὰ τοὺς πολλοὺς ἀδικία πάντως ἀναφαί-
νεται.

Quaestio et Solutio II: §6-§18

§6.   *Le Lemme Scripturaire.*   Gen 6, 2.   Ἰδόντες δὲ οἱ ἄγγελοι
τοῦ θεοῦ τὰς θυγατέρας τῶν ἀνθρώπων ὅτι καλαί εἰσιν, ἔλαβον
ἑαυτοῖς γυναῖκας ἀπὸ πασῶν, ὧν ἐξελέξαντο.
        "Les anges de Dieu voyant que les filles des hommes
étaient belles se prirent des femmes parmi toutes celles qu'ils
choisirent."

§6.   *Quaestio*

     Il n'y a d'autre lien entre cette partie et la partie
précédente que celui qui est fourni par le texte scripturaire
commenté.   Les apories qui forment la *quaestio* ne sont pas
introduites d'une façon technique, et partant, aussi nettement
que dans la *Quaestio et Solutio* précédentes.   Il faut formuler
ici la *Quaestio* en la construisant à partir de la *solutio* qui
en résout les difficultés.

La valeur allégorique de τὰς θυγατέρας τῶν ἀνθρώπων ayant été établie dans la partie précédente, ce qui fait difficulté ici c'est l'idée que des anges de Dieu aient pu épouser les filles des hommes qu'ils s'étaient choisies. L'allégorisation de "filles des hommes" rend impossible l'interprétation mythologique que la Bible suggère et que l'on rencontrera par exemple dans le *Livre des Jubilés* V, 1; I *Hénoch*, VI, 1, 2; VII, 5; X, 12; LXXXIX, 3, mais qui est totalement incompatible avec la nature même de l'exégèse de Philon. Mais alors comment peut-on entendre que des *anges de Dieu* aient *épousé* les *passions* des hommes?

Solutio

§6. L'élément de la réponse est fourni dès le §6 où Philon pose l'équation à trois termes: δαίμονες = ἄγγελοι = ψυχαί. Le terme le plus important de l'équation est le troisième. Il permettra d'établir que les "anges de Dieu" dont il s'agit sont simplement des âmes, répandues dans les airs, qui ont opté pour la vie incarnée.

§7. La proposition que l'air est peuplé d'âmes ne doit pas, à son tour, être considérée comme une imagination mythique. Toutes les parties de l'Univers sont peuplées d'êtres animés—non pas d'âmes comme l'écrit à tort A. Mosès dans son sous-titre—, qui sont propres à chacune d'elles, terre, eau, feu, éther.

§8. Les astres, habitants de ce dernier élément, sont de purs intellects comme le prouve leur mouvement circulaire.
L'air contient donc obligatoirement des "animaux" qui lui sont particuliers et qui comme lui sont invisibles.

§9. Mais le raisonnement supplée ici à la vue impuissante. L'air et le souffle sont le principe de vie de tous les animaux tant terrestres qu'aquatiques.

§10. La durée et la qualité de la vie dépendent de la qualité de l'air.

§11. L'air qui impartit la vie à tous les êtres ne saurait ne pas contenir d'âmes. Au contraire, par un privilège insigne que lui a conféré le Démiurge, il a en lui les semences de l'âme. C'est donc par excellence l'élément de l'âme et des âmes.

§12. Ce point établi, Philon rappelle qu'il existe deux
catégories d'âmes. Les unes qui se sont incarnées et sont les
âmes des hommes. Les autres qui ayant dédaigné la terre et
s'étant vouées au culte de Dieu sont les êtres divins que les
autres philosophes appellent δαίμονας et Moïse ἀγγέλους,
ministres de Dieu et gardiens des mortels.

§13. Pour les âmes qui se sont plongées dans le torrent
du corps, elles se répartissent à leur tour en deux catégories.
Celles qui s'y sont noyées et celles qui en ont remonté le
courant puis ont pu regagner à tire d'ailes le lieu d'où elles
s'étaient élancées.

§14. Ces dernières sont les âmes des philosophes
authentiques qui s'efforcent constamment de mourir à la vie
sensible pour participer à la vie incorporelle et éternelle.

§15. Les âmes qui ont coulé au fond, sont celles de
tous les autres hommes qui se sont voués à satisfaire les passions du corps-cadavre: gloire, argent, pouvoir, honneur, arts
plastiques.

§16. On a donc les moyens *d'échapper à la superstition
si l'on* admet l'équation établie au §6: ψυχὰς . . . καὶ δαίμονας καὶ ἀγγέλους = ἓν δὲ καὶ ταὐτὸν ὑποκείμενον.

La *superstition* consisterait précisément à admettre une
représentation mythique, *sacrilège* comme elles le sont toutes,
à savoir que des êtres divins tels que les anges ont pu con-
voiter la compromission avec le mal et les passions. Comme le
prouve le langage commun (οἱ πολλοί) qui applique la qualification de κακοί aux deux autres termes de l'équation (δαίμονας,
ψυχάς), il est légitime de parler de mauvais anges, indignes de
leur appellation.

§17. L'on a d'ailleurs la caution du Psalmiste qui
évoque des anges scélérats (ἀγγέλων πονηρῶν). Il s'agit en
fait de *mortels* scélérats masqués du nom d'anges (τὸ ἀγγέλων
ὄνομα ὑποδυόμενοι) représentants de la catégorie la plus basse
des âmes incarnées, celle qui, à la différence des âmes philosophiques, ignorent les *filles* de la *droite raison*, soit les

sciences et les vertus, pour courtiser les *descendantes mortelles*
des *hommes mortels* à savoir les plaisirs et les beautés sensibles.

§18. Le dernier paragraphe est consacré a l'exégèse de
l'expression du lemme, ἀπὸ πασῶν, ὧν ἐξελέξαντο. *Toutes* les
âmes vulgaires n'embrassent pas *tous* les plaisirs, le partitif
ἀπὸ πασῶν montre que ces épousailles sont limitées par la vocation hédonique--ὧν ἐξελέξαντο--, de chacune de ces âmes qui
obéit à des affinités électives: ἄλλων ᾠκειωμένων ἄλλαις.

Ainsi l'exégèse de Philon dans *Quaestio et Solutio* II
consiste à substituer, dans un but apologétique, au mythe de la
chute des anges des données dérivant du mythe du *Phèdre* et
présentées comme des vérités scientifiques (cf. §7 . . . μηδεὶς
ὑπολάβῃ μῦθον εἶναι τὸ εἰρημένον). Seules les pires des âmes
non divines se rendent définitivement infidèles à la vocation
de l'esprit. Cette proposition qui sauvegarde la dignité,
l'honneur, la sainteté des anges véritables, fidèles à leurs
fonctions d'intermédiaires entre la divinité et l'humanité; qui
nie l'existence de démons, au sens vulgaire et moderne du terme,
c'est-à-dire d'âmes à la fois divines, donc désincarnées, et
méchantes, ne va pas sans créer une certaine imprécision de
termes dans le développement philonien. En effet, alors que
dans le mythe du *Phèdre* le récit de la chute des âmes est
destiné à rendre compte de l'état spirituel de l'humanité
qu'elles sont allées animer, Philon, suivant le texte scripturaire, présuppose l'existence d'une nombreuse humanité (§1) et
d'une humanité mauvaise, à l'exception du juste Noé, préalable-
ment à l'union des âmes avec les passions humaines. Ce phénomène est ainsi apparemment privé d'une finalité très précise.
Ou alors il faut supposer que ces âmes viennent simplement
grossir les rangs de l'humanité, selon l'optique de Philon, la
plus basse ou la plus commune.

Quaestio et Solutio III: §19-§55

§19. *La Lemme Scripturaire.* Conformément à un procédé
technique dont il use fréquemment, Philon introduit le lemme
scripturaire qui fournira la matière de la *Quaestio III* par
quelques mots d'introduction qui dans le cas présent lient
logiquement la *Quaestio III* à la *Quaestio II*.

Ces mots d'introduction ont d'ailleurs encore une autre
importance. Ils montrent avec toute la clarté désirable que les
âmes qui se sont incarnées en épousant les "filles des hommes,"
ne constituent pas une catégorie à part au sein de l'humanité,
mais représentent le commun des hommes. Comparez Ἐν δὴ τοῖς
τοιούτοις ἀμήχανον . . . et οὐ καταμενεῖ . . . ἐν τοῖς ἀνθρώποις
du lemme.

εἶπε . . . κύριος ὁ θεός· Οὐ καταμενεῖ τὸ πνεῦμά μου
ἐν τοῖς ἀνθρώπους εἰς τὸν αἰῶνα διὰ τὸ εἶναι αὐτοὺς σάρκας (Gen
6, 3): "Le Seigneur Dieu dit mon souffle ne résidera pas chez
les hommes à jamais parce qu'ils sont chair."

Quaestio
Elle n'est pas ici non plus explicitement formulée.
Toutes les notions du verset sont considérées comme faisant
difficulté et seront l'objet des éclaircissements exégétiques
contenus dans la *Solutio*. Ce sont: οὐ καταμενεῖ (εἰς τὸν
αἰῶνα); τὸ πνεῦμά μου; διὰ τὸ εἶναι αὐτοὺς σάρκας.

§20. *Solutio*. Οὐ καταμενεῖ εἰς τὸν αἰῶνα. La phrase
implique que si le souffle de Dieu ne peut pas reposer à jamais
chez les hommes, il y réside à titre temporaire. Μένει μὲν γὰρ
ἔστιν ὅτε, καταμένει δ' οὐκ εἰσάπαν παρὰ τοῖς πολλοῖς ἡμῖν, tel
va être l'objet de la démonstration contenue dans les §§20-21.
Les pires des hommes ont parfois une vision instable et fugitive
du bien suprême.

§21. En effet le souffle de Dieu qui est descendu sur
eux pour les confondre, a vite fait de se détourner de leur âme
dont l'illégalité et l'injustice l'empêchent de le retenir.

§22. τὸ πνεῦμά μου. Les §§22-27 sont consacrés a la
définition du souffle de Dieu. Philon ne retient que deux défi-
nitions de τὸ πνεῦμά μου. Selon la première, le "souffle de
Dieu" est un *élément*. C'est le vent ou l'air en mouvement qui
était évoqué au debut du récit de la création et dont Moïse dit
très bien qu'il était porté au dessus de l'eau puisque sa
légéreté le situe, dans l'édifice des quatre éléments, précisément au dessus de l'eau Selon la seconde acception, le
"souffle de Dieu" est l'Esprit Saint et la Sagesse qui emplit
tout homme sage.

§23.   On en a la preuve du fait que l'Ecriture emploie l'expression πνεύματος θείου pour rendre compte du génie de Béçaléel. Mieux, les versets d'Exode, 31, 2-3 contiennent la définition même du πνεῦμα θεῖον.

§24.   Le πνεῦμα qui repose sur Moïse et dont Dieu dit (Nombres 11, 17) qu'il va en prélever pour le mettre sur les soixante-dix sages que pour cette raison l'Ecriture dénomme Anciens.

§25.   Le terme ἀφελῶ "j'enlèverai" ne doit pas induire en erreur. Il signifie non pas "retranchement," mais "communication," "propagation." Ce partage du souffle divin avec les disciples de Moïse n'implique aucun amoindrissement de la Sagesse de Moïse qui est une source inépuisable. Au contraire,

§26.   Elle semble s'accroître par l'exercice et l'enseignement. Du reste, si l'on peut concevoir qu'une sagesse réduite à n'être qu'une faculté humaine puisse s'amoindrir à être partagée entre tant de personnes, dans le cas de Moïse il en va autrement.

§27.   Bien que le verset de Nombres 11, 17 ne le spécifie pas, le πνεῦμα que Dieu va prélever sur Moïse est le πνεῦμα θεῖον qui emplit tout de sa présence et qui donne sans en être diminué.

§28.   L'exégèse de διὰ τὸ εἶναι αὐτοὺς σάρκας occupe les §§28-54.
Les exemples, cités en gradation ascendante, des plus criminels des hommes à Moïse, le sage suprême, montrent que le souffle de Dieu peut reposer sur les mortels. Mais il est certain qu'il partage la précarité et l'instabilité des choses humaines. Les hommes ne peuvent conserver durablement le souffle de Dieu davantage que le reste de leurs biens dont la possession est infiniment inconstante.

§29.   Mais il faut voir une très grande cause d'ignorance dans la chair et dans l'amitié avec la chair. Moïse ne dit-il pas que c'est parce que les hommes sont chair que le souffle divin ne peut se fixer durablement chez eux? La vie concrète

et ses obligations ou ses soucis font que la sagesse se flétrit
avant d'avoir pu s'épanouir.

§30. Mais le fondement premier de la vie concrète et,
par conséquent, la raison première de l'ignorance est la nature
de la chair.

§31. La preuve en est que les âmes désincarnées contem-
plent sans entraves le spectacle de l'univers tandis que les
âmes alourdies par la chair s'enracinent dans la terre.

Nous avons ici une transposition de *Phèdre* 247 et ss.
Il est frappant de constater que ces doctrines platoniciennes
répandues dans le public cultivé ont fini par acquérir la valeur
de vérités d'évidence et que Philon y a recours comme à des
arguments objectivement scientifiques.

§32. L'effet du poids de la chair explique que le
législateur soucieux de supprimer les relations illicites donne
à ces dispositions le préambule suivant:

᾿Ανθρωπος ἄνθρωπος πρὸς πάντα οἰκεῖον σαρκὸς αὐτοῦ
οὐ προσελεύσεται ἀποκαλύψαι ἀσχημοσύνην· ἐγὼ κύριος.

Selon une technique que nous retrouverons mise en oeuvre
avec plus d'ampleur encore à la fin du traité *Quod Deus*, Philon
utilise le commentaire d'un autre verset du Pentateuque, ici de
Lévitique 18, 6, pour éclairer le sens du verset considéré, à
savoir, en l'occurrence, de la fin de Gen. 6, 3.

La *Quaestio et Solutio* III est de la sorte une *Quaestio*
à tiroir.

C'est l'expression ἡ σάρξ καὶ ἡ πρὸς σάρκα οἰκείωσις du
§29 qui a provoqué la citation du verset de Lévitique qui
contient les mots analogues de πάντα οἰκεῖον σαρκὸς αὐτοῦ.

La *Quaestio* auxiliaire est introduite par une question
rhétorique à la louange de l'Ecriture: πῶς ἄν τις προτρέψαι τὸ
μᾶλλον σαρκὸς καὶ τῶν σαρκὸς οἰκείων καταφρονεῖν. La *Solutio*
consiste à commenter élément par élément Lévitique 18, 6.

§33. ᾿Ανθρωπος ἄνθρωπος οἰκεῖον σαρκός. L'emploi du
futur de l'indicatif dénote plus qu'une interdiction. Il exprime
une certitude exégétique. L'homme véritable ou, ce qui revient
au même l'homme vertueux *ne risque pas* de s'approcher de ces
amis et parents du corps que sont les plaisirs. Il apprendra au
contraire sans cesse à s'en aliéner. Comparez *De Ebrietate* 138.

§34. πάντα. Le text grec de Lévitique 18, 6 est un calque exact de l'original: *'iš 'iš el kāl šeēr besarô lo' tikrebu legalôt ʿerwâ 'anî 'adonāy.*

Philon qui ne se réfère pas à l'hébreu, ignore que πάντα . . . οὐ qui correspond à *kāl . . . lo'* signifie "aucun." Il comprend le verset des Septante comme si le texte portait οὐ προσελεύσεται πρὸς πάντα οἰκεῖον "il ne s'approchera pas sans discrimination de tout ce qui est parent de sa chair." A πάντα il oppose ἕνια et reconnaît qu'on ne peut éluder les plaisirs ou les soins liés au corps et nécessaires au maintien de la vie. Tout superflu qui alimente le désir doit être proscrit.

§35. αὐτός. Les plaisirs étant dangereux, il faut leur préférer la frugalité. Dans tous les cas, il ne faut pas *prendre l'initiative* de la recherche du plaisir. Car Moïse dit "il ne s'approchera pas de son propre chef": οὐ προσελεύσεται αὐτός. Nous avons ici une particularité remarquable. C'est que le texte qui est donné comme un texte scripturaire ne correspond ni à l'hébreu ni au texte des Septante correctement cité au §32 et n'autorisant pas l'exégèse développée dans les §§35-38. Y-a-t-il là une inadvertance de Philon ou une déformation volontaire du texte? Il est difficile d'en décider.

§36. L'argent, les honneurs, la force physique, tous ces biens qui sont du domaine du corps peuvent échoir à qui ne les a pas expressément recherchés.

§37. Dans ce cas il ne faut pas aller vers eux par la volonté et la pensée, ne pas les désirer ni vouloir en acquérir en quantité démesurée. Les biens du corps à qui l'on se soumet en esclave sont un très grand mal en ce sens qu'ils assujettissent l'âme à des réalité inanimées.

§38. Ces réalités ne sont même pas nécessaires au bonheur. La sagesse consiste dans tous les cas à les subordonner à l'esprit.

§39. ἀποκαλύψαι ἀσχημοσύνην. Puisque "s'approcher des parents de sa chair" est interprété comme étant une attitude philosophique: "*découvrir* la honte" est aussi appliqué à la philosophie. Quiconque recherche les biens du corps pervertit la philosophie et transforme la sagesse en sophistique vénale

et vaine, révélant du même coup, de façon manifeste, sa propre
honte.

§40. ἐγὼ κύριος. Ces mots qui terminent le verset
invitent à opposer aux biens du corps, le bien de l'âme et de
l'univers. Au plaisir irrationnel, l'esprit de l'univers qu'est
Dieu.

§41. Dès que l'on met en parallèle le plaisir et Dieu,
on ne peut que choisir le second terme, à moins que l'on ne
puisse comparer les contraires inférieurs aux contraires supé-
rieurs.

§42. Encore ces contraires sont à quelque égard comparables du fait qu'ils ont pour propriété commune d'appartenir
au devenir. Dieu situé hors de tout le créaturel et constamment
actif l'emporte sur ce que le devenir comporte de meilleur.

§43. Le bien consiste par conséquence à ne pas abondon-
ner les rangs de Dieu pour se vouer au plaisir efféminé nuisible
à ses amis, utile à ses ennemis.

§44. Il faut donc résister aux sortilèges du plaisir
et pratiquer la vertu jusqu'à ce qu'on en éprouve la passion.

§45. Moïse n'a pas terminé son verset par les mots ἐγὼ
κύριος pour rappeler que Dieu est le bien parfait, immortel et
véritable. Il ne désigne pas au hasard la divinité par son
attribut de Seigneurie. L'emploi de κύριος rappelle que Dieu
est aussi un maître redoutable.

§46. La présence du maître contraint à l'action droite.

§47. Or Dieu qui remplit tout est omniprésent. Il faut
donc agir conformément à la vertu pour empêcher le πνεῦμα θεῖον
de nous quitter trop rapidement.
    Conserver en soi le souffle divin présent, c'est imiter
dans le mesure de ses moyens la condition du sage Moïse.
    La question auxiliaire, c'est-à-dire le commentaire de
Lévitique 18, 6 est achevée. Les derniers mots nous ramènent,
à propos de Moïse, à la quaestio principale consacrée à la

résidence du souffle de Dieu en l'homme. Moïse a été attiré
ici parce qu'il a vécu 120 ans. Comparez, Gen. 6, 3 et Deut.
34, 7.

§48. *Moïse, le Sage chez qui le* πνεῦμα θεῖον *réside en
permanence.*

Moïse est le sage suprême qui ignore le changement
(τροπαί), c'est-à-dire le départ du πνεῦμα θεῖον. Il le conserve
dans *la paix* qu'il soit debout fermement (Nombres 14, 44 et cf.
au §49 Deuteronome 5, 31) ou assis (Cf. au §50 Exode 18, 14).
La vertu et le sage ignorent le changement.

§49. Comme le prouve l'Ecriture, Moïse trouve auprès de
Dieu stabilité et repos immuable.

§50. Jéthro, l'infatuation du superflu, s'étonne de cet
apanage du seul Moïse et s'en irrite.

§51. L'étonnement de Jéthro apparait comme fondé
lorsqu'au calme et à la stabilité de Moïse on oppose l'agitation
du reste des hommes dont la vie est une guerre en temps de paix.

§52. En dehors de Moïse, les plus éminents des hommes,
tel le grand-prêtre, ne peuvent retenir en permanence le πνεῦμα
θεῖον. Le grand-prêtre qui prononce une fois l'an le tétra-
gramme personnifie le langage proféré instable par nature puisque lié à la matière. Seule la contemplation de l'Etre qui a
dépassé le langage et atteint a l'unité--c'est le cas de Moïse--
jouit de la stabilité.

§53. On s'explique donc bien que la *multitude*, vouée à
la *multitude* des fins de la vie, soit incapable de retenir
longtemps le souffle de Dieu, à la différence de ceux qui se
dépouillent de tout ce qui appartient au devenir, et approchent
de Dieu par l'âme seule.

§54. Ainsi Moïse qui plante sa tente, c'est-à-dire son
âme, hors du camp du corps et devient l'hiérophante des plus
sacrés mystères.

Quaestio et Solutio IV: §55-§57

§55. *Le Lemme Scripturaire*. ῎Εσονται αἱ ἡμέραι αὐτῶν
ἔτη ἑκατὸν εἴκοσιν. Gen. 6, 3. "Leurs jours seront de cent
vingt ans."

§55. *Quaestio*. Est-il concevable que les pêcheurs
évoqués dans le paragraphe précédent et un sage parfait comme
Moïse aient vécu les uns et les autres cent vingt ans?
Il importe tout d'abord de remarquer qu'il n'y a aucun
rapport entre la *Quaestio* présente et la *Quaestio* précédente où
est discuté le problème de l'instabilité du souffle divin chez
les hommes.
Le sens obvie de l'Ecriture est que le caractère charnel
des hommes est incompatible avec la vie éternelle. C'est donc
la vie des hommes qui ne durera pas à jamais. Le souffle de
Dieu, πνεῦμα τοῦ θεοῦ, désigne ici le souffle vital. Il est
l'équivalent de la πνοὴ ζωῆς que Dieu souffle sur la face de
l'homme selon Gen. 2, 7 et que Philon en *Legum Allegoriae* I, 42
explique comme constituant une forme affaiblie du πνεῦμα.
"L'esprit vital" est une forme très affaiblie chez le premier
homme, de l'Esprit saint (Cf. *Legum Allegoriae* I, 33). C'est
probablement parce que dans le verset de Gen. 6, 3 ici commenté
les Septante emploient l'expression πνεῦμα τοῦ θεοῦ et non pas
πνοὴ ζωῆς que Philon n'admet pas que le souffle de Dieu puisse
avoir le sens d'esprit vital. La dernière partie du lemme est
donc complètement séparée de la partie précédente du verset.
L'interprétation de Philon est la même dans *Quaestiones in
Genesim* I, 91[6] où la dernière partie du verset de Gen. 6, 3
fair l'objet d'une *Quaestio* distincte, particularité qui justifie le découpage que nous proposons ici.
L'aporie réside dans le fait que les hommes ordinaires
qui sont incapables de retenir longuement le souffle divin voient
leur vie limitée a 120 ans. Mais Moïse sur lequel le souffle
reposait en permanence--

§56.--a émigré hors de la vie mortelle lui aussi au bout
de 120 ans, ainsi qu'en atteste Deutéronome, 34, 7. Les *pêcheurs*
semblent donc avoir joui de la vie aussi longtemps que l'homme
le plus parfait. La fin de *Quaestiones in Genesim* I, 91 nous
permet de comprendre la pensée de Philon. Philon est embarrassé
par le fait que les 120 ans qui selon notre verset constituent

la limite de la vie humaine contrastent avec la durée formidable
que le chapitre de Genèse 5 attribue à la vie des patriarches
antediluviens. D'autre part le très sage Moïse semble se contre-
dire lorsqu'il raconte par exemple que Sarah vécut 127 ans (Gen
23, 1), Abraham, 175 ans (Gen 25, 7) ou que Jacob a 130 ans (Gen
47, 9). C'est pourquoi il écrit: "But perhaps a hundred and
twenty years are not the universal limit of human life, but only
of the men living at that time, who were later to perish in the
flood after so great a number of years, which a benevolent bene-
factor prolonged, allowing repentance for sins. However, after
this limit they lived a more abundant life in later generations."

       Dans l'hypothèse où les 120 ans représentent une réduction
de la durée de la vie humaine et constituent un châtiment temporaire la durée relativement courte de la vie de Moïse fait en
effet difficulté.

       §56. *Solutio*. Philon laissera ici la question sans
réponse. Il se contente de noter que des éléments en apparence
identiques ont des valeurs diamétralement opposées selon qu'il
s'agit du méchant ou de l'homme de bien.

       §57. Philon promet d'expliquer en détail les 120 ans
de la vie de Moïse lorsqu'il écrira la biographie de Moïse.
Très vraisemblablement le *De Vita Mosis* où la promesse n'est
pourtant pas tenue. Peut-être aurions nous eu de considérations
arithmologiques du genre de celles qui sont contenues dans la
première partie de *Quaestiones in Genesim* I, 91, texte dans
lequel Philon commence par supposer que les 120 ans dont parle
Genèse 6, 3 sont une mention favorable à propos de la vie de
tous les hommes et où il analyse les vertus et l'excellence de
ce nombre.

Quaestio et Solutio V: §58-§67

       §58. *Le Lemme Scripturaire*. Οἱ δὲ γίγαντες ἦσαν ἐπὶ
τῆς γῆς ἐν ταῖς ἡμέραις ἐκείναις (Gen. 6, 4 a).
     "Les géants étaient sur la terre en ces jours."

   Quaestio

       §58. Comment Moïse peut-il avoir parlé des Géants qui
font penser aussitôt à la fable grecque? Or il n'est rien de

fabuleux dans l'Ecriture.   Le mythe est lié au mensonge et Moïse
déteste le mensonge.

§59. Au point d'avoir proscrit dans sa législation,
comme Platon dans sa *République*, la peinture et la sculpture qui,
dans le cas de Moïse, sont accusées probablement de propager
des idées fausses sur la divinité.

§60. *Solutio*. Moïse n'introduit pas de mythe au sujet
des Géants. Les Géants, selon la fable grecque, sont, comme les
Titans, des Γηγενεῖς des Fils de la Terre. Cette qualité
inspire le développement de Philon et lui permet de donner une
valeur allégorique aux Géants. Philon imagine en se référant à
la Bible et à Platon une classification tripartie de l'humanité.
Au plus bas de l'échelle appartiennent les Géants entièrement
voués à la terre, c'est-à-dire au domaine du corps. Les hommes
du ciel, savants et artisans, occupent la place intermédiaire.
La situation d'Abram/Abraham détermine la distinction des classes
2 et 3. Abraham est naturellement cité dans les §§62-64.

§61. Les hommes de Dieu sont les sages prêtres et
prophètes qui ont transcendé la République de l'Univers pour
accéder à la République des idées incorruptibles et incorporelles.

§62. A partir du §62 Philon commente et illustre le
classement qu'il vient d'établir. Il le fait à l'aide d'un
développement en chiasme. L'ordre des classes sera 2-3 pour
lesquelles vaut l'exemple d'Abraham, puis 1, plus liée à la
matière du traité et en ce sens plus importante.
Abram se vouait à la science des astres et de la nature.
Il appartenait à la 2° classe humaine.

§63. Abraham est devenu "homme de Dieu," comme on le
déduit du verset de Genèse 17, 1 où Dieu lui dit "je suis ton
Dieu."

§64. Si Dieu est le Dieu d'Abraham, Abraham est l'homme
de Dieu. Abraham est la raison vertueuse qui produit le langage,
mais est purifiée de tout le sensible et, de cette manière, dans
le lot de Dieu. Et en effet Abraham est un compagnon de Dieu

qu'il accompagne en suivant la voie droite de la route royale
sans en dévier ni à droite ne à gauche.

L'image de la route royale ne suggère pas la modération
de la philosophie du juste milieu, mais l'exactitude et la
constance de la vertu du "Père choisi du son."

§65. Les enfants de la terre ont assujetti l'esprit à
la chair et même l'ont transformé en la nature de la chair,
selon le verset de Genèse 2, 24 qui dit d'Adam, l'esprit, et
d'Eve, la sensation, ἐγένοντο γὰρ οἱ δύο εἰς σάρκα μίαν "car
les deux devinrent une seule chair." Ce sont des esprits qui
ont abandonné la vocation qui leur était propre et constituait
un degré supérieur de l'être pour passer en transfuges à une
condition inférieure et qui leur était contraire. L'initiateur
de cette désertion fut Nemrod.

§66. Selon Genèse 10, 8, en effet, ce fut Nemrod qui
commença à être un géant sur la terre. Nemrod est le symbole
de l'âme qui, ayant trahi l'esprit pour la chair, fait la guerre
à Dieu.[7] Le début du règne de Nemrod est donc justement appelé
Babylone puisque Babylone signifie "changement" et que le changement et l'altération sont le préambule de la désertion de
l'esprit.

§67. Il s'ensuit que, selon Moïse, le méchant est non
seulement un homme sans maison, sans cité, un vagabond et un
fugitif, mais encore un déserteur tandis que l'homme de bien est
un allié très sûr.

Après avoir traité des Géants, Philon passe au commentaire de la suite du texte.

B. *Quod Deus Sit Immutabilis*

Quaestio et Solutio VI: §1-§19

§1. *Le Lemme Scripturaire*. Genèse 6, 4 b. καὶ μετ'
ἐκεῖνο, φησίν, ὡς ἂν εἰσεπορεύοντο οἱ ἄγγελοι τοῦ θεοῦ πρὸς τὰς
θυγατέρας τῶν ἀνθρώπων, καὶ ἐγέννων αὐτοῖς;
"et après *celui-ci* quand les anges de Dieu venaient chez
les filles des hommes et qu'ils engendraient pour eux."

§1. *Quaestio*. Elle est introduite par une formule explicite: οὐκοῦν ἄξιον σκέψασθαι τίνα ἔχει λόγον. . . . Les mots qui font question sont μετ' ἐκεῖνο d'une part et καὶ ἐγέννων αὐτοῖς. Encore une fois l'interprétation de Philon n'est possible que si l'on fait abstraction de l'original hébreu. En effet μετ' ἐκεῖνο correspond à *wegam 'aḥarê ken*, c'est-à-dire (en ces jours là) "et encore après cela," "et ensuite encore."

L'embarras de Philon semble justifié lorsque l'on considère l'ensemble du verset 4. On a la séquence ἐν ταῖς ἡμέραις ἐκείναις, καὶ μετ' ἐκεῖνο qui peut sembler dure et insolite. On s'attendrait à lire καὶ μετ' ἐκείνας et le démonstratif neutre semble renvoyer à un autre antécédent qu'à ἡμέραις.

La verbe γεννάω signifie "engendrer" ou "enfanter" mais a principalement la première acception. Une confrontation avec l'original hébreu eût montré qu'il avait ici la seconde. En effet *weyaldû lahem* signifie que les filles des hommes enfantaient pour eux, les anges de Dieu.[8] Faute d'en être averti, Philon interprète ἐγέννωσαν αὐτοῖς "enfantaient pour eux," comme signifiant "engendraient pour eux" et est contraint de donner à αὐτοῖς la valeur du réfléchi αὐτοῖς.

Philon invite donc à rechercher l'antécédent du démonstratif ἐκεῖνο.

Solutio

§2. C'est le πνεῦμα θεῖον dont il avait été question dans le traité précédent et dont on avait montré qu'il était incapable de s'établir durablement dans une âme divisée par son union avec la chair. Lorsque le πνεῦμα quitte l'âme en y laissant les ténèbres, les anges entrent chez les filles des hommes, c'est à dire chez les passions.

§3. Lorsque la lumière de la sagesse éclaire l'âme et lui fait voir Dieu, les pseudo-anges[9] sont maintenus à distance. Ils profitent des ténèbres qui suivent le départ du πνεῦμα pour s'unir aux passions et en engendrer des enfants pour eux-mêmes et non pour Dieu.

§4. C'est à dire au lieu des vertus qui appartiennent à Dieu, les vices qui sont *de la famille* des méchants.

§5. Philon illustre ce que signifie "engendrer des vertus qui appartiennent à Dieu." Le premier exemple qu'il

donne est celui d'Abraham qui *restitue* à Dieu Isaac, la vertu
qu'a engendrée son âme.

§6.   Le second exemple, exposé beaucoup plus longuement,
est emprunté à l'histoire du "disciple et successeur" d'Abraham
que fut Anne. Fécondée par la semence divine, Anne dont le nom
signifie "son don gracieux"[10] *rend* au donateur ce qu'elle en a
reçu, Samuel, car elle sait bien qu'il n'est rien ici bas qui ne
soit présent gracieux de la divinité. Voilà pourquoi elle dit
de son fils en s'adressant à Dieu "Je te le donne à toi qui me
l'as donné" (I Samuel 1, 11) parole qui est conforme à l'ordre,
énoncé en Nombres 28, 2, d'offrir à Dieu les dons qu'il a faits.

§7.   Dieu seul, en effet, mérite des témoignages de
gratitude puisque tout de ce qui nous a été donné ne procède que
de lui seul. S'il nous demande de lui offrir *ses* dons dont il
n'a nul besoin, c'est afin que notre gratitude *purifie* nos
paroles, nos pensées et nos actes.

§8.   Cette purification de l'âme est absolument nécessaire comme on peut le déduire par un raisonnement *a fortiori* de
l'obligation faite à qui pénètre en un lieu sacré de se purifier
le corps. On ne saurait approcher Dieu avec une âme impure et
n'ayant pas renoncé au mal.

§9.   Car il est impossible que cette impureté échappe
à Celui qui voit jusque dans les tréfonds de l'âme et se promène
dans ses recoins secrets.

§10.   Une autre très claire description de la condition
d'une âme que Dieu aime se trouve dans le cantique où l'on
trouve cette parole: "la femme stérile a enfanté sept, mais la
multiple--en--enfants s'est épuisée."[11] Cette parole est étonnante concernant la mère du seul Samuel.

§11.   Mais Anne sait que le un est identique au sept
dans les nombres, l'harmonie de l'univers, les proportions de
l'âme vertueuse. Samuel consacré à Dieu seul est créé d'après
lui, c'est-à-dire conformément à l'un et la monade.

§12.   Or cette condition est celle de l'hebdomade, de
l'âme qui se repose en Dieu après avoir abandonné tout le sensible.

§13. Il était donc naturel que la stérile enfantât la
monade qui a la valeur de l'hebdomade.

§14. La multiple au contraire s'épuise en enfants. Il
s'agit de l'âme qui, suivant le chemin inverse de celui de la
précédente, s'éloigne de l'un et se trouve accablée par de
nombreux enfantements.

§15. C'est à dire par la mise au jour des innombrables
désirs liés aux sens.
     Après la description du comportement des âmes vertueuses,
Abraham et Anne, qui rendent à Dieu ce qu'elles ont conçu et mis
au monde, la peinture de la condition de l'âme multiple qui s'est
plongée dans le sensible, nous ramène au thème initial: ὅσοι
φθαρτοῖς ἑαυτοῖς φθαρτὰ γεννῶσιν. Philon en traite à nouveau en
l'envisageant, comme l'y invitaient les mots ἡ πολλὴ ἐν τέκνοις
ἠσθένησε, sous l'angle du châtiment de la philautie.

§16. Le châtiment de la philautie peut aller plus loin
encore que l'épuisement de l'âme dispersée dans le sensible.
Onan qui refuse d'engendrer lorsqu'il sait que sa postérité ne
sera pas à lui--ὅτι οὐκ αὐτῷ ἔσται τὸ σπέρμα Gen. 38, 9--, subit
la destruction totale, selon un châtiment tout à fait approprié.

§17. En effet ceux qui préfèrent leur intérêt propre
aux devoirs envers le prochain et envers Dieu connaîtront un
triste sort.

§18. Dieu détruira l'introduction scélérate de l'étrange
doctrine dénommée Onan.

§19. Philon condamne en conclusion tous ceux qui pro-
créent pour eux--πάντες οἱ γεννῶντες αὐτοῖς--, comme s'ils
étaient nés pour eux-mêmes--ὥσπερ αὐτοῖς μόνοις φύντες--, et non
pour d'innombrables êtres différents d'eux, des parents à
l'humanité, à l'Univers, aux sciences et aux vertus, jusqu'à
Dieu lui-même. Comme s'ils ne constituaient pas une partie
accessoir du Tout, mais à l'inverse, comme si l'Univers n'était
qu'une partie accessoire du tout personne.

Quaestio et Solutio VII: §20-§50

§20. *Le Lemme Scripturaire*. Gen. 6, 5-7. Philon passe
à la suite de son commentaire du texte biblique, qui décrit la
réaction de Dieu au spectacle des vices de l'humanité.

Ἰδὼν οὖν . . . κύριος ὁ θεὸς ὅτι ἐπληθύνθησαν αἱ κακίαι
τῶν ἀνθρώπων ἐπὶ τῆς γῆς, καὶ πᾶς τις διανοεῖται ἐν τῇ καρδίᾳ
ἐπιμελῶς τὰ πονηρὰ πάσας τὰς ἡμέρας, ἐνεθυμήθη ὁ θεὸς ὅτι ἐποίησε
τὸν ἄνθρωπον ἐπὶ τῆς γῆς, καὶ διενοήθη καὶ εἶπεν ὁ θεός· Ἀπαλείψω τὸν ἄνθρωπον ὃν ἐποίησα ἀπὸ προσώπου τῆς γῆς.

§20. *Quaestio*. La partie du traité qui correspond
proprement au titre *Quod Deus Immutabilis Sit* commence au paragraphe 20 et se termine avec le paragraphe 69. Elle comprend
deux *Quaestiones*.

Les mots qui font difficulté sont ἐνεθυμήθη ὁ θεὸς ὅτι
ἐποίησε τὸν ἄνθρωπον ἐπὶ τῆς γῆς, καὶ διενοήθη. Les deux formes
verbales soulignées ont une signification un peu ambiguë. La
première a pour acception "considéra," "prit à coeur" ou
"s'irrita," la seconde "réfléchit" ou "se repentit." H. Leisegang[12] estime que les LXX ont déjà volontairement affaibli le
texte original: "Iahvé se repentit d'avoir fait l'homme sur la
terre et il s'irrita en son coeur." Il semble[13] que Philon
donnait aux verbes ἐνεθυμήθη et διενοήθη dans l'interprétation
qui, dit-il, vient à l'esprit de certains et qu'il veut écarter,
un sens voisin: "Dieu fut préoccupé d'avoir créé l'homme et il
s'en repentit."

En effet, dans la partie constituée par les §§20-50,
il n'est pas question de la colère de Dieu, mais seulement de
son repentir. Le thème de la colère est abordé dans les §§51-69
qui représentent le commentaire de la fin du verset de Gen. 6, 7
où le texte de Philon avait la variante ἐθυμώθην "je suis irrité"
au lieu de ἐνεθυμήθην. On remarquera qu'au §20 Philon ne cite
pas la partie du verset qui contient cette forme verbale qui
aurait été déplacée dans un développement consacré au repentir.
Ἀπαλείψω opposé à ὅτι ἐποίησε s'accorde mieux avec l'idée du
repentir. Dieu *défait* ce *qu'il avait fait*. Voyez d'ailleurs
le §21 où la destruction de l'espèce humaine est liée au repentir de Dieu.

§20. *Solutio*. Contrairement à la plupart des éditeurs
nous considérons que les §§20-69 forment une partie unique, en

commentaire à Gen. 6, 5-7 cités pour l'essentiel au §20. Il est
vrai, cependant, que cette partie unique comporte elle-même deux
subdivisions:

    (a) §§20-32 sur ἐνεθυμήθη--διενοήθη.

        C'est une sorte de préface à la discussion du sens
véritable des mots ἐνεθυμήθη--διενοήθη qui emplira les §§33-49.
Philon expose ici les raisons qui empêchent de considérer que
ces formes verbales indiquent que Dieu s'est repenti.

    §21. Croire que Dieu puisse se repentir, c'est pro-
fesser une doctrine dont l'impiété dépasse l'impiété des hommes
du Déluge.

    §22. En effet penser que l'Etre immuable est capable
de changement c'est l'imaginer inférieur à certains hommes eux
mêmes auxquels une pratique authentique de la philosophie permet
d'atteindre à une fermeté inébranlable.

    §23. Mais la tranquillité et la fermeté inébranlable de
l'âme du sage sont également une conception et un idéal scripturaires. Le Legislateur rapporte la parole que Dieu dit à Moïse
"reste immobile ici avec moi" (Deut. 5, 31).

    §24. L'image de l'âme du sage accordée comme une lyre
à la connaissance des contraires et à la pratique du bien est
une illustration de sa *constante* justesse.

    §25. L'âme humaine bien accordée a servi de modèle aux
instruments de musique et elle transforme la pratique de la vie
humaine en une partition harmonieuse où est inscrite la plus
belle de toutes les symphonies.

    §26. Si la sagesse permet à l'âme d'abattre la tempête
des vices et de trouver le calme plat et la sérénité, Dieu dont
la sagesse, les vertus et la félicité ont une puissance incommen-
surablement supérieure aux *brises* du savoir et des vertus des
hommes doit, *a fortiori*, connaître le calme inséparable de la
constance du propos et par conséquent ignorer tout changement
intellectuel et tout repentir.

    §27. La versatilité ou l'inconstance d'esprit est un
phénomène inséparablement lié à la condition humaine. Les hommes

sont des êtres inconstants vivant au sein d'une société d'êtres
inconstants et leurs actes sont en conséquence.

§28. Ces variations nous convainquent de laisser-aller
frivole, défaut que l'on ne saurait attribuer à Dieu. Même
lorsque nous y échapperions nous-mêmes, l'inconstance d'autrui
entraîne la nôtre.

§29. L'homme ne saurait prévoir le futur ni deviner les
intentions du prochain. Mais Dieu voit tout dans une pure
lumière qui lui fait connaître avec évidence le fond le plus
secret des âmes; et l'incertitude touchant l'avenir est incompatible avec sa providence.

§30. Dieu, artisan de l'univers et Père des hommes,
connaît à ce titre son oeuvre et ses créatures. On ne saurait
invoquer contre la science divine l'obscurité du temps à venir
puisque le rapport du temps à Dieu est le même que celui du
monde et de l'humanité: Dieu a créé le temps.

§31. Il est le père du père du temps, à savoir de
l'univers dont le mouvement a mis en branle le temps; qui ainsi,
se trouve être le petit-fils de Dieu. Par univers on entend
l'univers sensible, le *fils cadet de Dieu*, le *fils aîné étant*
le monde intelligible resté auprès de son créateur.

§32. C'est donc le mouvement du monde sensible qui a
suscité le temps. Pour Dieu qui a en son pouvoir le commencement et la fin des temps, il n'est pas d'évènement futur.
D'ailleurs Dieu n'existe pas dans le temps, mais dans la durée
éternelle dont le temps n'est que l'image. L'éternité ignore
passé et avenir, elle permane dans un éternel présent.

(b) §§33-50--Quel est donc le sens de ἐνεθυμήθη--διενοήθη?

Cette deuxième partie de la *solutio* propose une
réponse positive quant au sens de ces deux formes verbales et de
la phrase qui les contient. On observera que cette partie est
introduite par la transition exégétique qui, ordinairement,
marque le passage d'une *Quaestio* à une autre: Ἱκανῶς οὖν
διειλεγμένοι περὶ τοῦ μὴ χρῆσθαι μετανοίᾳ τὸ ὂν ἀκολούθως ἀποδώσομεν, τί ἐστι τὸ ἐνεθυμήθη . . . κ.τ.λ.

Toutefois l'absence d'un nouveau lemme scripturaire et
la forme ἀποδώσομεν "nous allons rendre compte," indiquent que
nous avons affaire à une *solutio* ou plus exactement à la suite
d'une *solutio*.[14]

§33. Philon va examiner le sens des mots ἐνεθυμήθη et
διενοήθη puisqu'il tient pour démontré qu'on ne saurait leur
faire exprimer le repentir de Dieu.

§34. Ces deux mots correspondent respectivement à la
"notion" et à la "réflexion" divines, deux facultés très sûres
qui permettent au Créateur de *voir* constamment ses créatures et
de sanctionner leur fidélité ou leur désertion.

§35. Suivant le "regard" divin, Philon entreprend une
description de la condition des êtres matériels qu'il distingue
selon qu'ils sont constitués par une "manière d'être" ou un
"êtat" (ἕξις); une nature (φύσις); une âme (ψυχή); une âme
raisonnable (λογικὴ ψυχή).
L'*hexis* ou "état organique" est ce qui caractérise des
corps inanimés comme des pierres ou des fragments de bois. Leur
condition de matière organisée est due à la vertu du πνεῦμα qui
les enserre et assure leur cohésion. Ce πνεῦμα ne doit guère
différer du Logos qui maintient la cohésion de l'univers et de
toutes choses. L'activité du πνεῦμα qui assure l' ἕξις est
décrite d'une manière qui fait penser à la description de l'âme
du monde en *Timée* 34 b et du mouvement du Logos en *De Plantatione* 8.

§36. Les coureurs au théâtre illustrent la double course
du πνεῦμα.

§37. La *nature* caractérise les végétaux et se compose
de plusieurs facultés: nutrition, transformation, croissance.
L'arrosage ou la privation d'eau met en lumière la faculté de
nutrition ainsi que la faculté de croissance.

§38. Les transformations saisonnières mettent en
lumière la faculté de transformation. Au solstice d'hiver la
nature végétale entre en son repos.

§39. Elle se réveille au printemps et en été et ses variations sont couronnées par la production du fruit.

§40. Le fruit mûr se détache de lui-même de l'organisme végétal auquel il appartenait. Ses graines sont capables de produire des plantes semblables à celles qui l'ont produit.

§41. L'âme possède, en plus de la nature, la sensation, la représentation, l'inclination. Les plantes sont dépourvues d'âme; tous les animaux, au contraire.

§42. La sensation consiste en une introduction des phénomènes auprès de l'esprit qui les emmagasine.

§43. La représentation est la faculté qui interprète toutes les sensations introduites. Elle en marque l'âme comme un sceau marque de la cire.

§44. L'inclination est la réaction de l'âme à la représentation qui s'est imprimée en elle. Les animaux l'emportent sur les plantes parce qu'ils possèdent l'âme. On va voir ce qui fait la supériorité de l'homme sur les animaux.

§45. L'âme rationnelle. L'apanage de l'homme est l'intellect par lequel il comprend la nature des objets matériels et des réalités immatérielles. L'intellect est à l'âme ce que la vue est au corps et la lumière à la nature.

§46. Il est en effet la vue de l'âme. Formée à partir d'un élément supérieur commun aux natures divines, cette partie de l'âme est impérissable.

§47. A elle seule Dieu a donné liberté et libre arbitre. En effet, les autres créatures qui sont dépourvues de l'intellect destiné à la liberté, ont été livrées aux hommes comme des esclaves. L'homme qui a obtenu le libre-arbitre est par là même responsable du bien ou du mal qu'il fait.

§48. Les animaux, en effet, ne sont pas responsables[15] de leur actes. L'âme humaine qui a été affranchie par Dieu et rendue semblable à lui par la liberté qu'il lui a concédée,

seule peut être accusée d'ingratitude envers son Bienfaiteur et
subir le châtiment inexorable des affranchis ingrats.

§49. Le sens de ἐνεθυμήθη καὶ διενοήθη ὁ θεός est donc
que Dieu avait su et connu de tout temps quel être était l'homme
qu'il avait créé. L'homme a été créé affranchi et libre,
capable de discerner le bien du mal et de choisir le bien.

§50. La preuve en est le passage de Deut. 30, 15-19,
dans lequel Dieu laisse à l'homme le choix entre la vie et la
mort, le bien et le mal et lui conseille de choisir la vie. La
mention de la vie et de la mort mises devant lui présuppose que
l'homme a été créé avec la notion du bien et du mal. Le conseil
de choisir la vie et le bien montre que l'homme en a la liberté
grâce au juge incorruptible qu'il porte en lui, le jugement
fidèle aux suggestions de la droite raison.

Quaestio et Solutio VIII: §51-§69

§51. *Le Lemme Scripturaire*. Philon introduit la
Quaestio VIII par une des formules de transition qui lui sont
familières Δεδηλωκότες οὖν ἀποχρώντως περὶ τούτων τὰ ἐξῆς ἴδωμεν.
Le lemme de la question est la fin du verset 7 qui est
à présent cité complètement. Le verbe ἀπαλείψω est cette fois
considéré comme une manifestation de la colère de Dieu.

Ἀπαλείψω τὸν ἄνθρωπον ὃν ἐποίησα ἀπὸ προσώπου τῆς γῆς,
ἀπὸ ἀνθρώπου ἕως κτήνους, ἀπὸ ἑρπετῶν ἕως πετεινῶν τοῦ οὐρανοῦ,
ὅτι ἐθυμώθην ὅτι ἐποίησα αὐτόν.

"J'effacerai l'homme que j'ai créé de la face de la
terre, depuis l'homme jusqu'au bétail, depuis les reptiles
jusqu'aux oiseaux du ciel, parce que je suis irrité de l'avoir
créé." Le lemme, à la différence de Deus 70 et QG I, 95 n'est
pas exactement cité. Le texte correct est ὅτι ἐποίησα αὐτούς.
Le singulier marque plus clairement que la menace a pour cause
l'homme et lui seul.

§52. *Quaestio*. Le verbe ἐθυμώθην variante ancienne,
pour le répéter, de ἐνεθυμήθην ne peut signifier que "je me suis
irrité," je suis irrité." Il est donc inévitable que certains
pensent que Dieu est sujet à des accès de colère. Mais Dieu ne
connaît aucune passion. La passion est liée à la faiblesse

humaine, tandis que le caractère incorporel de Dieu le rend
inaccessible à la passion.

§52. *Solutio*. Le Législateur ne parle de cette manière
de la divinité qu'eu égard à l'état d'impréparation spirituelle
des hommes auxquels s'adresse son instruction.

§53. La partie législative du Pentateuque comporte deux
propositions capitales concernant la Cause première. L'une
affirme que Dieu *n'est pas comme l'homme* (Nombres 23, 19);
l'autre qu'il *est comme l'homme* (Deut. 8, 5).

§54. La première proposition est l'expression de la
pure vérité; la seconde est alléguée pour l'instruction du
vulgaire.

§55. Les hommes se répartissent en effet selon deux
catégories. L'une est celle des *amis de l'âme* capables d'abstraction et qui n'ont besoin pour concevoir Dieu de la médiation
d'aucune représentation empruntée au domaine du sensible. Ils
appréhendent l'existence de Dieu purifiée de tout attribut
hétérogène.

§56. Les hommes impliqués dans les *réalités corporelles*
et incapables de concevoir rien qui en soit indépendant, pro-
jettent dans le domaine divin l'image qu'ils se font d'eux-mêmes.
Prêtant à Dieu une pluralité de facultés, ils ne se doutent pas
qu'ils lui attribuent ainsi une pluralité d'organes correspondant
à ces facultés.[16] Mais ces facultés et ces organes n'auraient
de sens qu'eu égard au sensible. Or Dieu n'a besoin de rien de
ce qui se trouve dans le sensible.

§57. Prêter à Dieu des organes serait aboutir à des
absurdités. A quoi lui serviraient des pieds à lui qui emplit
l'univers et ne saurait aller nulle part? Des mains, à lui qui
ne saurait rien recevoir et qui a tout donné, non de ses mains,
mais par l'intermédiaire du Logos?

§58. Aurait-il besoin d'yeux? Mais il voyait, avant
que fût la lumière sensible nécessaire à la vision charnelle,
grâce à la lumière qu'il est lui-même.

§59. Faut-il parler des organes de la nutrition? Celui
qui en possède est sujet à la faim et à l'évacuation. C'est donc
une fiction mythique impie que de prêter à Dieu des organes qui,
plus encore qu'à la forme humaine, le soumettent aux servitudes
humaines.

§60. Pourtant Moïse attribue à Dieu précisément des bras
et des jambes. Il le montre en train de se déplacer. Il lui
prête des armes dont certaines ont leur équivalent dans la
mythologie. Il le montre animé de sentiments de jalousie et de
colère analogues à ceux qu'éprouvent les hommes. Philon s'en
explique de la manière suivante:

§61. Moïse désire être utile à tous ses disciples. Or
ceux-ci, nous l'avons vu, constituent deux classes. La classe
supérieure *des amis de l'âme* chemine sur la route royale sous
la conduite de la vérité qui les initie aux mystères authentiques
de l'Etre, c'est à dire à cette vérité que Dieu n'a d'analogie
avec rien de ce qui est dans le devenir.

§62. *Ces amis de l'âme* professent que "Dieu n'est pas
comme un homme," en fait comme rien de sensible. On ne peut
saisir de lui que son existence pure et simple.

§63. *Les amis du corps* dont, du fait de leur éducation,
l'esprit est infirme, ont besoin de moniteurs en guise de médecins.

§64. De même que les esclaves sans éducation ni discernement sont incités à la sagesse par la crainte que leur
inspire le maître, que *les amis du corps* y soient conduits par
des mensonges s'ils ne peuvent l'être par la vérité.

§65. Il y a là un procédé comparable à ce que l'on
observe dans la pratique des médecins. Les médecins pour conduire les malades vers la guérison leur mentent sur leur état.

§66. Ces mensonges rehaussent le moral des patients
et leur permettent de supporter les traitements médicaux les
plus pénibles.

§67. De même le parfait médecin des passions qu'est le Législateur, recourt au mensonge comme à un artifice pédagogique dont la fin est l'éradication des maladies de l'âme.

§68. Les représentations où Dieu apparaît animé de colère, proférant des menaces, brandissant des armes contre les transgresseurs, constituent l'unique moyen d'amender l'insensé.

§69. Tels sont les procédés pédagogiques qi'il faut appliquer à ceux qui croient que "Dieu est comme un homme." Les Lois pour exhorter les hommes à la piété s'adressent soit à la crainte soit à l'amour.
Ceux qui imaginent *Dieu comme un homme* pourvu de membres, capable d'éprouver des passions humaines et d'infliger des châtiments matériels servent Dieu par crainte.
Ceux qui savent que *Dieu n'est pas comme un homme* et qu'ils n'ont à en redouter aucun des maux qui peut infliger un homme, ceux-là rendent à Dieu un culte désintéressé et qui n'est mêlé d'aucune considération extrinsèque. Ils servent Dieu par amour.

Quaestio et Solutio IX: §70-§85

§70. *Le Lemme Scripturaire.* ἐθυμώθην ὅτι ἐποίησα αὐτούς (Gen. 6, 7). Νῶε δὲ εὖρε χάριν (Gen. 6, 8).
La présente *Quaestio* est sans doute architectoniquement la moins claire et exégétiquement la plus faible et la moins convaincante de tout le traité.

§70. *Quaestio.* Il est certain que dans la *Quaestio* précédente Philon a plutôt traité de l'anthropomorphisme et de l'anthropopathie dans l'Ecriture, qu'il n'a indiqué le sens intrinsèque de ἐθυμώθην ὅτι ἐποίησα αὐτούς. Certes, Moïse prête parfois des sentiments de colère à la divinité par concession à la grossièreté spirituelle *des amis du corps*. Mais il s'agit ici d'un récit et non d'une interdiction ou d'une parénèse destinée à les impressionner. De toute façon, comment peut-on dire que Dieu s'est irrité d'une action qu'il a faite lui-même? Il faut donc proposer une explication des mots dont se sert ici l'Ecriture. Philon le fait dans les §§71-72 qu'il présente comme constituant la conclusion des *Quaestiones* précédentes où il voit un ensemble de considérations préalables: Ἃ μὲν οὖν προκαταστήσασθαι τῆς ζητήσεως ἁρμόττον ἦν, τοιαῦτά ἐστιν. Ἐπανιτέον δὲ ἐπὶ τὴν ἐξ ἀρχῆς σκέψιν καθ' ἣν ἡποροῦμεν, τίνα ὑπογράφει νοῦν τὸ "ἐθυμώθην ὅτι ἐποίησα αὐτούς."

Le verbe προκαταστήσασθαι s'applique certainement à toute la partie du texte qui va du paragraphe 20 au paragraphe 69. Les *Quaestiones* que nous y avons distinguées, sont, de fait, organiquement liées. Comme il apparaît du §72, Philon considère que la colère n'est qu'une espèce du genre qu'est le changement d'opinion ou repentir: τοῦτο μὲν γὰρ μετανοοῦντος ἦν. . . .

On serait donc tenté de considérer que les §§70-72 appartiennent à la partie précédente consacrée à élucider le sens de la colère divine. En fait cette conclusion apparente constitue l'introduction d'une partie de transition qui traite d'un problème différent. Philon y prend comme lemme scripturaire la fin du verset de Gen. 6, 7 et le début de Gen. 6, 8 auquel sera consacrée la *Quaestio* X (§§86-103). La juxtaposition des mots ἐθυμώθην ὅτι ἐποίησα αὐτούς et de Νῶε δὲ εὗρε χάριν montre que ce qui est réellement traité dans la présente partie est la signification de *l'apparition* des méchants et du juste par rapport à la providence divine dont il est improprement parlé en termes de sentiments, colère ou plaisir.

§70. *Solutio*. Moïse veut peut-être dire que la colère de Dieu est une façon de mentionner l'apparition des méchants, comme la grâce trouvée auprès de lui, l'apparition des gens de bien.

§71. Il emploie à propos de Dieu improprement, mais de façon excellente dans la perspective de son sens figuré, le mot θυμός entendu au sens de passion. Grâce à quoi il peut en effet révéler une très nécessaire vérité, à savoir que tout ce que nous faisons sous l'empire de la passion est mauvais, tandis qu'est louable tout ce que nous faisons guidés par la droite raison et la connaissance.

§72. Le style de Moïse confirme une telle interprétation. Il écrit, on l'a vu, ἐθυμώθην ὅτι ἐποίησα αὐτούς et non Διότι ἐποίησα αὐτούς, ἐθυμώθην. La première formulation engage à comprendre la phrase de la façon suivante: "J'étais en colère, *comme le prouve* le fait que je les ai créés"; dans la seconde, la phrase eût immanquablement signifié "c'est parce que je les ai créés que je suis irrité"[17] et impliqué un changement d'état

d'esprit incompatible avec l'omniscience divine. La phrase dont
a fait usage Moïse suggère seulement un lien de cause à effet
entre la passion et les fautes, les oeuvres droites et la
raison.[18]

§73. Ces vérités philosophiques établies, Philon revient
au sujet propre de la présente *quaestio*, tel qu'il l'avait
indiqué au §70: οἱ μὲν φαῦλοι θυμῷ γεγόνασι θεοῦ, οἱ δ᾽ ἀγαθοὶ
χάριτι. Lorsque tous les hommes allaient succomber sous les
péchés qu'ils avaient volontairement commis,[19] Dieu ne permit
pas que l'humanité pérît tout entière.

§74. C'est ainsi que Noé trouva grâce tandis que les
autres hommes étaient détruits du fait de leur ingratitude. De
la sorte la miséricorde de Dieu contrebalance sa rigueur.

§75. C'est là chose nécessaire, car sans la miséricorde
divine nul homme ne saurait subsister.

§76. Pour que l'humanité ne soit pas à tout jamais
effacée, pour sauver le genre humain même lorsque sont engloutis
de nombreux individus, Dieu fait don aux hommes, même s'il en
sont indignes, de sa miséricorde en la personne de Noé. Le don
de Noé précède le châtiment de l'humanité, parce que Dieu use
de miséricorde avant que de juger.

§77. Ce qui signifie que sa miséricorde consiste à
adapter son jugement à la faiblesse humaine. Il tempère ses
puissances lorsqu'il a affaire aux créatures. Ces dernières
sont en effet incapables de les accueillir dans leur intégrité
sans mélange.

§78. L'homme qui est incapable de contempler les rayons
du soleil, lequel n'est pourtant qu'une oeuvre de Dieu, serait-
il capable de considérer dans leur pureté les puissance inengen-
drées dont la divinité rayonne?

§79. Pour le soleil lui-même, Dieu a tempéré d'air
froid la chaleur de ses rayons afin de rendre la perception
visuelle possible. Il est donc évident que nul homme, pas plus
que le ciel et l'univers tout entiers, n'est capable d'accueillir
dans son absolu aucune des vertus de Dieu.

§80. C'est pourquoi, connaissant la faiblesse humaine,
Dieu proportionne ses bienfaits et ses châtiments à la capacité
de ceux qui vont les subir ou en bénéficier.

§81. L'humanité ne saurait prétendre à autre chose qu'à
ces puissances divines diluées en proportion de sa faiblesse,
les puissances pures étant du domaine de Dieu.

§82. Cette vérité que ce qui est pur et sans mélange
est du domaine de Dieu, tandis que ce qui est mixte est du
domaine de la créature, est prouvée par le verset 12 du psaume
61: "Le Seigneur a parlé une seule fois, deux ai-je entendu
cela."

§83. La parole de Dieu qui ne met pas en jeu des
organes de phonation ni l'air est incorporelle et une.

§84. Mais nous, nous entendons grâce à la dyade. Nous
avons besoin des organes de la parole et de l'air et notre parole
comporte des sons aigus et des sons graves.

§85. Philon explique à présent, pour conclure, pourquoi
la grâce divine a consisté en l'apparition d'un *seul* juste opposé
à la multitude des *raisonnements* injustes. S'il est inférieur
par le nombre, le juste est supérieur par la valeur à toute la
masse des injustes. Il suffit donc à faire contrepoids et à
empêcher que le mal ne l'emporte.

Quaestio et Solutio X: §86-§103

§86. *Le Lemme Scripturaire*. Le Lemme est apparemment
le même que dans la *Quaestio* précédente et que dans la *Quaestio*
suivante. En particulier si l'on compare les deux formules intro-
ductoires:
Τί δέ ἐστι τὸ "Νῶε εὗρε χάριν ἐναντίον κυρίου τοῦ θεοῦ"
       συνεπισκεψώμεθα (§86)
Τί δέ ἐστι τὸ "Νῶε εὗρε χάριν παρὰ κυρίῳ τῷ θεῷ" διαπορητέον
       (§104) la pensée semble n'avoir pas progressé.

§86. *Quaestio*. En réalité, il n'en est rien. Nous
avons vu que la partie précédente était consacrée à éclaircir
l'idée que les méchants apparaissaient selon la colère de Dieu

et les justes selon sa grâce. La majeure partie du passage a
trait à la signification cosmique de l'apparition du juste et
constitue le commentaire du mot Νῶε de Gen. 6, 8. La présent
partie propose l'interprétation de εὖρε. Dans la *Quaestio et
Solutio* XI: §§104-121 Philon commente χάριν ἐναντίον κυρίου τοῦ
θεοῦ. Qu'est ce que *trouver* dans le cas de Noé?

§86. *Solutio*. Philon propose de distinguer entre
εὕρεσις "découverte" et ἀνεύρεσις "redécouverte"[20] comme le font
ceux qui ont à coeur la propriété des termes.

§87. Ἀνεύρεσις. La loi du Nazir (Nombres 6, 2) concernant le grand voeu fournit un bon exemple de ce qu'est la
redécouverte. Le *voeu* est une prière pour demander des biens;
le *grand voeu* consiste à professer que Dieu seul est l'unique
cause des biens que l'on reçoit.

§88. C'est que Dieu peut faire que les causes secondaires produisent des effets contraires à leurs effets ordinaires.
L'homme qui prononce ce voeu est "saint": il a l'obligation de
faire croître en son esprit les principes *capitaux* des vertus
qui forment comme une chevelure.

§89. Parfois il les perd soudainement par suite d'une
inconstance spirituelle dont il n'est pas maître, qui souille
son esprit et qu'il appelle mort.

§90. Mais il reconquiert son intégrité spirituelle.
Les jours qui séparent sa chute de son rétablissement sont
appelés *alogoi* c'est-à-dire "en discordance avec la droite
raison" ou "nuls et non avenus" parce que dépourvus de valeur
et de ce fait n'entrant pas en ligne de compte.

§91. Εὕρεσις. La découverte peut être une aubaine
matérielle inespérée comme dans le cas du laboureur qui trouve
un trésor en creusant la terre pour y planter un arbre fruitier.

§92. Le cas de Jacob fournit, sur le plan de l'esprit,
un autre exemple. Jacob trouve sans effort au cours de sa
chasse spirituelle le trésor de parfaite félicité dont Dieu lui
fait don.

§93. C'est une illustration de ce que nous observons
sous nos yeux. Certains ne découvrent rien malgré de laborieuses
recherches. D'autres sans y penser font d'abondantes et faciles
découvertes grâce à un pouvoir d'intuition qui fait défaut aux
premiers.

§94. C'est à ceux qui trouvent sans chercher que fait
allusion l'Ecriture lorsqu'elle parle des Israélites qui vont
jouir de biens qu'ils n'ont pas produits. (Deut. 6, 10-11):
cités, maisons, citernes, vignes et oliviers.

§95. Les cités sont les vertus génériques; les maisons
les vertus individuelles.

§96. Les citernes non creusées sont les réservoirs des
eaux célestes et délicieuses des vertus; les vignes symbolisent
l'allégresse que les vertus procurent et les oliviers, qui sont
à l'origine de l'huile, la lumière dont elles emplissent l'âme.

§97. Heureux sont ceux-ci: le monde leur est donné
sans peine. Mais ceux qui s'acharnent après des biens qui leur
sont inaccessibles et auxquels ils prétendent par une sorte
d'esprit de contestation sont des infortunés.

§98. Non seulement ils n'obtiennent pas ce qu'ils
recherchent, mais encore ils s'infligent des dommages qui ré-
jouissent leurs ennemis.

§99. Tel est le cas de ceux des Israélites qui, montés
malgré l'ordre reçu, sur la montagne de l'Amoréen s'en font
chasser par les habitants qui les mettent à mal comme feraient
des abeilles (Deut. 1, 43-44).

§100. Philon propose une explication allégorique de ces
deux versets qu'il vient de citer. La montagne de l'Amoréen et
l'état d'esprit des Israélites qui y montent symbolisent la
démarche des gens qui forcent leur talent pour pratiquer des
arts et métiers; la déroute symbolise l'échec honteux auquel
ils sont voués; la poursuite des Amoréens qui piquent leurs
agresseurs comme des abeilles, les morsures du sentiment que
l'on a de la contrefaçon commise et qui empêche la supercherie
de réussir.

§101. Philon illustre cette dernière proposition par
l'attitude des gens qui restituent des dépôts de peu de valeur
parce qu'ils sont à l'affût d'une spoliation plus importante.
Lorsqu'ils restituent le dépôt, ils font violence à leur mauvaise foi naturelle qui ne saurait jamais cesser de les percer
de son dard.[21]

§102. Les hypocrites religieux souffrent eux aussi
lorsqu'ils contrefont une piété qu'ils n'éprouvent pas.

§103. Après avoir donné le change un court moment, ils
se démasquent et sont confondus. Toute violence est de courte
durée.[22]

Quaestio et Solutio XI: §104-§116

§104. *Le Lemme Scripturaire*. Comme nous l'avons noté,
bien que le lemme scripturaire allégué soit le même pratiquement
que dans la *quaestio* précédente, le commentaire ne porte pas sur
la même partie du verset. Dans la *Quaestio et Solutio* X (§86)
le lemme était cité sous sa forme exacte: Νῶε εὗρε χάριν ἐναντίον κυρίου τοῦ θεοῦ. La dernière partie du verset, de χάριν à
θεοῦ n'étant pas commentée. Ici nous avons le verset en grec
plus classique: ἐναντίον κυρίου τοῦ θεοῦ est correctement
interprété et rendu par παρὰ κυρίῳ τῷ θεῷ.

§104. *Quaestio*. Bien que dans le §104 le commentaire
semble encore porter sur la notion de *trouver* et bien que le
verbe εὑρίσκειν figure dans les versets d'Ex. 33, 7 et Gen. 39,
20-21 qui commandent les articulations du passage, la vraie
Quaestio porte ici sur χάριν--παρὰ κυρίῳ τῷ θεῷ.
    A Νõε qui est le sujet de cette phrase, s'opposent en
bien Moïse qui a trouvé χάριν--παρὰ τῷ θεῷ (§109) et en mal
Joseph qui a trouvé χάριν--παρὰ τῷ ἀρχιδεσμοφύλακι (§§111-116).

§104. *Solutio*. Le lemme au premier regard, peut se
prendre en deux sens:
        (a) *Νõε a obtenu la grâce*. Cette acception n'est
pas recevable, puisque Νõε n'a pas, sous le rapport de la grâce,
de situation privilégiée. Toutes les créatures sans exception

one bénificié dans une mesure égale de la grâce de leur Créateur.

       (b) *Noé a été jugé digne de la grâce.*

§105. Cette interprétation du lemme est meilleure.[23]
Dieu juge dignes de sa grâce ceux qui restent fidèles à la
nature morale qu'il leur a assignée. Mais il est impossible
d'entendre cette proposition en rigueur.

§106. Pour être digne, au sens propre, de la grâce de
Dieu, il faut posséder une perfection dont la première, la plus
grande, la plus parfaite des oeuvres de Dieu, à savoir l'Univers,
est peut-être elle-même dépourvue.

§107. Il faut donc chercher un troisième sens au lemme
scripturaire examiné. C'est peut-être le suivant:
       (c) *Noé découvrit ce qu'est la grâce ou plutôt
quelle est sa fonction cosmique.* Noé, la sage ami de la recherche
et de la science, a découvert que la grâce divine est à l'origine
de tout ce qui existe et vit dans l'univers. C'est la faveur par
laquelle Dieu a donné le monde au monde.

§108. Le monde n'y a eu aucun mérite, aucun droit qui
l'eût rendu digne de le recevoir. Mais Dieu a créé le monde avec
une générosité, une bonté qui dépassait de très loin l'évalua-
tion des mérites. La Bonté est la vertu divine suprême et la
source de toutes ses grâces.

§109. A Gen. 6, 8, verset selon lequel Noé a plu au
Seigneur et à Dieu, qui sont des puissances de l'Etre, s'oppose
le verset d'Exode, 33, 17 selon lequel Dieu dit à Moïse: "Tu
as trouvé grâce auprès de moi," ce qui implique que Moïse a plu
à l'Etre qui est au delà des puissances dénommées Seigneur et
Dieu et qui se désigne ici à l'exclusion de tout autre attribut.

§110. La Sagesse de Moïse est donc jugée digne de l'Etre
lui-même tandis que celle de Noé qui n'est qu'une image de la
précédente et a une envergure plus individuelle, trouve l'agré-
ment du Seigneur et de Dieu, puissances subordonnées par lesquelles l'Etre manifeste sa souveraineté et son rôle de bienfaiteur.

§111. A Noé et à Moïse qui ont trouvé grâce auprès de
Dieu s'oppose Joseph qui a trouvé grâce auprès de geôlier en
chef. Joseph est l'esprit ami du corps et des passions, esclave
de l'eunuque chef-cuisinier. Il est conduit à la prison des
passions où il trouve une grâce infamante auprès du maître de
ces lieux.

§112. Les prisonniers qui y sont détenus sont ceux que
la nature a condamnés pour les dispositions de leur âme emplie
de vices.

§113. Quant au chef-geôlier c'est une figure qui symbolise l'ensemble des vices qui emprisonnent l'âme. Il est tout
à fait funeste de lui plaire et de le seconder, tâche que certains tiennent pour louable.

§114. En fait cette autorité et ce commandement en
second sont pire que l'insupportable esclavage. Il faut se
proposer toujours un idéal de vie libre des passions.

§115. Si l'on succombe à la passion, mieux vaut être
prisonnier que geôlier. Ressentir les souffrances de la prison
est le signe que tout espoir de libération n'est pas perdu. Se
faire au contraire geôlier c'est, sous les espèces de la course
aux emplois et aux honneurs, consentir à sa captivité et la
rendre perpétuelle.

§116. Il est donc nécessaire de fuir les faveurs du
chef geôlier et de rechercher celles de la Cause première. A
défaut de pouvoir y parvenir, il faut se faire le suppliant des
puissances de la Cause Première, du Seigneur et de Dieu, qui
touchés du culte authentique et sans défaillance qui leur sera
ainsi rendu, mettront leur suppliant au nombre de ceux qui leur
ont plu comme l'a fait Noé dont les enfants sont cités d'une
manière très étonnante et très inédite.

Quaestio et Solutio XII: §117-§121[24]

§117. *Le Lemme Scripturaire.* Αὗται αἱ γενέσις Νῶε·
Νῶε ἄνθρωπος δίκαιος, τέλειος ὢν ἐν τῇ γενεᾷ αὐτοῦ· τῷ θεῷ
εὐηρέστησε Νῶε. (Gen. 6, 9)

"Voici les générations de Noé[25]: Noé fut un homme, juste,
parfait en sa génération, Noé plut a Dieu."

§117. *Quaestio*. Philon ne tient compte ni dans les
Quaestiones in Genesim ni dans notre passage du verset de Gen.
6, 10: Ἐγέννησε δὲ Νῶε τρεῖς υἱοὺς, τὸν Σὴμ, τὸν Χάμ, τὸν
Ἰάφεθ, qu'il avait pourtant commenté implicitement lorsqu'en
De Gigantibus 1, il avait mentionné la naissance de Noé et de
ses fils par référence à Gen. 5, 32.

Détaché de son contexte, le verset de Gen. 6, 9 a une
allure étrange. Après l'annonce "voici les générations de Noé"
on se serait attendu à voir énumérer des noms de descendants,
or on lit la mention de quatre vertus:

1: ἄνθρωπος
2: δίκαιος
3: τέλειος
4: τῷ θεῷ εὐηρέστησε

§117. *Solutio*. Cet énoncé est pourtant naturel. De
même que des organismes donnent naissance à des organismes qui
leur sont semblables,

§118. une âme vertueuse donne naissance à l'humanité,
à la justice, à la perfection, à la grâce aux yeux de Dieu. Ces
vertus sont énumérées en gradation ascendante. Voilà pourquoi
la dernière en laquelle culminent toutes les autres est, dans
le verset, citée en dernier lieu.

§119. Après l'énumération des "générations" de Noé,
Philon revient sur le sens du mot γένεσις. Le vocable comporte
une acception positive comme dans le cas de Noé et du reste de
toutes les plantes et de tous les animaux. Il peut désigner
aussi une évolution négative que suggère le verset de Gen 37, 2[26]
à propos de Jacob. La formulation de ce verset est en effet
tout à fait parallèle à celui qui concerne les générations de
Noé. Αὗται δὲ αἱ γενέσεις Ἰακώβ· Ἰωσὴφ δέκα ἑπτὰ ἐτῶν ἦν
ποιμαίνων μετὰ τῶν ἀδελφῶν τὰ πρόβατα, ὢν νέος μετὰ τῶν υἱῶν
Βαλλᾶς καὶ τῶν υἱῶν Ζελφᾶς τῶν γυναικῶν πατρὸς αὐτοῦ.

"Voici les générations de Jacob: Joseph âgé de dix-sept
ans faisait paître avec ses frères, étant un jouvenceau, avec
les fils de Bilha et Zilpah, les femmes de son père."[27]

Le début du verset qui concerne les générations de Jacob est, au nom propre près, le même que celui qui est relatif aux générations de Noé, et bien que dans le cas de Jacob, la formule soit suivie de la mention d'un être apparemment concret, il y a entre la formule et la mention une sorte d'hiatus logique que Philon interprète comme si la phrase signifiait que Jacob suscite Joseph âgé de dix-sept ans: Cf. §120 Ἰωσὴφ εὐθὺς ἀπογεννᾶται.

§120. Joseph en effet n'est que l'image amoindrie, rétrécie, infidèle de la vertu de Jacob. Il apparaît aussitôt que Jacob se relâche et abandonne le domaine de Dieu, cher aux disciples de Moïse, pour le domaine du corps et des biens du corps auquel se dévouent ceux qui, quel que soit leur âge, restent des jeunes gens dans l'ordre spirituel.

§121. Voilà pourquoi Moïse dépeint Joseph comme paissant son troupeau en compagnie non des fils d'Israël, ses frères légitimes, mais des fils des concubines Bilhah et Zilpah.

Quaestio et Solutio XIII: §122-§139

§122. *Le Lemme Scripturaire*. Ἐφθάρη ἡ γῆ ἐναντίον τοῦ θεοῦ καὶ ἐπλήσθη ἀδικίας.
"La terre se corrompit devant Dieu et se remplit d'injustice." (Gen. 6, 11)[28]

§122. *Quaestio*. Pourquoi immédiatement après la mention des quatre "générations" de Noé, Moïse dit-il que la terre se corrompit et se remplit d'injustice? Philon affecte de voir dans cette juxtaposition une relation de cause à effet,[29] et déclare que l'intention de l'auteur sacré n'est pas difficile à apercevoir pour qui a reçu une formation philosophique.

§123. *Solutio*. Lorsque l'élément incorruptible se lève dans l'âme l'élément mortel se corrompt ou se détruit aussitôt.

§124. Selon la même doctrine, si de la couleur vive apparait sur le corps du lépreux, il sera souillé (Lev. 13, 14). Moïse précise que "la couleur vive souillera"[30] (*Lev.* 13, 15) au contraire de toutes les idées reçues.

§125. Mais c'est là une manifestation de l'originalité
de la sagesse de Moïse. Il veut dire que la couleur saine et
vive qui apparait dans l'âme est le témoin qui la confond.

§126. Ce témoin recense toutes les fautes de l'âme et
ne cesse de lui en faire le reproche et l'âme se rend compte
qu'elle est pleine d'injustice et de souillures.

§127. Ce principe explique aussi la règle très paradoxale formulée par Moïse et selon laquelle le lépreux partiel
est considéré comme *impur*, tandis qu'est *pur* le malade dont le
corps est entièrement recouvert par la lèpre.

§128. Le corps entièrement recouvert par la lèpre
symbolise les transgressions involontaires qui sont, en quelque
manière, *pures* et échappent au reproche de la conscience; la
lèpre partielle est le symbole des fautes volontaires qui sont,
si limité que soit leur domaine, condamnées par le juge qui
siège dans l'âme et les déclare *impures*.

§129. La lèpre qui a une double nature et se couvre
d'efflorescences de deux couleurs désigne le vice volontaire,
puisque l'âme qui possède en elle la raison vivifiante la récuse
comme pilote et confie le gouvernail à ceux qui ignorant tout de
l'art de naviguer conduiront au naufrage l'esquif de sa vie.

§130. La lèpre qui a viré tout entière au blanc[31]
figure la défaillance involontaire: l'esprit est alors amputé
de tout pouvoir de réflexion et se trouve plongé dans une nuit
totale où il subit des chutes incessantes et involontaires.

§131. Un autre commandement analogue se trouve en Lév.
14, 35-36[32] concernant la plaie de lèpre affectant une maison.
Le propriétaire de la maison atteinte doit avertir le prêtre qui
fait vider tout le mobilier pour qu'il ne devienne pas impur,
puis entre examiner l'habitation.

§132. C'est donc l'entrée du prêtre qui, d'une manière
paradoxale, rend impur ce qui était pur.

§133. Il y a là une importante vérité "naturelle," même
si elle ne s'accorde pas avec le sens littéral de la prescription.

§134. Aussi longtemps qui le prêtre, l'ἔλεγχος, guide de l'âme, n'est pas entré dans la maison de notre âme aucune de nos actions commises dans l'ignorance du bien, n'est blâmable.

§135. La lumière de l'ἔλεγχος au contraire agit comme un révélateur et fait prendre à l'âme conscience de son impureté. Le prêtre ordonne de vider la maison afin de la débarrasser de ses fautes et de pouvoir soigner ses maladies.

§136. Philon trouve une autre illustration de sa doctrine dans l'épisode d'Elie et de la veuve de Sarepta (I Rois, 17, 9-24). La femme de Sarepta est une *veuve en esprit*, c'est-à-dire une femme qui a fait son deuil des passions qui corrompent et souillent l'âme. Apparentée à la figure de la veuve de Sarepta est celle de Tamar.

§137. En effet, Tamar devenue veuve s'établit dans la maison de son Père céleste en renonçant à tout ce qui est mortel jusqu'à ce que, ayant reçu la semence divine, elle enfante les vertus qui lui feront acquérir la palme à laquelle elle doit son nom.

§138. Toute âme désireuse de devenir une veuve en esprit, dépourvue de tous les vices, dit au prophète avec la femme de Sarepta: "O homme de Dieu, tu es entré chez moi pour rappeler mon iniquité et ma faute" (I Rois 17, 18).[33] En effet l'entrée dans l'âme de ce personnage sacré, interprète et prophète de Dieu, oblige l'âme à gémir sur ses errements passés et à en haïr les conséquences.

§139. Les anciens désignaient le prophète tantôt par l'appellation d'"homme de Dieu" tantôt par celle de "voyant" qui toutes deux en décrivaient excellemment le caractère inspiré et le don de vision.[34]

Quaestio et Solutio XIV: §140-§183

§140. *Le Lemme Scripturaire*. Après une phrase qui est la conclusion apologétique de la partie précédente et qui sert de transition aux paragraphes qui suivent, Philon introduit le verset de Gen. 6, 12: ἦν δὲ κατεφθαρμένη, ὅτι κατέφθειρε πᾶσα σάρξ τὴν ὁδὸν αὐτοῦ ἐπὶ τῆς γῆς.[35]

"Elle était corrompue parce que toute chair avait
corrompu sa voie sur la terre."

§141. *Quaestio*. Les mots τὴν ὁδὸν αὐτοῦ semblent renvoyer à l'expression πᾶσα σάρξ et pourtant l'anaphorique au
génitif masculin ne semble pas pouvoir s'accorder avec un sub-
stantif féminin.

§142. *Solutio*. En réalité, cette apparente impropriété
montre qu'il n'est pas seulement question dans le verset de la
chair qui corrompt sa propre voie,[36] mais encore qui corrompt sa
voie à Lui, la voie qui conduit à Dieu.

§143. Cette voie est la sagesse dont le terme est la
connaissance et la science de Dieu. Tout compagnon de la chair
s'efforce de la corrompre, car la science[37] est l'ennemie par
excellence du plaisir de la chair.

§144. La notion de la voie de Dieu évoque dans l'esprit
de Philon un épisode fameux de l'itinéraire spirituel de la
nation horatique--Israël dans sa progression vers Dieu au long
de la voie royale est combattu par le terrestre Edom qui menace
de rendre la route impraticable.

§145. Les messagers d'Israël lui demandent de traverser
à pied ses terres sans passer à travers champs ni vignes, sans
boire l'eau de sa citerne. Ils suivront la voie royale sans
s'en détourner à droite ni à gauche. Edom leur interdit le
passage et les menace de la guerre. Les Israélites reviennent à
la charge en spécifiant qu'ils désirent suivre le chemin de la
montagne et s'engagent à payer à Edom une compensation pour
l'eau qu'eux et leurs troupeaux pourraient boire. Mais,
assurent-ils, il n'y a ici rien qui vaille. Ils ne feront que
suivre le chemin de la montagne. Nouveau refus d'Edom.

§146. Philon commente désormais Nombres 26, 17-20. Il
commence par rappeler l'anecdote selon laquelle Socrate désignait
les richesses exhibées au cours d'une fastueuse procession comme
tout ce dont il n'avait pas besoin.

§147. Cette victoire définitive sur les richesses est
le fait d'une âme admirable.

§148.   Mais si chez les Païens il ne s'est trouvé qu'un
seul homme exceptionnel pour triompher des richesses, à l'école
de Moïse, c'est toute une nation très populeuse qui, ayant appris
les préliminaires de la sagesse accomplit le même exploit. C'est
ce que montre l'audace des paroles que l'âme de chaque disciple
adresse au terrestre Edom, le roi de tous les biens d'apparence
que sont les biens de la terre.

§149.   "Je vais traverser ton territoire." Israël se
fait fort, de la sorte, de dépasser tous les biens terrestres
d'un irrésistible élan.

§150.   Il méprisera les biens de convention: richesses,
distinctions sociales, noblesse, gloire. Il méprisera même les
biens dit "indifférents": santé, exactitude des sens, beauté,
force physique.

§151.   L'idéal d'Israël est celui de la Migration qui lui
fait quitter la région terrestre pour vivre au milieu des natures
divines.

§152.   Cet idéal doit procéder d'un choix délibéré et
non de la paresse ou du manque de goût pour les biens dont on
s'abstient.

§153.   C'est pourquoi Israël dit: "je dépasserai ces
biens en passant à travers ton territoire" c'est-à-dire en connaissance de cause de ce qu'il méprise.

§154.   Mais, selon le lemme scripturaire, Israël s'engage
au contraire à ne pas dépasser les champs et les vignes symboli-
sant la culture qui fait mûrir les vertus et l'allégresse que
l'exercice des vertus procure.

§155.   Israël qui boit l'eau du ciel et sur qui Dieu
répand sa manne n'a que faire de la citerne d'Edom qui ne
recueille que l'eau matérielle, l'eau de la terre.

§156.   L'idée même de thésauriser de l'eau dans une
citerne est une marque de défiance à l'égard de Dieu dispensa-
teur de l'eau de son trésor céleste.

§157. Mais Israël[38] que ni le ciel ni la pluie ni la
citerne ni rien de créé n'est capable de nourrir entièrement,
compte sur le Dieu qui l'a rassasié depuis son enfance. Il
n'aura aucun regard pour l'eau amassée sous terre.

§158. Il ne risque pas de boire à la citerne d'Edom,
lui à qui Dieu dispense l'ivresse soit par l'entremise d'un
ange soit directement.

§159. Il veut donc marcher au long de la voie royale en
méprisant les biens terrestres. La voie royale est celle qui a
pour maître le vrai Roi.

§160. C'est la sagesse, qui permet aux âmes suppliantes
de se réfugier en Dieu vers lequel mène la voie royale.

§161. Ceux qui auront accédé à Dieu connaîtront aussi
sa béatitude et leur peu de valeur comme Abraham qui ayant
approché Dieu sut aussitôt qu'il n'était que terre et cendre.[39]

§162. Il faut avancer sur la voie royale en en suivant
l'exact milieu sans en dévier ni à droite ni à gauche. La dévi-
ation est blâmable quel que soit le sens selon lequel elle
s'écarte de l'exact milieu.

§163. Les gens qui vivent inconsidérément versent dans
les excès opposés: témérité, avarice, fourberie, superstition
en déviant à droite; lâcheté, prodigalité, naïveté, impiété, en
déviant à gauche.

§164. Pour éviter de tomber dans les vices opposés, il
faut avancer droit sur la route médiane.[40] Celle qui, bordée
par la témérité et la lâcheté, la dissipation et l'avarice, la
fourberie et la naïveté, la superstition et l'impiété, passe
par le courage, la modération, la prudence et la piété.

§165. Chacune de ces vertus constitue une avenue prati-
cable située à égale distance entre les deux excès opposés, et
que les organes corporels ne sauraient emprunter, mais bien les
mouvements d'une âme qui toujours désire le bien suprême.

§166. Edom hait la vertu. Il craint qu'Israël en
traversant son territoire ne saccage les fruits qu'il a produits

pour ruiner la sagesse et qui sont encore sur pied. Il menace
donc de s'opposer à Israël par les armes.

§167. Sans se laisser intimider, Israël déclare qu'il
veut suivre le chemin de crête de la montagne. Marcher au haut
de la montagne lui convient à lui qui contemple la nature la
plus sublime et dédaigne comme trop basses les réalités corporelles. Mais le même mot signifie à la fois "montagne" et
"définition." La seconde acception est, elle aussi, très appro-
priée à la vocation d'Israël qui définit tout ce qui existe.
Il ne touchera donc à aucun des biens d'Edom.

§168. Y toucher serait en effet honorer Edom qui
pourrait se vanter d'avoir séduit les amants de la vertu par
les appâts du plaisir.

§169. C'est pourquoi il dit "si je bois de ton eau je
te rendrai hommage." Par τιμήν il entend "l'honneur."

§170. En effet, lorsqu'un débauché ou un coquin voit
un homme qui avait l'apparence de la vertu céder à la malhonnêteté ou au vice il se réjouit et croit en être honoré, puisque
le personnage respectable semble conférer une garantie morale
aux vices qu'il pratique comme lui.

§171. Il faut donc dire à tout coquin: "Boire de ton
eau ou toucher à tes biens reviendrait à t'honorer et à t'approu-
ver." Mais tout ce qui fait l'objet de tes soins n'est qu'un
néant absolu.

§172. En effet tout ce qui est mortel est dans une
oscillation continuelle et a l'inconsistance des songes trom-
peurs.

§173. Les vicissitudes des pays et des peuples en
fournissent une preuve frappante. En Europe les Macédoniens
brisent la Grèce; puis leur Empire mondial est partagé entre
les Diadoques.

§174. Les Empires ou royaumes barbares offrent le même
spectacle. Les Perses vaincus par les Macédoniens sont dominés
par les Parthes. La grandeur de l'Egypte n'est plus qu'un

souvenir. Les Ethiopiens, Carthage, la Libye, les rois du Pont
ne sont plus rien.

§175. L'Europe, L'Asie, le monde entier sont aussi
instables qu'un navire balloté par la tempête.

§176. C'est la ronde du Logos divin que le commun des
hommes désigne du nom de Fortune qui explique ces vicissitudes
historiques. Le Logos redistribue sans cesse à chacun les biens
de tous de sorte que le monde semblable à une cité unique soit
soumis au juste régime de la démocratie.

§177. Le résultat est que toutes les affaires humaines
sont oeuvre de néant et chose nulle. Elles n'ont pas plus de
consistance que le vent ou que l'ombre. Elles sont inconstantes
comme le flux et le reflux.

§178. Pareille à eux, la prospérité se retire complètement d'une nation qu'elle avait d'abord couverte.

§179. Seuls entendent la raison de ces phénomènes les
Israélites qui disent à Edom que tout le devenir est chose de
rien et qu'ils suivront le chemin de crête.

§180. Il faut en effet emprunter les chemins de crête
des definitions philosophiques pour être capable de renoncer à
ce qui est mortel et émigrer vers les réalités incorruptibles.
De même que le terrestre Edom veut barrer la route à
Israël, le Logos divin[41] veut barrer la voie d'Edom et de ses
émules.

§181. Au nombre des émules d'Edom il faut compter Balaam
qui même lorsqu'il aperçoit l'ange qui lui barre la route, continue son chemin pour accomplir ses oeuvres perverses.[42]

§182. C'est que lorsque la maladie spirituelle a
atteint un certain point de gravité nous sommes incapables
d'obéir aux admonestations de l'*Elenchos* qui veut nous détourner
de notre voie mauvaise.

§183. Le résultat est "la mort avec les blessés" qu'ont
transpercés les passions. La triste fin de Balaam doit inciter

ceux dont les maux spirituels ne sont pas comme les siens
incurables, à se rendre favorable le juge intérieur et à ne pas
contester ses sentences.

C. *Récapitulation et Conclusions Générales*

Nous avons cru bon de pratiquer l'analyse des deux
traités de Philon d'une manière beaucoup plus détaillée qu'il
n'est habituel. Ce n'est qu'ainsi, pensons-nous, qu'il devient
possible de formuler un jugement précis sur l'exégèse de Philon
d'Alexandrie dans *De Gigantibus* et *Quod Deus*.

(a) *Gig. Deus et QG*

La première constatation que cette analyse nous permet
de faire, c'est qu'elle confirme, nous semble-t-il, d'une façon
très nette l'impression que nous avions retirée d'une lecture
courante de notre texte. Les deux traités sont constitués par
une suite de quatorze *quaestiones et solutiones* sur quelques
versets de la Genèse.

L'objet, la méthode et souvent la teneur de cette suite
de commentaires exégétiques sont les mêmes dans *De Gigantibus--
Quod Deus sit Immutabilis* d'une part et dans *Quaestiones in
Genesim* I, 89-99 d'autre part. Il est indéniable cependant que
des différences existent entre les deux séries.

Le commentaire dans les deux traités est, d'une manière
générale, plus ample, plus élaboré, plus riche que dans *QG*. Si
l'on n'y trouve pas de développement arithmologique sur les cent
vingt ans de la vie de l'homme comparable à celui qui se lit en
QG, I, 91, Philon a au contraire étoffé et élargi le commentaire
dans les traités, de parties qui n'ont rien qui leur corresponde
dans les *QG*, ainsi les passages concernant la grâce trouvée par
Moïse en opposition à celle de Noé ou celle de Joseph con-
trastée avec celle de Noé; "les générations" de Jacob; l'épisode
d'Edom et celui de Balaam.

Considérés globalement *Quaestiones in Genesim* I, 89-99
font figure d'ébauche lorsqu'on les compare à *De Gigantibus* et
à *Quod Deus sit Immutabilis*. Pour la raison, probablement, que
les premières ont précédé les seconds dans le temps.

Articulées entre elles au moyen de formules de transition, transformées en texte suivi, les quatorze *quaestiones et
solutiones* qui forment la trame des deux traités n'en constituent pas moins une paraphrase et un commentaire philosophique

perpétuel du texte scripturaire. Le lemme est décomposé en
parties secondaires dont chacune est analysée dans le développement exégétique qu'elle balise en quelque sorte et dont elle
jalonne le progrès. Ces références constantes au lemme commenté,
ces mots-échos[43] qui parsèment le discours permettent souvent
d'en percevoir les intentions et la signification exactes. Il
arrive même, comme nous l'avons noté a propos d' ἔγγονα (§138)
ou de ὅτι τὸ τῆς ψυχῆς μεμυκὸς ὄμμα ἀναβλέψας (§181) que les
termes du commentaire philonien réfèrent à des parties du lemme
qui ne sont pas citées.

  Quant à l'art de composer, notre analyse a fait apparaître, pensons-nous, que le jugement de Massebieau est plus
près de la vérité que l'appréciation négative d'E. Herriot.
Philon pratique en fait l'art de composer et même, dans la
perspective réelle de sa pensée qui est celle des *quaestiones
et solutiones*, il le pratique d'une façon parfaitement cohérente et rigoureuse, avec une logique sans faille. C'est un
auteur clair.

  Les deux traités n'apparaissent comme déconcertants,
pleins de matières hétéroclites, dépourvus de cohérence, que
lorsqu'on y cherche une pensée systématique exposée synthétique-
ment. Et, réellement l'unité interne existe si peu que, nous
l'avons mentionné, son absence a peut-être été responsable de
la scission en deux écrits distincts de ce qui, à l'origine,
était un seul traité.

(b) *Problèmes de l'allégorie*

  "La méthode allégorique chez Philon, écrit E. Bréhier[44]
ne prouve rien et ne veut rien prouver, ce n'est pas un instrument apologétique. . . ."

  Le commentaire allégorique dans nos deux traités permet
de s'inscrire en faux contre l'assertion de Bréhier. L'allégorie dans *De Gigantibus--Quod Deus* apparaît avec des fonctions
apologétiques non équivoques dans le propos commun et principal
qui est de fournir un recours contre le mythe.

  Le *De Gigantibus* évacue grâce à l'allégorie des representations concernant la révolte des anges du genre de celles
qui remplissent la littérature de l'Intertestament, la littérature chrétienne et la littérature midrashique.[45] La gigantomachie appartient au domaine de la fable avec tout ce que cette
notion implique de périls pour la raison et la piété humaines.[46]

C'est pourquoi, lorsque le Législateur met en scène des géants,
la fabulation ne lui en reste pas moins étrangère.

Les conceptions anthropomorphiques et anthropopathiques
sont elles aussi, et entre toutes, liées au mythe. Elle con-
duisent à des représentations impies de la divinité, à un culte
inadéquat et servile, en un mot à la superstition.[47]

L'interprétation allégorique permet à Philon, même
lorsqu'elle dépasse le sens littéral de l'Ecriture, de louer la
lettre du texte sacré et d'en porter les étrangetés apparentes
au compte de l'incomparable originalité philosophique de Moïse.
Nos deux traités contiennent toute une série d'expressions lau-
datives à la gloire du texte scripturaire dont elles soulignent
la vérité que l'allégorie, surtout, fait resortir.[48]

Ceci dit, il n'est pas douteux que Philon considère
l'exégèse allégorique comme un instrument de découverte spirituelle et le plus puissant outil au service de la philosophie
entendue comme une interprétation de la parole de Dieu et une
contemplation de l'univers.

L'usage qui est fait dans nos deux traités de l'exégèse
allégorique pose avec une particulière netteté le problème de
la légitimité de cette méthode, de ses droits par rapport au
sens littéral de l'Ecriture, du rôle, du statut et de la dignité
de ce dernier et, de façon concomitante, la problème de la Bible
de Philon dans le *De Gigantibus* et le *Quod Deus*.

Philon soulève lui-même en *Deus* 133 la question de savoir
si son exégèse allégorique de la Loi sur la lèpre des maisons
s'accorde avec la signification littérale de ce commandement.

᾿Αλλὰ ταῦτα μὲν εἰ συνᾴδει τῇ ῥητῇ καὶ προχείρῳ διατάξει,
σκέψονται οἷς ἔθος καὶ φίλον. . . .

On aurait sans doute tort de conclure de cette formule
que Philon n'éprouve que mépris à l'endroit du sens littéral en
tant que tel. Ce qui est visé ici est non pas le texte littéral
lui-même, que Philon ne dédaigne pas, comme le laissent apparaître plusieurs de ses remarques, mais l'objection qui viserait
à déclarer irrecevable une interprétation allégorique inspirée
par la droite raison au nom de son incompatibilité avec le sens
littéral. Méritent d'être qualifiés de *littéralistes* non pas
les exégètes qui admettent et tiennent en estime le sens
littéral de l'Ecriture, mais ceux qui emprisonnent l'Ecriture
dans les limites de ce qu'ils croient être le sens obvie, qui
rejettent toute interprétation à laquelle il serait possible
d'opposer le sens littéral.

Pour Philon, l'interprétation allégorique d'une loi n'en
annule pas en principe la validité légale et le plus souvent une
disposition qui a été interprétée allégoriquement dans ce qu'on
est convenu d'appeler le Commentaire allégorique est commentée
sur le plan de la pratique dans l'Exposition de la Loi. Mais il
existe aux yeux de Philon quelques cas qui font exception. A
tort ou à raison il estime que la loi concernant la nécessité
de restituer avant le coucher du soleil un manteau donné en gage
est dans sa teneur littérale indigne de la sublimité et de la
pitié de Dieu. C'est pourquoi il s'attache fort longuement en
De Somniis I, 92-102 à mettre en lumière les difficultés du sens
littéral, à l'intention des littéralistes évoqués au paragraphe
102. Il estime que la loi édictée en Exode XXII, 26-27 n'en est
pas véritablement une et il n'en traite pas dans le *De Specialibus Legibus*.

Il peut arriver qu'une inconséquence dans un détail de
la partie narrative lui paraisse appeler les mêmes remarques et
inviter à un abandon du sens littéral. Ainsi lorsqu'il lit en
Genèse 9, 25 que Canaan est maudit et destiné à servir ses frères
pour une faute commise par Cham. Il laisse aux littéralistes,
avec une ironie assez perceptible,[49] le plaisir de débrouiller
la difficulté et il feint d'admettre qu'il y sont parfaitement
parvenus. Quant à lui-même il suivra l'inspiration de la droite
raison.

La loi sur la lèpre devait sembler à Philon assez
étrange dans sa formulation littérale et surtout assez dépourvue
d'application pratique possible pour appeler le même jugement.
La Loi sur la lèpre, qu'il s'agisse de la lèpre des personnes
ou de la lèpre des maisons ne reçoit dans le corpus philonien
de commentaire qu'allégorique[50] et le *De Specialibus Legibus*
l'ignore.

Voilà pourquoi nous pensons que la formule qu'il emploie
en *Deus* 133 signifie surtout qu'il ne sait pas ce que la loi sur
la lèpre peut bien vouloir dire littéralement[51] et qu'il
n'accepte pas qu'on puisse opposer le sens littéral à l'interprétation qu'il propose lui-même et qui est *garantie* par la
profonde vérité naturelle sur laquelle elle débouche: συνῳδὸν
οὕτως οὐδὲν ἄλλο ἄλλῳ, ὡς τὸ εἰσελθόντος τοῦ ἱερέως τὰ κατὰ τὴν
οἰκίαν μιαίνεσθαι. C'est là, bien entendu, encore une façon de
sauver le texte de l'Ecriture, mais surtout une telle attitude
est à la fois l'origine et l'explication du caractère en apparence contradictoire de l'exégèse de Philon. Philon propose

d'une part une interprétation minutieuse, qui est attentive aux
moindres détails de texte sacré, qui en valorise la lettre à
l'extrême et pourrait être qualifiée de *lecture talmudique*. Mais
d'autre part, il parait ne pas hésiter à adapter de diverses
manières le texte scripturaire au propos du développement où il
est lui-même engagé, allant jusqu'à omettre tel ou tel verset
dont la teneur lui semble incompatible avec sa pensée du moment.
Cette liberté déconcertante[52] unie à une extrême soumission à
la lettre du texte scripturaire, ne doit pas s'expliquer par la
désinvolture ou la suffisance de Philon. Il croit au caractère
inspiré des suggestions de la droite raison et il estime que le
texte de Moïse qui enferme toute la nature, qui est inépuisable
comme elle, souffre d'être ainsi--*non pas manipulé*, comme nous
serions tentés de qualifier un tel traitement, mais mis dans une
perspective légitime, qui en dévoile une dimension supplémentaire,
qui le révèle en profondeur au lieu de le trahir.

　　　Pour le lecteur moderne, à quoi tiennent les sentiments
mêlés, où la fascination le dispute à la déception, que provoque
souvent Philon?

　　　Si hasardeux qu'il soit toujours de comparer auteurs
anciens et auteurs modernes et des auteurs aussi éloignés dans
le temps et l'espace que Philon d'Alexandrie et Franz Kafka,
nous tenterons tout de même un parallèle. Comme Philon, Kafka
est un extraordinaire créateur de symboles. Sa puissance
d'envoûtement et le sentiment d'insatisfaction qu'il laisse
parfois à certains lecteurs que l'"indétermination" met particulièrement mal à l'aise, proviennent de l'obscurité du sens qui
sous-tend les paraboles et dont aucune exégèse rationnelle ne
parvient à rendre compte d'une façon convaincante ou exhaustive.

　　　Les représentations plastiques sont mises au service
d'un langage qui est proprement musical et qui, autant que la
musique, semble rebelle à toute traduction discursive. Qui
suggère et se dérobe.

　　　Philon quant à lui, fascine par sa virtuosité exégétique,
par sa faculté d'apercevoir des rapports inattendus entre le
texte biblique et des réalités apparemment très éloignées, par
la puissance avec laquelle il invente des symboles originaux,
souvent baroques, mais toujours expressifs ou frappants, tandis
que le discours philosophique auquel ces éléments correspondent
risque de sembler trop clair, au contraire de celui de Kafka,
trop pauvre et décevant eu égard aux moyens mis en oeuvre.

Il serait toutefois équitable de ne pas perdre de vue
que ces défauts sont, en partie au moins, inséparables du caractère d'apologie de l'Ecriture qui est propre à l'allégorie de
Philon et en vertu duquel l'exégèse s'efforce, au moyen des
symboles qu'elle invente de retrouver dans le texte sacré des
vérités reconnues. En définitive d'ailleurs, les thèmes exégétiques par quoi surtout Philon a influencé la postérité, com-
binent en une création nouvelle les idées philosophiques et des
symboles scripturaires. C'est à cela que devra prendre garde le
lecteur soucieux de dépasser les préjugés modernes et de ne pas
perdre de vue que, selon la fameuse formule d'Ernest Renan, il
n'est d'admiration qu'historique.

NOTES

[1]Cette singularité s'explique peut-être par le fait que le *De Gigantibus* et le *Quod Deus* ne constituaient à l'origine qu'un seul et même traité. Le Catalogue d'Eusèbe (*Histoire ecclésiastique* II, 18, 4) les mentionne sous le titre commun de Περὶ γιγάντων ἢ [ou καὶ] περὶ τοῦ μὴ τρέπεσθαι τὸ θεῖον. L'auteur du florilège dit de *Johannes Monachus ineditus* introduit des extraits du *Quod Deus* par la formule ἐκ τοῦ περὶ γιγάντων: voyez E. Schürer, *A History of the Jewish People in the Time of Jesus Christ* translated by Sophia Taylor and Rev. Peter Christie, Vol. III, Edimbourg 1891, p. 326, 334-35. H. Leisegang (Philo von Alexandria *Die Werke in Deutscher Übersetzung*, Band IV, 2. Auflage, Berlin 1962, pp. 53-54) qui renvoie au catalogue d'Eusèbe estime que la partition actuelle du traité a été opérée par quelque copiste. Il souligne qu l'on ne trouve jamais entre deux traités consécutifs, mais distincts de Philon une formule comparable aux trois derniers mots du *De Gigantibus*.

[2]Voyez notre article "L,Exégèse de Philon d'Alexandrie" *Revue d'Histoire et de Philosophie Religieuses* LIII (1973) pp. 309-29 spécialt. pp. 323-24; et notre ouvrage *Le Commentaire de l'Écriture chez Philon d'Alexandrie* Leyde 1977, pp. 1, 170 et ss.

[3]Voyez *Die Werke in Deutscher Übersetzung, Inhaltsübersicht* p. 55 et s; *Loeb Philo* II, pp. 443-45; *De Gigantibus*; *Quod Deus*, éd A. Moses p. 21 (non paginée), "Analyse du traité" dont le texte fournit aux intertitres.

[4]Depuis l'édition de R. Marcus, indispensable, mais souvent très imparfaite, dans la Bibliothèque Loeb (1953), les *Quaestiones* ont suscité récemment des travaux significatifs. On mentionnera ceux de F. Petit, "Les fragments grecs du livre VI des Questions sur la Genèse de Philon d'Alexandrie" *Le Museon* 84 (1971) 93-150; ce travail sur *QG* IV, 154-248 a été étendu à l'ensemble des fragments grecs dans *Philon d'Alexandrie 33, Quaestiones Fragmenta Graeca*, Paris 1978. F. Petit a publié aussi une édition critique et un commentaire d'une ancienne version latine partielle datant du IV° siècle des *Questions sur la Genèse* qui contient quelques fragments remarquables non conservés dans la version arménienne. Voyez *L'ancienne version latine des Questions sur la Genèse de Philon d'Alexandrie I Edition Critique II Commentaire* TU 113-14 Berlin 1973. E. Lucchesi "La division en six livres des *Quaestiones In Genesim* de Philon d'Alexandrie" *Le Museon* 89 (1976) 384-95. On trouvera aussi des remarques utiles dans l'ouvrage du même auteur: *L'usage de Philon dans l'oeuvre exégétique de Saint Ambroise, Arbeiten zur Literatur und Geschichte des hellenistischen Judentums* IX, Leyde 1977. CH. MERCIER, *Philon d'Alexandrie 34 A Quaestiones in Genesim* Livres I-II, Paris 1979 contient le texte latin de J. B. AUCHER et une traduction française faite sur la version arménienne. P. BORGEN--R. SKARSTEN, "Quaestiones et solutiones: some observations on the Form of Philo's Exegesis," *Studia Philonica* 4 (1976-1977), 1-13; J. ROYSE "The Original Structure of Philo's *Quaestiones*, Ibid., 41-78.

[5]Voyez note complémentaire 1.

[6]Philon n'a pas commenté ailleurs le verset de Genèse VI, 3.

[7]Voyez note complémentaire 2.

[8]*Quaestiones in Genesim* I, 92 semble très en retrait, par rapport à notre texte, relativement aux géants issus de l'union des anges avec des femmes mortelles. Philon commence par indiquer que pour Moïse les Géants ne sont pas les êtres nés du sol et fils de la terre, mais que le prophète emploie ce nom au sens figuré pour désigner des hommes dont la taille hors du commun semble imiter celle d'Hercule. Hercule était selon la fable un demi-dieu; les géants sont, d'après Moïse, les enfants des anges et des femmes. Les anges, créatures spirituelles, peuvent, cependant prendre l'apparence humaine pour les nécessités du moment telles que connaître des femmes pour en engendrer des Hercules.
Il est très frappant de constater que dans la suite de la *Quaestio* les anges ne sont pas blâmés pour leur commerce charnel. Philon ne stigmatise que la perversité des mères mortelles. Les "géants" placés entre la vertu paternelle et le vice maternel sont condamnés s'ils s'écartent de la première et méprisent l'Etre Suprême. La réalité mythologique, apparemment conservée, semble déboucher sur une allégorie morale analogue à l'apologue de Prodicos. Il paraît en tout cas évident que Philon se refuse, même aux dépens de la clarté ou de la logique, à impliquer ici les anges dans le mal et le péché.

[9]Le texte de *Quaestiones in Genesim* I, 92 permet de se rendre compte que c'est Philon lui-même qui doit avoir été responsable de l'altération du verset de Genèse 6, 2 (*De Gigantibus*, 6) ou au moins de Genèse 6, 4 (*Quod Deus* 1) où les mots υἱοὶ τοῦ θεοῦ que donnent la majorité des manuscrits de la LXX, ont été remplacés par l'expression équivalente d' ἄγγελοι τοῦ θεοῦ. En effet, la fin de la *Quaestio* est constituée par une discussion de υἱοὶ τοῦ θεοῦ. Philon y observe que Moïse appelle parfois les anges *Fils de Dieu* parce que ce sont des êtres incorporels qui ne doivent leur naissance à aucun mortel. Surtout, Philon voit dans l'appellation de *Fils de Dieu* une signification morale. Moïse qualifie les hommes excellents et vertueux de *Fils de Dieu*, tandis qu'il appelle "corps" les hommes méchants et pervers; les hommes vertueux étant incorporels comme les anges.
Il est évident que, de la sorte, οἱ ἄγγελοι τοῦ θεοῦ devait dans la perspective de l'interprétation philonienne de *De Gigantibus--Quod sit Deus*, paraître préférable a υἱοὶ τοῦ θεοῦ.

[10]Voyez note complémentaire 3.

[11]Sur la question de la stérilité d'Anne, nous nous permettons de renvoyer à notre étude "Στεῖρα, Στερρά, πολλὴ et l'exégèse de 1 Samuel 2, 5," *Sileno*, Roma, Aprile-Dicembre 1977 (paru 1979) pp. 149-85.

[12]Voyez la note de Leisegang dans *Philon von Alexandria, Die Werke in Deutscher Übersetzung* Band IV 2. Auflage, Berlin 1962, p. 76 n. 2.

[13]Nous avons en *Quaestiones in Genesim* I 93 l'équivalent des §§20-49.

Toutefois le partie de *QG* I, 93 qui correspond aux §§33-49 de *Quod Deus*, traite plutôt que la responsabilité de l'homme, de sa nature mixte irrésistiblement, du fait du corps, entraînée au mal.

[14]*QG* I, 93 confirme ce jugement. Toutefois Philon omet en *Deus* de commenter les mots ἀπὸ ἑρπετῶν ἕως πετεινῶν τοῦ οὐρανοῦ (Gen 6, 7) qui ne sont pas cités en §§20-49, qui sont cités au §51 mais ne font l'objet d'aucun commentaire en §§51-69. Philon leur consacre la *Quaestio* 1, 94, où il les explique au sens littéral, puis au sens allégorique. Le commentaire allégorique qui diffère des explications que nous lisons en *Deus* §§33-49, lui est cependant, un peu analogue.

[15]Ces remarques correspondent à une partie du texte scripturaire (verset 7) concernant les animaux qui n'est pas citée, comme nous l'avons noté, dans la *Quaestio* VII, qui sera citée, mais non commentée dans la *Quaestio* VIII. Comparez §47 τὰ μὲν γὰρ ἄλλα ζῷα . . . ὥσπερ οἰκέται δεσπόταις et *QG* I, 94: ". . . not necessarily and primarily were beasts made but for the sake of men and for their service."

[16]Tous ces paragraphes de Philon nous paraissent revêtus d'une très grande importance. Les facultés dont il est question ici sont, bien entendu, essentiellement conçues comme analogues aux facultés ou fonctions organiques humaines et dont chacune implique l'existence d'organes corporels destinés à en permettre la mise en oeuvre. Mais le texte, qui insiste sur le fait qu'on ne saurait à propos de Dieu concevoir rien d'autre que son existence pure et simple, semble bien indiquer que les facultés que Philon distingue ailleurs à propos de la divinité n'ont pas d'existence véritablement objective. Ce sont des propositions théologiques que l'esprit humain dégage de l'Ecriture, ce miroir parfait qui réfléchit la nature. L'allusion au Logos dans le §57 ne nous paraît pas infirmer cette observation. Parler du Logos est une façon d'indiquer sans rien en dire d'autre, que Dieu dispense ses biens sans recourir à des organes corporels et d'une manière qui lui est entièrement particulière. Le Logos est Dieu lui-même et nullement un instrument de Dieu au sens propre du terme.

[17]Il va sans dire que ces explications peuvent sembler à la fois forcées et débouchant sur une banalité philosophique. Mais il est certain que Philon se heurtait à des versets dont il était particulièrement difficile de rendre compte à la lumière de la doctrine de l'immutabilité de Dieu. *QG* I 95 témoigne d'un embarras analogue et d'une pauvreté philosophique comparable. On y trouve d'ailleurs la doctrine de nos §§71-72.

[18]Cette proposition, comme la fin de *QG* I, 95 a une portée purement générale et ne concerne naturellement pas les oeuvres de Dieu. Les fautes des hommes qui procèdent non de la divinité, mais comme l'indique le §73, du libre arbitre humain, sont mises en relation avec la passion par la formule que Moïse emploie tout à fait improprement de Dieu: "J'ai été passionné (ou irrité) comme le montre le fait que je les ai créés."

[19]Philon n'explique pas clairement, à l'inverse de ce qu'il fait pour l'apparition de Noé, par la grâce de Dieu, le sens de la proposition οἱ φαῦλοι θυμῷ γεγόνασι θεοῦ. A moins qu'il ne s'agisse que de la manifestation des φαῦλοι en tant

que tels qui résulte du seul jeu de leur libre arbitre (§73) et
n'est mise en relation avec la colère de Dieu que pour les
raisons philosophiques énoncées aux §§71-72.

Il ne dit pas non plus comment il conçoit qu'un Dieu
immuable et dépourvu de sentiments comparables a ceux de l'homme
inflige des châtiments ou dispense des grâces. Nous nous mouvons
d'ailleurs sur un plan qui semble situé tantôt dans la réalité
concrète tantôt sur le plan de l'allégorie psychologique. Ainsi
au §85 l'humanité est désignée par les mots τῷ πλήθει τῶν ἀδίκων
λογισμῶν: "la foule des raisonnements injustes" et au §123 Noé
est l'élément immortel qui pénétrant dans l'âme corrompt l'élément mortel.

[20]Voyez note complémentaire 4.

[21]Voyez note complémentaire 5.

[22]Il peut sembler que ce développement nous ait consi-
dérablement éloignés de la recherche sur "trouver" et du contexte
du traité. En réalité il n'en est rien. Les paragraphes §§92-
103 illustrent *a contrario* le cas de ceux qui trouvent sans avoir
eu à chercher. Dans tous les exemples cités, qu'il s'agisse de
nazir qui "retrouve," du laboureur, de Jacob ou des Israélites
héritant des villes, maisons, citernes, vignes et oliviers qu'ils
n'ont ni bâties ni creusées ni plantées, l'idée de "retrouver"
ou de "trouver" est liée à celle de la grâce divine et n'en constitue qu'un aspect. Voilà pourquoi si Philon commente dans ce
passage le verbe εὖρε cette forme verbale est, très significa-
tivement liée au mot χάριν.

[23]Le texte de *Quaestiones in Genesim* I, 96 contient une
interprétation plus simple et de caractère littéral du verset.

Il nous semble donc légitime de penser que nos *Quaestiones* IX, X, XI représentent une interprétation qui sous une
forme approfondie et élargie procède de *QG* I, 96.

La *Quaestio* X, §§86-103 qui est une méditation sur εὖρε
n'a pas de correspondant dans *QG* I, 96. Inversement la deuxième
explication mentionnée en *QG* I, 96 n'a pas été reprise en *Deus*
70, 116, etc.

[24]Nous distinguons dans les §§117-121 une *Quaestio et
Solutio* distincte comme dans les *Quaestiones in Genesim* où le
commentaire de Gen. 6, 9 constitue une *Quaestio* à part.

Il convient de remarquer que le présent passage est lié
au précédent non seulement par la dernière phrase du §116 qui
l'annonce, mais encore par le fait que le troisième descendant
spirituel de Noé est τῷ θεῷ εὐηρέστησε Νῶε qui est un équivalent
de Νῶε εὖρε χάριν παρὰ κυρίῳ τῷ θεῷ telle que cette phrase est
commentée dans les §§104-116. On relèvera les termes εὐαρεστῆσαι §109; τὸ εὐαρεστῆσαι §113; τὰς εὐαρεστήσεις et τῶν εὐαρεστη-
σάντων §116. Mais le sujet réel de ce passage est tout à fait
indépendant de celui qui est traité dans la *Quaestio* précédente.

[25]En *QG* I, 97 il s'agit, dans le lemme, non des descendants de Noé, mais de ses ancêtres. Mais dans le corps de *QG*
I, 97 les générations de Noé désignent comme dans notre passage
les vertus auxquelles donne naissance l'âme du sage. *QG* I, 97
distingue trois vertus (au lieu de quatre comme dans notre passage) qui par leur nombre correspondent aux trois fils de Noé
mentionnés dans l'Ecriture.

[26]La citation de Philon ne reproduit pas tout à fait
exactement le texte des LXX. Voyez le tableau que nous donnons
à la section C. 2.

[27]Les frères dont il est question dans ce verset sont les
mêmes que ceux qui sont désignés ensuite sous le nom de fils de
Bilha et Zilpah comme le montre bien le §121.

[28]Philon omet, comme on l'a signalé, la première partie
du verset de Genèse 6, 11: Ἐγέννησε δὲ Νῶε τρεῖς υἱοὺς, τὸν
Σημ, τὸν Χαμ, τὸν Ιαφεθ. Comme, nous l'avons constaté, il
n'ignore ni dans les *Quaestiones in Genesim* ni dans le *De Gigantibus* l'existence de Sem, Cham et Japhet qu'il interprète allégoriquement quoique de façon divergente. Ici, il semble considérer
que la particule δὲ introduit d'autres "générations spirituelles"
de Noé qu'il a déjà commentées et sur lesquelles il n'a plus à
revenir. *QG* 1, 98 propose une exégèse assez insignifiante de
Gen 6, 11.

[29]Il est donc nécessaire de traduire les deux aoristes
du lemme biblique par des passés simples et non par des impar-
faits. Les vertus de Noé manifestent *instantanément* la corruption de la terre.

[30]Le texte exact de Lév. 13, 15 est: καὶ μιανεῖ αὐτὸν
ὁ χρὼς ὁ ὑγιής. Sur ce passage, voyez encore la section C. 2.

[31]Le blanc était le couleur de la lèpre ainsi qu'il
apparaît d'un épisode tel qu'Exode 3, 6. Il va sans dire que
l'exégèse de Philon est elle-même paradoxale. Une âme couverte
de toutes les fautes, même involontaires, devrait être tenue pour
irresponsable plutôt que "pure." Sur ce passage, voyez encore
la section C. 2.

[32]Pour l'évacuation du mobilier, on notera, bien entendu,
la distorsion du sens littéral. L'Ecriture recommande de vider
la maison de tout son mobilier afin de préserver celui-ci de la
contagion du mal qui affecte l'édifice. Philon explique qu'il
faut évacuer le mobilier pour que l'entrée du prêtre ne le rende
pas impur et il tire de cette disposition la *preuve* que l'entrée
du prêtre implique *ipso facto* la souillure de la maison et de
son contenu. Seule cette *preuve* compte parce que l'Ecriture n'en
comporte pas d'autre de la proposition que le prêtre souille le
lieu où il pénètre. On se gardera donc de pousser à sa conséquence logique la proposition de Philon et de faire observer
qu'évacuer le mobilier de la maison revient à préserver des
fautes involontaires de la justice de l'ἔλεγχος.

[33]Il serait peut-être nécessaire de mettre les guillemets
fermants après τὸ ἀδίκημά μου et de considérer que les mots τὸ
ἁμάρτημά μου appartiennent à Philon. En effet, le texte des LXX
est le suivant . . . "τί ἐμοὶ καὶ σοί, ἄνθρωπε τοῦ θεοῦ; εἰσῆλθες πρὸς μὲ τοῦ ἀναμνῆσαι ἀδικίας μου, καὶ θανατῶσαι τὸν υἱόν
μου."

    Il est probable que τὸ ἁμάρτημά μου est une interpréta-
tion que Philon fait de θανατῶσαι τὸν υἱόν μου. Un détail
montre qu'il avait cette expression à l'esprit. Il note en effet
que la veuve prend horreur non seulement de son ancienne infidélité (τὴν παλαιὰν τροπήν) mais qu'elle hait *les enfants* de
cette infidélité (τὰ μὲν ἐκείνης ἔγγονα μισήσασα) ou si l'on
préfère les "enfants" qu'elle a eus elle-même lorsqu'elle était
sous l'empire de cette infidélité. Le mot ἔγγονα correspond
donc, avec un pluriel plus "naturel" en l'occurrence, au vocable
υἱόν. L'"homme de Dieu," appellation qui chez Philon désigne
le "prêtre" et le "prophète," pénètre chez la veuve de Sarepta,

établie, telle Thamar dans la *maison* de son père, comme le
prêtre de la Loi sur la Lèpre pénètrait dans la maison contami-
née: afin d'obliger l'âme à avoir conscience ou mémoire de son
iniquité et afin d'en tuer les fruits. On voit donc comment
Philon a été amené à rapprocher les deux textes.

[34]Le §139 est une sorte de note explicative, visant à
justifier la double appellation de l'ἔλεγχος dans le §138:
"Homme de Dieu" et "Prophète." Philon rappelle que les anciens
le qualifiaient aussi de "voyant." Dans le Chap. 9 de I Samuel
où Samuel est appelé tantôt "homme de Dieu" (6, 8, 10) tantôt
voyant (9, 18, 19) le verset 9 précise "le prophète d'aujourd'hui,
on l'appelait autrefois le voyant."

[35]Philon adapte la citation scripturaire à son texte.
Les LXX ont: καὶ ἦν κατεφθαρμένη. Les *Quaestiones in Genesim*
I, 99 ont une exégèse de Gen. 6, 11 très analogue à celle qui
se lit ici.

[36]*QG* I, 99 cité ci-dessus admet aussi que la voie
corrompue est à la fois celle de l'homme réduit à la chair et
la voie de Dieu.

[37]C'est une paraphrase du lemme scripturaire. Cf.
encore *QG* I, 99.

[38]Cf. Gen. 48, 15. L'homme dont il s'agit est Jacob,
donc Israël. Philon faisant fi de l'ordre du texte, place ce
passage après la prière de Moïse en Deut. 28, 12 et considère
que la profession d'Israël "Dieu qui me nourrit depuis mon
enfance" atteste que Moïse a été exaucé. Israël est nourri non
par l'eau de terre, mais par l'eau du Ciel.

[39]Gen. 18, 27: ἐγὼ δὲ εἰμι γῆ καὶ σποδός. Il ne s'agit
donc pas d'une citation explicite. Sur le sentiment du néant
humain on pourra voir notre étude "Les suppliants chez Philon
d'Alexandrie" *Revue des Etudes Juives*, 1963, pp. 241-78.

[40]Voyez note complémentaire 6.

[41]Il n'est pas certain qu'il s'agisse ici du Logos de
Dieu: tout ange peut être qualifié de l'appellation de λόγος
θεῖος et c'est d'un ange qu'il s'agit dans Nombres 22, 31 cité
au §181. Au §182 le λόγος θεῖος est évoqué en des termes qui
constituent une citation implicite de Psaumes 90, 11-12 et qui
s'appliquent dans ce poème *aux anges* de Dieu.

[42]Le texte de la LXX contient certaines analogies
d'expression qui ont pu favoriser le rapprochement de l'épisode
de Balaam avec celui d'Edom.
L'ange de Dieu s'oppose à Balaam l'épée à la main, comme
Edom s'oppose à Israël (Nombres 22, 22, 23, 31, 32). Au verset
32, il déclare: καὶ ἰδοὺ ἐγὼ ἐξῆλθον εἰς διαβολήν σου, ὅ τι
οὐκ ἀστεία ἡ ὁδός σου ἐναντίον μου.
L'attitude de Balaam dans tout l'épisode a beau
paraître respectueuse de la volonté de Dieu et de son ange;
il a beau ne se mettre en route vers le roi de Moab qu'avec
l'expresse permission de Dieu (versets 20, 21), son voyage est
jugé condamnable par Dieu qui s'en irrite (v. 22) et l'ange lui
déclare que sa voie n'est pas sage (v. 32). Il n'en continue
pas moins à la suivre avec la permission conditionnelle de

l'ange. La tradition juive considère que Balaam, malgré sa
bénédiction forcée, est un ennemi d'Israël et elle le traite
sévèrement. Comme le rappelle Philon, il trouve la mort de la
main d'Israël.

[43]Il serait naturellement trop long d'en dresser ici un
catalogue complet. Nous nous contenterons de quelques exemples.
A οἱ ἄνθρωποι πολλοί du lemme (*Gig.* 1) correspondent les mots
πολυανθρωπίαν (*ibid.*); πάμπολυ (*ibid.*); μυρίους, ἄπειρον ὅσην
πληθῦν (§2); τὸ μυρίον, πολλούς (§3); τοὺς πολλούς (§5).
        A θυγατέρες du lemme (*Gig.* 1) correspondent les mots
θηλυγονοῦσιν, θηλυδρίαι, γυναικώδες (§4); θυγατέρας, θηλυτόκος
(§5).
        Le mot ἱερεύς de *Deus* 131 est repris aux paragraphes 132,
133, 134 et paraphrasé au paragraphe 135 par les expressions ὁ
ἱερεὺς ὄντως ἔλεγχος et ὁ ἱερώμενος ἔλεγχος. Le mot οἰκίαν de
Deus 131 est paraphrasé au paragraphe 134 par καθάπερ τινὰ ἑστίαν.
Le mot ἀκάθαρτα de *Deus* 131 est prolongé par καθαρά, ἀκάθαρτα,
κεκαθαρμένου, ἀκαθάρτων, καθαρά (§132); μιαίνεσθαι (§133); καθαρωτάτη, καθαράν (§135).

[44]E. Bréhier, *Etudes de Philosophie antique*, Paris 1955:
"Philo Judaeus," p. 212.

[45]Voyez καὶ μηδεὶς ὑπολάβῃ μῦθον εἶναι τὸ εἰρημένον à
propos d'une représentation philosophique liée à l'interprétation allégorique que Philon fait de l'union des anges de Dieu
avec les filles des hommes (*De Gigantibus* 7). Surtout *De
Gigantibus* 58-60.
        Le texte de *Quaestiones in Genesim* I, 92 auquel nous
avons déjà eu l'occasion de faire allusion est très intéressant
à comparer avec le passage de notre traité. Pour autant qu'il
soit possible d'en juger avec certitude à partir de la traduction
latine de J. B. Aucher, l'esprit de ce texte est foncièrement le
même que celui du traité, malgré une sorte d'incertitude qui
domine l'ensemble de *QG* I, 92. Philon y indique d'abord que
Moïse emploie le terme de géants improprement pour désigner les
hommes d'une taille exceptionnelle. Mais il semble admettre
que les anges puissent s'unir à des femmes pour en engendrer
des "géants." Nous paraissons être en plein mythe, bien que
la suite du texte le dilue en allégorie morale. Mais ce qui
reste le plus remarquable, c'est que, comme nous avons eu l'occasion de le noter, Philon n'a pas un mot pour qualifier morale-
ment l'action des anges. Il se tait, croyons-nous, parce que
sa pensée lui interdit de penser que des messagers de la divinité
puissent être compromis dans des actions déshonorantes. L'exégèse de *De Gigantibus* est en progrès par rapport à *QG* I, 92,
dans la perspective propre à Philon, parce qu'elle est parvenue
à surmonter les résidus de mythe qui subsistaient dans la *Quaestio*. Il s'agit d'une exégèse arrivée à maturité plutôt que
d'une différence volontaire explicable par le fait que les deux
oeuvres auraient eu des destinataires qualitativement distincts.

[46]D'après Philon, l'interdiction mosaïque des images a
été motivée par les liens qui existent entre les arts plastiques
et le mythe. La poésie lui est parfois suspecte pour la même
raison. Il va sans dire que Philon n'hésite pas à emprunter à
la mythologie des éléments d'ordre culturel ou stylistique. En
Deus 155 il éclaire que la nourriture que le Ciel prodigue à
Israël est supérieure au nectar et à l'ambroisie de la fable:
τὴν νέκταρος καὶ ἀμβροσίας τῶν μεμυθευμένων ἀμείνω τροφήν. On
lit en *Deus* 60 une allusion plus obscure et de valeur plus

incertaine à l'ouragan et à la foudre dont les poètes font les
armes de la divinité.   Partout ailleurs, dans les deux traités,
la mythologie est rejetée avec horreur comme une manifestation du
mensonge et de l'impiété.   Dans le cas de la trahison des anges,
le mythe en accordant une volonté personnelle et perverse à des
êtres ressortissant à la sphère divine pouvait sembler mettre en
danger le dogme du monothéisme lui-même.   Les représentations
anthropomorphiques et anthropopathiques de la divinité procèdent
de la mentalité mythique installée par une éducation défectueuse
(Cf. *a contrario Deus* 61).   Elles restent liées au mythe et à
l'impiété: ἀσεβῶν αὗται μυθοποιίαι (*Deus* 59).

Leurs conséquences les plus funestes sont d'emprisonner
les âmes dans l'erreur et de soumettre l'amour pour Dieu à la
peur, l'une des redoutables passions énumérées en *Timée* 69 d et
dont Philon déclare, faisant écho au passage de Platon, que si
Dieu n'a assorti les commandements de Décalogue d'aucune pré-
vision pénale c'est pour que l'on choisisse le Bien librement
en échappant à la contrainte de la peur, ce conseiller insensé:
μή πως φόβῳ τις ἄφρονι συμβούλῳ χρησάμενος . . . (*De Decalogo*,
177).

[47]Comme l'indique le nom même de δεισιδαιμονία, la
crainte est le moteur premier de la superstition.

[48]La sagesse du Législateur est tout à fait nouvelle:
καινότατος δ'ἐν ἅπασι τὴν σοφίαν ὁ νομοθέτης (*Deus* 125).   Son
originalité s'exprime volontiers par le paradoxe sous lequel se
dissimule une vérité profonde: παραδοξότατον νόμον (*Deus* 127).
On relèvera les expressions suivantes d'intention apologétique
et destinées à mettre en lumière la conformité de l'Ecriture à
la nature, la vérité, l'exactitude, la raison, la beauté,
l'excellence pédagogique: Εἰκότως οὖν (*Gig.* 3); ὥς ἂν τις
προτρέψαιτο μᾶλλον . . . ἢ τοῦτον τὸν τρόπον (*Gig.* 33); παγκάλως καὶ σφόδρα παιδευτικῶς εἴρηται (*Gig.* 40); φυσικώτατα (*Deus*
11); ἀψευδῶς καὶ σφόδρα ἐναργῶς (*Deus* 14); ὀρθῶς καὶ προσηκόντως
(*Deus* 16); ἀκριβέστατα (*Deus* 123); Δηλοῖ δὲ . . . διὰ συμβόλων
τούτων ἀληθέστατον ἐκεῖνο (*Deus* 128); κύρια ὀνόματα καὶ ἐμπρεπῆ
(*Deus* 139); προσηκόντως (*Deus* 140).   Une étude systématique de
ces expressions ou d'expressions analogues dans tout le corpus
philonien serait très souhaitable.

[49]Voyez *Sob.* 33: Ἀλλ' ἐσκέψαντο μὲν ἐφ' ἑαυτῶν ἴσως
οἷς ἔθος ἀκριβοῦν τὰς ῥητὰς καὶ προχείρους ἀποδόσεις ἐν τοῖς
νόμοις. . . .

[50]Outre les passages du *Deus*, la loi sur la lèpre des
personnes est commentée en *Post.* 47; *LA* 3, 7; *Plant.* 111; *Sob.*
49; la loi sur la lèpre des maisons en *Det.* 16.

[51]Voyez note complémentaire 7.

[52]Voyez le tableau donné en section C. 2.

NOTES COMPLÉMENTAIRES

[1]La situation chronologique des *Quaestiones* par rapport
aux autres écrits exégétiques de Philon, fait toujours problème.
Au siècle dernier, H. EWALD, *Geschichte des Volkes Israel*, 3.
Aufl. Band VI, S. 294 les considérait comme plus anciennes;
A. F. Dähne, "Einige Bemerkungen über die Schriften des Juden
Philo, angeknüpft an eine Untersuchung über deren ursprüngliche
Anordnung" *Theologische Studien und Kritiken* VI (1833) p. 1037
soutenait au contraire qu'elles étaient plus récentes. Voyez
aussi Chr. GROSSMAN, *De Philonis Judaei operum continua serie
et ordine chronologico comment.* I II Leipzig, 1841-1842, II p. 14-17.
Le fait est que certains traités, essentiellement des
traités perdus, sont mentionnés dans les *Quaestiones* ou à la
fois dans les *Quaestiones* et dans le *Commentaire*. Ainsi dans
QG II, 4 Philon renvoie à propos de l'Arche du Temple "au
traité qui concerne ce sujet." Il n'apparaît pas clairement
s'il s'agit d'un traité consacré à l'Arche du Temple ou, ce qui
serait peut-être plus vraisemblable et comme semble le penser
R. Marcus qui donne une référence inadéquate, d'un traité du
Commentaire, où se trouverait un développement relatif à l'Arche.
En *QG* II, 34 Philon mentionne qu'il a déjà parlé en détail du
pacte d'alliance avec Dieu. R. Marcus (*Supplement* II, 76, a)
renvoie à *De Mutatione Nominum* 53, où se lit la phrase suivante:
τὸν δὲ περὶ διαθηκῶν σύμπαντα λόγον ἐν δυσὶν ἀναγέγραφα συντά-
ξεσι soit "j'ai écrit tout ce qu'il y a à dire sur les alliances
en deux ouvrages (ou deux livres d'un ouvrage)." Particulièrement intéressant est le cas d'un ouvrage Περὶ ἀριθμῶν que Philon
cite sous ce titre à la fois dans le *Commentaire* et dans les
Quaestiones. On lit en effet en *De Vita Mosis* II, 115, à propos
de la tétrade, ἔχει δὲ καὶ τὰς ἄλλας ἀμυθήτους ἀρετὰς ἡ τετράς,
ὧν τὰς πλείστας ἠκριβώσαμεν ἐν τῇ περὶ ἀριθμῶν πραγματείᾳ. "La
tétrade a encore d'innombrables vertus dont nous avons examiné
la plus grande partie dans le traité sur les nombres." Dans le
De Opificio Mundi 52 il parle d'un traité qu'il doit écrire
particulièrement sur le sujet de la tétrade, πολλαῖς δὲ καὶ
ἄλλαις κέχρηται δυνάμεσι ἡ τετρὰς ἃς ἀκριβέστερον καὶ ἐν τῷ περὶ
αὐτῆς ἰδίῳ λόγῳ προσυποδεικτέον. "La tétrade possède beaucoup
d'autres propriétés que l'on exposera encore avec plus de pré-
cision dans le traité spécial qui lui sera consacré."
Il est possible qu'au moment où Philon écrivait cette
phrase il n'avait pas encore une vue très claire du traité qu'il
se proposait de composer. D'où cette formulation qui ne permet
pas d'être absolument certain que le traité de la tétrade et le
traité des nombres sont un seul et même ouvrage. La chose est
cependant vraisemblable. Elle permettrait d'établir que le *De
Opificio Mundi* est antérieur au *De Vita Mosis*. Le περὶ ἀριθμῶν
est encore mentionné comme publié dans *QG* IV, 110: "Now, what
sort of nature the decad has both in respect of intelligible
substance and in respect of sense perceptible (substance) has
already been stated in the book *On Numbers*."
Le traité sur les nombres est allégué aussi dans le
fragment 9 de l'ancienne version latine. Ces allusions ont, en
tout état de cause, l'intérêt de montrer que lorsque Philon
rédige certaines Questions il a déjà publié des traités du type

de ceux qui sont contenus dans le *Commentaire*: Ainsi *QG* IV, 110
serait postérieur à *De Opficio Mundi* etc.
         Voilà pourquoi Schürer, *op. cit.* III (trad. anglaise)
p. 329 n. 82 a peut-être raison de soutenir que les *Quaestiones*
sont pour partie plus anciennes et pour partie plus récentes que
le *Commentaire*. Voyez aussi R. Marcus, *Supplement* I, X, n. a.
         On s'est intéressé aussi à l'origine, à la forme des
Quaestiones ainsi qu'à leur rapport littéraire avec le *Commentaire*. Quelles que soient les similarités extérieures qui existent entre les *Quaestiones* et les scholies des grammairiens grecs
aux textes classiques, l'origine des Questions doit très vraisemblablement être cherchée à la Synagogue. Le lecture publique
de l'Ecriture y était, lors des sabbats, suivie d'un commentaire
où le texte biblique était repris verset par verset et expliqué
en tout détail ou toute partie qui, dans ses données littérales,
semblait appeler un éclaircissement. Puis le commentateur pas-
sait à une exégèse moins étroite et exposait tous les problèmes
d'ordre moral ou religieux qui lui semblaient liés au passage
considéré. Philon dans les *Quaestiones* paraît avoir conservé
cette démarche caractéristique. Son apport propre pourrait avoir
consisté dans le caractère philosophique et allégorique de
l'exégèse πρὸς διάνοιαν dont il fait suivre son élucidation du
sens littéral (τὸ ῥητόν). Quant aux traités du *Commentaire*, ils
constituent une adaptation étudiée et littéraire des *Quaestiones*.
Il semble que les Questions de Philon aient donné naissance à un
genre littéraire de la littérature patristique, qui a été étudié
par G. Bardy: voyez E. Lucchesi, *L'usage de Philon . . .* p. 122
et n. 4; p. 130. H. Savon l'a retrouvé dans la correspondance
de St. Ambroise; voyez *Saint Ambroise devant l'Exégèse de Philon
le Juif* 2 vol. Paris 1977 I, p. 13 et, plus généralement, p. 27
et suivante.
         La "simplicité" de l'exégèse dans les *Quaestiones* nous
paraît avoir été fort exagérée. H. Savon (*op. laud.* I p. 216)
qui relève avec justesse que la démarche de Philon reste semblable dans les *Quaestiones* et dans le *Commentaire* croit pouvoir
écrire: "Le genre particulier des *Quaestiones in Genesim* impose
une autre démarche. Philon s'y tient beaucoup plus près du sens
obvie des récits qu'il commente; il n'allégorise que là où il y
voit une nécessité impérieuse." La description de S. Sandmel
(*Philo of Alexandria An Introduction*, New York--Oxford 1979,
p. 79) nous paraît beaucoup plus proche de la réalité philologique. "Philo's ordinary manner in *Questions and Answers*,"
écrit Sandmel, "is to ask why the biblical verse says what it
does, or else, what is the meaning of the verse as he quotes it.
Almost invariably his answer respecting the literal is very
brief, and he gives an elaborate philosophical explanation, and
frequently proceeds to an allegorical interpretation."
         Quant à la fonction ou aux destinataires des *Quaestiones*,
il n'existe pas d'opinion unanime pour en rendre compte. L'avis
traditionnellement répandu est que les *Quaestiones* représentent
une exégèse populaire, non-scientifique, s'adressent à un public
plus populaire que le *Commentaire*. On trouve ce jugement sous
sa forme classique chez Schürer (*op. cit.* III, trad anglaise,
p. 329) qui écrit: "while this shorter explanation in a cate-
chetical form was intended for more extensive circles, Philo's
special and chief scientific work is his *large allegorical commentary on Genesis. . . .*" La nature philologique réelle des
Quaestiones que Sandmel caractérise si justement empêche de
croire aux "more extensive circles."
         Sandmel fait une autre proposition (*ibid.*) "Since there
is so much overlap in content between *Questions and Answers to
Genesis* and *The Allegory*," écrit-il, "scholars have wondered

why the two presentations. My published suggestion that *Questions and Answers* is mostly on the order of preliminary notes for treatises, some of which Philo wrote and others he planned but did not get around to, has met with approval by those who have seen it." Cette suggestion est effectivement séduisante. Toutefois, avant de l'accepter, il serait nécessaire de faire une étude comparée, systématique et sans préjugés de l'exégèse que Philon propose pour les mêmes textes scripturaires dans chacune des deux séries.

Un progrès très important pour l'étude des *Quaestiones* et la connaissance de Philon en général nous semble avoir été accompli par Peder Borgen et Roald Skarsten dans leur étude des *Studia Philonica* que nous citons supra à la note 4. Nous y voyons l'amorce de recherches formelles très fructueuses qui devraient trouver leur place dans le Philo Project de Claremont animé par Burton Mack. La dernière phrase de l'article en indique très clairement l'enjeu: "On the base of these findings," écrivent les auteurs, "the issue of the essential distinction between the *Quaestiones* and the Allegorical Commentary must be raised anew in relation to formal structure, content and intention." Dans leur note finale (*Studia Philonica* 4, 15) ils font observer que "Carsten Colpe, 'Philo,' *Religion in Geschichte und Gegenwart* 5. 342, makes too sharp a distinction when he writes 'Ph's wissenschaftliches Hauptwerk ist der grosse allegorische Kommentar zur Genesis . . . Nicht wissenschaftlich, sondern kateketisch gemeint sind die Quaestiones in Genesin und in Exodum (armen).'" Ce que Borgen et Skarsten mettent ici en question c'est en fait le jugement de Schürer scolastiquement transmis par Colpe. Rien ne saurait mieux indiquer que les recherches projetées marquent un tournant dans l'étude de Philon.

[2]La traduction d'André Mosès pour *De Gigantibus* 65-66 n'est pas adéquate. Les mots ἄρξαντος τοῦ ἔργου Νεβρώδ ne signifient pas "Nemrod dirigeait l'opération," mais bien "Nemrod fut l'initiateur de ce processus." Le participe ἄρξαντος anticipe sur le verset de Gen 10, 8 qui le justifie: Οὗτος ἤρξατο εἶναι γίγας ἐπὶ τῆς γῆς. En outre τῇ παναθλίᾳ ψυχῇ est dit de Nemrod: il faudrait traduire "à cette âme infortunée." Quant à la révolte de Nemrod contre Dieu, elle est très clairement décrite en *Quaestiones in Genesim* II, 82. Il est probable que Philon rattache le nom de Nemrod à la racine hébraïque *marad* "se rebeller." Il déduit l'hostilité de Nemrod à l'endroit de la divinité de Gen X, 9 où γίγας κυνηγὸς ἐναντίον κυρίου τοῦ θεοῦ est interprété comme "un géant chasseur *contre* le Seigneur Dieu." De même au verset 10. Dans le texte des *Quaestiones* Philon déduit en outre le caractère sauvagement passionné de Nemrod de sa qualité de chasseur. Il faut noter encore que Philon y propose une deuxième étymologie du nom de Nemrod qui signifierait "Ethiopien" et indiquerait que le géant n'a aucune part à la lumière. On a souvent fait observer que cette étymologie convient non à Nemrod, mais à Cush, son père. Il y a certainement ici une confusion, car il est évident que le nom de Nemrod ne peut signifier à la fois "désertion" et "Ethiopien." Mais d'après le début de la *Quaestio*, il semble que Nemrod ne soit qu'un aspect de l'âme de Cush l'Ethiopien et, de la sorte, éthiopien lui aussi. On a l'impression qu'il y a eu interférence ici d'une tradition concernant Cush l'Ethiopien et d'une étymologie, peut-être particulière à Philon, qui explique le nom de Cush par le grec χοῦς "amas de terre." Voyez *Quaestiones in Genesim* II 81 et 82 (début). Voici d'ailleurs le texte de la *Quaestio* 82 dans la traduction de R. Marcus où nous corrigeons la formulation du lemme.

82 (Gen. X 8-9) Why did Cush beget Nimrod who began to be "a giant hunter" *against* the Lord, wherefore they said "like Nimrod a giant hunter *against* God?"

It is proper that one having a sparse nature, which a spiritual bond does not bring together and hold firmly, and not being the father of constancy either of soul or nature or character, but like a giant valuing and honouring earthly things more than heavenly, should show forth the truth of the story about the Giants and Titans. For in truth he who is zealous for earthly and corruptible things always fights against and makes war on heavenly things and praiseworthy and wonderful natures, and builds walls and towers on earth against heaven. But those things which are here are against those things which are there. For this reason it is not ineptly said "a giant *against* God," which clearly is opposition to the Deity. For the impious man is none other than the enemy and foe who stands against God. Wherefore it is proverbial that everyone who is a great sinner should be compared with him as the chief head and fount, as when they say "like Nimrod." Thus the name is a clear indication of the thing (signified) for it is to be translated as "Ethiopian" and his skill is that of the hunter. Both of these are to be condemned and reprehended., the Ethiopian because pure evil has no participation in light, but follows night and darkness while hunting is as far removed as possible from the rational nature. But he who is among beasts seeks to equal the bestial habits of animals through evil passions. Παρὸ καὶ ἀρχὴν τῷ Νεβρὼδ τῆς βασιλείας ὑπογράφει βαβυλῶνα. Ici encore la traduction d'A. Mosès doit être corrigée: ἀρχήν ne signifie pas "capitale" mais bien "commencement." La phrase réfère à Genèse 10, 10: καὶ ἐγένετο ἀρχὴ τῆς βασιλείας αὐτοῦ βαβυλῶν . . . qui, à son tour, correspond à l'hébreu . . . *watehî rē'sit mamlaktô bābel*. Il est certain que Philon entendait ici ἀρχή comme signifiant "commencement," puisqu'il explique ce mot par le vocable Προοίμια "préambule."

Ceci dit, il importe de remarquer que Philon ignore le nom de Babel et ne connaît que celui de Babylone. La raison, qui est une preuve supplémentaire de son ignorance de l'hébreu, est que le verset de Genèse XI, 9 où l'on trouve le nom de *bābel* rapproché de *bālal* est traduit par les Septante de la manière suivante: Διὰ τοῦτο ἐκλήθη τὸ ὄνομα αὐτοῦ (scil. τοῦ πύργου) σύγχυσις (ou Σύγχυσις), ὅτι ἐκεῖ συνέχεε κύριος τὰ χείλη πάσης τῆς γῆς. Philon ne donne jamais la preuve qu'il est au courant du fait que la tour Σύγχυσις est la tour de Babylone puisque le mot Βαβυλῶν de Genèse 10, 10 correspond comme Σύγχυσις de Genèse XI, 9 à l'original *bābel*. Contrairement à la littérature judéo-hellénistique et au midrash, Philon ne rapproche jamais le texte relatif à Nemrod et à Babylone (dont il n'explique allégoriquement le nom que dans le seul passage du *De Gigantibus* 66) de l'épisode de la Tour de Babel, pour lequel on verra *De Posteritate Caini* 53, 81; *De Confusione Linguarum* 1, 9, 158; *De Somniis* II, 283-290. Un seul texte pourrait faire hésiter, c'est le passage de *Quaestiones in Genesim* II, 82 que nous avons cité où se lisent les mots "builds walls and towers on earth against heaven." Mais la traduction n'est ici pas assurée et R. Marcus note que "walls and towers" devrait être peut-être "heaps and mounds." Ces mots correspondent à la phrase suivante de la traduction latine de J. B. Aucher "aggerem construens terram contra caelum," soit "faisant de la terre une terrasse d'assaut contre le ciel." L'image a été suscitée par la comparaison des actions de Cush-Nemrod avec celles des Géants et des Titans de la fable. Nemrod préfère les choses terrestres aux célestes, la terre entière lui sert de tremplin pour se conduire

hostilement contre le ciel. *QG* II, 82 prouve précisément que
le rapprochement de Nemrod et des Géants procède des expressions
de Genèse X "géant chasseur contre Dieu" et non de l'épisode de
la tour Σύγχυσις narré au chapitre XI de la Genèse.

En somme nous avons ici une évacuation totale de la
gigantomachie mythologique. L'histoire des géants et de Nemrod
est entièrement allégorisée.

[3]"Αννα, τῆς τοῦ θεοῦ δώρημα σοφίας. Le vocable δώρημα
permet de préciser le sens de χάρις αὐτῆς: il s'agit du "don
gracieux." Cette acception n'est pas compatible avec l'hébreu
ḥinnāh. Reste à savoir comment il faut interpréter ici les mots
τῆς τοῦ θεοῦ δώρημα σοφίας appliqués à Anne. On trouve une
exégèse allégorique de la figure d'Anne en *De Ebrietate* 145 et
ss; *De Mutatione Nominis* 143 et ss; *De Somniis* I, 254. Dans ces
trois traités le nom d'Anne est expliqué étymologiquement par
χάρις. En *De Somniis* I, 254 et *De Ebrietate* 145, on trouve une
justification du nom de χάρις appliqué à Anne.

Soit *Ebr.* 145: οὗτος μητρὸς γέγονεν "Αννης, ἧς τοὔνομα
μεταληφθέν ἐστι χάρις· ἄνευ γὰρ θείας χάριτος ἀμήχανον ἢ λιποτακτῆσαι τὰ θνητὰ ἢ τοῖς ἀφθάρτοις ἀεὶ παραμεῖναι. "Celui-ci
(Samuel) eut pour mère Anne dont le nom traduit est *grâce*: en
effet, sans la grâce divine, il est impossible soit de déserter
les choses mortelles soit de se maintenir parmi les choses im-
mortelles." Le nom de grâce qualifie donc ici le comportement
d'Anne et le §146 montre qu'Anne est à la fois la grâce qui
permet de s'évader du mortel et l'âme à qui la grâce a permis
cette fuite. En *De Somniis* I, 254 Philon invoque le témoignage
d'Anne: ἡ προφῆτις καὶ προφητοτόκος "Αννα, ἧς μεταληφθέν τοὔνομα
καλεῖται χάρις. τὸν γὰρ υἱὸν διδόναι φησὶ τῷ ἁγίῳ δῶρον Σαμουὴλ
(I Sam I, 28) "la prophétesse et mère de prophète, Anne dont le
nom en traduction est *grâce*. Elle dit, en effet, qu'elle fait
don au Saint de son fils Samuel." Il est possible que la grâce
soit ici, comme dans notre passage, le "don gracieux."

En *Deus* 5 et ss on pourrait interpréter τῆς τοῦ θεοῦ
δώρημα σοφίας comme signifiant qu'Anne est un don de la Sagesse
divine ou que l'âme atteint la divine sagesse lorsqu'à s'y
manifeste le type d'Anne ou encore que le don de la sagesse
divine est réalisé lors qu'Anne enfante Samuel et qu'elle le
donne à Dieu. Il est peut-être plus probable qu'on a ici une
explication analogue à celle *d'Ebr.* 145 citée *supra*. Anne
s'appelle "don de la sagesse divine" parce qu'elle sait que tous
les accomplissements spirituels loin de représenter son oeuvre
propre sont des dons gracieux de Dieu: μηδὲν ἴδιον ἑαυτῆς κρίνουσα ἀγαθόν, ὃ μὴ χάρις ἐστὶ θεία. En d'autres termes, son
nom décrit comportement ou sa profession de foi qu'elle
exprime en "donnant à Dieu son fils donné." Du même coup elle
est aussi "grâce-gratitude" comme le montrent les termes du §7
qui font écho au paragraphe précédent: εὐχαριστητέον διὰ τῶν
ὑπ' αὐτοῦ δοθέντων; εὐχαριστητικῶς ἔχειν.

La particule γάρ au début de la deuxième phrase du §5
réfère aux termes μαθητρὶς καὶ διάδοχος de la première.

[4]Philon attribue cette distinction à "des gens qui se
soucient de la propriété des mots." Par une très curieuse
ironie, la distinction que Philon répète en leur nom relève
d'une très détestable grammaire grecque.

'Ανεύρεσις est un mot rare en grec. Chez Philon il ne
se rencontre que dans notre passage, mais il y a dans le corpus
philonien cinquante neuf exemples du verbe ἀνευρίσκειν: sur les
nuances théoriques qui distinguent les synonymes ἀνευρίσκειν,

ἐξευρίσκειν ἐφευρίσκειν on verra Jean BRUNEL, *L'aspect verbal et
l'emploi des préverbes en grec, particulièrement en attique* Paris,
1939, p. 59, 103 et 144.

Le préverbe ἀνά a des valeurs fort diverses: "mouvement
de bas en haut"; "valeur privative"; "de nouveau." Dans le cas
d'ἀνευρίσκειν le préverbe sert simplement à souligner "l'effort
pour faire aboutir le procès ou pour le mettre en train." Le
verbe ἀνευρίσκειν, entre dans le même catégorie que les verbes
ἀναφαίνεσθαι "se découvrir"; ἀναβράττειν, "mettre à bouillir";
ἀνερωτᾶν, "interroger"; ἀναβοᾶν, "pousser un cri." Cf. P. Chan-
traine, *Dictionnaire Etymologique de la Langue Grecque*, I, p. 83
s. v. ἀνα-.

La différence que Philon prétend établir entre εὕρεσις
"découverte" et ἀνεύρεσις "redécouverte" est donc simplement
impossible.

Il n'y a dans l'usage philonien aucune différence perceptible entre εὑρίσκειν et ἀνευρίσκειν. Le sentiment que Philon
avait de la langue grecque est en effet bien meilleur que la
réflexion théorique sur la langue à laquelle il affirme ici
donner son approbation.

Le verbe ἀνευρίσκειν a chez lui les acceptions suivantes
a, "trouver, découvrir, inventer" et au passif "être trouvé"
etc. b, exclusivement au passif: "se révéler, apparaître avec
telle ou telle qualité."

Certains emplois excluent totalement qu' ἀνευρίσκειν
puisse signifier "redécouvrir." Ainsi en *Opif.* 114 où il est
question des navigateurs qui découvrent des terres auparavant
inconnues: τὰς πρὶν ἀδηλουμένας χώρας ἀνεῦρον. D'ailleurs,
dans certains contextes Philon emploie côte à côte et sans
différence de sens εὑρίσκειν et ἀνευρίσκειν. Par exemple en
De Plantatione 78, à propos du "puits du serment," μὴ ἀνευρίσκειν le commentaire philonien du lemme biblique: οὐχ
εὕρομεν ὕδωρ. En *De Confusione* 75, Philon emploie lui-même,
sans distinction de sens εὑρεῖν et ἀνευρίσκει.

Le caractère fautif de l'analyse d' ἀνεύρεσις que l'on
ne retrouve ni dans la littérature grecque ni chez Philon semble
rendre très douteuse la valeur technique de l'expression οἱ
ζητητικοὶ τῶν κυρίων ὀνομάτων. Le terme ζητητικοί ne désigne
pas des "spécialistes," mais des "gens qui recherchent" "qui se
soucient ou sont curieux de." Comparez l'emploi de l'adjectif
ζητητικός en *Leg. All.* III 3, 249; *Deus* 107; *Confus* 5; *Migr.*
214-16.

Il n'est pas impossible que Philon qui avait à placer
ses exemples de redécouverte découverte, ait imaginé ici lui-
même, de façon malheureuse et fugitive, la différence dont il
fait état entre εὕρεσις d'une part et, sous l'influence,
probablement d' ἀνάμνησις, ἀνεύρεσις d'autre part. Dans cette
perspective l'expression οἱ ζητητικοὶ τὴν κυρίων ὀνομάτων dont
Philon se sert aussi en *Quod Deterius* 76, pourrait n'être pas
une supercherie, mais avoir simplement une valeur indéfinie.
Elle signifierait "lorsqu'on est soucieux d'employer les mots
exacts." Philon pourrait s'inclure dans cette catégorie de
personnes et de désigner lui-même par cette expression géné-
ralisante.

[5]Les Amoréens qui blessent les fuyards à la façon des
abeilles et symbolisent la conscience, correspondent ici à
l' ἔμφυτος ἀπιστία des escrocs. C'est cette malhonnêteté innée
qui souffre lorsque lui faisant violence, ils restituent un
dépôt. C'est pourquoi, si l'on admet que dans le §100 les mots
κατορθοῦν et πρὸς τοῦ συνειδότος désignent respectivement une
conduite droite et la conscience morale, on devra convenir que

l'interprétation symbolique que Philon fait de Deut. I, 43-44 au
§100 n'est illustrée que bien imparfaitement par les exemples
allégués dans les §§102-103.

Il nous semble donc plus probable que μὴ κατορθοῦν et
πρὸς τοῦ συνειδότος sont dépourvus ici de coloration morale.
Philon emploie en effet quelquefois le verbe κατορθοῦν dans le
sens de "réussir" dans le bien comme le mal.   Nous nous contenterons ici de quelques exemples.   D'abord au sens de "bonne
réalisation" ou de "réussite technique" avec une valeur favorable:
à propos des saisons qui mènent tout à bonne fin: Αἱ δ'ὧραι
πάντα τελεσφοροῦσαι κατορθοῦσιν . . . ; Op. 59; des yeux qui permettent à toutes les parties du corps de fonctionner convenable-
ment: ὀφθαλμοὶ . . . τὴν τοῦ δύνασθαι κατορθοῦν αἰτίαν . . .
παρέχουσιν, Spec. 1, 340; des chefs-d'oeuvre de la peinture ou
de la sculpture: ὅσα γραφικῆς ἔργα καὶ πλαστικῆς ἐν ἑκατέρᾳ
τέχνῃ κατορθούμενα, Abr. 267; d'admirables exécutions musicales
. . . μουσικὴν ἐπιδεικνύμενόν τινα δι' αὐλῶν ἢ λύρας καὶ σφόδρα
κατορθοῦντα . . . Spec. II, 246.

Mais Philon peut employer le verbe κατορθοῦν pour
désigner le succès des malfaiteurs.   Ainsi en Spec. 1, 314,
εἰκὸς δὲ καὶ ἀναξίους ὄντας κατορθοῦν . . . ὑπὲρ τοῦ λυπεῖσθαι
. . . ἡμᾶς, ou en Flacc. 1: οἷς γὰρ ἰσχὺς οὐ πρόσεστι τῶν τὰς
φύσεις τυραννικῶν, πανουργίαις τὰς ἐπιβουλὰς κατορθοῦσιν.   Quant
à σύνοιδα et à τὸ συνειδός, il est indéniable que la plupart des
exemples que l'on trouve chez Philon concernent la conscience
morale.   Parfois cependant ces deux vocables sont employés pour
désigner le sentiment intime sans qualification morale.   Le verbe
σύνοιδα peut alors signifier "avoir conscience" c'est à dire
"savoir bien" et fonctionne comme un synonyme renforcé de οἶδα.
Par exemple Συνίσασι δ' οἱ ταῖς ἱεραῖς βίβλοις ἐντυγχάνοντες,
"De cela ont parfaitement conscience ceux qui pratiquent les
Livres sacrés" . . . De Vita Mosis II, 11; Μαρτυρήσω δὲ καὶ
αὐτὸς ὅσα σύνοιδα . . . "j'y joindrai le témoignage de mes
informations personnelles . . . " In Flaccum, 99.   En De Iosepho
265, Joseph cite Dieu comme témoin de ses dispositions intimes:
ὃν μάρτυρα καλῶ τοῦ συνειδότος ἐπ' ἀψευδέσι καταλλαγαῖς.   Surtout en De Decalogo 91 τὸ συνειδὸς désigne les dispositions
intimes mauvaises, par lesquelles le parjure prétend faire de
Dieu l'associé de ses crimes . . . ὑπερβολὴν ἀσεβείας οὐκ ἀπο-
λέλοιπας λέγων, εἰ καὶ μὴ στόματι καὶ γλώττῃ, τῷ γοῦν συνειδότι
πρὸς θεόν· τὰ ψευδῆ μοι μαρτύρεις etc.

C'est pourquoi malgré la phrase de Deus 134 où "avoir
le sentiment immédiat," "avoir conscience" est exprimé par ποι-
οῦνται κατάληψιν et où la réussite (κατορθοῦν opposé à πταί-
ουσι) s'entend certainement d'une réussite morale, nous croyons
que dans notre passage les personnages mis en scène sont torturés
par le sentiment intime qu'ils ont de ne pas réussir dans les
entreprises perverses qui les contraignent à forcer leur nature
véritable.   Agissant contre leurs véritables instincts, appétits
ou dispositions d'esprit, ils ne cessent d'avoir la conscience
déplaisante de faire ce que réellement ils n'aiment pas.   Ce
sentiment les empêche de durer très longtemps dans leur simula-
tion.   Mettant bas le masque, ils dénoncent eux-mêmes leur
comédie et se laissent confondre.   Il ne s'agit pas ici de
remords, mais de l'impossibilité de faire violence à sa vraie
nature.   Le mot de Deut. 1, 43-44 qui est ici réellement commenté est παραβιασάμενοι.   Le thème du passage est résumé à
la fin du §103.   La violence est de peu de durée: tout ce qui
est βίαιον est βαιόν c'est à dire ὀλιγοχρόνιον.

[6]Philon met souvent en rapport la loi de Moïse et la
doctrine du juste milieu.   Selon Spec. IV, 102, le Législateur
a cherché une voie moyenne entre l'austérité de Sparte et le

luxe et l'hédonisme des Ioniens et des Sybarites. Les Thérapeutes eux-mêmes atténuent la rudesse des moeurs spartiates
(*Cont.* 69). A la mort de Sarah (*Abr.* 257-261) la douleur
d'Abraham se maintient à une égale distance des convulsions et
de l'impassibilité.

On comparera à notre passage les textes suivants: *Post.*
101-102; *Gig.* 64; *Deus* 61; *Fug.* 203; *Mig.* 146, s.; *Abr.* 269;
Spec. IV, 144, 167-168; *QE* 2, 26.

Mais le "juste milieu" qui est intelligible lorsqu'il
s'agit de caractériser le comportement recommandé par Moïse à
des hommes contingents, Israélites, Thérapeutes ou Abraham décrit
comme un personnage historique, est plus difficile à entendre
lorsqu'il s'agit, comme dans notre passage de τρόποι de l'âme.
Tout le discours au terrestre Edom est ici placé sous le signe
de *l'apatheia* et non de la *metriopatheia*. C'est un hymne non à
la modération, mais à la migration. C'est pourquoi il faut ou
considérer qu'il y a ici, chez Philon, une certaine inconséquence, au moins dans la présentation, ou supposer que la voie
royale est moins la voie du compromis que celle de l'exacte
mesure et de l'harmonie. La vertu est atteinte lorsque l'âme
est ajustée rigoureusement comme une lyre. Le ciel et sa
musique sont les archétypes de l'âme vertueuse et la notion du
"tempérament" au sens musical du terme, qui est présente dans
certains passages de Platon comme *Rep.* 410 D-E est à plusieurs
reprises liée chez Philon à l'idée de la voie moyenne ou de la
vertu. Ainsi en *Deus* 24-25 ou *Spec.* 4, 102. Il est du reste
frappant de constater (*Mig.* 147) que Philon semble dissocier
la philosophie de Moïse et celle des philosophes qui pratiquent
τὴν ἥμερον καὶ κοινωνικὴν . . . φιλοσοφίαν c'est à dire des
aristotéliciens dont le témoignage n'est invoqué que pour con-
firmer une vérité découverte par le Législateur.

Une autre valeur de la *voie médiane* est celle de la
fidélité à l'ordre reçu. En *Post.* 102 c'est le verset de Deut.
28, 14 qui est allégué: "tu ne te détourneras ni à droite ni
à gauche de la parole que je t'ordonne aujourd'hui." Comparez
Spec. 4, 167.

[7]On trouve chez Philon quelques formules frappantes pour
exprimer l'embarras où le plonge la signification de la lettre
de la Loi. On peut citer les passages suivants: *Det.* 167: καὶ
τοῦτο τίνα ἔχει λόγον πρὸς τὰς ῥητὰς διερμηνεύσεις οὐκ οἶδα
Agr. 131: καίτοι γε πρὸς τὴν ῥητὴν ἐπίσκεψιν οὐκ οἶδ' ὃν ἔχει
λόγον ἡ προσαποδοθεῖσα αἰτία . . . *Fug.* 106: ἡ προθεσμία . . .
πολλὴν ἐν τῷ ῥητῷ μοι παρέχουσα δυσκολίαν.

Chaque fois qu'il estime la chose possible, Philon ne
manque pas de louer le sens littéral. Voyez *LA* 2, 14: Ἔστι
δὲ καὶ ἡ τροπικὴ καὶ ἡ ῥητὴ ἀπόδοσις ἀξία τοῦ θαυμάζεσθαι;
Ebr. 130: θαυμάσαι μὲν οὖν εἰκότως ἄν τις καὶ τὸ ῥητὸν τῆς
προστάξεως; *Sob.* 65: καὶ τὸ ῥητὸν μέντοι συνᾴδειν ἔοικεν;
Conf. 190: ἴσως γὰρ ἀληθεῖ καὶ αὐτοὶ χρῶνται λόγῳ; Somn 1,
120: θαυμάσαι ἄν . . . καὶ τὴν ῥητήν.

Philon parle avec le plus grand respect et l'admiration
la plus fervente des docteurs juifs qui scrutent le sens littéral de l'Ecriture. En *Spec.* 1, 8 il rapporte les motivations
médicales et morales de la circoncision, qui, transmises en des
traditions anciennes remontant à des hommes admirables, qui ont
scruté très diligemment les écrits de Moïse, sont parvenues à
ses oreilles. Après quoi Philon expose deux interprétations
allégoriques du même rite. Il n'est pas certain qu'il soit
légitime de voir comme on le fait quelquefois des *Littéralistes*
dans ces maîtres qui rapportent d'antiques justifications d'un

commandement. Rien n'indique qu'ils eûssent rejeté les deux
interprétations allégoriques, complémentaires et non contradictoires, que propose Philon. Le problème du littéralisme ne
se pose qu'au cas où le sens littéral et le sens allégorique
sont en conflit et, pour le répéter, le littéralisme consiste
alors à rejeter le second au nom du premier. En *Spec*. 3, 178
Philon qualifie d'hommes admirables les exégètes qui voient dans
la plupart des dispositions de la Législation les symboles
visibles de réalités invisibles. En *Spec*. 1, 314 les hommes
admirables sont les exégètes juifs en général sans qu'il soit
fait de distinction entre les tenants du sens littéral ou les
allégoristes.

Chaque fois que la chose apparaît possible, Philon
utilise les deux types d'exégèse. Il est des cas, comme nous
l'avons noté, où son embarras l'incline à penser que le sens
littéral doit être abandonné. Citons, outre les exemples que
nous avons allégués dans le texte, *LA* 2, 19; *Det*. 15; *Plant*.
113; *Agr*. 157. Mais, plus souvent encore, dans la partie législative elle-même de son commentaire, Philon fait suivre l'explication ou la motivation littérale d'une disposition légale, d'une
interprétation allégorique en laquelle l'exégèse culmine et qui
est censée proposer les aperçus les plus profonds, la motivation
fondamentale et transcendante du commandement. On comparera les
textes suivants: *Mig*. 89, 93; *Somn*. 1, 164; *Abr*. 68, 88, 119,
200, 217, 236; *Ios*. 23, 125; *Spec*. 1, 200, 287; 2, 129, 147;
Praem. 61, 65; *Cont*. 28, 78. Par une exception notable, en *Abr*.
131, le sens littéral est donné après l'interprétation allégorique et mystique qu'il renforce.

Dans le cas de la Loi sur le lèpre, il nous paraît
probable que ce qui a incité Philon à en répudier le sens littéral, c'est moins son caractère paradoxal ou son apparence
étrange que le fait qu'elle ne devait correspondre à rien
d'intelligible dans le milieu de Philon et dans la pratique
médicale qui y était courante. Au contraire une disposition
aussi singulière pour la raison que la purification par les
cendres de la vache rousse (Nombres XIX, 2-10) mais qui, a
l'époque de Philon, était toujours en vigueur, est commentée
en *Spec*. 1, 268, cependant qu'au paragraphe 269 il est fait
allusion à une exégèse allégorique qui ne nous est pas parvenue.

V. Nikiprowetzky

B. *The Formal Structure of Philo's*
Allegorical Exegesis

That Philo of Alexandria is dependent to at least some
extent on Greek rather than traditional Jewish models for the
specific form of his allegorical exegesis of the Pentateuch has
been recognised long before this, and is accepted by such authorities as Zeller, Bréhier and Leisegang.[1] These have suggested
in particular the Stoic exegesis of the Homeric poems as likely
models for Philo's remarkable enterprise, and I believe that
they are right. However, the formal structure of Philo's exegesis and the precise characteristics which he derives from his
presumed sources has not, it seems to me, been up to now sub-
jected to sufficiently detailed examination. A number of
scholars have set out to analyse Philo's methods;[2] their studies
have borne interesting titles such as "The Allegorical Exegesis
of Philo of Alexandria" (Stein), "The Literary Form of Allegorical Exegesis in Philo's Commentary on *Genesis* (Adler), or "The
Technique of Allegorical Interpretation in Philo of Alexandria"
(Irmgard Christiansen), but when one turns to examine the contents one is disappointed. Stein gives an excellent survey,
but confines himself to the Hellenistic Jewish antecedents of
Philo, and is unwilling to grant Philo any great measure of
originality. Adler makes a useful five-fold division of types
of exegesis, according to the degree of complexity of the individual *lemma*, and whether or not Philo introduces the exegesis
of parallel passages, but he does not relate Philo's method to
any other. Fräulein Christiansen seeks the roots of Philo's
method of allegory in the Platonic diaeresis, a rather desperate
suggestion which may or may not have some merit as a general
principle, but does not contribute to the explanation of the
particular form which Philo employs. These and other studies
have failed, in my judgement, to contribute much to the solution of the question, through failing to take into account one
class of evidence which seems to me to be capable of throwing

---

Note: This section first saw the light as a talk to the
American Philological Association, which will explain its lack
of particular reference to the present treatises.

77

considerable light on the problem here to be examined, to wit, the Neoplatonic commentaries on Plato.

In this essay I propose to go through what appear to be the salient formal characteristics of Philo's exegetical method, in each case giving sufficient examples from both Philo himself and from the Neoplatonic commentators, primarily Proclus, to make clear the essential unity of the tradition of commentary which each exemplifies.

II

(i) First, the text to be commented upon is divided up into *lemmata*, short passages, from one line to a paragraph, on which the commentary is then based. The text of the lemma is taken either phrase by phrase--sometimes word by word--or first as a whole, and then in detail, depending on the nature of the subject-matter. A.-J. Festugière, in a most useful article published some time ago,[3] analyses the practice of Proclus and Olympiodorus in this matter. Olympiodorus is very schematised in his procedure, while Proclus is much freer, and thus more closely analogous to Philo, so I will confine my comparisons to him. The subject matter of the whole lemma is referred to by Proclus as the θεωρία (and often, also, simply as τὰ πράγματα), as opposed to the details of the text, which he terms λέξις or τὰ ῥήματα. He may adopt any of three possibilities: (i) *theoria* first, then *lexis*; (ii) *lexis* first, then *theoria*; (iii) a mixture. Festugière documents the first two possibilities fully on pp. 86ff. of his article; the third possibility does not concern him. When we turn to Philo, we find that he uses the same procedure, in the same free way as Proclus does, but with enough unmistakable technical expressions to make it clear that he is aware of what he is doing. At *LA* 1.65 for instance, we pass from the general comment to the particular with the phrase ἴδωμεν δὲ καὶ τὰς λέξεις. At *LA* 2.31, on the question of Adam's trance (*Gen.* 2:21), we make a similar transition with the phrase: τούτων εἰρημένων ἐφαρμοσ- τέον τὰς λέξεις. At *Fug.* 38, we pass from a general discussion of the "endurance" of the ἀσκητικός to a consideration of the text with the bridge-passage: τοιαῦτα ὑφηγεῖται τῷ ἀσκητικῷ ἡ ὑπομονή, τὰς δὲ λέξεις ἀκριβωτέον. With these we may compare such phrases as ἐπὶ δὲ τὴν λέξιν ἐπανίωμεν καὶ τὰ ῥήματα τοῦ Σωκράτους (Procl. *In Tim.* I 32, 19 Diehl); ταῦτα μὲν περὶ τῆς

ὅλης τῶν ἐκκειμένων ῥημάτων διανοίας· ἐπεξέλθωμεν δὲ καὶ τοῖς
καθ' ἕκαστον συντόμως (ibid. 187, 12); or ἀλλ' ἐπειδὴ περὶ τῆς
τῶν πραγμάτων τάξεως εἴρηται, φέρε καὶ τὴν λέξιν θεωρήσωμεν
αὐτήν (In Parm. 776, 1-3 Cousin).

Philo, we may note, also uses the opposition of πράγματα
to ῥήματα, e.g., Somn. 2.97, Her. 72, though not, admittedly, in
such a technical way.

I do not find Philo, on the other hand, making the progression from the particular to the general that Proclus makes
on occasion; what he does often do is to break up the lemma into
phrases and discuss them consecutively. This procedure of his
is too common to require documentation. Similarly, Proclus will
not rigidly observe a distinction between *theoria* and *lexis* if
the text does not seem to require it. Nevertheless, the tradition in which both these men are working does seem to have
employed this distinction, for use when the text required it.

(ii) Within the individual section (κεφάλαιον) of commentary, one proceeds from the literal interpretation (ἡ ῥητὴ
ἐξήγησις), which may include historical or philological comment,
to the "ethical" (ἠθική), which considers the moral lessons to
be derived from the passage--this level of commentary may be
either literal or allegorical--and then to the "physical"
(φυσική) or allegorical proper, in which the subject matter
of the lemma is taken to represent metaphysical truths. In a
commentary on Plato, this progression is only fully relevant to
the introductory portions (προοίμια) of the dialogues, and other
similar passages, where non-philosophical activities are being
described which make a distinction between a literal and an
allegorical interpretation necessary. In the case of Genesis
or the Homeric Poems, on the other hand, such a distinction is
constantly necessary. However, there is quite enough of this
sort of material in the Platonic commentaries to allow this
method ample exercise. Again, in the cases both of Homer and
of Genesis, the literal meaning often has to be explained away
as something of an embarrassment, which is not really the case
with the Platonic dialogues, so that Philo may be presumed to
be nearer than the Neoplatonists in this feature to the common
source.

Sometimes the literal interpretation is tolerable
(though it never comprises the complete sense), e.g., LA 2.14:
ἔσει δὲ καὶ ἡ τροπικὴ καὶ ἡ ῥητὴ ἀπόδοσις ἀξία τοῦ θαυμάζεσθαι;

more often it has to be explained away, e.g., *ibid*. 19 (Eve
being formed out of Adam's rib): τὸ ῥητὸν ἐπὶ τούτου μυθῶδές
ἐστι or *Det*. 95 (Exod. 2:23, the Children of Israel mourning the
death of the Pharaoh): πρὸς μὲν οὖν τὸ ῥητὸν ἡ λέξις τὸ εὔλογον
οὐ περιέχει. Cf. also *Deus* 71: εἴρηται τροπικώτερον (see note
ad loc.). We may note here that Proclus does not employ the
terms ῥητός or τροπικός in this sense (although Olympiodorus
does use ῥητός).[4] Proclus simply begins with philological or
historical comments on the literal level of the text (usually
replies to criticisms of Plato; see below under *aporiai*), and
then passes on to the allegorical interpretation, whether ethical or physical, with some such formula as ἀλλὰ τούτων ἄδην
(I 82, 19), or χαρίεντα μὲν οὖν πάντα ταῦτα καὶ ὅσα τοιαῦτα ἄν
τις ἐπινοήσειεν εἰς θεωρίαν τῆς προκειμένης ῥήσεως (I 15, 22f.),
in which latter passage the word ῥῆσις is used more or less to
mean the literal text. A commentator on Plato does not have to
worry as much as Philo does about the historicity or otherwise
of details of the text, although in the case of such an event
as the War with Atlantis in the *Timaeus*, Proclus feels the need
to discuss whether this actually happened (I 75, 30ff.), while
taking it primarily as a symbol of cosmic truth.

At any rate, one passes from the literal to the ethical
interpretation. In Philo we find such bridge-formulas as ἡ δὲ
πρὸς τὸ ἦθος ἀπόδοσίς ἐστι τοιαύτη (*LA* 1.16); λεκτέον οὖν
ἠθικῶς μὲν τοῦτο, or *Mos*. 2.96. As I have said, the ethical
interpretation may be based on either a literal or an allegorical interpretation of the text, from either of which moral
lessons may be drawn. In Proclus' *Timaeus Commentary* the ethical interpretations, while given, are usually being disparaged,
since, following Iamblichus, Proclus has settled rigidly for a
"physical" interpretation of the whole *Prooimion*. Porphyry,
however, commenting more loosely, had given ethical interpretations, and these are faithfully reported (e.g., I 16, 31ff.;
24, 12ff.; 29, 31ff.; etc.). That such comment was recognised
normally as being respectable, however, can be seen from such a
passage as the comment of Proclus' comrade Hermeias on *Phaedrus*
229B[5] (the Myth of Boreas and Oreithyia), where he offers first
an ἠθικωτέρα διάπτυξις and then ἡ ἐπὶ τὰ ὅλα μεταβιβάζουσα τὸν
λόγον. The ethical interpretation here is literal, the physical
allegorical.[6] Proclus himself accepts an ethical interpretation of the very first *lemma* (the whole *kephalaion* is a very
good, because very full, example of his exegetical method), at

I 15, 25 f.: οὐκοῦν ἠθικὰ μὲν λάβοις ἂν ἐντεῦθεν Πυθαγόρεια
δόγματα τοιαῦτα. As is often the case, the comment here is on
the literal interpretation of the text.

　　　　To return to Philo, we find him also moving formally
from the ethical to the "physical" level, e.g., *LA* I, 39:
φυσικῶς μὲν (actually preceding ἠθικῶς δέ); *ibid.* 100: καὶ
φυσικῶς (following an ethical exegesis); *ibid.* 2.12: φυσικῶς
δὲ ἐκεῖνο (following λεκτέον οὖν ἠθικῶς μὲν τοῦτο, quoted above),
etc. The "physical" level of exegesis, as we have said, is
always allegorical. Proclus makes the same progression. In
the first *kephalaion* of his *Timaeus* Comm., mentioned above, we
find the following bridge passage: ταῦτα μὲν οὖν καὶ ὅσα τοιαῦτα, ἠθικά· φυσικὰ δὲ τοιαῦτα (I 16, 20).[7] In the *Timaeus*
Commentary, however, the "physical" interpretation is often
attributed in the first instance to Iamblichus, who is often,
in turn, correcting the "ethical" interpretation of Porphyry
(e.g. I 117, 18: ὅ γε μὴν φιλόσοφος Ἰάμβλιχος φυσικῶς ταῦτα
ἀξιοῖ θεωρεῖν, ἀλλ᾽ οὐκ ἠθικῶς). Proclus normally agrees with
Iamblichus, however, though often modifying him. That all
three levels were fully recognised by the Neoplatonists appears
from a significant passage at the beginning of Olymp. *Commentary
on the Alcibiades* (2, 16f. West.), where he explains that the
full significance of Plato has often escaped earlier commentators because they have not realised that he must be understood 'καὶ φυσικῶς καὶ ἠθικῶς καὶ θεολογικῶς καὶ ἁπλῶς πολλα-
χῶς', even as is the case with Homer. The Neoplatonist commentators make a distinction between "physical" and "theological" comment (e.g., Procl. *In Tim.* I 8, 5) which Philo does not
make explicitly. Obviously he is not satisfied with what the
Stoics thought of as "physical" exegesis, but he merely extends
the significance of the word to comprise "theology." On a
number of occasions, indeed, he takes issue with Stoic physical
interpretations (whether genuine or fabricated by himself will
be discussed further below), as in the case of The Tree of Life
(*QG* I 10), or of the Cherubim and the Flaming Sword (*Cher.*
25ff.), or of the Fathers of Abraham (*QG* 3, 11), and proposes
a better, theological exegesis, though without using the word.

　　　　(iii) The next notable characteristic is the following:
near the beginning of a *kephalaion*, normally within the area of
the literal interpretation, but not necessarily so, there may
occur the criticism of previous commentators, and the raising

and solving of "problems" (ἀπορίαι) arising from the text. In
the Neoplatonic tradition we find two classes of commentators,
those individually named, and those left unidentified, normally
designated as οἱ μέν, οἱ δέ, or ἄλλοι. Of those who are raising
aporiai, some may be termed friendly, that is to say Platonists
who are genuinely baffled by something, and others "hostile" or
"eristic," that is, non-Platonist critics who are trying to
make a fool of Plato. We have ample evidence that Homer too
was beset by such gadflies.

     A perusal of a Neoplatonic commentary, in particular
of Proclus' *Comm. on the Timaeus*, where Proclus deals with his
predecessors, both named and unnamed, very fully, will show how
this aspect of the commentary form has developed by their time.
For the later Platonists, there was no lack of previous comment, both constructive and hostile. They could base their own
positions on the criticism and further refinement of a long
line of predecessors. In the very first *kephalaion* of Proclus'
Timaeus Commentary, one finds, first, *aporiai* by Longinus and
one Praxiphanes, and then an answer to these and an ethical
comment by Porphyry, before Proclus contributes his own thoughts.
Proclus often presents elaborate doxographies, comprising both
anonymous and named commentators, before stating his own view
(e.g. I 75, 30 ff., on the Atlantis Myth). The anonymous οἱ
μέν and οἱ δέ seem in the Timaeus Commentary to designate
chiefly Middle Platonic commentators, while Proclus' immediate
Neoplatonic predecessors, Amelius, Porphyry, Iamblichus and
Syrianus are usually mentioned by name, though in the Parmenides
Commentary everyone is made anonymous, save for occasional
references to "my revered teacher," Syrianus. In either case,
however, there is no question about the existence of a long
line of predecessors.

     When we turn to Philo, on the other hand, we find a
curious situation: properly speaking, he had no predecessors,
that is, no one who indulged in allegorical interpretation of
the Old Testament on anything like the scale that he did. I
realise that this is still a controversial question, but the
fact remains that, outside of the evidence of Philo's own
writings, we are unable to uncover any authority who seems to
anticipate his particularly comprehensive type of commentary
--one Aristobulus, I would maintain, does not make an exegetical tradition. And yet Philo undoubtedly appears to make reference repeatedly to previous authorities.[8]

Certainly, the Therapeutae and the Essenes indulged in allegorical interpretation; we have no reason to doubt Philo's testimony on this point. It may, indeed, have been his contact with the Therapeutae that turned his mind to his own great enterprise. There were also some, to whom he objects, who chose to take everything in the Pentateuch as "spiritual" and thus felt themselves free of the provisions of the Law (*Mig.* 89). But what we find on a number of occasions in Philo's commentary also is an apparent class of exegete who interprets the text of the Pentateuch in a Stoic sense, giving a determinedly material- istic explanation of the text, and showing in the process more than a passing acquaintance with the details of Stoicism. Such a class of critic appears, for instance, in *LA* 1,59 and *QG* 1,10, identifying the Tree of Life of *Gen.* 2:9 with the heart, wherein they situate τὸ ἡγεμονικόν. At *QG* 1,10 there are in fact three other "physical" (in the Stoic sense) explanations given as well, amounting to a set of four anonymous groups of critics. On the question of the Cherubim and the Flaming Sword, again, (*Cher.* 25ff.) we find two unsatisfactory materialistic exegeses--one, that the Cherubim are the spheres of the fixed stars and of the planets respectively, and the sword the principle of their motion; the other that the Cherubim are the two hemispheres, and the sword the Sun--both of which Philo rejects before coming to his own explanation. *QG* 3,11 (on the "fathers" of Abraham) and *ibid.* 13 (a suggestion that Moses accepted the Stoic doc- trine of εἱμαρμένη) are further instances of this curious class of criticism. Such passages are not to be confused with others where Philo is criticising literal interpreters, who are doubt- less orthodox rabbis, or certain "pious" and "admirable" men (e.g. *Abr.* 99, *Jos.* 151, *Spec.* 3, 178, *Spec.* 2, 147) who may very well be none other than the Therapeutae, though Philo does venture modestly to dispute their interpretations. The Stoic interpreters, then, are a special problem. The suggestion that I have to make in their regard may seem extreme, and I emphasise that it is speculative, but our alternative is to postulate, as scholars have indeed done, a class of Stoicising (and, in orthodox Jewish eyes, godless and blasphemous) interpreters of the Pentateuch, of whose existence we have really no other evidence than that of Philo himself.

Before presenting my suggestion, I wish to turn back briefly to Proclus. One is from time to time inclined to doubt, when faced by an anonymous *aporia* or by a list of anonymous

doxai, whether in fact they represent the views of any real
person. Especially when Proclus presents us with an extended
list, as he does, for instance, at *In Tim.* II 104, 17 ff. (on
the identity of τὸ μέσον at *Tim.* 34B) or *ibid.* 212, 12 ff. (on
the seven ὅροι of the soul at *Tim.* 35B). In each case *five*
anonymous opinions are mentioned. The difficulty of even theoretically attaching names to all these putative critics leads
one to wonder if perhaps he is not just listing all the possible
interpretations that occur to him of the important passage in
question. I wish to suggest that Philo is doing in the passages
I have referred to above what I feel that Proclus is doing here,
setting up straw men in order to shoot them down. In Philo's
case I would view such a procedure as a way of attacking the
Stoics, and I would suggest that he may be adapting it from a
Neopythagorean tradition of commentary on Homer (which we know
to have existed later from the evidence of Numenius, and of such
a passage as Origen, *Contra Cels.* VII 6, but which may already
have existed in Philo's time, in which the Pythagorean commentator would naturally systematically attack Stoic physical interpretations and substitute his own theological ones. My suggestion is that Philo, who criticises Stoic materialism from a
Pythagorean standpoint on many other occasions, is here adapting to his own purposes a characteristic of Neo-Pythagorean, not
Stoic, Homer commentary.

        The problem of *aporiai* is similar. Philo uses formulae
for introducing *aporiai* that are familiar from Neoplatonic commentary, e.g. ζητήσειε δ᾽ἄν τις (*LA* 1, 48), or ἄξιον δὲ διαπορῆσαι (*ibid.* 85) or ἄξιον δὲ σκέψασθαι (*ibid.* 2, 42, cf. *Gig.* 1).
These formulae are picked up, when the solution is presented,
by phrases like λεκτέον οὖν (*LA* 1, 86) or μήποτ᾽ οὖν ἀλληγο-
ροῦντες λύσωμεν τὸ ἀπορηθέν (*ibid.* 3, 60, cf. *Deus* 106,122).
Many of these *aporiai* seem to presuppose a tradition of
"eristic," hair-splitting, criticism of the books of Moses such
as certainly existed in respect of both Homer and Plato. Now
it is quite possible that some Jew-baiter of the type of Apion
had got to work on the books of Moses by Philo's time, but my
suggestion is that it is not necessary that there should be any
real author for most of these *aporiai*; it was simply part of
the tradition which Philo was adapting that problems, both constructive and destructive, should be dealt with and "solved."

(iv) We come now to a characteristic of Philo's exegesis
which is not paralleled in the Neoplatonic tradition, and which
was, on the other hand, a part of Jewish (or at least Essene)
tradition, that is, his systematic etymologising (which
involves translating), of the proper names in the Pentateuch.
Philo himself plainly did not know Hebrew to any significant
extent, so that for these translations he is dependent on a
word-list compiled by someone who did. Not that all the etymologies are accurate--some are very strange--but they are plainly
the work of someone who knew Hebrew well. On the translations
thus provided, Philo builds many remarkable interpretations.

The Neoplatonists make no use of such a tool in the
exegesis of Plato's dialogues; they took the characters in the
dialogues as symbols of metaphysical realities, but they made
no effort to interpret the actual names of Socrates, Timaeus,
Zeno or Parmenides in such a way as to support their exegesis.
On the other hand, we know that the Stoics were much given to
the etymologising at least of the names of the Homeric gods,
though I know of no such attempt on the names of, say, Achilles,
Agamemnon, or Penelope.

It seems to me in this case that Philo is making a
genuine synthesis between a native Jewish form and a Greek one,
which results simply in a more elaborate application of the
existing Stoic exegetical device. Philo does in fact try a
Greek etymology of Jewish names on six occasions (Stein, p. 60),
for no obvious reason, and with no apparent consciousness that
he is doing anything absurd or remarkable. For instance,
Pheison, the river of Eden, he derives at *LA* 1, 66 from φεί-
δεσθαι, and Leah, Rachel's sister, from λεῖος (*ibid.* 2, 59),
although he knows also a Hebrew etymology for her (e.g. *Mig.* 26;
Mut. 253-5).

Here, then, as also, I think, in the case of his very
extensive use of parallel passages, Philo is employing a native
Jewish exegetical form which happens also to be a Greek one.
In the matter of the use of parallel passages, which Philo uses
very diffusely, we are faced, I think, with another instance of
cross-fertilisation. We can certainly observe in the Neoplatonists the practice of bringing in other Platonic texts to
explain a particular position (the *Phaedrus* myth, for example,
to elucidate the psychology of the *Timaeus*), and the copious
quotation of parallel passages of Homer in the pseudo-Plutarchan
Life and Poetry of Homer shows this to be a characteristic of

Homeric commentary, but it is undeniable that the Midrashic
tradition also made much use of parallel passages, so that here
we see rather a synthesis of two traditions than a wholesale
adoption of the Hellenic one.

III

I have tried to show, in summary fashion, that the tradition of commentary with which Philo on the one hand, and the
Neoplatonists on the other, are working is essentially the
same. Even if we make ample allowance for the idiosyncrasies
of such figures as Philo and Proclus, it is possible, I think,
to see in broad outline the formal characteristics of their
common source. This, I suggest, was the tradition of commentary
developed by Stoic scholars of the last two centuries B.C.E., in
particular Crates of Mallos and his pupil Herodikos of Babylon,
of whose work the *Homeric Allegories* of Herakleitos (probably
of the late first century C.E.) is a reflection.[9] Even Herakleitos, however, preserves sufficient traces of literal, ethical and, above all, physical exegesis to constitute good evidence in confirmation of my thesis.

NOTES

[1]Edward Zeller, *Philosophie der Griechen* III[2], pp.
300-6; Emile Bréhier, *Les Idées philosophiques et religieuses de
Philon d'Alexandrie*, ch. III; Hans Leisegang, *RE* article, Philon
41, Vol. 20:1 cols. 36-9.

[2]E.g. Edmund Stein, *Die allegorische Exegese des Philo
aus Alexandreia*, Beihefte zur Zeitschr. f. die alttest. Wiss.
51, 1929; Maximilian Adler, *Studien zu Philon von Alexandreia*,
Breslau, 1929; Irmgard Christiansen, *Die Technik der allegorischen Auslegungswissenschaft bei Philon von Alexandrien*,
Beitr. z. Gesch. d. Bibl. Herm. 7, Tübingen 1969.

[3]"Modes de composition des Commentaires de Proclus,"
Mus. Helv. XX 1963, pp. 77-100.

[4]See index to Westerink's ed. of Olymp. *Comm. on the
Alcibiades*, s.v.

[5]Hermeias, *In Phaedrum*, p. 28, 24-5 Couvreur.

[6]The use of τὰ ὅλα here to mean the general truths
behind the particular text is common also in Proclus (e.g. *In
Tim.* I 37,18; 53, 24; 73, 12.

[7]Cf. also *In Parm.* 677,13: ἀπὸ δὲ τῆς ἠθικῆς λάβοις ἄν . . . ; 678,11: ἔτι τοίνυν φυσικῶς ἐπισκεψώμεθα; 718,5: τὸ μὲν ὅσον ἠθικὸν ἐν τούτοις . . . 27 εἰ δὲ καὶ ταῦτα ἐθέλοις ἀνάγειν ἐπὶ τὰ θεῖα. . . .

[8]The evidence is well set out by Stein in his monograph, pp. 26-41.

[9]Cf. Buffière's introduction to his Budé ed. of Herakleitos, *Allégories d' Homère*, pp. xxxii-xxxvii.

J. Dillon

C. *Philo's Bible in the* De Gigantibus *and the*
Quod Deus sit Immutabilis

1. *The Textual Tradition of*
   Philo's Biblical Citations

It is notorious that while the text of Philo's biblical
citations presented by some Philonic manuscripts follows the
standard LXX translation, the text presented by other Philonic
manuscripts differs widely from the LXX in many places. To
complicate matters further, manuscripts do not consistently
present the same text-type throughout all the treatises, but
follow now one text-type and now the other. In our two treatises the manuscripts MAPHG are those which present the citations in the LXX-tradition, while the manuscripts UF present a
text of another kind.

The nature of this different text was long the subject
of debate. As late as the middle decades of this century it
was being argued by some (i) that Philo must have had access to
a Greek translation different from the LXX; (ii) that sometimes
he used this different translation for his citations from the
Old Testament; and (iii) that in the course of the transmission
of the text, passages cited from this other translation were
"corrected," in most manuscripts, though mercifully not in all,
to bring their wording into line with that of the LXX.

That this is no longer thought to be so is due largely
to the work of two scholars: the late P. Katz (Walters) and
D. Barthélemy. Katz in his *Philo's Bible, The Aberrant Text of*
Bible Quotations in Some Philonic Writings and its Place in the
Textual History of the Greek Bible, Cambridge University Press,
1950, showed that the characteristic readings of the non-LXX
text-type occur in the *lemmata* preceding Philo's expositions,
and are often in conflict with the wording of the citations
adopted by Philo in the course of the expositions themselves;
and that secondly, these characteristic readings are in fact
the result of a revision, based on some translation like that
of Aquila, and aimed at bringing the original LXX-translation

into greater conformity with the Hebrew. Katz thought that this
revision was the work of some Christian reviser living towards
the end of the fifth century A.D.

In this latter particular Katz, who was working before
the evidence from the manuscripts discovered in the Judaean
Desert became generally available, was mistaken. Barthélemy
in an article entitled 'Est-ce Hoshaya Rabba qui censura le
"Commentaire Allegorique"?', first published in Philon d'Alexandrie, Lyon 11-15 Septembre 1966, in Editions du Centre National
de la Recherche Scientifique, Paris, 1967, pp. 45-78, reissued
as pp. 140-73 of 'Etudes d'histoire du texte de l'Ancien Testament,' Orbis Biblicus et Orientalis 21, Göttingen 1978, has
shown (i) that the hebraizing readings in question are not
merely like Aquila's renderings: they are taken from him and
from him only; and (ii) that the reviser who substituted these
readings for the LXX readings in Philo's citations was in fact a
Jew, who, not to put too fine a point on it, moved in the circle
of both the Christian scholar Origen and the Jewish scholar
Hoshaya Rabba in Caesarea in the first half of the third century
A.D. But Katz's main contention that the non-LXX readings did
not come from some different Greek translation available in
Philo's time, but were introduced by some later reviser of
Philo's text, has been amply confirmed by Barthélemy.

The tracing of this hebraizing revision to its source
has opened a very interesting window on to the study of Philo
by both Jews and Christians in the third century A.D.; but since
the revision was made long after Philo's time, its readings are
irrelevant to the ascertaining of Philo's meaning, and further
study of them would be out of place in this volume.

                                                    D. Gooding

2. *Philo's Citations of and allusions to the Bible in the* De Gigantibus *and* Quod Deus

La meilleure manière d'apercevoir les problèmes qu'impliquent les citations scripturaires contenues dans le *De Gigantibus* et le *Quod Deus sit Immutabilis* nous a paru être de dresser le tableau que nous donnons ci-dessous.

La première colonne de ce tableau indique le paragraphe du traité où se trouve une citation ou une allusion scripturaire. La deuxième colonne contient les références bibliques à la version des LXX. Les textes correspondants sont consignés pratiquement d'apres A. Rahlfs dans la colonne trois, tandis que dans la quatrième colonne se trouvent les textes de Philon qui les reproduisent ou s'en inspirent.

Gig.	LXX	Texte des LXX	Texte de Philon
1	Gen 6,1	καὶ ἐγένετο ἡνίκα ἤρξαντο οἱ ἄνθρωποι πολλοὶ γίνεσθαι ἐπὶ τῆς γῆς, καὶ θυγατέρες ἐγενήθησαν αὐτοῖς	« καὶ δὴ ἐγένετο, ἡνίκα ἤρξαντο οἱ ἄνθρωποι πολλοὶ γίνεσθαι ἐπὶ τῆς γῆς, καὶ θυγατέρες ἐγεννήθησαν αὐτοῖς»
6	Gen 6,2	ἰδόντες δὲ οἱ υἱοὶ τοῦ θεοῦ τὰς θυγατέρας τῶν ἀνθρώπων, ὅτι καλαί εἰσιν, ἔλαβον ἑαυτοῖς γυναῖκας ἀπὸ πασῶν, ὧν ἐξελέξαντο	« ἰδόντες δὲ οἱ ἄγγελοι τοῦ θεοῦ τὰς θυγατέρας τῶν ἀνθρώπων ὅτι καλαί εἰσι ἔλαβον ἑαυτοῖς γυναῖκας ἀπὸ πασῶν, ὧν ἐξελέξαντο»
17	Ps 77,49	Ἐξαπέστειλεν εἰς αὐτοὺς ὀργὴν θυμοῦ αὐτοῦ, θυμὸν καὶ ὀργὴν καὶ θλῖψιν, ἀποστολὴν δι᾿ ἀγγέλων πονηρῶν	« Ἐξαπέστειλεν εἰς αὐτοὺς ὀργὴν θυμοῦ αὐτοῦ, θυμὸν καὶ ὀργὴν καὶ θλῖψιν, ἀποστολὴν δι᾿ ἀγγέλων πονηρῶν»

Gig.	LXX	Texte des LXX	Texte de Philon
	Gen 6,3	καὶ εἶπεν κύριος ὁ θεός Οὐ μὴ καταμείνῃ τὸ πνεῦμά μου ἐν τοῖς ἀνθρώποις τούτοις εἰς τὸν αἰῶνα διὰ τὸ εἶναι αὐτοὺς σάρκας	« Εἶπε κύριος ὁ θεός Οὐ καταμενεῖ τὸ πνεῦμά μου ἐν τοῖς ἀνθρώποις εἰς τὸν αἰῶνα διὰ τὸ εἶναι αὐτοὺς σάρκας »
22	Gen 1,2	καὶ πνεῦμα θεοῦ ἐπεφέρετο ἐπάνω τοῦ ὕδατος	« Πνεῦμα θεοῦ ἐπεφέρετο ἐπάνω τοῦ ὕδατος »
23	Ex 31,2	[2] ἰδοὺ ἀνακέκλημαι ἐξ ὀνόματος τὸν Βεσελεηλ τὸν τοῦ Ουριου τὸν Ωρ τῆς φυλῆς Ἰούδα. [3] καὶ ἐνέπλησα αὐτὸν πνεῦμα θεῖον σοφίας καὶ συνέσεως καὶ ἐπιστήμης ἐν παντὶ ἔργῳ [4] διανοεῖσθαι,	« ἀνεκάλεσεν ὁ θεὸς τὸν Βεσελεὴλ καὶ ἐνέπλησεν αὐτὸν πνεύματος θείου, σοφίας, συνέσεως, ἐπιστήμης, ἐπὶ παντὶ ἔργῳ διανοεῖσθαι »
24	Nombres 11,17	καὶ ἀφελῶ ἀπὸ τοῦ πνεύματος τοῦ ἐπὶ σοὶ καὶ ἐπιθήσω ἐπ᾽ αὐτούς	« ἀφελῶ ἀπὸ τοῦ πνεύματος τοῦ ἐπὶ σοὶ καὶ ἐπιθήσω ἐπὶ τοὺς ἑβδομήκοντα πρεσβυτέρους »

Gig.	LXX	Texte des LXX	Texte de Philon
32	Lev 18,6	Ἄνθρωπος ἄνθρωπος πρὸς πάντα οἰκεῖα σαρκὸς αὐτοῦ οὐ προσελεύσεται ἀποκαλύψαι ἀσχημοσύνην· ἐγὼ κύριος ὁ θεὸς ὑμῶν	« Ἄνθρωπος ἄνθρωπος πρὸς πάντα οἰκεῖον σαρκὸς αὐτοῦ οὐ προσελεύσεται ἀποκαλύψαι ἀσχημοσύνην· ἐγὼ κύριος»
48	Nombres 14,44	ἡ δὲ κιβωτὸς τῆς διαθήκης κυρίου καὶ Μωυσῆς οὐκ ἐκινήθησαν ἐκ τῆς παρεμβολῆς	« Μωυσῆς καὶ ἡ κιβωτὸς οὐκ ἐκινήθησαν»
49	Deut 5,31	σὺ δὲ αὐτοῦ στῆθι μετ᾽ ἐμοῦ	« Σὺ δὲ αὐτοῦ στῆθι μετ᾽ ἐμοῦ»
50	Ex 18,14	διὰ τί σὺ κάθησαι μόνος	« Διὰ τί σὺ κάθησαι μόνος;»
55	Gen 6,3	ἔσονται δὲ αἱ ἡμέραι αὐτῶν, ἑκατὸν εἴκοσιν ἔτη	« Ἔσονται αἱ ἡμέραι αὐτῶν ἔτη ἑκατὸν εἴκοσιν»
56	Deut 34,7	Μωυσῆς δὲ ἦν ἑκατὸν καὶ εἴκοσι ἐτῶν ἐν τῷ τελευτᾶν αὐτόν· οὐκ ἠμαυρώθησαν οἱ ὀφθαλμοὶ αὐτοῦ, οὐδὲ ἐφθάρησαν τὰ χελύνια αὐτοῦ	« Ἀλλὰ καὶ Μωυσῆς τῶν ἴσων γενόμενος ἐτῶν τοῦ θνητοῦ βίου μετανίσταται»
63	Gen 17,1	ἐγώ εἰμι ὁ θεός σου· εὐαρέστει ἐναντίον ἐμοῦ, καὶ γίνου ἄμεμπτος	« ἐγώ εἰμι ὁ θεός σου· εὐαρέστει ἐναντίον ἐμοῦ, καὶ γίνου ἄμεμπτος»

Gig.	LXX	Texte des LXX	Texte de Philon
65	Gen 2,24	καὶ ἔσονται οἱ δύο εἰς σάρκα μίαν	« ἐγένοντο γὰρ οἱ δύο εἰς σάρκα μίαν»
66	Gen 10,8	οὗτος ἤρξατο εἶναι γίγας ἐπὶ τῆς γῆς	« οὗτος ἤρξατο εἶναι γίγας ἐπὶ τῆς γῆς»

Deus	LXX	Texte des LXX	Texte de Philon
1	Gen 6,4	καὶ μετ᾽ ἐκεῖνο, ὡς ἂν εἰσεπορεύ-οντο οἱ υἱοὶ τοῦ θεοῦ πρὸς τὰς θυγα-τέρας τῶν ἀνθρώπων, καὶ ἐγεννῶσαν ἑαυ-τοῖς· ἐκεῖνοι ἦσαν οἱ γίγαντες οἱ ἀπ᾽ αἰῶνος, οἱ ἄνθρωποι οἱ ὀνο-μαστοί	« καὶ μετ᾽ ἐκεῖνο ὡς ἂν εἰσεπορεύοντο οἱ ἄγγελοι τοῦ θεοῦ πρὸς τὰς θυγατέρας τῶν ἀνθρώπων, καὶ ἐγέννων αὐτοῖς» _La fin du verset manque_
4	Gen 22,2-9	[9] καὶ συμποδίσας Ἰσαὰκ τὸν υἱὸν αὐτοῦ ἐπέθηκεν αὐτὸν ἐπὶ τὸ θυ-σιαστήριον ἐπάνω τῶν ξύλων	συμποδίσας, ὥς φησιν ὁ νόμος
4	Gen 15,6	καὶ ἐπίστευσεν Αβραμ τῷ θεῷ καὶ ἐλογίσθη αὐτῷ εἰς δικαιοσύνην	ὅτε τὴν περὶ τὸ ὂν ἀνενδοίαστον ἔγνω βεβαιότητα, ἢ λέγε-ται πεπιστευκέναι
6	1 Sam 1,11	δώσω αὐτὸν ἐνώ-πιόν σου δοτόν	« Δίδωμί σοι αὐτὸν δοτόν» ἐν ἴσῳ τῷ δοτὸν ὄντα, ὥστ᾽ εἶναι « τὸν δεδομέ-νον δίδωμι»

Deus	LXX	Texte des LXX	Texte de Philon
6	Nombres 28,2	τὰ δῶρά μου δόματά μου, καρπώματά μου εἰς ὀσμὴν εὐωδίας διατηρήσετε προσφέρειν ἐμοί ἐν ταῖς ἑορταῖς μου	« τὰ δῶρά μου, δόματά μου, καρπώματά μου διατηρήσετε προσφέρειν ἐμοί»
10	1 Sam 2,5	ὅτι στεῖρα ἔτεκεν ἑπτά, καὶ ἡ πολλὴ ἐν τέκνοις ἠσθένησε	« στεῖρα ἔτεκεν ἑπτά, ἡ δὲ πολλὴ ἐν τέκνοις ἠσθένησε»
16	Gen 38,9	Γνοὺς δὲ Αυναν, ὅτι οὐκ αὐτῷ ἔσται τὸ σπέρμα	ʹΟ γοῦν Αὐνάν, « αἰσθόμενος ὅτι οὐκ αὐτῷ ἔσται τὸ σπέρμα»
20	Gen 6,5-7	ʹΙδὼν δὲ κύριος ὁ θεὸς ὅτι ἐπληθύνθησαν αἱ κακίαι τῶν ἀνθρώπων ἐπὶ τῆς γῆς, καὶ πᾶς τις διανοεῖται ἐν τῇ καρδίᾳ αὐτοῦ ἐπιμελῶς ἐπὶ τὰ πονηρὰ πάσας τὰς ἡμέρας· [6] καὶ ἐνεθυμήθη ὁ θεός, ὅτι ἐποίησεν τὸν ἄνθρωπον ἐπὶ τῆς γῆς, καὶ διενοήθη· [7] καὶ εἶπεν ὁ θεός, ἀπαλείψω τὸν ἄνθρωπον, ὃν ἐποίησα, ἀπὸ προσώπου τῆς γῆς ἀπὸ ἀνθρώπου ἕως κτήνους καὶ ἀπὸ ἑρπετῶν ἕως πετεινῶν τοῦ	« ʹΙδὼν κύριος ὁ θεὸς ὅτι ἐπληθύνθησαν αἱ κακίαι τῶν ἀνθρώπων ἐπὶ τῆς γῆς, καὶ πᾶς τις διανοεῖται ἐν τῇ καρδίᾳ ἐπιμελῶς τὰ πονηρὰ πάσας τὰς ἡμέρας, ἐνεθυμήθη ὁ θεὸς ὅτι ἐποίησε τὸν ἄνθρωπον ἐπὶ τῆς γῆς, καὶ διενοήθη. καὶ εἶπεν ὁ θεός ʹΑπαλείψω τὸν ἄνθρωπον ὃν ἐποίησα ἀπὸ προσώπου τῆς γῆς»

Deus	LXX	Texte des LXX	Texte de Philon
		οὐρανοῦ· ὅτι ἐνε- θυμήθην, ὅτι ἐποί- ησα αὐτούς	
23	Deut 5,31	σὺ δὲ αὐτοῦ στῆθι μετ' ἐμοῦ	« σὺ δὲ αὐτοῦ στῆθι μετ' ἐμοῦ»
50	Deut 30,15-19	[15] Ἰδοὺ δέδωκα πρὸ προσώπου σου σήμερον τὴν ζωὴν καὶ τὸν θάνατον, τὸν ἀγαθὸν καὶ τὸν κακόν	« Ἰδοὺ δέδωκα πρὸ προσώπου σου τὴν ζωὴν καὶ τὸν θάνα- τον, τὸν ἀγαθὸν καὶ τὸν κακόν, ἔκλεξαι τὴν ζωήν»
		[19] Διαμαρτύρομαι ὑμῖν σήμερον τόν τε οὐρανὸν καὶ τὴν γῆν, τὴν ζωὴν καὶ τὸν θάνατον δέδωκα πρὸ προσώπου ὑμῶν· τὴν εὐλογίαν καὶ τὴν κατάραν· ἔκ- λεξαι τὴν ζωὴν σύ . . .	
51	Gen 6,7	ἀπαλείψω τὸν ἄν- θρωπον, ὃν ἐποίησα, ἀπὸ προσώπου τῆς γῆς ἀπὸ ἀνθρώπου ἕως κτήνους, καὶ ἀπὸ ἑρπετῶν ἕως πετεινῶν τοῦ οὐρα- νοῦ· ὅτι ἐθυμώ- θην ὅτι ἐποίησα αὐτούς	« Ἀπαλείψω τὸν ἄν- θρωπον ὃν ἐποίησα ἀπὸ προσώπου τῆς γῆς, ἀπὸ ἀνθρώπου ἕως κτήνους, ἀπὸ ἑρπετῶν ἕως πετει- νῶν τοῦ οὐρανοῦ, ὅτι ἐθυμώθην ὅτι ἐποίησα αὐτόν»

Deus	LXX	Texte des LXX	Texte de Philon
53	Nombres 23,10	οὐχ ὡς ἄνθρωπος ὁ θεός	«οὐχ ὡς ἄνθρωπος ὁ θεός»
54	Deut 8,5	ὡς εἴ τις παιδεύ- σαι ἄνθρωπος τὸν υἱὸν αὐτοῦ, οὕτως κύριος ὁ θεός σου παιδεύσει σε	«Ὡς ἄνθρωπος παιδεύ- σει τὸν υἱὸν αὐτοῦ»
70	Gen 6,7	ἐθυμώθην ὅτι ἐποί- ησα αὐτούς	«ἐθυμώθην ὅτι ἐποί- ησα αὐτούς»
	Gen 6,8	Νῶε δὲ εὗρε χάριν	«Νῶε δὲ εὗρε χάριν»
74	Ps 100,1	Ἔλεον καὶ κρίσιν ᾄσομαί σοι	«Ἔλεον καὶ κρίσιν ᾄσομαί σοι»
77	Ps 74,9	Ὅτι ποτήριον ἐν χειρὶ κυρίου, οἴνου ἀκράτου πλῆ- ρες κεράσματος	«Ποτήριον ἐν χειρὶ κυρίου, οἴνου ἀκρά- του πλῆρες κεράσμα- τος»
82	Ps 61,12	Ἅπαξ ἐλάλησεν ὁ θεός, δύο ταῦτα ἤκουσα	«ἅπαξ κύριος ἐλά- λησε, δύο ταῦτα ἤκουσα»
86	Gen 6,8	Νῶε δὲ εὗρε χάριν ἐναντίον κυρίου τοῦ θεοῦ	«Νῶε εὗρε χάριν ἐναντίον κυρίου τοῦ θεοῦ»
87	Nombres 6,21	ὃς ἐὰν μεγάλως εὔξηται εὐχήν	περὶ τῆς μεγάλης εὐχῆς
88	Nombres 6,5	ἅγιος ἔσται τρέ- φων κόμην τρίχα κεφαλῆς	«τρέφοντα κόμην τρί- χα κεφαλῆς»

Deus	LXX	Texte des LXX	Texte de Philon
89	Nombres 6,9	'Εὰν δέ τις ἀποθά- νη ἐξάπινα ἐπ' αὐτῷ παραχρῆμα μιανθήσεται ἡ κε- φαλὴ εὐχῆς αὐτοῦ	ὁ δὲ τυφῶν οὗτος τροπή τίς ἐστιν ἀκούσιος παραχρῆμα τὸν νοῦν μιαίνουσα, ἣν καλεῖ θάνατον
90	Nombres 6,12	καὶ αἱ ἡμέραι αἱ πρότεραι ἄλογοι ἔσονται, ὅτι ἐμι- άνθη κεφαλὴ εὐχῆς αὐτοῦ	ὡς τὰς προτέρας τῆς τροπῆς ἡμέρας ἀλό- γους ἐξετάζεσθαι
92	Gen 27,20	εἶπεν δὲ Ισαακ τῷ υἱῷ αὐτοῦ Τί τοῦτο, ὃ ταχὺ εὗρες, ὦ τέκνον; ὁ δὲ εἶπεν Ὁ παρέδωκεν κύριος ὁ θεός σου ἐναντί- ον μου	ὁ γοῦν ἀσκητὴς πυ- θομένου τοῦ πατρὸς αὐτοῦ τῆς ἐπιστήμης τὸν τρόπον τοῦτον· "τί τοῦτο ὃ ταχὺ εὗρες, τέκνον;" ἀποκρίνεται καὶ φησιν· «ὃ παρέδωκε κύριος ὁ θεὸς ἐναν- τίον μου»
94	Deut 6,10-11	δοῦναί σοι πόλεις μεγάλας καὶ καλὰς ἃς οὐκ ᾠκοδόμησας [11] οἰκίας πλή- ρεις πάντων ἀγαθῶν, ἃς οὐκ ἐνέπλησας, λάκκους λελατομη- μένους οὓς οὐκ ἐξελατόμησας, ἀμπε- λῶνας καὶ ἐλαιῶνας οὓς οὐ κατεφύτευ- σας	τούτοις ὁ νομοθέτης φησὶ δίδοσθαι «πό- λεις μεγάλας καὶ καλάς, ἃς οὐκ ᾠκο- δόμησαν οἰκίας πλή- ρεις τῶν ἀγαθῶν, ἃς οὐκ ἐνέπλησαν λάκκους λελατομη- μένους οὓς οὐκ ἐξελατόμησαν, ἀμπε- λῶνας καὶ ἐλαιῶνας, οὓς οὐκ ἐφύτευσαν»

Deus	LXX	Texte des LXX	Texte de Philon
99	Deut 1,43-44	καὶ παραβιασάμενοι ἀνέβητε εἰς τὸ ὄρος. [44] καὶ ἐξῆλθεν ὁ Ἀμορραῖος ὁ κατοικῶν ἐν τῷ ὄρει ἐκείνῳ εἰς συνάντησιν ὑμῖν καὶ κατεδίωξαν ὑμᾶς ὡς εἰ ποιήσαισαν αἱ μέλισσαι, καὶ ἐτίτρωσκον ὑμᾶς ἀπὸ Σηειρ ἕως Ερμα	« παραβιασάμενοί τινες ἀνέβησαν ἐπὶ τὸ ὄρος καὶ ἐξῆλθεν ὁ Ἀμορραῖος ὁ κατοικῶν ἐν τῷ ὄρει ἐκείνῳ, καὶ ἐτίτρωσκεν αὐτούς, ὡς ἂν ποιήσειαν αἱ μέλισσαι, καὶ ἐδίωξεν αὐτοὺς ἀπὸ Σηειρ ἕως Ἑρμᾶ »
104	Gen 6,8	Νωε δὲ εὗρε χάριν ἐναντίον κυρίου τοῦ θεοῦ	« Νῶε εὗρε χάριν παρὰ κυρίῳ τῷ θεῷ »
109	[Gen 6,9]	[τῷ θεῷ εὐηρέστησεν Νωε]	παρατηρητέον δ᾿ ὅτι τὸν μὲν Νῶέ φησιν εὐαρεστῆσαι ταῖς τοῦ ὄντος δυνάμεσι, κυρίῳ τε καὶ θεῷ
	Exode 33,17	εὕρηκας γὰρ χάριν ἐνώπιόν μου	« εὕρηκας χάριν παρ᾿ ἐμοί »
111	Gen 39,1	καὶ ἐκτήσατο αὐτὸν Πετεφρὴς ὁ εὐνοῦχος Φαραω, ὁ ἀρχιμάγειρος	Ἕτερος δέ τις φιλοσώματος καὶ φιλοπαθὴς νοῦς πραθεὶς τῇ ἀρχιμαγείρῳ τοῦ συγκρίματος ἡμῶν ἡδονῇ καὶ ἐξευνουχισθεὶς τὰ ἄρρενα καὶ γεννητικὰ τῆς ψυχῆς μέρη πάντα

Deus	LXX	Texte des LXX	Texte de Philon
117	Gen 6,9	Αὗται δὲ αἱ γενέσεις Νωε· Νωε ἄνθρωπος δίκαιος, τέλειος ὢν ἐν τῇ γενεᾷ αὐτοῦ· τῷ θεῷ εὐηρέστησεν Νωε.	« Αὗται αἱ γενέσεις Νῶε· Νῶε ἄνθρωπος δίκαιος, τέλειος ὢν ἐν τῇ γενεᾷ αὐτοῦ τῷ θεῷ εὐηρέστησε Νῶε»
	Gen 6,10	Ἐγέννησεν δὲ Νωε τρεῖς υἱούς, τὸν Σημ, τὸν Χαμ, τὸν Ιαφεθ	*Manque*
119	Gen 37,2	Αὗται δὲ αἱ γενέσεις Ιακωβ· Ιωσηφ δέκα ἑπτὰ ἐτῶν ἦν ποιμαίνων μετὰ τῶν ἀδελφῶν αὐτοῦ τὰ πρόβατα ὢν νέος, μετὰ τῶν υἱῶν Βαλλας καὶ μετὰ τῶν υἱῶν Ζελφας τῶν γυναικῶν τοῦ πατρὸς αὐτοῦ	« Αὗται δὲ αἱ γενέσεις Ἰακώβ· Ἰωσὴφ δέκα ἑπτὰ ἐτῶν ἦν ποιμαίνων μετὰ τῶν ἀδελφῶν τὰ πρόβατα, ὢν νέος, μετὰ τῶν υἱῶν Βαλλᾶς καὶ μετὰ τῶν υἱῶν Ζελφᾶς τῶν γυναικῶν πατρὸς αὐτοῦ»
122	Gen 6,11	Ἐφθάρη δὲ ἡ γῆ ἐναντίον τοῦ θεοῦ, καὶ ἐπλήσθη ἡ γῆ ἀδικίας	« ἐφθάρη ἡ γῆ ἐναντίον τοῦ θεοῦ καὶ ἐπλήσθη ἀδικίας»
123	Lev 13,14	καὶ ᾗ ἂν ἡμέρα ὀφθῇ ἐν αὐτῷ χρὼς ζῶν, μιανθήσεται	« ἐὰν ἀνατείλῃ χρὼς ζῶν ἐν τῷ λεπρῷ, μιανθήσεται»
124	Lev 13,15	καὶ μιανεῖ αὐτὸν ὁ χρὼς ὁ ὑγιής	« Καὶ μιανεῖ ὁ χρὼς ὁ ὑγιής»

Deus	LXX	Texte des LXX	Texte de Philon
127	Lev 13,11-13	[11] λέπρα παλαιου-μένη ἐστίν, ἐν τῷ δέρματι τοῦ χρωτός ἐστιν. [12] ἐὰν δὲ ἐξανθοῦσα ἐξανθήσῃ ἡ λέπρα ἐν τῷ δέρ-ματι, καὶ καλύψῃ ἡ λέπρα πᾶν τὸ δέρ-μα τῆς ἀφῆς ἀπὸ κεφαλῆς ἕως ποδῶν καθ᾽ ὅλην τὴν ὅρα-σιν τοῦ ἱερέως, [43] καὶ ὄψεται ὁ ἱερεὺς καὶ ἰδοὺ ἐκάλυψεν ἡ λέπρα πᾶν τὸ δέρμα τοῦ χρωτός, καὶ καθα-ριεῖ αὐτὸν ὁ ἱερεὺς τὴν ἀφήν, ὅτι πᾶν μετέβαλεν λευκόν, καθαρόν ἐστιν	Διὸ καὶ παραδοξό-τατον νόμον ἀνα-γράφει, ἐν ᾧ τὸν μὲν ἐκ μέρους ὄντα λεπρὸν ἀκάθαρτον, τὸν δὲ ὅλον δι᾽ ὅλων ἀπὸ ἄκρων ποδῶν ἄχρι κεφαλῆς ἐσχάτης καὶ ἐσχη-μένον τῇ λέπρᾳ καθαρόν φησιν εἶναι
131	Lev 14,34-36	[34] ῾Ως ἂν εἰσ-έλθητε εἰς τὴν γῆν τῶν Χαναναίων, ἣν ἐγὼ δίδωμι ὑμῖν ἐν κτήσει, καὶ δώσω ἀφὴν λέπρας ἐν ταῖς οἰκίαις τῆς γῆς τῆς ἐγκτήτου ὑμῖν, [35] καὶ ἥξει τίνος αὐτοῦ ἡ οἰκία καὶ ἀναγ-γελεῖ τῷ ἱερεῖ λέγων ῞Ωσπερ ἀφὴ ἑώραταί μου ἐν τῇ οἰκίᾳ [36] καὶ προστάξει ὁ ἱερεὺς	« ἐὰν γένηται ἀφὴ λέπρας ἐν οἰκίᾳ ἀφέξεται ὁ κεκτημέ-νος καὶ ἀναγγελεῖ τῷ ἱερεῖ λέγων· ὥσπερ ἀφὴ λέπρας ἑώραταί μοι ἐν τῇ οἰκίᾳ. καὶ προστά-ξει ὁ ἱερεὺς ἀπο-σκευάσαι τὴν οἰκίαν πρὸ τοῦ εἰσελθόντα τὸν ἱερέα εἰς τὴν οἰκίαν ἰδεῖν καὶ οὐ γενήσεται ἀκά-θαρτα ὅσα ἐν τῇ οἰκίᾳ. Καὶ μετὰ

Deus	LXX	Texte des LXX	Texte de Philon
		ἀποσκευάσαι τὴν οἰκίαν πρὸ τοῦ εἰσελθόντα ἰδεῖν τὸν ἱερέα τὴν ἀφὴν καὶ οὐ μὴ ἀκάθαρτα γένηται ὅσα ἐὰν ᾖ ἐν τῇ οἰκίᾳ, καὶ μετὰ ταῦτα εἰσελεύσεται ὁ ἱερεὺς καταμαθεῖν τὴν οἰκίαν	ταῦτα εἰσελεύσεται ὁ ἱερεὺς καταμαθεῖν
136	1 Rois 17,40	καὶ ἀνέστη καὶ ἐπορεύθη εἰς Σαρεπτα εἰς τὸν πυλῶνα τῆς πόλεως, καὶ ἰδοὺ ἐκεῖ γυνὴ χήρα συνέλεγεν ξύλα καὶ ἐβόησεν ὀπίσω αὐτῆς Ηλιου καὶ εἶπεν αὐτῇ Λαβὲ δή μοι ὀλίγον ὕδωρ εἰς ἄγγος καὶ πίομαι	Μεμίμηται δὲ τοῦτο καὶ ἡ ἐν ταῖς Βασιλείαις ἐντυγχάνουσα τῷ προφήτῃ γυνὴ <χήρα>
137	Gen 38,11	Εἶπε δὲ Ιουδας Θαμαρ τῇ νύμφῃ αὐτοῦ, κάθου χήρα ἐν τῷ οἴκῳ τοῦ πατρός σου . . . Ἀπελθοῦσα δὲ Θαμαρ ἐκάθητο ἐν τῷ οἴκῳ τοῦ πατρὸς αὐτῆς	καὶ γὰρ ταύτῃ προστέτακται χηρευούσῃ καθέζεσθαι ἐν τῷ τοῦ μόνου καὶ σωτῆρος οἴκῳ πατρός,

Deus	LXX	Texte des LXX	Texte de Philon
138	1 Rois 17,18	καὶ εἶπε πρὸς Ηλιου, τί ἐμοὶ καὶ σοὶ ἄνθρωπε τοῦ θεοῦ; εἰσῆλθες πρὸς μὲ τοῦ ἀναμνῆσαι τὰς ἀδικίας μου, καὶ θανατῶσαι τὸν υἱόν μου	« Ἄνθρωπε τοῦ θεοῦ, εἰσῆλθες πρὸς μὲ ἀναμνῆσαι τὸ ἀδίκημά μου καὶ τὸ ἁμάρτημά μου »
139	1 Sam 9,9	. . . ὅτι τὸν προφήτην ἐκάλει ὁ λαὸς ἔμπροσθεν, ὁ βλέπων	τοὺς γὰρ προφήτας ἐκάλουν οἱ πρότεροι τοτὲ μὲν ἀνθρώπους θεοῦ, τοτὲ δὲ ὁρῶντα
140	Gen 6,12	Καὶ εἶδεν κύριος ὁ θεὸς τὴν γῆν, καὶ ἦν κατεφθαρμένη, ὅτι κατέφθειρεν πᾶσα σὰρξ τὴν ὁδὸν αὐτοῦ ἐπὶ τῆς γῆς	ἦν δὲ κατεφθαρμένη, ὅτι κατέφθειρε πᾶσα σὰρξ τὴν ὁδὸν αὐτοῦ ἐπὶ τῆς γῆς
145	Nombres 20,17-20	[17] παρελευσόμεθα διὰ τῆς γῆς σου, οὐ διελευσόμεθα δι᾿ ἀγρῶν οὐδὲ δι᾿ ἀμπελώνων οὐδὲ πιόμεθα ὕδωρ ἐκ λάκκου σου, ὁδῷ Βασιλικῇ πορευσόμεθα, οὐκ ἐκκλινοῦμεν δεξιὰ οὐδὲ εὐώνυμα, ἕως ἂν παρέλθωμεν τὰ ὅριά σου. [18] Καὶ εἶπεν πρὸς αὐτὸν Εδωμ Οὐ διελεύσῃ δι᾿ ἐμοῦ· εἰ δὲ μή, ἐν πολέμῳ	« παρελευσόμεθα διὰ τῆς γῆς σου· οὐ διελευσόμεθα δι᾿ ἀγρῶν, οὐ δι᾿ ἀμπελώνων, οὐ πιόμεθα ὕδωρ λάκκου σου· ὁδῷ Βασιλικῇ πορευσόμεθα, οὐκ ἐκκλινοῦμεν δεξιὰ οὐδὲ εὐώνυμα ἕως ἂν παρέλθωμέν σου τὰ ὅρια » Ὁ δὲ Ἐδὼμ ἀποκρίνεται φάσκων· « οὐ διελεύσῃ δι᾿ ἐμοῦ εἰ δὲ μή, ἐν πολέμῳ ἐξελεύσομαί σοι

Deus	LXX	Texte des LXX	Texte de Philon
		ἐξελεύσομαι εἰς συνάντησίν σοι. [19] Καὶ λέγουσιν αὐτῷ οἱ υἱοὶ Ἰσραηλ Παρὰ τὸ ὄρος παρελευσόμεθα· ἐὰν δὲ τοῦ ὕδατός σου πίωμεν ἐγώ τε καὶ τὰ κτήνη, δώσω τιμήν σοι· ἀλλὰ τὸ πρᾶγμα οὐδέν ἐστιν παρὰ τὸ ὄρος παρελευσόμεθα. [20] Ὁ δὲ εἶπεν Οὐ διελεύσῃ δι᾽ ἐμοῦ.	εἰς συνάντησιν». Καὶ λέγουσιν αὐτῷ οἱ υἱοὶ Ἰσραήλ· «παρὰ τὸ ὄρος παρελευσόμεθα. Ἐὰν δὲ τοῦ ὕδατός σου πίω ἐγώ τε καὶ τὰ κτήνη, δώσω σοι τιμήν· ἀλλὰ τὸ πρᾶγμα οὐδέν ἐστι, παρὰ τὸ ὄρος παρελευσόμεθα. Ὁ δὲ εἶπεν· Οὐ διελεύσῃ δι᾽ ἐμοῦ»
148	Nombres 20,17	Παρελευσόμεθα διὰ τῆς γῆς σου	«Ἤδη παρελεύσομαι διὰ τῆς γῆς σου»
156	Deut 28,12	Ἀνοίξαι σοι κύριος τὸν θησαυρὸν αὐτοῦ τὸν ἀγαθόν, τὸν οὐρανόν, δοῦναι τὸν ὑετὸν τῇ γῇ σου ἐπὶ καιροῦ αὐτοῦ	«ἀνοίξῃ κύριος ἡμῖν τὸν θησαυρὸν αὐτοῦ τὸν ἀγαθόν, τὸν οὐρανόν, δοῦναι ὑετόν»
157	Gen 48,15	ὁ θεὸς ὁ τρέφων με ἐκ νεότητος	«ὁ θεὸς ὁ τρέφων με ἐκ νεότητος»
161	Gen 18,27	καὶ ἀποκριθεὶς Ἀβρααμ εἶπε Νῦν ἠρξάμην λαλῆσαι πρὸς τὸν κύριόν μου· ἐγὼ δὲ εἰμι γῆ καὶ σποδος	καὶ γὰρ Ἀβραὰμ ἐγγίσας τῷ θεῷ ἑαυτὸς εὐθὺς ἔγνω γῆν καὶ τέφραν ὄντα

Deus	LXX	Texte des LXX	Texte de Philon
181	Nombres 22,31	Ἀπεκάλυψεν δὲ ὁ θεὸς τοὺς ὀφθαλμοὺς Βαλααμ, καὶ ὁρᾷ τὸν ἄγγελον κυρίου ἀνθεστηκότα ἐν τῇ ὁδῷ	« εἶδε τὸν ἄγγελον τοῦ θεοῦ ἀνθεστῶτα»
183	Nombres 31,8	καὶ τὸν Βαλααμ υἱὸν Βεωρ ἀπέκτειναν ἐν ῥομφαίᾳ σὺν τοῖς τραυματίαις αὐτῶν	« φθορὰν τὴν μετὰ τῶν τραυματιῶν»

Ce tableau nous paraît appeler une observation générale. C'est que les guillemets que contient le texte de Philon et qui sont ceux du texte de P. Wendland et de la traduction de J. Leisegang d'où il sont passés dans l'édition de F. H. Colson et dans celle d'A. Mosès sont, d'une manière générale, très gravement inadéquats et constituent des facteurs d'erreur. Tous les textes qu'ils encadrent ne sont pas, il s'en faut parfois de beaucoup, des citations véritables. Les renvois de Philon au texte scripturaire sont de nature diverse et vont de l'allusion fugitive à la citation implicite, de la paraphrase à la citation vraie. L'emploi erroné des guillemets peut être à l'origine de jugements inexacts concernant le texte biblique auquel se référait Philon et, par suite, l'histoire de la Septante elle-même.

Il nous paraît donc utile d'examiner un à un chacun des passages contenus dans le tableau et d'en discuter individuellement tous les problèmes.

*   *   *   *   *

1. *Gig 1 = Gen 6,1.* Il s'agit ici d'une vraie citation à un minime détail près: le καί des Septante a été renforcé, vraisemblablement par Philon lui-même, à l'aide de la particule δή pour former la locution très fréquente καὶ δή: "et voici que."

Rahlfs écrit ἐγενήθησαν au lieu du causatif ἐγεννήθησαν.
Sur le problème, on verra Peter Walters (formerly Katz), *The
Text of the Septuagint its Corruptions and Their Emendation*,
edited by D. W. Gooding, *Cambridge University Press*, 1973, p.
115 et ss.

Il nous paraît toutefois assuré que Philon lisait ici
l'aoriste passif, non de γενέσθαι mais de γεννᾶν. En effet, en
Gig. 5 la phrase καὶ θυγατέρες ἐγεννήθησαν αὐτοῖς est reprise
de la manière suivante: οὗ χάριν θυγατέρας οἱ ἄνθρωποι οὗτοι
γεννῆσαι λέγονται. . . . La forme ἐγεννήθησαν nous semble
indiquer d'une manière beaucoup plus décidée et plus claire
qu'ἐγενήθησαν la responsabilité des géniteurs incapables d'engendrer autre chose que des femelles.

2. *Gig 6 = Gen 6,2.* C'est une vraie citation, mais
ici, comme en *Deus 1*, à l'expression οἱ ἄγγελοι τοῦ θεοῦ du
texte de Philon correspond οἱ υἱοὶ τοῦ θεοῦ dans le texte de
Rahlfs. On verra sur la question, Peter Katz, *Philo's Bible,
The Aberrant Text of Bible Quotations in Some Philonic Writings
And Its Place In the Textual History of The Greek Bible*, Cam-
bridge University Press, 1950, p. 20 et s.; et Peter Walters
(formerly Katz), *The Text of the Septuagint . . . p. 255.*

Nous résumons les arguments que Katz-Walters développe
contre le texte de Rahlfs qui lui paraît étonnant et qu'il est
enclin à rejeter.

La traduction de בְּנֵי הָאֱלֹהִים est ἄγγελοι τοῦ θεοῦ pour
Gen 2 dans A[nas], la tradition lucianique, la version bohaïrique,
le *Speculum* et Philon, Josèphe, Clément d'Alexandrie. Pour
Gen. 6 elle est υἱοὶ τοῦ θεοῦ chez tous les témoins à l'exception de Philon et du manuscrit minuscules (72).

Katz-Walters considère que pour Gen 6, 2, comme pour
Gen 6, 8 la traduction ancienne est ἄγγελοι τοῦ θεοῦ. Il fonde
ce jugement sur des considérations d'ordre théologique. Aux
yeux des traducteurs anciens Dieu ne pouvait avoir ni fils ni
compagnons égaux à lui-même. L'existence de créatures sur-
humaines n'était naturellement pas niée, mais l'on exigeait que
leur subordination à la divinité fût indiquée sans hésitation
possible par les termes servant à les désigner. C'est le cas
de l'appellation d'ἄγγελοι τοῦ θεοῦ. Avec les Trois (Symmaque,
Aqila, Théodotion) les préoccupations changent du tout au tout.
Ce dont il est désormais question, ce n'est plus d'éviter des
énoncés choquants, mais seulement de coller à l'hébreu d'aussi

près que possible. Quant aux difficultés exégétiques et théologiques qui peuvent résulter de cette fidélité absolue à l'original, les traducteurs laissent le soin d'en traiter et de les
résoudre aux docteurs dont c'est l'office propre. Il est donc
certain qu'ἄγγελοι représente dans les deux passages le texte
authentique, tandis que υἱοί procède d'une révision d'une date
certainement plus récente (il se trouve chez les Trois et chez
Origène (Syr. Hexapl. etc.). Au contraire une transformation
d'υἱοί en ἄγγελοι eût été inconcevable. Rahlfs agit donc d'une
manière surprenante lorsqu'il introduit, pour les deux passages,
υἱοί dans son texte. Peut-être, suppose Katz, Rahlfs a-t-il
voulu harmoniser Gen 6,2 et Gen 6,4 où, comme il a été signalé,
tous les témoins à l'exception de Philon et de m (72) ont υἱοί.
Katz explique cette particularité en invitant à y voir une
inconséquence du procès de modernisation subi par la plupart
des témoins.

     Ce qui nous empêche d'accepter sans réserves de telles
explications c'est l'existence du texte de Philon dans *Quaestiones in Genesim* I, 92 sur Gen 6,4.

     Les בְּנֵי הָאֱלֹהִים y sont décrits à la fois comme des anges
et des "fils de Dieu": "Caeterum aliquando *Angelos* vocat *Dei
filio* quoniam non ab ullo facti sunt mortali incorporei, quum
sint spiritus corpore carentes. Potius autem exhortator iste
(sive praeceptor Moyses) optimos praeditosque virtute viros
filios Dei nominat, pessimos vero et pravos, corpora (vel
carnes)." Tout se passe en somme comme si Philon lisait dans
sa Bible ἄγγελοι τοῦ θεοῦ en Gen 2 et υἱοί τοῦ θεοῦ en Gen 6,4.
C'est lui-même qui aura pu ramener Gen 6,4 à Gen 6,2 pour la
raison qu'il indique. L'appellation de "fils de Dieu" désigne
surtout des hommes de sagesse et de vertu, ce que les "anges
de Dieu" mis en scène dans le *De Gigantibus* ne sont pas. Que
ce soit entre autres dans notre passage que Moïse a appelé les
anges "fils de Dieu" l'allusion à "corpora vel carnes" semble
l'indiquer, puisqu'il fait probablement écho aux mots διὰ τὸ
εἶναι αὐτοὺς σάρκας de Gen. 6,3.

        3. *Gig. 17 = Ps. 77,49.* Citation vraie.

        4. *Gig. 19 = Gen 6,3.* C'est une véritable citation avec
quelques particularités de peu d'importance. (a) Philon ne cite
pas le καί initial du verset. (b) Il substitue à la forme hel-
lénistique εἶπεν avec la nasale éphelcystique devant un mot à
initiale consonantique (Cf. F. M. Abel, *Grammaire du Grec*

Biblique, Paris 1927, p. 24) la forme classique. (c) A οὐ μὴ καταμείνῃ du verset correspond οὐ καταμενεῖ dans le texte de Philon. Voyez Peter Katz *Philo's Bible* . . . p. 17 et s. Katz suppose que la forme καταμενεῖ a pu s'introduire ici sous l'influence du présent καταμένει de *Gig.* (2). (d) La variante ou la divergence la plus remarquable est constituée par l'omission du démonstratif τούτοις du verset. Ce vocable grec ne correspond du reste à rien du texte original qui a le collectif בָאדָם. Peut-être la traduction des Septante représente-t-elle une interprétation comparable à celle de Philon en ce se qu'elle suggère que les anges ou les fils de Dieu n'étaient que des hommes. Cette tendance est nettement perceptible chez Symmaque qui traduit בְּנֵי הָאֱלֹהִים par οἱ υἱοὶ τῶν δυναστευόντων et dans le Targoum d'Onkelos qui a בְּנֵי רַבְרְבַיָּא. Chez Philon la disparition de τούτοις peut avoir été purement accidentelle. Il paraît évident qu'il connaissait le texte exact des LXX dont on trouve un écho indubitable dans la phrase initiale de *Gig* 19 qui annonce la citation de Gen 6,3: Ἐν δὴ τοῖς τοιούτοις ἀμήχανον τὸ τοῦ θεοῦ καταμεῖναι καὶ διαιωνίσαι πνεῦμα, ὡς δηλοῖ καὶ αὐτὸς ὁ νομοθέτης.

5. *Gig 22 = Gen 1,2.* Citation vraie qui laisse en dehors la conjonction de coordination initiale du verset.

6. *Gig 23 = Ex 31,2-4.* Sur ce passage, voyez Peter Katz, *Philo's Bible* . . . p. 18.

(a) Philon commence par ne pas rapporter la filiation de Βεσελεηλ parce qu'elle n'importait pas à son propos.

(b) Il corrige le solécisme qui consiste à faire suivre, d'après l'hébreu, le verbe ἐμπιμπλᾶν d'un double accusatif: πνεῦμα θεῖον du verset devient πνεύματος θείου.

La traduction des LXX est sans doute soucieuse de serrer l'original hébreu qui a: וָאֲמַלֵּא אֹתוֹ רוּחַ אֱלֹהִים בְּחָכְמָה וּבִתְבוּנָה וּבְדַעַת וּבְכָל מְלָאכָה "et je l'ai empli d'esprit divin dans le domaine de l'intelligence, du discernement, du savoir et de tout métier" . . . πνεῦμα θεῖον σοφία etc. est une tentative d'exprimer le même rapport; ἐν παντὶ ἔργῳ est une interprétation qui consiste à supprimer la dernière copule ו et a lire וּבְדַעַת בְּכָל מְלָאכָה.

Philon considère que les génitifs σοφίας, συνέσεως, ἐπιστήμης sont des appositions à πνεύματος dont ils décrivent le contenu.

(c) ἐν παντὶ ἔργῳ du verset devient chez Philon ἐπὶ
παντὶ ἔργῳ peut-être, selon P. Katz, sous l'influence du vocable
ἐπιστήμης qui précède.

(d) La forme διανοεῖσθαι constitue le premier mot du
verset d'Ex. 31,4.

(e) P. Katz considère que Philon cite ici, avec les
modifications que nous venons de signaler non pas Ex. 31,2-4
mais Exode 35,30 où l'énoncé se trouve à la 3ᵉ personne, le
discours étant placé dans la bouche de Moïse qui rappelle aux
Israélites que Dieu a appelé Bezaléel par son nom etc.
L'hypothèse de Katz n'est peut-être pas absolument indispensable.
Une adaptation consistant en un changement de personne est fa-
cilement concevable de la part de Philon. L'autre part ἐν/ἐπὶ
παντὶ ἔργῳ διανοεῖσθαι appartient sans conteste à Ex 31,3-4.
En Ex. 35,30 on a ἀνακέκληκεν au lieu de ἀνεκάλεσεν chez Philon,
qui n'a pas non plus ἐξ ὀνόματος d'Ex 31,2 et 35,30.

En résumé il est difficile de dire en quelle mesure la
citation de Philon mérite les guillemets: on devrait en rigueur
les placer à partir de σοφίας.

7. *Gig 24 = Nombres 11,17.* Philon omet la conjonction
de coordination καί. Il remplace αὐτούς par les mots τοὺς
ἑβδομήκοντα πρεσβυτέρους qui appartiennent de façon manifeste
non au verset, mais au texte de Philon. Les guillemets fermants auraient donc dû à l'évidence être placés après ἐπιθήσω.

8. *Gig 32 = Lev 18,6.* Sur ce passage cf. Katz, *Philo's
Bible* . . . p. 18 etc.

Katz fait observer que la leçon manuscrite majoritaire
des LXX πάντα οἰκεῖα est unique, car partout ailleurs l'original
שְׁאֵר "parent" est rendu correctement par un masculin ou un féminin et jamais par un neutre ainsi en Lévitique 18, 12, 13, 17;
21,2; 25,49; Nombres 25,5; 27,11. Il estime donc que le texte
de Philon permet ici de reconstruire le texte original du verset
qu'il propose de lire, d'une manière conforme à la citation de
Philon πάντα οἰκεῖον au lieu de πάντα οἰκεῖα.

9. *Gig 48 = Nombres 14,44.* C'est une citation incomplète qu'il eût fallu écrire: «Μωυσῆς καὶ ἡ κιβωτός . . . οὐκ
ἐκινήθησαν . . .» C'est aussi une citation libre dans laquelle
les mots Μωυσῆς et ἡ κιβωτός sont donnés dans l'ordre inverse
de celui du verset.

10. *Gig 50 = Ex 18,14*.   Citation exacte.

11. *Gig 55 = Gen 6,3*.   Citation exacte, sauf que le
verset pour ἑκατὸν εἴκοσιν ἔτη suit l'ordre des mots de l'hébreu,
tandis que Philon probablement par souci d'élégance, inverse et
écrit: ἔτη ἑκατὸν εἴκοσιν.   Cf. γεγονὼς ἔτη τρία ἀπολείποντα
τῶν ἑκατόν Isocrate, 12, 270.

12. *Gig 56 = Deut 34,7*.   Il ne s'agit pas d'une citation.

13. *Gig 63 = Gen 17,1*.   Citation exacte.

14. *Gig 65 = Gen 2,24*.   Les guillemets ont été abusive-
ment placés devant ἐγένοντο.   Il eût fallu écrire: «οἱ δύο εἰς
σάρκα μίαν»

15. *Gig 66 = Gen 10,8*.   Citation exacte.   Notons que la
traduction des LXX rend d'une manière apparemment assez gauche
le TM: הוּא הֵחֵל לִהְיוֹת גִּבֹּר בָּאָרֶץ "ce fut lui qui commença a être
un puissant héros sur la terre."   Mais comme l'original hébreu,
la version grecque suggère que γίγας désigne plutôt un comportement qu'une nature physique, particularité qui a pu être à l'origine de l'interprétation allégorique de Philon.

16. *Deus 1 = Gen 6,4*.   Citation exacte sauf que l'imparfait ἐγεννῶσαν avec la désinence de la 3ᵉ pers du pluriel
-σαν peut-être d'après ἦσαν, qui est une forme de la κοινή
fréquente chez les LXX, a été remplacé par l'imparfait classique
ἐγέννων.   La fin du verset a été volontairement omise.

17. *Deus 4 = Gen 22,2-9*.   Le texte de Philon ne constitue qu'une allusion à un récit scripturaire.   Le mot συμποδίσας aurait pu être mis entre guillemets.

18. *Deus 4 = Gen 25,6*.   Le texte de Philon constitue
une simple allusion au passage scripturaire.

19. *Deus 6 = 1 Sam 1,11*.   Le texte de *Deus* 6 "Δίδωμί σοι
αὐτὸν δοτόν" est une adaptation non de 1 Sam 1,28, mais de 1 Sam
1,11 où se lisent les mots δώσω αὐτὸν ἐνώπιόν σου δοτόν.
     La référence erronée figure dans l'édition de
P. WENDLAND et la traduction allemande de H. Leisegang; dans

l'édition de COLSON et dans celle de MOSÈS. Elle est aggravée
par une note de COLSON (PHILO III, 483 sur le §6 "I give him to
thee a gift." The stress which Philo lays on δίδωμι and δοτόν
suggests that he had in mind a different version of the text
from that of LXX, where, though in v. 27 we have "the Lord gave
me my request," v. 28 runs "I lend him (κιχρῶ) to the Lord, a
loan (χρῆσιν) to the Lord."

         L'allusion à Anne et à Samuel qui se lit en *De Somniis*
I, 254, réfère elle aussi à I Samuel I, 11.

         La traduction allemande (t. VI, p. 224) et l'édition
de Lyon (Philon d'Alexandrie 19, p. 126) renvoient toujours à
I Samuel I, 28, mais COLSON (Philo V, 429) donne la référence
correcte et propose l'observation suivante à la p. 605 du même
volume.

         §254 I Sam I, 11--WENDLAND erroneously gives the refer-
ences as to v. 28 ("I lend him as a loan"), as also in *Quod Deus*
6, on which passage, carelessly following WENDLAND, I suggested
in a note that Philo in v. 28 had a different text from the LXX.
A German reviewer pointed out the mistake."

         Les INDICES de J. W. Earp (Philo X, 259 et s.) reflètent
les variations de COLSON.

         Le verset de I Samuel I, 11 est donné pour commenté
dans I *De Somniis*, 254. EARP renvoie à la note de COLSON que
nous venons de citer et dans laquelle l'éditeur reconnaît son
erreur initiale. Chose plus curieuse, *Deus* 6 continue à être
rattaché, sans aucun éclaircissement à I Sam I, 27, 28.

         Les erreurs, une fois établies, sont vivaces et cer-
taines références fautives ont pu parfois être transmises d'une
édition savante à une autre durant des siècles. On reprochera
à MOSÈS et, plus encore, à P. SAVINEL, l'éditeur du *De Somniis*,
de n'avoir pas pris garde à l'importante rétractation de COLSON
et d'avoir de la sorte contribué à la perpétuation scolastique
d'une erreur qui n'était pas tout à fait sans conséquence pour
l'étude de Philon.

         20. *Deus 6 = Nombres 28,2.* C'est une citation véritable,
mais incomplète. Outre les derniers mots du verset, Philon
omet l'expression εἰς ὀσμὴν εὐωδίας. Sur cette omission voyez
P. Katz, *Philo's Bible* . . . p. 21-23.

         Philon omet régulièrement la traduction de רֵיחַ נִיחֹחִי
lorsqu'il cite Nombres 28,2 en *LA III*, 196; *Cher* 84; *Sacr* 111;
Migr 142.

Il cite incomplètement Gen 8,21 en *Congr* 115: Ὠσφράνθη
κύριος ὀσμὴν εὐωδίας et note que l'expression est employée par
Moïse au sens figuré et signifie que Dieu a "approuvé" (συναινέ-
σαι): οὐ γὰρ ἀνθρωπόμορφος οὐδὲ μυκτήρων ἤ τινων ἄλλων ὀργανι-
κῶν μερῶν χρεῖος.

Notons d'ailleurs que κύριος au lieu de κύριος ὁ θεός
des LXX est conforme au TM qui a seulement יהוה. Toutefois en
QG II, 53, le verset est cité complètement et l'essentiel de
l'aporie consiste dans le fait que Noé sacrifie τῷ θεῷ et non
τῷ κυρίῳ (Cf. Gen 8,20: καὶ ᾠκοδόμησεν Νωε θυσιαστήριον τῷ
θεῷ, commenté dans la *Quaestio* 51), mais qu'il rend grâce κυρίῳ
τῷ θεῷ. L'explication fournie dans la *Solutio* II, 53 implique
une interprétation allégorique d'ὀσμὴ εὐωδίας analogue à celle
de *Congr* 115 et qui est indiquée dans la *Quaestio* II, 53 elle-
même: "*l'acceptation* se fait par les deux puissances, du
Seigneur et de Dieu." Il eût donc été facile à Philon de conserver, au prix de la même interprétation allégorique, cette
expression dont le caractère anthropomorphique était choquant
lorsqu'on l'entendait littéralement. Simplement, elle n'aurait
rien ajouté à l'idée que Philon voulait tirer ici de l'Ecriture
à savoir la "propriété" des offrandes que Dieu commandait de
lui offrir. Il est donc vraisemblable que, pour emprunter les
termes de Peter Katz, Philon "l'a négligée comme un détail de
peu d'importance."

21. *Deus* 10 = I Sam 2,5. Citation exacte. Philon "met
une virgule" après ἡ δὲ πολλή.

22. *Deus* 16 = Gen 38,9. Les guillemets doivent être
placés à « ὅτι οὐκ αὐτῷ etc.

23. *Deus* 20 = Gen 6,5-7. Sur quelques divergences
entre le verset et Philon voyez Peter Katz *Philo's Bible* . . .
p. 24. Nous les indiquerons toutes.

Tout d'abord la première phrase du verset est extra-
ordinairement gauche puisqu'elle est constituée par une période
participiale d'où le verbe principal est absent. On le trouve
au début de la seconde phrase après la conjonction καί. Philon
corrige Ἰδὼν δὲ κύριος . . . πάσας τὰς ἡμέρας. Καὶ ἐνεθυμήθη
. . . en Ἰδὼν κύριος . . . πάσας τὰς ἡμέρας, ἐνεθυμήθη ὁ
θεός . . . La particule δέ a été supprimée et remplacée par
οὖν qui appartient sans doute au texte de Philon.

La construction διανοεῖται . . . ἐπὶ τὰ πονηρά "médite
. . . en vue du mal" est remplacée par la construction directe
plus courante.

L'expression ἐν τῇ καρδίᾳ αὐτοῦ est réduite à ἐν τῇ
καρδίᾳ, plus classique. Philon supprime, dans le même esprit
le *nu* éphelcystique d'ἐποίησεν devant le mot suivant à initiale
consonantique.

24. *Deus 23 = Deut 5,31*. Citation exacte.

25. *Deus 50 = Deut 30,15-19*. Citation exacte, mais
"éclectique." Il eût fallu mettre des points de suspension
après προσώπου σου après τὸ κακόν et après τὴν ζωήν.

Sur l'omission de σήμερον de Deut 30,15, on verra
l'excellente remarque de Peter Katz, *Philo's Bible* . . . p. 24
note 2.

26. *Deus 51 = Gen 6,7*. Citation exacte. Le mot αὐτόν
n'en fait pas partie et les guillemets fermants devraient être
placés après le mot précédent. Pour Philon la colère de Dieu n'a
pour origine que l'homme et les autres créatures n'en sont
atteintes que par voie de conséquence.

27. *Deus 53 = Nombres 29,19*. Citation exacte.

28. *Deus 54 = Deut 8,5*. Ce n'est pas une citation au
sens technique du terme, mais une phrase récrite à partir du
verset où tous les mots de Philon figurent dans la forme qu'ils
ont dans son texte.

29. *Deus 70 = Gen 6,7*. Citation exacte.

30. *Deus 70 = Gen 6,8*. Citation exacte.

31. *Deus 74 = Ps 100,1*. Citation exacte.

32. *Deus 77 = Ps 74,9*. Citation exacte avec omission de
ὅτι du verset.

33. *Deus 82 = Ps 61,12*. Le verset a ὁ θεός conformément au TM. Dans le texte de Philon on a κύριος, peut-être
parce que ce mot suggérait mieux la puissance de la divinité.

L'ordre verbe, sujet est inversé. Le *nu* éphelcystique est
supprimé. Sur ce passage et son contexte, voyez le réflexions
de Peter Katz, *Philo's Bible* p. 24-25. Katz considère comme
des changements opérés volontairement par Philon les divergences
minimes qui séparent le texte de Philon de celui du verset.

      34. *Deus 86 = Gen 6,8*. Citation exacte. La particule
δέ du verset est supprimée.

      35. *Deus 87 = Nombres 6,2*. Il ne s'agit naturellement
pas d'une citation. Philon forge l'expression de μεγάλη εὐχή
à partir de μεγάλως εὔξηται εὐχήν.
      Deus 88 = Nombres 6,5. Citation exacte adaptée à la
tournure infinitive. Le verbe sustantif passe à l'infinitif
conformément à la construction et au sens.

      36. *Deus 89 = Nombres 6,9*. Le texte de Philon est une
allusion au verset. Le vocable παραχρῆμα lui appartient; les
mots μιαίνουσα, θάνατον s'en inspirent.

      37. *Deus 90 = Nombres 6,12*. Citation implicite. Les
mots τὰς προτέρας . . . ἡμέρας ἀλόγους s'inspirent du verset.

      38. *Deus 92 = Gen 27,20*. Paraphrase du verset avec
des éléments de citation incomplète. Dans la question d'Isaac
ὦ est omis devant τέκνον.
      Dans la réponse de Jacob le *nu éphelcystique* devant le
mot suivant à initiale consonantique est supprimé. Jacob dit
κύριος ὁ θεός et non comme dans le verset κύριος ὁ θεός σου,
formule qui, au premier regard, pouvait laisser penser que Jacob
se dissociait de son père et ne reconnaissait pas la même
divinité.

      39. *Deus 94 = Deut 6,10-11*. Le texte de Philon est une
citation adaptée du verset. Le verbe δοῦναι est repris sous la
forme δίδοσθαι. Avec le discours indirect les deuxièmes personnes du singulier deviennent des troisièmes personnes et
passent, *ad sensum*, au pluriel. L'expression πλήρεις πάντων ἀγαθῶν est récrite en πλήρεις τῶν ἀγαθῶν qui a le même sens.

      40. *Deus 99 = Deut 1,43-44*. C'est une paraphrase des
versets avec des éléments de citations exactes. Le discours est

transformé en récit avec les changements de personnes verbales
que cette transposition implique. Philon corrige ἀνέβητε εἰς
τὸ ὄρος en ἐπὶ τὸ ὄρος. On a une citation exacte du début du
verset 44 avec omission de εἰς συνάντησιν ὑμῖν. Pour la seconde
partie du verset, les pluriels verbaux collectifs sont trans-
formés en singuliers. Philon change l'ordre des actions. Les
ennemis blessent les Israélites et les poursuivent de Séir à
Herma. La fin de la phrase pouvait sembler quelque peu dure
sur le plan de la logique. La forme verbale à préverbe du verset est ramenée à la forme simple. Philon conserve la métaphore
des abeilles, mais il récrit ὡς εἰ en ὡς ἂν et ramène la forme
d'aoriste optatif en -αισαν à la forme classique.

41. *Deus 104 = Gen 6,8*. La fin de la citation est
récrite en style plus classique.

42. *Deus 109 = Gen 6,9 = Exode 33,17*. Le texte fait
allusion à Gen 6,8. Le verbe εὐαρεστῆσαι du texte s'inspire de
Gen 6,9 verset qui, pourtant, interdirait l'interprétation que
propose Philon. Dans la citation d'Ex 33,17, Philon fait subir
au verset une modification analogue à celle du verset de Gen
6,8 en *Deus* 104.

43. *Deus 111 = Gen 39,1*. Le texte de Philon est une
allusion au verset, ἀρχιμαγείρῳ reprenant ὁ ἀρχιμάγειρος et
ὁ εὐνοῦχος donnant lieu au commentaire qui chez Philon commence
à ἐξευνουχισθείς.

44. *Deus 117 = Gen 6,9*. Citation exacte. Philon supprime le *nu* éphelcystique devant un mot à initiale consonantique.
    Le verset 10, incompatible avec l'interprétation de
Philon, n'est pas cité.

45. *Deus 119 = Gen 37,2*. Citation exacte avec de minimes
retouches. Philon supprime αὐτοῦ après τῶν ἀδελφῶν et τοῦ devant
πατρὸς αὐτοῦ.

46. *Deus 122 - Gen 6,11*. Citation exacte avec deux
minimes simplifications. Philon supprime la particule δέ et
les termes ἡ γῆ répétés devant le dernier mot du verset.

47. *Deus 123 = Lev 13,14.* C'est une "citation" entièrement récrite. Seuls les mots χρὼς ζῶν ἐν et μιανθήσεται devraient être pourvus de guillemets.

48. *Deus 124 = Lev 13,15.* Sur ce passage, voyez P. Katz *Philo's Bible* . . . p. 27-28.

P. Katz fait observer que les LXX se trompent sur la signification de TM בָּשָׂ֥ר חַ֖י qui désignerait des "bourgeons de chair" se manifestant sur l'endroit lépreux. La Septante traduit par conséquent l'expression hébraïque par χρὼς ζῶν et χρὼς ὑγιής.

Ignorant l'hébreu, Philon entend χρὼς ζῶν et χρὼς ὑγιής au sens de "chair saine," au contraire de ce que font le TM et même dans une certaine mesure les LXX. En effet, le texte original des LXX était peut-être, comme le pense Grabe, conforme dans sa signification à l'hébreu. La distorsion des LXX par rapport au TM, que l'on constate aujourd'hui, a pour origine la ponctuation, élément extérieur et postérieur au texte lui-même.

On aurait eu de la sorte, primitivement: καὶ ὄψεται ὁ ἱερεὺς τὸν χρῶτα τὸν ὑγιῆ καὶ μιανεῖ αὐτὸν (*scil.* τὸν λεπρὸν) ὁ χρὼς ὁ ὑγιῆς [ὅτι] ἀκάθαρτός ἐστιν, λέπρας ἐστίν. Donc ce serait ici ὁ χρὼς ὁ ὑγιής qui serait objet d'impureté parce que manifestation de la lèpre. Philon a lu et compris καὶ μιανεῖ αὐτὸν ὁ χρὼς ὁ ὑγιής comme si la chair saine souillait le malade; provoquant la corruption de la chair malade et, par voie de conséquence, le détérioration de l'organisme tout entier. Katz voit dans tout le passage une prémonition de la doctrine de l'Epitre aux Romains, 3, 20: "Car nul ne sera justifié devant lui par les oeuvres de la loi, puisque c'est par la loi que vient la connaissance du péché" et de 5, 20: "Or la loi est intervenue pour que l'offense abondât, mais là où le péché a abondé, la grâce a surabondé, afin que, comme le péché a régné par la mort, ainsi la grâce régnât par la justice pour la vie éternelle par Jésus-Christ notre Seigneur."

La ressemblance nous paraît assez superficielle et les textes de Philon semblent bien éloignés de la profondeur et des implications mystiques de l'Epitre.

Philon omet αὐτὸν après μιανεῖ. Cette omission, probablement volontaire, donne une portée générale à sa proposition.

49. *Deus 127 = Lev 13,11-13.* Il ne s'agit pas d'une citation, mais d'un résumé et d'une appréciation du passage biblique.

50. *Deus 131 = Lev 14,34-36.* Sur ce passage, on verra
P. Katz, *Philo's Bible . . .* p. 28-30. P. Katz souligne bien
que la "citation" de Philon est une paraphrase de caractère
abrégeant, et que le texte de Wendland ne fait pas un usage
très précis des guillemets.

Philon omet toute la première partie du verset 34 qui
semble restreindre l'application de la disposition légale concernant la lèpre des maisons au seul pays de Canaan. Il préfère la formule impersonnelle ἐὰν γένηται ἃ καὶ δώσω qui semble
impliquer Dieu dans le mal. Seuls les mots ἀφὴ λέπρας ἐν méritent les guillemets. Encore le cas du premier est-il adapté
au contexte de Philon.

Dans les versets 35-36 ἥξει τίνος αὐτοῦ ἡ οἰκία est
remplacé par le tour classique ἀφίξεται ὁ κεκτημένος. Suit, de
"καὶ ἀναγγελεῖ τῷ ἱερεῖ ἃ ἀποσκευάσαι τὴν οἰκίαν," une citation
véritable avec deux variantes minimes. Au lieu du texte scripturaire ὥσπερ ἀφὴ ἑώραταί μου ἐν τῇ οἰκίᾳ on a chez Philon ὥσπερ ἀφὴ λέπρας ἑώραταί μοι ἐν τῇ οἰκίᾳ.

P. Katz suggère que Philon a pu ici conserver le texte
original du verset; il a le soutien de certains MSS des LXX,
des Pères et des traductions.

La suite du verset 36 est elle aussi réellement citée
par Philon, mais avec des modifications qui sont le fait de
l'Alexandrin lui-même πρὶν (τοῦ εἰσελθόντα) est remplacé par
πρό; τοῦ εἰσελθόντα ἰδεῖν τὸν ἱερέα· τὴν ἀφὴν devient τοῦ
εἰσελθόντα τὸν ἱερέα εἰς τὴν οἰκίαν ἰδεῖν; καὶ οὐ μὴ ἀκάθαρτα
γένηται devient καὶ οὐ γενήσεται ἀκάθαρτα; dans ὅσα ἐὰν ᾖ ἐν
τῇ οἰκίᾳ les mots ἐὰν ᾖ sont supprimés, de même que τὴν οἰκίαν
à la fin du verset.

51. *Deus 136 = Lev 17,10.* Seuls les mots γυνὴ <χήρα>
pourraient être mis entre guillemets.

52. *Deus 137 = Gen 38,11.* Paraphrase du verset que
rappellent les mots χηρευούσῃ καθέξεσθαι ἐν τῷ τοῦ . . . οἴκῳ
πατρός.

53. *Deus 138 = 1 R 17,18.* Citation partielle du verset.
Philon remplace τὰς ἀδικίας μου par τὸ ἀδίκημά μου. Les derniers mots καὶ τὸ ἁμάρτημά μου semblent devoir être exclus des
guillemets. Comme nous l'avons indiqué, ce sont, croyons-nous,

l'équivalent de τὸν υἱόν μου, interprété plus loin comme τὰ
μὲν ἐκείνης (= τροπῆς) ἔγγονα.

54. *Deus 189* = *I Sam 9,9*. Simple allusion au verset.

55. *Deus 145* = *Nombres 20,17-20*. Sur ce passage, voyez
P. Katz *Philo's Bible . . .* p. 31-32.
   Pour le verset 17, on note quelques modifications
minimes du verset chez Philon: οὐδὲ . . . οὐδὲ devient chez
Philon οὐ . . . οὐ; ὕδωρ ἐκ λάκκου σου est simplifié en ὕδωρ
λάκκου σου; τὰ ὅρια σου est modifié en σου τὰ ὅρια.
   Le début du verset 18 jusqu'au discours d'Edom est
récrit. La fin est exactement citée. Au verset 19 Philon a
πίω pour πίωμεν du verset; δώσω σοι τιμήν pour δώσω τιμήν σοι.

56. *Deus 148* = *Nombres 20,17*. Philon ajoute Ἤδη et
met le verbe au singulier, peut-être pour souligner l'unanimité
de la résolution de disciples de Moïse: ἡ ἑκάστου ψυχὴ τῶν
γνωρίμων αὐτοῦ.

57. *Deus 156* = *Deut 28,12*. Citation adaptée au contexte de Philon: Ἀνοίξαι σοι κύριος est modifié en ἀνοίξῃ
κύριος ἡμῖν. La fin du verset τῇ γῇ σου ἐπὶ καιροῦ αὐτοῦ n'est
pas citée.

58. *Deus 157* = *Gen 48,15*. Citation exacte.

59. *Deus 161* = *Gen 18,27*. Allusion au verset que rappellent les mots γῆν καὶ τέφραν ὄντα.

60. *Deus 181* = *Nombres 22,31*. Allusion au verset et
citation partielle. Comme on l'a signalé, les mots du texte
de Philon τὸ τῆς ψυχῆς μεμυκὸς ὄμμα ἀναβλέψας réfèrent à
Ἀπεκάλυψεν . . . ὁ θεὸς τοὺς ὀφθαλμοὺς Βαλααμ; ἀνθεστῶτα
remplace ἀνθεστηκότα ἐν τῇ ὁδῷ et devrait être exclu des
guillemets.

61. *Deus 183* = *Nombres 31,8*. Les mots du texte de
Philon ne devraient pas être mis entre guillemets: ils ne constituent pas une citation de Nombres 31,8, mais une simple
allusion à ce verset.

                                              V. Nikiprowetzky

3. *Philo's Knowledge of the Hebrew*
   underlying the Greek

Next the question arises whether in all his citation and exposition of the Old Testament Philo shows any awareness of the Hebrew underlying the Greek translation which he so uniformly quotes, or any evidence of having had access to the meaning of the Hebrew independently of the Greek translation. On both counts the answer must be no.

In the first place Philo himself as good as tells us that the Hebrew was to him irrelevant. In his account of the origin of the LXX translation he maintains that the Greek was directly and equally inspired as the original Hebrew: the translators "like men possessed prophesied not each man something different but all of them the same actual nouns and verbs, as though some invisible prompter were dictating to each one of them" (*De Vit. Mos.* II, 7, 37). Obviously, if a translation is produced by direct inspiration of God, there is no need to refer to the original.

Moreover, as evidence of the complete detailed accuracy of the translation Philo cites the verdict always given, so he claims, by "any Chaldaeans who learn Greek, or Greeks who learn Chaldaean, and then come across both Scriptures, the Chaldaean and the (Greek) translation . . ." (*op. cit.*, 7, 40). Interesting here is the way he phrases himself: it suggests that he himself was not among those who have learned what he calls "the Chaldaean." And if that is so, it further suggests that Philo could not have consulted the Hebrew himself, even if he had thought it necessary or desirable to do so.

Furthermore, he asserts that as a result of the divine inspiration with which the translators were favoured, the Greek words they chose corresponded with the "Chaldaean" with the precision of geometrical or philosophical terminology. Granted that Philo may have allowed himself some exaggeration here for the sake of propaganda, one must conclude that the man who could write these words had no conception of the material differences that exist in many places between the Hebrew original and the LXX translations.

This conclusion is borne out by what we find when we turn to his actual expositions. First, there is the general evidence, amply set forth in (ii) above, that he uniformly cites the Old Testament in the LXX translation, which, given the frequent inadequacy of the LXX, he would surely not have done, or

not have done without protest or explanation, had he known the
underlying Hebrew. Secondly, from time to time he offers expositions of the Greek which the Hebrew, had he known it, would
have forbidden him. Here are some representative samples:

(a) He will expound a passage by playing on the (supposed) etymology of a word in the Greek translation regardless
of whether the Hebrew word which it represents has a similar
etymology. So in *Quod Deus* 3:13 he suggests that the true meaning of στεῖραν, "barren" is στερράν, "firm." Etymologically
there may be some connection between στεῖραν and στερράν (though
such etymology would not justify his exposition); but the Hebrew
עֲקָרָה has no such etymology. Again, in *Quod Deus* 22:103, Philo
cites Deut 1:43, where for וַתָּזִדוּ "they acted presumptuously,"
the LXX has παραβιασάμενοι, "acting by force or violence against
(*scil*. what God had said)." The context indicates that immediately after taking this attitude Israel was repulsed by the
enemy; and had Philo been content with that observation, all
would have been well. But on the basis of the Greek word παραβιασάμενοι he maintains that all such violence (τὸ βίαιον) is
short-lived (ὀλιγοχρόνιον), "as the very word shows derived as
it is from βαιόν: and βαιόν was a word the ancients used for
short-lived." Well, to start with, βαιόν has nothing to do
etymologically even with Greek βίαιον; but what is more to our
point the Hebrew √זיד has no etymological connection with either
the notion of "violence" or that of "short-lived."

(b) Where a Greek word has more than one meaning Philo
will sometimes select and insist on one of those meanings against
any of the others, regardless of whether the underlying Hebrew
word can have the meaning which he insists on. So in *Quod Deus*
35:168-36:171 Philo refers to Israel's attempted negotiations
with Edom: "But if I and my cattle drink of your water, I will
give you the price of it" (Num 20:19). For the "price of it"
the LXX has simply τιμήν. τιμή, however, is a word of many
connotations: worship, esteem, honour, worth, value, price,
compensation, satisfaction, penalty, fine, punishment. Obviously the connotation intended by the LXX is that which corresponds to the underlying Hebrew מִכְרָם which means "the price,"
or "value of them." But Philo explicitly insists that τιμήν
does not mean "the pelf, to use the poet's word, silver or gold
or aught else which the purchaser is wont to give in exchange

to the vendor, but by τιμήν he here means 'honour' (γέρας)"
(translation by Colson and Whitaker). He seems totally unaware
that the Hebrew מכר only means "price" or "value," or "merchan-
dise"; it does not have the connotation "honour."

    (c) Philo sometimes quotes a phrase from the LXX, where
the Hebrew, or at least the MT, has something quite different;
and Philo does not show himself aware of the difference. For
instance, as its last phrase in Num 20:19 the LXX has παρὰ τὸ
ὄρος παρελευσόμεθα, thus repeating a phrase which comes earlier
in the verse. Philo, *Quod Deus* 31:145, follows the LXX. But
the MT has the quite different בְּרַגְלַי אֶעֱבֹרָה "let me pass through
on foot."

    In the light, then, of evidence such as this that Philo
had no conception of the Hebrew underlying the Greek, the fact
that from time to time he quotes the meaning of Hebrew proper
names (see, for example, *De Gigantibus* 14:62, where the name
Αβράμ is interpreted as meaning πατὴρ μετέωρος) cannot be taken
to imply that Philo had a detailed knowledge of Hebrew. Jews in
Alexandria would be aware that their own personal names meant
something in Hebrew, even if they themselves did not know much
Hebrew. Indeed, in Hellenistic times it was common for Jews to
use Greek translations (and not transliterations) of their
names, e.g., Theodotion, or, Theodoros, for Jonathan. There may
well have been "dictionaries" giving Greek equivalents of Hebrew
proper names which they and Philo could have consulted.

    Finally, there is one place in our treatises where, had
Philo been aware of the Hebrew underlying the Greek and had he
been competent to discuss the exact meaning of the Hebrew, sheer
honesty, one would have thought, must have obliged him to cite
the meaning of the Hebrew. In *Quod Deus* 5:20ff. he quotes the
LXX translation of Gen 6:6, which runs: "And God had it in his
mind (ἐνεθυμήθη) that he had made man on the earth, and he
bethought him (διενοήθη)." He then comments "Perhaps some of
the uncritical (τῶν ἀνεξετάστων) will suspect that the Lawgiver
is hinting (αἰνίττεσθαι) that the Creator repented (μετέγνω) of
the creation of man . . . ." The comment is interesting. Why
should people, we may ask, suspect this? One reason could be
the unnaturalness of the sense in the Greek. Another could be
that even in Philo's day it is possible that some people were
faintly aware that the LXX Greek translations were apt in places
to use euphemistic paraphrases, as the Targums do; and that the

unnaturalness of the Greek expressions in this verse suggested
to them that here was one of those euphemisms. However that may
be, the fact remains that the LXX rendering here *is* a euphemistic paraphrase; the Hebrew says: "And the Lord repented (וַיִּנָּחֶם;
or, was sorry) that he had made man on the earth, and it grieved
him (וַיִּתְעַצֵּב) at his heart." In other words, the meaning of the
Hebrew is exactly that which Philo is at pains to deny that the
LXX rendering is hinting at. Had Philo known Hebrew, he must
have admitted that at least there was some superficial difficulty
here, and he must have invented some argument to explain it, or,
as is more normal with him, to explain it away. Instead he
speaks as if the Lawgiver himself had used the terms found in
the LXX, and then he denies that in using these (Greek) terms
the Lawgiver was hinting at the meaning which (we can see, even
if he could not) the Hebrew conveys.

4. *Philo's Misuse of the Greek
   Translation*

     Philo, then, bases himself entirely on the Greek trans-
lation. But is he always fair to the intended meaning of the
Greek? Here it may be helpful to make a distinction between:
(a) instances where all would agree over what the Greek says,
but Philo with his hermeneutical principles makes what the Greek
says mean what the Greek never meant; and (b) instances where
Philo misconstrues Greek grammar and syntax to make the Greek
say what it never intended to say. The distinction is a fine
one, and not, perhaps, ultimately valid. But from a practical
point of view it may be useful. Under both heads, Philo is not
seldom unfair to the Greek.

     Examples under (a) are so numerous in the treatises, and
so obvious, that it is almost arbitrary to cite anything less
than the whole of Philo's work. Nevertheless let us take one
small example. When in *De Gigantibus* 11:50-51 he cites the
words of Jethro to Moses "Why do you sit (κάθησαι) alone?"
(Ex 18:14), all would agree, Philo included, as to what the
Greek says: it says "Why do you sit alone?" But the question
arises, what does "sit" mean in this context? The context is
one of judicial proceedings, and to common sense it is clear
that "sit" means "sit as judge." But Philo's hermeneutical
principles allow him to disregard the context, and interpret
"sit" to mean "to be stable," "to be able to maintain fair
weather in a storm, or calm in the swell of a raging sea." Here,

then, is no question of what the Greek says, but only of what
it means; and Philo's interpretation is arbitrary and far-fetched.

Under (b), however, one might list instances where Philo
misconstrues the syntax of the Greek in order to make it say
something other than what it was intended to say. In Gen 6:7
the Greek quotes God as saying "I will wipe out man whom I made
from the face of the earth, from man unto beast, from creeping
things unto the fowl of heaven, ὅτι ἐθυμώθην, ὅτι ἐποίησα αὐτούς." The question arises, how the two ὅτι-clauses are to be
understood. The natural way would be to understand both as
causal clauses, the first giving God's reason for destroying
mankind: he was wroth; the second giving the reason for the
wrath: he was angry because he had made man. But such an understanding of the syntax would offend Philo's philosophical pre-
suppositions, and so he sets out to show that the syntax should
be construed differently (*Quod Deus*, 11:51 and particularly,
15:72): "You see what great caution he has employed even over
his form of expression. He says ὅτι ἐθυμώθην ὅτι ἐποίησα αὐτούς," and not in the reverse order "διότι ἐποίησα αὐτοὺς ἐθυμώθην." This latter order, Philo goes on to explain, would imply
change of mind on God's part, a thing impossible in Philo's
philosophy. In other words, put the ὅτι-ἐποίησα-αὐτούς-clause
first, and change the ὅτι, as Philo does, to διότι, then the
clause is undeniably a causal clause giving the reason for the
wrath: "because I made them, I was wroth." Leave the order of
the clauses as it is in the LXX, and then Philo claims, it
"brings before us a most essential doctrine that wrath is a
source of errors." In other words Philo is claiming that the
ὅτι-ἐποίησα-αὐτούς-clause is not to be understood as a causal
clause giving the cause of the wrath, but as an explanatory
clause offering the evidence that justifies the statement, "I
was wroth." Thus: "I was wroth, as is proved by the fact that
I made them" or, "I was wroth in that I made them." Now it is
true that a ὅτι-clause can in certain contexts be used in this
sense. Liddell-Scott cite *Iliad* 16.35: γλαυκὴ δέ σε τίκτε
θάλασσα . . . ὅτι τοι νόος ἐστὶν ἀπηνής . . . "as is proved by
the fact that . . . " But to insist on this meaning of the ὅτι-
clause in our context is to pervert the plain straightforward
meaning of the Greek in the interests of preconceived philosophical views.

5. *Where Philo's dependence on the Greek*
    translations leads him to misrepresent
    the meaning of the original Old Testament,
    how far is this the fault of the poor
    quality of the Greek translations?

          The answer here is that there are several places where
the poor quality of the LXX translations has led Philo to make
wrong deductions from what they appear to say. In fairness to
Philo, of course, we should remember that his belief that the
translation was equally inspired as the original, would prevent
him from suspecting that the translation could on times be mistaken, and from regarding its literalistic renderings as mis-
leadingly inadequate translations: to him oddities and seeming
imperfections in the Greek translation would appear as indicators
of profound meaning. Two examples will suffice.

          In Lev 13:14, 15, in the course of instructions on the
diagnosis of leprosy, the Hebrew talks of בָּשָׂר חַי, literally,
"living flesh," meaning "raw flesh." It is clearly something
bad. The LXX, however, translates it literalistically in 3:14
as χρὼς ζῶν, "living flesh," and then, misinterpreting what
"living flesh" means, puts in 13:15 τὸν χρῶτα τὸν ὑγιῆ, "the
healthy flesh." Philo can hardly be blamed for the use which
he proceeds to make of the LXX's misinterpretation, even if he
does manage to introduce an additional misinterpretation of his
own: the Greek word χρὼς can mean "skin" or "flesh," or "the
colour of the skin, complexion," or simply "colour"; Philo
chooses to understand it as "colour."

          Again, an idiomatic way of saying in Hebrew "Not a
single man shall do so-and-so," is to use the expression, "A man,
a man shall not do so-and-so." This is not, however, a Greek
idiom, and therefore when in Lev 18:6 the LXX translates the
idiom literalistically ἄνθρωπος ἄνθρωπος πρὸς πάντα οἰκεῖον
σαρκὸς αὐτοῦ οὐ προσελεύσεται, it sounds very strange. As might
be expected, Philo is sure that this strange-sounding phrase is
full of deep significance, and he comments (*De Gigantibus* 8:34):
"The repetition ἄνθρωπος ἄνθρωπος, instead of the single expression, shows that he is indicating not the man compounded of body
and soul, but the man who practices virtue. For he indeed is
the true man. . . ."

          But to be fair to Philo, in this instance we should
recognise that he was not alone in misinterpreting the significance of the repetition. And for him there is the excuse that
he did not know Hebrew. But later Jewish rabbis, who had expert

knowledge of Hebrew, followed hermeneutical principles that led
them likewise to see all kinds of strange significance in this
same Hebrew idiom. In Num 5:12, for instance, the repetition
"man, man" occurs as an idiomatic way of expressing a generali-
sation: "If any man." The *Midrash Rabbah*, Numbers IX, 2,3,4,5,
offers no less than six different, and to us equally unwar-
ranted and far-fetched, interpretations of the significance of
the repetition.

But the relation of Philo's exegetical principles to
those of later rabbis takes us beyond our present concern. The
topic is dealt with elsewhere.

D. Gooding

II. PHILO'S STYLE AND DICTION

A. *Philo's Knowledge of Rhetorical Theory*

Philo's acquaintance with rhetorical theory might be inferred both from his interest in Hellenic education, dominated in his time by grammar and rhetoric, and from his frequent use of poetic and rhetorical devices in his own writing.[1] But Philo has left far more specific evidence of his knowledge of the details of rhetorical theory in his use of terms and in his many reflections on language and persuasion in the texts of his essays. His own comments leave the reader in little doubt of his awareness not only of the basics of rhetorical theory as a branch of preliminary education, but also of the philosophical debates on the value and perils of rhetoric that began in the speeches and dialogues of Plato and Isocrates and were still very much alive in the time of Quintilian. In various passages scattered throughout the essays, Philo gives a definition of rhetoric that is reminiscent of that assigned to Theodorus in Quintilian II.15.16, enumerates the divisions of the subject (Invention, Arrangement, Diction, Judgment, Memory, and Delivery), refers to rhetorical genres (Judicial, Deliberative, and Epideictic, including encomiastic speeches in praise of the Lord, like the later prose hymns of Aristeides and Julian), and uses the terms for the parts of an oration (*prooimia, diegēseis, pisteis, epilogoi*).[2] There can be little question that Philo was conversant with schoolroom rhetoric and that he used the terminology freely in later life. His interest in the interpretation of texts and his habit of labelling his own divisions and proofs led him to use rhetorical terms where even the best trained Greek orators would have avoided them.

In the area of rhetorical invention, Philo was aware of the reliance of Aristotelian rhetoric on the acceptability of probable rather than necessary premises in arguments aimed at a popular audience. The possibility of making formally valid arguments from probable premises is at the very heart of Aristotle's method in rhetoric and dialectic, and Philo is very uncomfortable with this aspect of conventional rhetorical theory. To Philo, probability arguments are associated with the hired lawyer whose aim is to trick the jury into accepting a bad case

(*Agr.* 13) or with the more sinister worldly wise sophists who corrupt the morals of their hearers (*Det.* 38, in contrast to the Egyptian sophists, Moses has no talent for τὴν τῶν εὐλόγων καὶ πιθανῶν εἰκαστικὴν ῥητορείαν), or even the clever-talking serpent in the Garden of Eden (*Agr.* 96). This, along with his frequent use of the contrast between appearance (*to dokein*) and reality (*to einai*), places him firmly in the camp of the philosophers who were hostile to conventional rhetoric rather than those who sought to tame and analyze it. Philo's figures of the "Egyptian" sophists and Jethro are strongly reminiscent of Plato's attacks on probability and sophistical rhetoric in the *Gorgias* and *Phaedrus*.[3] His attitude toward pathos, which he knows as an integral part of the conventional rhetoric, is similar, and is in keeping with the Platonic and Stoic attitudes on rhetoric rather than the tradition represented by Aristotle, Isocrates and Cicero. The only justification for pathos appeals would be in bringing the ignorant and undeveloped souls closer to a perception of the truth that would free them from the domination of the passions.[4]

Whatever his feelings about conventional rhetoric, Philo makes use of the language of rhetorical invention. He knows the terms *enthymema, paradeigma, parabolē*, and *tekmērion*, all of them Aristotelian or conventional in origin. In his near parody of a philosophical debate on the theme "Will the wise man indulge in drunkenness?", he refers to the distinction between "artistic" and "inartistic" proofs, a specific piece of Aristotelian lore which he probably includes in order to characterize his imaginary speaker.[5] The same debate reveals that Philo or his source was thoroughly trained in the use of formal topics for philosophical and rhetorical argumentation. Again the pedantic introduction of the actual rules and definitions of the arguments employed seems to be intended as a reflection of the sophistical character of the imaginary speaker. The topics employed are definition (*Plant.* 154-155), synonymy (*Plant.* 150), etymology (*Plant.* 165, cf. Aristotle *Topica* 112a32ff. and Cicero *Topica* 35), and the joint applicability of contraries within a genus (*Plant.* 172, cf. Aristotle *Topica* 111a14ff. and 113a33ff.). Formal topics belong to the inner mysteries of rhetorical invention and are not adequately covered in most rhetorical textbooks. They are especially at home in Aristotelian rhetoric and dialectic, in the debating techniques of the New Academy, and in Ciceronian rhetoric (*Topica* and

De oratore II.39,162). Cicero comments that the Stoics were
very deficient in this regard, and I would suspect that Philo,
like Cicero, came into contact with this method through the
Academic and Peripatetic practice of debating theses through
topical reasoning rather than through Stoic logic or rhetoric.[6]

Philo uses a good many of these formal topics in *Deus*,
though he is much more subtle than in the set-piece debate in
De plantatione. Among the more obvious instances of formal
topics are *a fortiori* (*Deus* 105-106; 148), definition (*Deus* 83,
86, 179-180), cause and effect (*Deus* 77-79, cf. topics 17 and 24
in Aristotle *Rhetoric* II.23), genus-species (*Deus* 95, 117-119,
cf. Aristotle *Topica* 111a14ff.), contraries (*Deus* 124, cf.
Aristotle *Topica* 112a26ff.), results (*Deus* 75-76, cf. topic 13
in *Rhetoric* II.23), incredible but true (*Deus* 91, cf. Aristotle
Rhetoric II.23, topic 21), and etymology (*Deus* 103, cf. Aristotle *Topica* 112a32ff., though here the influence of Stoic
grammar may be at work). Most of these were known to Cicero
as well as Aristotle and may have been current in Philo's time,
but this is advanced rhetoric or dialectic, not the schoolroom
variety. The proper use of these topics is not taught in basic
schoolroom rhetoric and the texts that seek to explain it are
very difficult; the best way to learn this system is to *use* it
in the defense or destruction of theses with a teacher practiced
in this art. It seems to me very likely that such debating
formed a part of Philo's education.

Philo's Knowledge of the Terminology of Diction

Philo uses the actual terminology of Greek grammar and
rhetoric more frequently than is customary in literary prose.
This is not, as in the case of invention, out of any tendency
to label his own rhetorical devices, but results from the
necessity of interpreting particular passages in his text. This
is Philo the commentator rather than Philo the debater of theses.
Most of the stylistic terms that Philo uses throughout his essays
are found in the immediate context of an interpretation of a
Biblical text. Philo's technique here is closer to that of the
Stoic allegorist or the grammarian glossing the text of a classical author for his class than to the style of the sophists and
philosophers, like Plutarch, Maximus of Tyre, or Dion

Chrysostomus, who sometimes use Homer or exotic mythologies as
texts from which to preach a lesson.

Philo's acquaintance with the technical language of
grammar and style seems to have been very wide indeed. He knows
phonology (the seven vowels, semi-vowels, etc.), the parts of
speech, the Stoic classification of questions and statements,
the terms for grammatical errors, and a large repertoire of
figures of speech.[7] He has a large vocabulary, as might be
expected, for allegory and types of comparison: *ainigma*, *allēgoria*, *analogia*, *eikōn*, *metaphora*, *symbolon*, *tropos*, and *hypo-
noia*. For most of these terms he has verbal, adjectival, and
adverbial forms as well. These terms, however, must already
have been established in the allegorical tradition well before
Philo; most of them are found in Heraclitus, in allegorical
contexts in Plutarch, and in the scholia to authors like Homer,
Hesiod, and Aratus, as well as in late, Neo-Platonic allegorists,
like Iamblichus, Porphyry, Sallustius, and Proclus. This is a
fairly consistent tradition, and there would be little need for
an author like Philo to go directly to the rhetoricians who also
use these terms. Allegory, symbol, and such like terms already
had quite distinct applications for the allegorist and the rhetorician.[8]

Another class of terms that occur in the analysis of
particular passages seems to belong to grammar and the Greek
manuals of style, material common to rhetoric, poetics, and
literary criticism: *anastrophē*, *glaphyrotēs*, *episphragizō*,
epiphoneō, *makrologia*, *ogkos*, *homonymia*, *paroimia*, *parabolē*,
periplokē, *ptōsis*, and *sunuphainō*. Almost all of these terms
can be found in the Greek literature on style, from Book III of
Aristotle's *Rhetoric*, through Demetrius *On Style* and Dionysius
On Verbal Composition.[9] Terms not attested in Greek authors
before Philo often have their Latin equivalents already in the
Fourth Book of *Rhetorica ad Herennium* and also occur in late
Greek rhetoricians like Hermogenes. Taken as a whole, the
grammatical and stylistic lore employed by Philo belongs to the
specialized Hellenistic tradition on those subjects rather than
to the philosophical and literary rhetorics, like Aristotle's
or Cicero's, which try to place rhetorical techniques and
stylistic devices in the context of a general theory of persuasion. Some of the terms listed above are distinctively grammatical, like *homonymia* and *ptōsis*, while others are found in
the Hellenistic doctrine of the virtues of style, like

glaphyrotēs and *ogkos*. It is unlikely that Philo followed only
one grammar or manual of style; his acquaintance with the tradition was rich enough that he could be somewhat eclectic in his
use of it.

      The Greek rhetorician treated figures of speech and
thought as intentional devices of the author aimed at producing
a particular effect in the souls of the audience. Appropriate-
ness of style to subject matter or to the level of style sought
by the author was the standard against which Demetrius or
Dionysius judged the use of stylistic devices in the authors
studied. This is not generally Philo's aim in using rhetorical
terms; for Philo the important thing is to find a grammatical
or rhetorical justification for his interpretation of a specific
text. A consideration of some of the rhetorical and grammatical
terms used in *Deus* is offered in illustration:

      Deus 1 *anaphora*: *Anaphora* occurs as the name of a
rhetorical figure in Demetrius *On Style* 141 and Longinus *On the
Sublime* 20.1 (cf. also *repetitio* in *Ad Herennium* 4.13.19). To
the rhetorician, this term means repetition of a word or phrase
for emphasis or stylistic effect. In Philo, the word seems not
to mean repetition at all, but, as Colson translates, "reference back." At any rate, there is no instance of rhetorical
anaphora in the Septuagint text cited; *met'ekeino* is not
repeated for emphasis at the beginning of adjacent clauses.
Anaphora does occur as a grammatical term in Dionysius Thrax
(637b16) in a sense parallel to this use in Philo.

      Deus 20 *sunuphainō*: This word belongs to a family of
terms that refer to interweaving of words, sounds, or ideas
(*Rhetorica ad Alexandrum* 33.8; Dionysius of Halicarnassus *On
Verbal Composition* 18, 23; *enuphainō* in Demetrius *On Style* 166).
Frequent in Philo, who knows *sunuphainō* also as a music term,
as a word for making connections between ideas or interpretations in the course of his exegesis. Not precisely equivalent
to the rhetorical usage.[10]

      Deus 71 *tropikos* and *kuriologoumenon*: For the history
of these terms, see the note *ad loc*. The kind of distinction
made here is already expressed (in different language) in
Isocrates, Aristotle and the *Rhetorica ad Alexandrum* (*haplous*
and *metapherōn* 23.1434b34). There is no doubt about the

rhetorical and grammatical background of these terms, but, again,
Philo's use of them may not be a direct application of his rhetorical training. The distinction between figurative and proper
discourse may already have become a commonplace in allegorical
exegesis. Plutarch has *kuriōs . . . legousin* in his interpretation of the Egyptian habit of associating the dog with Hermes in
De Iside 11.355b and says that Plato in his *Laws* speaks *ou di'
ainigmōn oude sumbolikōs, alla kuriois onomasin* (*De Iside* 47.
370f.). Similar contrasts are to be found in other Greek allegorizing texts.

     Deus 72 *prophora*: See note *ad loc.* for the details.
Prophora is more a grammatical term than a rhetorical one. Here
it is used to introduce a point about the precise word order of
the text which is intended to support Philo's interpretation of
the passage.

     Deus 72 *anastrophē*: In Quintilian 8.6.65 (cf. *Rhetorica
ad Herennium* 4.32.44 *perversio*) and Hermogenes *Peri ideōn* I.12
this is the name of a figure of speech in which the normal word
order is deliberately reversed for stylistic effect. In Philo,
a reversal of the order of clauses is meant, and that is important in this instance because of the implication of the text for
the consistency of Moses' description of God's relationship with
man. Philo's interpretation removes the suggestion that God is
capable of repenting of actions, a suggestion that a more
literally-minded reader might pick up from reading the narrative
of the Creation and the Flood. There is no rhetorical point to
be made in Philo's analysis: again he has used a familiar rhetorical term in a non-rhetorical application that suits his
needs as a commentator.

     Deus 141 *ptōsis*: Philo's use of this term is perfectly
regular and fits both the rhetorical (Aristotle *Rhetoric* II.23,
1364b34) and the grammatical traditions (Dionysius Thrax 12.634b
and 636b3). The analysis of inflexions for their argumentative
implications was a feature of Aristotelian dialectic (*Topica*
106b29) and it would seem natural that one educated in debating
theses would look for significance in the gender or case of a
word. Argument from grammatical cases, however, may already
have been established in the allegorical method before Philo.

Cicero uses it in his explanation of the name of Jove in *De natura deorum* II.25.64.

Deus 146 *dia brakheias phōnēs*: This is perhaps a genuinely rhetorical observation as well as an ethical one. Philo makes a similar comment about Moses' brevity in *Op.* 130, and Plutarch has an extensive discussion of loftiness of thought with brevity of expression in his *Phocion* 5.2-4, cf. also Demetrius *On Style* 103.

The main inspiration in Philo's use of terms shared by grammarians and rhetoricians seems to have been grammatical. Philo rarely uses these terms to introduce a point about Moses' style. This may be attributed to Philo's needs as a commentator building a case for his interpretation of the text rather than to any lack of interest in style on Philo's part. Philo's appreciation of style is displayed in his own use of figures and in his own diction rather than in his analysis of texts. As grammatical analysis is really part of Philo's invention or proofs, it should be noted that what he is doing is closely parallel to the analysis of premises and arguments in Greek dialectic as well as to the application of rhetorical techniques in the Greek allegorical tradition. Verbal objections, arguments from etymology, from names, and from inflexions, and analysis of the forms of statements are all used in constructing dialectical proofs in Aristotelian and Stoic logic. In the latter school, grammatical learning was a *sine qua non* for both dialectic and allegorical interpretation. It should not be surprising that Philo uses much grammatical terminology in the Genesis commentary and that, in doing so, his aim is more philosophical than literary.

NOTES

[1]Rhetoric in the *encyclius paedeia*: *Agr.* 18; *Cher.* 105; *Cong.* 11-19. See I. Heinemann, *Philo's griechische und jüdische Bildung*, Breslau, 1932, pp. 436ff. and 519ff. and T. Conley, "'General Education' in Philo of Alexandria," *Colloquia of the Center for Hermeneutical Studies in Hellenistic and Modern Culture*, 15 (March 1975).

[2]The divisions of rhetoric: *Som.* I.205. The parts of the oration: *Plant.* 128; *Mos.* II.51. Epideictic speeches in praise of the Lord: *Plant.* 130-131.

[3]For probability as an issue, see Plato *Gorgias* 454D-455A, *Phaedrus* 272D-274A; Isocrates 13.1-3; 15.184, 271-274;

Aristotle *Rhetoric* I.1-3; II.24; Cicero *De oratore* I.30; II.
107-109; Quintilian II.14-21.

[4]Pathos vs. logos: *L.A.* III.116, 155; *Agr.* 78; *Cher.*
105.

[5]Enthymeme: *Det.* 40; *L.A.* III.230. Example: *Plant.*
134. Parable: *Conf.* 99. Token: *Deus* 148 and frequently.
Artistic/Inartistic proofs: *Plant.* 173-174.

[6]For the various types of topics employed by Philo, see
section 'E' below. The formal topics I refer to here correspond
to those characterized as "dialectical" by Prof. Conley.

[7]Phonology and basic grammar: *L.A.* II.16; *Op.* 126-127.
Stoic doctrine on statements: *Agr.* 140-141.

[8]See below, section 'D', for a fuller discussion of
allegorical terms.

[9]*Anaphora* (*Deus* 1), *anastrophē* (*Deus* 72), *glaphyrotēs*
(*Cong.* 16, 78), *episphragizō* (cf. *Deus* 124), *epiphoneō* (*Plant.*
51, cf. Demetrius *On Style* 106-111), *makrologia* (*Plant.* 153),
ogkos (*Plant.* 157, cf. Aristotle *Rhetoric* III.6), *homonymia*
(*Gig.* 56), *paroimia* (*Exs.* 150), *periplokē* (*Det.* 41), *ptōsis*
(*Deus* 141), *sunuphainō* (*Deus* 20).

[10]*Sunuphainō* occurs also as a music term in *Post.* 104.
It should be noted that by this time *sunuphainō* may have been a
very dead metaphor and that in logical and grammatical contexts
it may do no more than refer to a grammatical conjunction or a
logical connection.

B. *Philo's Vocabulary and Word Choice*

The richness of Philo's vocabulary has frequently been
noticed both in this commentary and in the older literature on
Philo. Philo not only draws upon a rich and eclectic fund of
philosophical terms from the Academic, Peripatetic, and Stoic
traditions, but also rejoices in a fullness of expression that
is one of the chief ornaments of his style. Like Plutarch and
"Longinus," Philo is very fond of verbal antithesis, synonymy,
and other types of "doubled" expression; he rarely uses one
word where two will serve.[1] Lists and catalogues of virtues,
vices, duties, attributes, and philosophical classifications
abound in Philo's essays, and the words in the lists are often
arranged in sets of three or five with the last member in the
list suitably amplified for a crescendo effect. Such are the
"triads" which have been identified in a number of the notes in
the commentary.[2] Philo is also very free with metaphors,
similes, and extended comparisons, and develops these with
great fullness of style. Where Teles or Epictetus would be
content with a few nautical or weather terms in a storm at sea
comparison, Philo regularly continues the figure, often with
every idea doubled through synonymy and with a richer selection
of nautical words, some of them paralleled only in the poets.[3]
Each of these factors contributes to the richness of Philo's
vocabulary, and the frequency both of Platonic and poetic echoes,
and of words first attested in Philo is reflected on almost
every page of the commentary.

On the whole, Philo's grammar and word choice are consistent with a mildly atticizing type of literary Greek. He
does not restrict himself to a narrowly classical word list
culled from the prose writers of the fifth and fourth centuries
B.C.E., but, on the other hand, he generally avoids vulgar and
koinē forms and expressions. Considering his subject matter,
he is remarkably free of the influence of the Greek of the Septuagint, which he sometimes corrects in quotations from memory
and paraphrases.[4] One might say that his Greek is influenced
both by the authority of the classical prose writers and by the
educated usage of Hellenistic and contemporary authors who were

not strict atticists. Aside from Stoic terminology, which even
a strict atticist might well use despite its late origin, Philo
uses many words which are found first in such sources as Polybius,
Strabo, Diodorus Siculus, or Dionysius of Halicarnassus.[5] Some
of his rhetorical and grammatical terms occur first in Dionysius
or Philodemus and are the likely products of the elaboration of
the technical language of these subjects that took place in the
Hellenistic period. Since Stoic philosophy, grammar, and allegorical technique are important influences on Philo's approach
to his subject matter, it seems only natural that Philo's diction as a whole should have been influenced by educated Hellenistic prose style.

        Aristotle and the Stoics seem to contribute mainly
technical terms to Philo's language, though there are a few
favorite Stoic metaphors and similes, like wax impressions for
the mechanics of Stoic *phantasia* (*Deus* 43). The Platonic tradition, on the other hand, supplies Philo both with technical
terms and with a rich source of poetic language and imagery.
There is a distinctly Platonic coloring to much of Philo's
diction, and this derives both from the use of many individual
words and phrases that are familiar from Plato's dialogues and
from the extensive use of Platonic similes and imagery.[6] The
chariot, the light imagery, and the struggles of the soul in its
journey from the *Phaedrus* myth are favorite sources of imagery
for Philo, just as they are for Plutarch, Dion, and Maximus
Tyrius, and Philo's allusions to Plato's poetic phrases and
images from Socrates' "dithyrambic" second speech in that dialogue would have been readily recognized and appreciated by his
audience.[7] In Philo, poetic passages, usually from Plato's
myths, are offered as similes or extended comparisons and are
shorn of their context in a mythical utterance and the warnings
that usually accompany such speeches in Plato's dialogues. The
distinction between myth and dialectic, so important for Plato
and maintained by Plutarch and some later Platonists, seems not
to be very important for Philo. In Philo, the poetic imagery
from Plato's myths is translated into figurative language with
no fictional context. Philo also transforms some of his Platonic material. In *Gig.* 31, for instance, he develops the Platonic image of the world seen from above by the liberated soul
(*Phaedo* 109B-110E) into the elaborate figure of the universe as
a theater.

A great many words have been designated in the commentary
as "first attested in Philo." Some of these are the result of
stylistic *variatio* and Philo's need to fill out a doubled expression, as in *Deus* 59, where we find the Hellenistic term *anthrō-
pomorphon* balanced by the apparently original coinage *anthrōpo-
pathes*. Other pairs also include a previously attested word and
a new word, such as *aklines* and *arrepes* (*Deus* 23) and *philosō-
matos* and *philopathēs* (*Deus* 111). Fullness of expression must
often have been a factor in Philo's choice of words which are
either unattested in surviving predecessors or actually coined
by Philo himself. There is a much larger category of words,
however, which are first attested in Philo, but occur also in
Plutarch. Siegfried lists some of these and others have been
noted in the commentary.[8] As Plutarch is neither too remote
in date from Philo nor likely to have been influenced by his
diction, it seems likely that both authors are drawing upon the
diction of educated but non-archaizing Greek prose writers from
the third century B.C.E. and after. This supposition receives
occasional support from words like *libas* (*Deus* 155), which
occurs in Strabo, *philautia* (*Deus* 16), which is one of the Greek
words in Cicero's letters, and *phruattomai* applied to persons
(*Deus* 168), which is in Diodorus Siculus. Philo seems to preserve for us something of the quality of educated and literary
prose before the strong influence of the Atticist movement of
the first century B.C.E.

NOTES

[1]Antithesis and synonymy: C. Siegfried, *Philo von
Alexandria*, Jena, 1875, pp. 132-137.

[2]Triads: *Gig.* 27, 37; *Deus* 107, 114, 126, 149, 182.
Classical examples may be found in Demosthenes 3.26 and Cicero
Pro Archia 16. A similar style is often adopted by "Longinus,"
cf. *On the Sublime* 9.6; 10.3.

[3]Compare Teles in Stobaeus III.1.98 (p. 41.9-14) with
Philo *Gig.* 13ff. and *Deus* 26, 60, 89, 98, 129, 177.

[4]For Philo and LXX, see the notes on *Gig.* 34, 61; *Deus*
9, 28, 54, 89, 137, 158, 165.

[5]For Hellenistic diction, see the notes on *Gig.* 31 and
Deus 1, 2, 4, 5, 7, 16, 17, 18, 59, 72, 95, 138, 141, 144, 154,
155.

[6]For individual words and phrases, see *Gig.* 33, 35, 39,
50; *Deus* 4, 22, 27, 28, 30, 67, 86, 156, 162. There is a list
of Platonic words in Philo in Siegfried, *op. cit.*, pp. 31-37.

Platonic imagery: *Gig.* 12, 17, 31, 46, 61; *Deus* 2, 78, 79, 105, 135, 137, 151, 181. For Platonic similes in Philo, see Billings, *The Platonism of Philo Judaeus*, Chicago, 1919, pp. 88-103.

[7]*Gig.* 31, 61; *Deus* 2, 135.

[8]Siegfried, *op. cit.*, pp. 38-45.
Commentary: *Deus* 23, 34, 56, 60, 72, 75, 76, 79, 83, 111, 115, 150.

C. *Characteristics of Philo's Style in the*
De Gigantibus *and* Quod Deus

The ancient literary critics maintained that style and word choice should be appropriate to the genre and subject matter of the speaker. From this point of view, Philo's style poses some interesting problems. By Philo's time, the scope of rhetorical theory had expanded to include new genres of literature, but there is no evidence that allegorical or philosophical commentaries were ever regarded as a distinct literary genre by Greek rhetoricians. The surviving ancient commentaries on authors like Homer, Hesiod, and Aratus, and the fragments of Didymus' Demosthenes commentary are largely lacking in literary pretensions of their own. Comment on classical authors is found in more literary types of writing, especially the dialogue, the symposium, and the literary or philosophical letter, but, though Philo is plainly influenced by these genres and actually makes use of the dialogue and letter forms elsewhere, he has not chosen to imitate them closely in the form of his essays in the Genesis commentary. The literary effort that Philo puts into his commentaries can be paralleled in some of the more ambitious Neo-Platonic and Christian commentaries, but even in the fourth century, when such attempts were more common, there are no literary canons for the commentary. In his own time, Philo is unique.

If one were to compose a rhetoric for philosophical commentaries of a more literary type, certain parallels might be drawn from the comments on dialogue and epideictic writing in the literary critics. A conversational style, employing periods of moderate length and an unobtrusive prose rhythm, rich in question figures, apostrophe, exempla, and analogies would seem the appropriate style for up-grading the textbookish prose of a commentary and presenting the material in an appealing way. Cicero, Seneca, and Plutarch approached the problem of translating textbook philosophy into literary prose by adopting the dialogue or letter forms, already recognized as literary genres, and in the case of Cicero, there is direct evidence that non-literary textbooks and hypomnemata have been re-written as speeches in the mouths of characters. The style is Cicero's

141

and usually involves a florid style for the exposition of doctrine and a grander style where the subject matter provides
opportunities for praise or exhortation. On at least one occasion, Cicero actually presents a commentary in literary form;
in *De legibus* II-III, he explicates his own model law code,
based on the Twelve Tables. The full dialogue form allows him
to recite and explain the laws himself, while Quintus and
Atticus raise objections and ask the questions that maintain
the flow of the argument.[1] The letter form provides similar
opportunities for Seneca in his *Moral Letters* and for authors
like Dionysius of Halicarnassus in his works of literary criticism. Interlocutors in a dialogue and the recipient of a letter
lend dramatic significance to many of the question figures,
objections, and exhortations employed by the author and justify
their presence in a philosophical or scientific work. Philo seems
to have been influenced by the dialogue tradition both directly,
from his reading of Plato's dialogues, and indirectly, from what
modern scholars have called the diatribe tradition, which makes
use of many of the rhetorical devices of the dialogue style.
The dialogue style offers the most obvious and effective technique for translating the textbookish subject matter of a commentary into a recognized literary form and also allows for the
discussion of problems and difficulties through the speeches of
the interlocutors. Plato also serves as a model for the poetic
treatment of philosophical themes, and later practitioners of
the dialogue form were not deterred by the criticisms of Caeci-
lius and Dionysius in this regard. Cicero, Plutarch, and Dion
Chrysostomus all include highly poetic passages in their dialogues on the model of the very *Phaedrus* myth attacked by the
critics who sought to set literary standards for the dialogue
style. Philo, in his own non-dramatic essays, is also an imi-
tator of this aspect of Plato's style.[2]

        The dialogue is, however, a dramatic form. Conversa-
tional diction, apostrophe, "*Du-Stil*," and illustrative comparisons from daily life all fit the dramatic situation of a ficti-
tious conversation among friends. The same devices occur, for
similar reasons, in the symposia of Plutarch and Athenaeus, and,
to a lesser degree, in non-dramatic but conversational literary
letters. Philo's writing is non-dramatic in form and there are
some non-dramatic models for what he is doing. The diatribe is
not a form specifically recognized by surviving Greek rhetoricians, but it may be broadly subsumed under the handling of

general themes in display oratory and mingles some of the techniques of dialogue with those of the school orations on theses,
or general questions.[3] The dramatic features of the dialogue
are maintained to some degree in a non-dramatic form by the fiction that the speaker is addressing the individual member of the
audience. Philo often adopts this style when he has already
proven his point through allegorical exegesis and wants to bring
home the moral to his audience. In many of his essays, there
is a kind of rising and falling rhythm of exegetical passages
in conversational but technical style and more rhetorical passages, either poetic flights of the Platonic type or diatribe
passages. Diatribe style offered Philo a technique for conveying the impression of a philosophical dialogue without the need
for interlocutors. This is one of the important differences
between Philo and the real diatribists like Maximus of Tyre and
Epictetus; Philo is writing long, continuous discourses that
form a fairly complete system of Mosaic philosophy, much more
ambitious than any treatment of subject matter in the diatribists. Philo's treatment is extended and exhaustive, and the
diatribe elements are not isolated sermons on the conventional
themes of popular philosophy, but extended lessons based on the
exegesis of a continuous text. For Philo, the diatribe technique is a method of breaking out of the textbook style and
making his work more literary and more philosophical. Without
fiction, he succeeds in giving something like the impression of
a philosophical dialogue. I think that the more important model
for Philo in this respect is Plato rather than the contemporary
diatribists whose methods permit Philo to seem more Platonic in
his exegesis of Jewish law.

     Under the heading of appropriateness to subject matter,
one might mention the various rhetorical aims which Philo assigns
to Moses himself in various places. Moses teaches the Law
itself and suggests its various levels of significance, he
praises the Lord and His creation, he advises his people and
exhorts them to virtue.[4] For teaching, the plain style of the
textbook or the conversational passages in dialogue would be
appropriate; for some deeper levels of significance, the teaching may take on the form of allegory. Praise is served by a
grander style, with fullness of diction and thought and poetic
language to lend dignity. For the praise of the gods and of
divine works, the Greek rhetoricians actually recommend the use
of allegorical language, which in both Moses and Philo, can

excite awe as well as conveying a message. Advice and exhortation seem to call for a more vehement and forceful style, like
the style of Demosthenes' courtroom speeches or the diatribes
of the Cynics.[5] In general Philo uses the plain style in passages of exegesis, a richer more poetic style in the exposition
of philosophical doctrine, and the vehemence of the diatribists
in drawing the moral, especially when it involves warning or
reproof. The diatribe style also serves him in the refutation
of alternative and inferior interpretations of the text. Philo
actually has many styles, not only in the whole corpus of his
works, but within the individual essays. Long stretches of his
essays are in the florid style, richly decorated with metaphors
and similes, but devoid of question figures, apostrophe, and
the short kola and kommata that are characteristic of the diatribe. These passages bear a stronger resemblance to Plutarch's
essays or the long speeches in Cicero's dialogues than to Epictetus or Paul. In other places, Philo mixes the diatribe figures with the more Platonic flights of poetic fancy that are
found in Plutarch and Dion, but not in Teles or Epictetus.
There is more than one way of giving philosophical themes rhetorical treatment, and Philo's extended pursuit of philosophical
subject matter in Jewish law is too grand a plan to be contained
in the form or style of the diatribist.

Levels of Style and Major Figures

Though Philo's essays in the Genesis commentary sometimes have a recognizable proem and epilogue, the arrangement of
material and its stylistic treatment rarely resemble the structure of a formal speech. In Philo, style and argument follow
the order of the Biblical citations in the continuous commentary
and each of the members of the series is developed individually.
A Biblical text is explained allegorically in the plain style,
its meaning is further expounded with the aid of philosophical
doctrine and parallel Biblical texts, and, where appropriate, a
moral lesson is driven home in a more vehement style, employing
figures that have been associated with the diatribe form. In
some sections of *Gig.* and *Deus*, the middle style predominates
almost to the exclusion of diatribe elements, while in others
the diatribe style is followed more consistently as if Philo
were delivering a short sermon drawn from the lesson in his text.
In general, the individual sections of his commentary follow the

same pattern, with similar figures repeated at similar points in
the development of his argument. The level of style rises and
falls in rhythm with the introduction of sections of text in the
commentary.

In both the middle style passages and the diatribe passages, Philo's style is rich in metaphors and similes, a general
characteristic of the florid style of writing which Cicero associates especially with Demetrius of Phalerum and the oratory of
those trained in the schools of philosophy.[6] The similes often
grow into extended comparisons which also serve as illustrative
comparisons (*parabolai*) and analogies to support the proof.
While it is possible to find parallels to this technique in the
Stoic *similitudines*--most of them serving the double function of
ornamentation and analogy--discussed by Cicero in *De natura
deorum* and *De finibus* and in the diatribes of Epictetus, none of
the writers in this tradition uses these devices as frequently
or with the same fullness of expression as Philo.[7] In *Deus* 33-
50, for instance, Philo takes a bit of philosophical doctrine
which might occupy a single short paragraph in a textbook and
exploits it for its full value as a rhetorical distribution in
which each part is made to yield its lesson. The passage begins
with praise of order in God's plan for the universe, developed
further through a metaphor from war, the rewards for those who
keep their place in the rank to which God has assigned them and
the punishment meted out to deserters. The distribution of the
four principles that apply to bodies follows, with each of the
four illustrated with similes and extended comparisons. The
operation of *hexis* is like the circuit of the *diaulos*, which is
itself a human imitation of the divine order of the universe
(35-36). *Phusis*, personified as the power of growth and recalling Lucretius' Venus and the *Natura* of Cicero *De natura deorum*
II, is the subject of a highly poetic passage which describes
the growth of plants according to the seasons (37-40). Two
related similes compare the buds of the plants to eyes and the
yearly cycle of plant life to waking and sleeping; a further
comparison from human or animal life refers to the unseen
channels through which plants take their nourishment as analogous to breasts. The whole treatment of plant life is done in
a very fulsome rhetorical style, with elaborate periodic structure and doubling of expression through synonymy and many minor
metaphors. This richness of expression in the description of
natural phenomena recalls Vergil's *Georgics* and Lucretius' *De*

rerum natura as well as the style attributed to Poseidonius, but
not well-illustrated, in Strabo and Cicero.[8] *Psukhē* is also
explained with the aid of extended comparisons; the mind is like
a treasure house for perceptions (42) and *phantasia* leaves its
print on the mind like the impression of a sealing ring in wax
(43). The rational principle, last of the series and the best,
has its similes as well: light and darkness imagery (46) and
another comparison elaborated almost to a parable, the slave and
master analogy applied first to the relationship between men and
animals and then to men themselves, when they abuse their priv-
ileges as ungrateful freedmen of the cosmic community (47-48).
Even the brief conclusion to this section, which returns to a
consideration of the Genesis text, has a simile of its own--the
reason as an incorruptible judge. In addition to the similes
and extended comparisons that serve as important illustrations
for Philo's proofs, there are many minor metaphors throughout
the passage. As a whole, the style of this section, with its
strongly figurative language and periodic structure falls into
the middle style described by Cicero in the *Orator* as typical or
the orators who emerge from the schools of philosophy.

     Deus 33-50 is almost entirely in the middle style and
diatribe figures like apostrophe, hypophora, rhetorical question,
and prosopopoiia are absent, but Philo often mixes the two styles,
enlivening his exposition with occasional appeals to the audience.
This applies to much of *Gig.* (1-5, 6-18, and 58-67) and to parts
of *Deus* (20-32, 70-85, and 122-139). In these sections the exposition of doctrine in the middle style is occasionally enlivened
with brief appeals to the audience through apostrophe, clusters
of questions, and the use of first and second person "communica-
tive" plurals. Here I believe some caution should be exercised
in attributing figures to the diatribe or homiletic styles.
When Philo introduces an objection through *hypophora* or *prokata-
lepsis* at the beginning of a passage of exegesis (*Gig.* 20, 58;
Deus 21-22, 51, 122), uses "*Wir-Stil*" in a transitional passage
(*Gig.* 28; *Deus* 20, 33), or puts a syllogistic argument in the
form of a series of questions (*Gig.* 10-11), he is doing no more
than following the common practice of writers of Greek argumentative prose from the author of the Hippocratic essay *On Ancient
Medicine* and Aristotle in his esoteric works through later
writers like Dionysius and Strabo.[9]

     This applies equally to an argumentative device which
Philo uses repeatedly in *Deus*. When he has already made his

interpretation of the text and expounded its philosophical meaning, he often drives home the moral in an *a fortiori* comparison
expressed as a conditional sentence ending in a question--if you
can accept *x*, how can you fail to accept the greater truth in *y*?
He repeats this device at similar points in the development of
the argument in *Deus* 8, 26, and 78. The most felicitous of
these is *Deus* 26, which begins with an extended comparison
between the soul in its resistance to wickedness and a sudden
storm at sea that gives way to calm, bright weather. The comparison is developed through a long series of metaphors from
weather lore arranged in balanced clauses with great fullness of
expression. The continuous interweaving of moral terms with
weather imagery, as in the chiastic arrangement of πνεῦμα τὸ
κακίας and ἐπιστήμης καὶ σοφίας αὔραις in successive clauses,
maintains our attention and carries us along with the flow of
the argument as no simple analogy could. In the second half of
the sentence, we are asked, just when we are most under the
influence of Philo's eloquence, how we could doubt that the consistency we have observed in the human soul applies even more
to a God whose very titles suggest that He is unchanging. Again
there is great fullness of expression, especially in the catalogue of divine attributes, and the whole passage ends in a
series of balanced clauses illustrating some of Philo's favorite
rhythms (γνώμης μεταβολῇ, . . . ἀρχῆς ἐβουλεύσατο . . . αὐτῶν
μετατιθεῖς;). Bultmann and Thyen allude briefly to this sort of
argument in the diatribe style, and similar arguments are indeed
found in Stoic fragments, in Dion, and in Epictetus, but the
same type of argument is also found in writers outside this
tradition, including Aristotle, Dionysius, the Pseudo-Aristotelian
De Mundo, and Ptolemy.[10] This device might reasonably be attributed as much to the characteristics of Greek argumentative prose
in general as to the diatribe tradition.

There are, however, sections of *Gig.* and *Deus* which bear
a stronger resemblance to the diatribe style. These include the
digression on Moses' *pneuma* in *Gig.* 24-57 and parts of *Deus*
51-69, 86-121, and 140-183. In passages like these, Philo's
style rises from the florid tones of the philosophical lecturer
to the force and vehemence of the orator in the grand style.
Metaphors and Philo's characteristic fullness of expression are
still in evidence, and far more so than in the typical authors
of the diatribe style, but in these passages, Philo is actively
trying to involve his audience in the argument rather than

merely presenting them with weighty thoughts in beautiful and
impressive language. Clusters of question figures grow more
frequent, second person singular and first and second person
plural forms occur continuously rather than in isolated transitional passages, types of apostrophe peculiar to the diatribe
style appear (*O psykhē*, *Gig.* 44 and *Deus* 114; *O dianoia*, *Deus* 4),
and the sentence structure is broken up, here and there, into
shorter *kola* and *kommata*. It is also in passages like these
that Philo makes use of Greek chriae (*Gig.* 33, *Deus* 146),
proverbs (*kat' ikhnos bainein*, *Gig.* 39), and exempla (*Deus* 91),
as well as the figures prosopopoiia and personification, devices
rare in the florid style. While most of these devices can be
paralleled in Greek political oratory and, to a lesser extent,
in philosophical writing that does not fall within the diatribe
tradition, there is a fairly close correspondence between Philo's
practice here and that of the diatribists as characterized by
Wendland, Bultmann, and Thyen.[11]

        In the digression on Moses' *pneuma*, for instance, Philo
drops into "*Du-Stil*" immediately after introducing his text
(25). He then moves rapidly through a series of similes from
cutting, from transferring a flame from torch to torch (25),
from drawing water (25), and from shredding (26). These are
introduced in short *kola* and are not elaborated as are the
similes in *Deus* 33-51. The moral is drawn in characteristically
diatribe fashion; in the sentence beginning *nun de* . . . , we
get a kommatic catalogue of six attributes of Moses' *pneuma* with
asyndeton, balanced by an equally rapid set of antitheses in
short verbal clauses (27). The use of a rapid series of metaphors or similes to characterize Moses' *pneuma* is a particular
feature of the use of metaphor in the diatribe style, and
Bultmann mentions clauses with *nun de* . . . as typical of the
way in which diatribists draw conclusions from analogies.[12]
The argument in 28-31 begins with a rhetorical question in the
first person plural (28) and continues through a brief comparison of human affairs with a scale (28) and a catalogue of
worldly concerns that distract men from continuously receiving
the divine spirit as Moses did (29). The argument is rounded
off neatly in a short metaphorical epigram: πρὶν σοφίαν ἀνθῆσαι, κατεμάραναν.[13] In 30-31, Philo grows more expansive, and
the contrast between free souls and those still burdened with
the flesh is developed in longer periods and with the rich
imagery Philo uses elsewhere in the middle style passages. At

section 32, a new text is introduced, followed by a rhetorical
question and Philo's usual exegesis is enlivened with a Cynic
chria (34). A moral lesson follows, very much in diatribe
style, with first person plural hortatory subjunctives, short
kola, and vulgar diction (*skorakisteon* 34, and the unlovely comparison of the appetites with rabid dogs, 35).

Sections 36-43 continue in much the same vein, developing particular points from the text of Leviticus 18.6, but at
43-44 Philo employs devices new to this digression, but perhaps
quite old in the diatribe tradition. If this passage were preserved in some author like Stobaeus, we might well take it as
a portion of a lost diatribe. The short sentences, the stock
metaphors (*lipotaktēsai* and *automolēsai*, *tōn hēdonēs philtrōn*,
and *hōs sideritis lithos.* . . .), the love of paradoxical antithesis (*blaptei men gar hotan didōi*), the personification of
Pleasure, and the apostrophe of the soul combined with second
person singular imperatives are all typical of this style and
difficult to parallel elsewhere.[14] The apostrophe of the soul,
for instance, is found in Theognis, but is rare in later Greek
or Roman writers; the closest parallels to Philo's use of
apostrophe are in Seneca, Epictetus, M. Aurelius, and Tertul-
lian.[15] The type of personification used here is found in Plato
and Xenophon, and may be at home in Greek didactic literature
as far back as Hesiod, but in the First and Second Centuries of
the Common Era, it is especially typical of Dion, Seneca, Epictetus, and M. Aurelius.[16]

Diatribe figures and short *kola* continue in the remainder
of the digression on Moses' *pneuma* (45-57), though they are
increasingly rare and subordinated to key Biblical texts and the
lessons to be derived from them. The typical short and commonplace metaphors continue with the master and slave terminology
at 46 (also found in Teles and Epictetus), and the proverbial
measuring stick, a standby of Greek wisdom literature from
Theognis to Plutarch, at 49.[17] The war within the soul (57)
and the storm at sea imagery in the same passage are also found
in the diatribists. While these images are commonplace enough
in all types of Greek literature that they cannot serve as
direct evidence of Philo's use of the diatribe as a model, it
may be significant that Philo has not given these figures the
full poetic treatment here. In this section he introduces an
image briefly and moves quickly on to his next point and his
next image in the rapid-fire style familiar to readers of

Epictetus. This does not hold true, however, for the mystery
imagery in 53-54; this is the sort of fully developed comparison
in periodic style that is especially characteristic of Philo and
not so easy to find, nor as impressive to read when it is found,
in authors like Teles and Epictetus. In Philo, too, we get not
only the full battery of mystery terms and images, but also the
tent from the Exodus text and the allusion to an audience whose
ears are "purified," elements which lend a specifically Jewish
coloring to the otherwise Platonic mystery imagery. The effect
here is of the grandeur of the poet-philosopher rather than the
speed and vehemence of the Cynic preacher.

        The digression on Moses' *pneuma* ends with a transitional
passage which is not in a very vehement style. It does pose a
paradox for the audience--Moses' life spanned only one hundred
and twenty years, a degree of longevity matched by many mortals
who were no match for him in spirit. The paradox is stated as
a question, as if it were one of Aristotle's dialectical problems and a fuller exposition, or initiation (*mueisthai*) is
promised in the future. This is a nice pedagogical style, but
not at all typical of the Stoic-Cynic sermons, which are complete in themselves rather than parts of a continuous discourse.
For an epilogue more suitable to the diatribe, one might turn
to *Deus* 172-183, where the mutability of human affairs is made
the subject of a kind of peroration. Philo sets out to prove
that to be concerned with pleasure and the things of this world
is the pursuit of a false dream. He states his conclusion in
the form of a rhetorical question in the second person singular
at 172 and offers exemplary proofs from the vicissitudes of the
nations and empires of the past in 173-175. Short, commonplace
metaphors, brief rhythmical clausulae, and clusters of questions
and answers abound. This passage could have been declaimed by
a student of Polemon:

$$\text{Μακεδονία πάλιν ἤνθησεν,}$$
$$\text{ἀλλὰ διαιρεθεῖσα}$$
$$\text{κατὰ μοίρας ἠσθένησεν,}$$
$$\text{ἕως εἰς τὸ παντελὲς ἀπεσβέσθη.}$$

This fast-paced catalogue of fallen glory ends with a final
question about the present in similarly Gorgianic style, employing Philo's favorite storm at sea imagery:

$$\text{καὶ συνελόντι φράσαι πᾶσα ἡ οἰκουμένη;}$$
$$\text{Οὐκ ἄνω καὶ κάτω κλονουμένη}$$

καὶ τινασσομένη
ὥσπερ ναῦς θαλαττεύουσα
τοτὲ μὲν δεξιοῖς
τοτὲ δὲ καὶ ἐναντίοις πνεύμασι χρῆται;

After this series of examples in question form, Philo presents
his major premise, a maxim about the cyclical dance of the divine
Logos that recalls similar maxims in Herodotus and Aristotle
(176). The conclusion is then re-stated and amplified. Philo
has presented us in t..is passage with a full-fledged rhetorical
epicheireme, a syllogism with all of the parts present and each
premise proven or illustrated in its turn, and with the conclusion at the beginning and repeated, with amplification, at the
end. This is the rhetorician's syllogism, not the logician's,
and even the examples brought in to prove the premises are put
in a highly ornamented rhetorical form. At 177, Philo amplifies further on his theme of mutability, this time picking up
the sea imagery from 175 and developing it more fully. In 179-
180, he is back with the figure of the road, which has dominated
the earlier part of this diatribe section (the whole of 140-183).
The conclusion of the essay as a whole comes in 181-183, with
Balaam and the personified Elenchos, the bad example that serves
as a warning and the divine reason that should serve as a guide
on the right road. While there is no summary of the contents
of the essay as a whole, as required by rhetorical theory, this
figure serves as a fitting conclusion to the spirit of *Deus*,
which combines exhortation with warnings in the vehement style
in most of the diatribe passages.

Like his teacher and the subject of his essays, Moses,
Philo expounds doctrine, offers praise of the Lord and His creation, admonishes the wicked and the ignorant, and exhorts the
audience to virtue and the pursuit of knowledge. He has many
styles, plain, florid, solemn, poetic, and vehement, and he
must have had many models, Plato and later Academics as well as
the Stoic-Cynic diatribists, but, in Philo, it strikes me that
the *tribōn* of the philosopher is almost always embroidered with
the fancy stitching of the poet, who needs a metaphor to
denounce even the least of the vices.

NOTES

[1]Cicero on his own technique in translating from textbook to dialogue style: *Ad Atticum* 12.52; 13.19; *De natura deorum* II.7.20; *De finibus* I.3.7-10; II.1.1-3; *De legibus* II.14-18.

[2]Rhetorical canons for the dialogue: Aristotle *Rhetoric* III.16; Demetrius *On Style* 19-21, 223-227, 296-298; Dionysius of Halicarnassus *De Demosthene* 2, 5-8; "Longinus" *On the Sublime* 32.5-8.

Poetic flights: Cicero *Somnium Scipionis*; Plutarch *De genio Socratis* 591A-529E; *Amatorius* 764D-765E; Dion Chrysostomus 36.39-61.

[3]I am taking as my main authorities for the diatribe style P. Wendland, *Philo und die Kynisch-Stoische Diatribe*, Berlin, 1895; R. Bultmann, *Der Stil der Paulinischen Predigt und die Kynisch-Stoische Diatribe* (in *Forschungen zur Religion und Literatur des Alten und Neuen Testaments* 13), Göttingen, 1910; and H. Thyen, *Der Stil der Jüdisch-Hellenistischen Homilie* (in *Forschungen zur Religion und Literatur des Alten und Neuen Testaments* 65), Göttingen, 1955. There is a recent discussion of the problem of the diatribe as a literary genre in G. Kustas, "Diatribe in Ancient Rhetorical Theory," *Center for Hermeneutical Studies in Hellenistic and Modern Culture: Colloquy* 22 (1976).

I prefer to regard the diatribe as a useful modern construct rather than as a recognized genre of classical rhetoric. The stylistic devices of authors like Teles, Maximus Tyrius, Epictetus, Musonius, and M. Aurelius are distinctive and tend not to occur in the same combinations in authors outside the tradition. When Philo uses the same devices in the same combinations, I think that it is useful to associate his style with theirs. The diatribe is, however, not the only way of dealing with philosophical themes rhetorically, nor is it even the only way of defending an ethical thesis in popular form. Writers like Cicero, Plutarch, Dion Chrysostomus, and Seneca have a much wider range and are capable of dealing with the same theme in various styles and genres. Some of their efforts resemble the diatribe style and some do not. The remarks of Synesius on Dion (Dion Chrysostomus, *Discourses*, V., ed. H. L. Crosby, London, 1951, pp. 364-387) are instructive in this respect; a late antique reader of great rhetorical sophistication finds Dion a very difficult author to classify according to the conventional types of the philosopher, the political orator, and the sophist. To solve the problem by classifying Dion as an author of diatribes did not occur to him.

[4]For Moses' various rhetorical aims, see *L.A.* I.93-101; II.67, 98, 105; III.244-245; *Gig.* 13, 38; *Deus* 32-33, 125; *Plant.* 128 ff.

[5]For solemnity and the associated stylistic devices, see Hermogenes *De ideis* I.6 (pp. 242 ff. Rabe); vehemence is discussed in I.8 (pp. 260 ff. Rabe).

[6]Cicero *Orator* 26.91-27.96. The importance of the Academic and Peripatetic schools in relation to the rhetorical treatment of philosophical themes, both in the origin of thesis declamations and in the development of the florid style is often neglected in discussions of possible models for Philo. Demetrius of Phaleron was not only an orator bred in the Peripatetic school, but a pioneer in the collection of chriae and apophthegmata, later mainstays of the so-called diatribe style.

[7]Zeno in Cicero *De natura deorum* II.8.22; Stoics generally in *De finibus* III.6.22; IV.27.75-76; Epictetus 4.5.16-18;

4.8.35-40. For Cicero's terminology in these passages, see
McCall, *Ancient Rhetorical Theories of Simile and Comparison*,
Camb., Mass., 1964, pp. 121-129.

[8]For Philo's nature imagery, cf. especially the breast
analogy in Lucretius *De rerum natura* 5.807-815. Cicero *De
natura deorum* II is replete with rhetorical amplification on
natural themes as are some of the essays in Seneca *Quaestiones
naturales*. Strabo mentions and partially illustrates the rhetorical fullness of Poseidonius' treatment of natural phenomena
in II.3.5 and III.2.9.

[9]Rhetorical questions: *On Ancient Medicine* III.49.54;
VII.1-16; Aristotle *An. post.* 89a11 ff.; *Topica* 158a28-30;
Dionysius *De Demosthene* 13; Strabo I.2.5; I.2.6; I.3.6. Dionysius and Strabo use questions in syllogistic arguments and
in refutations.
    Wir-Stil: On Ancient Medicine XIII.26 ff.; Aristotle
Topica 101b11; Strabo I.2.31; Pseudo-Aristotle *De mundo* 391b3-9;
394a7.

[10]Stoic: Cicero *De natura deorum* II.8.22; Epictetus
1.9.7; 1.14.10; 2.18.29.
    Elsewhere: Aristotle *Physica* 199b26-30; Dionysius *De
Demosthene* 37; I. Cor. 14.7-9; *De mundo* 6.398a6-398b14; 399b9;
400b25 (all without the question figure--question figures are
unusually rare in *De mundo*); Ptolemy *Tetrabiblos* I.2.5.
    The theory of the *a fortiori* comparison is dealt with
by Quintilian VIII.4.9-14, but all of his illustrations are
from courtroom speeches; Quintilian regards this as a figure
of amplification.

[11]See esp. Bultmann, *op. cit.*, pp. 20-46 and Thyen, *op.
cit.*, pp. 47-63.

[12]For *nun de*, see Bultmann, pp. 42 ff.

[13]For this image, cf. Plutarch *Praec. ger. reip.* 804E.
The strikingly similar epigrams in Plutarch and Philo may have
their origin in the commonplaces of the Hellenistic funerary
epigram, a number of examples, including one from the First
Century B.C.E., are collected by R. Lattimore *Themes in Greek
and Latin Epitaphs*, Urbana, Ill., 1962, pp. 195 ff.

[14]Stock metaphors: M. Aurelius 11,9, 20 (desertion);
Plato *Ion* 533D and Achilles Tatius I.17 (magnet); Plutarch *Numa*
16 (philtre).

[15]*Thumĕ*: Theognis 695-696; 1029-1036; *Psukhē*: M. Aurelius 2.6; 11.1; *Vita*: Seneca *Ad Marciam* 20.3; *Phantasia*: Epictetus 2.18.24.

[16]Personification of Pleasure: *Kakia*: Xenophon *Mem.*
II.1.21-34 (Prodicus); *Hēdonē*: Dion Chrysostomus 16.1; Maximus
Tyrius 14.1a ff.; Seneca *De vita beata* 11.2; 13.4-5 (*Voluptas*
and *Virtus*). This sort of personification is very common in
the diatribe tradition and in Philo (cf. *Elenchus* in *Deus* 181-
183); there is a discussion in Bultmann, p. 34.

[17]Master and Slave: Plutarch *Mor.* 46E, 692E; Epictetus
2.1.24-28; 3.24.66-77; 4.1.33 etc.

Measuring Stick: Theognis 805-810, 995-996; Pindar *Pythian* I.62; Demosthenes 18.296; Plutarch *Praec. ger. reip.* 807D; Epictetus 1.28.28.

D. *Rhetoric and Allegory*

Many of the terms and techniques of allegorical exegesis belong also to the rhetoricians and are sometimes attested earlier in rhetorical sources than in the surviving allegorists. Riddles, similes, analogies, metaphors, and name arguments are all found in the Greek literature on style from Book III of Aristotle's *Rhetoric* through Dionysius of Halicarnassus. *Rhetorica ad Herennium*, Cicero, and Quintilian provide further evidence, especially for allegory as extended comparison and allegory as a technique of indirection in political speeches and poetry. Philo and the rhetoricians appear to be speaking a common language and, if other evidence were lacking, it would seem reasonable to suppose that Philo applied his rhetorical training directly to his work as commentator. While this may be true of some of the details in Philo's exegesis, I think there is some reason to doubt that Philo is making any large-scale adaptation of rhetoric to the ends of allegory on his own. The Greek allegorical tradition, despite some important distinctions between Platonic and Stoic allegorizers, is remarkably consistent in its terminology and methods. The same groups of allegorical terms and characteristic phrases turn up in the Scholia to Homer, Pindar, and Aratus, in Heraclitus and Cornutus, in Philo and in Plutarch's *De Iside*. Some of these words and phrases are translated into Latin in Cicero's *De natura deorum* and appear also in the Neo-Platonic allegorists like Porphyry and Sallustius. When Heraclitus, Cicero, and Philo make similar comments about the "invented fables of the poets," or make similar arguments from etymology or from cases (*ptōseis*), it seems doubtful that any of them is being original. Indeed, the *physica ratio* of the Stoics produces similar etymologies of Kronos (from Khronos), similar explanations of the battle of the Gods with the giants, and similar interpretations of Homeric epithets like "swift Night" in many of the later authors in this tradition.[1]

Granted that Philo gets his terms and methodology partly from a pre-existing tradition and partly from his own knowledge of rhetoric and grammar, there is the further question of

Philo's awareness of the rhetorical perspective on allegory.
The rhetorical accounts of allegory, riddle, symbol, and similar
devices assume that all of these devices will be used deliberately by the author in order to communicate some message to his
audience indirectly. Indeed, the rhetorical textbook definition
of allegory, shared also by Heraclitus as a *starting* definition,
is saying one thing in order to communicate another.[2] There are
many techniques for doing this, but the one most often mentioned
by the theorists of style is extended metaphor or extended comparison. Both Quintilian and Heraclitus quote poems which
employ an extended use of the ship of state image as examples
of *literary* allegory. For the rhetorician, there are distinct
stylistic criteria for using and identifying allegory, a point
which is partially acknowledged in the allegorical tradition by
the frequent use of figurative analysis to identify an allegory
in Homer or Moses. There are also specific rhetorical ends for
the use of riddles and allegories. The most primitive and
obvious of these is represented by Hesiod's fable of the Hawk
and is actually stated in Phaedrus' collection of Aesop's
fables--to criticize the powerful indirectly. Since the fable,
myth or allegory may be interpreted in various ways by the
audience, it is up to the object of the criticism to admit that
it applies to him by taking offense. This is the root of the
type of political allegory discussed by Cicero and Quintilian,
an extended innuendo expressed in figurative language, often
with the names of important men concealed under mythical or
historical *personae*. When the rhetoricians speak of allegory
and *ainigma*, they refer above all to this type of allegory,
which was employed in political orations, in comedy and satire,
and even in letters written in politically dangerous times.[3]
Similarly, an allegory may be used to convey in brief or popular form a philosophical message that would otherwise require
a long dialectical proof or even a life-time's study. Dionysius
refers to Plato's use of allegory and the Stoics, from Zeno on,
seem to have been very fond of the extended comparison in their
teaching.[4] The secrets of a mystery religion may be recalled
for the initiate and at the same time protected by the use of
myths, symbols and allegories. The last of these motives
derived from subject matter is the probable source of a peculi-
arly rhetorical motive for allegory--allegory arouses fear,
reverence, and a sense of the mysterious in the audience. The

specific connection between rhetorical allegory and religion is
made in two Greek rhetoricians, Demetrius and Hermogenes.[5] For
Demetrius, allegory inspires awe because of its indirection and
ambiguity, because people are more frightened by hints and suggestions than by direct statements. The mysteries derive their
impressiveness from this technique, which inspires in the audience something like fear of the dark, since "allegory resembles
darkness and night." Hermogenes actually advises the use of
consistent allegory in order to achieve the rhetorical ideal of
Solemnity with religious or philosophical subject matter (the
Gods and their works, nature, the deeds of great men in which
the Gods took a hand). The rhetorical doctrine on allegory
implies an author with a message to be conveyed indirectly, a
stylistic effect to be achieved through figurative language,
and an audience that will recognize that something non-literal
is being said. The orator who uses these techniques must signal
clearly to his audience that he is shifting from the literal to
the figurative or the message will not be conveyed and the
audience will not be impressed.

        The allegorists vary considerably in the extent to
which they show an awareness of the rhetorical implications of
the type of analysis they employ. Heraclitus, Cornutus, and
the author of the Pseudo-Plutarchian *De vita et poesi Homeri*,
having once decided that Homer and Greek mythology contain a
systematic account of Greek philosophy, medicine, and natural
history, look for allegorical interpretations throughout the
text and not only in the obviously figurative passages. Heraclitus makes a clear distinction between literary allegory, for
which he quotes the textbook definition and a textbook example
from Archilochus, and the allegories in Homer. The poetic
allegories are mainly for stylistic effect and are subject to
more than one interpretation, whereas Homer is always clear and
systematic in his allegories. Allegory is not a mere figure
for Homer, but a consistent technique of philosophical instruction. For Demetrius, allegory must be ambiguous to work; for
Heraclitus it is important that Homer be represented as not
speaking in ambiguities or giving allegories that are subject
to debate.[6] As a consequence, the allegorist cannot rely mainly
on stylistic criteria for identifying allegories. The chief
criteria for the Greek allegorists are the resemblances between
the poet's "system" of myth and legend and the philosophical
system it is supposed to express and the existence of apparently

impious or inappropriate elements in the myths that demand
allegorical interpretation. If Homer has a representation of
the world on the Shield of Achilles, that must encode a philosophical world with similar subdivisions. If Homer represents
the gods at war, that must represent the conflicts among the
elements of which the world is made or the cosmic conflict
between intelligence and stupidity; this is determined both by
the symbolic significance of the gods involved and by the need
to refute the accusation that the story is blasphemous.[7] In
all of this, the rhetorical perspective on allegory tends to
get lost and it is often forgotten that Homer is an author com-
municating with an audience.

Plutarch and Philo both use the old Stoic system of
physical and ethical allegory and both accept the idea of systematic allegory in Egyptian myth or Jewish law, but both are
also aware of the problem of author and audience and take some
care in their explanations of how the allegorical message got
into the text. Plutarch's Egyptian priests do hint that their
wisdom is enigmatic by setting up sphinxes before their temples
as a sort of prooemium to the mysteries concealed in their
myths and rituals (*De Iside* 354C). Isis-Athena declares in the
inscription on her statue at Sais: "I am all that has been,
and is, and shall be, and my robe no mortal has yet uncovered."
The wisdom conveyed in the Egyptian lore is still a mystery even
after it has been interpreted allegorically and, like the inner
mysteries of Platonism itself, it is not perfectly grasped even
by the initiates. Plutarch has the advantage of defending and
explicating a body of myth and ritual rather than a single text;
he is at liberty to reject some versions of the myths entirely
and, like Philo, he discusses alternative interpretations more
than the Allegorists of Homer do. Perhaps the difference
between Plutarch and the Stoic allegorists is illustrated most
clearly by Plutarch's handling of the objectionable stories of
wanderings and dismemberments of the gods. The Stoics saved
these stories through physical allegory; Plutarch advances a
theory which explains both the stories and *how they came to be
told*. Isis and Osiris were once demi-gods, subject to the same
trials and tribulations, actions and passions as mortals. After
the sufferings hinted at in the myths, they were transformed
into demi-gods, but before her transformation, Isis herself
mixed in with the Egyptian rituals reflections (*eikonas*)
allegories (*huponoias*), and representations (*mimēmata*) of her

sufferings to serve as a lesson in piety and a consolation in
trouble for mankind. She is herself the author of the mysteries,
but clarity and system were less important to her purpose than
the permanent invitation and training offered by enigmas.[8] This
may help to explain Plutarch's marked preference for *ainigma* as
opposed to *allēgoria* in comparison to Heraclitus and Philo. In
fact, Plutarch refers to "allegory" mainly to criticize those
who place too much reliance on facile allegories derived from
the *physica ratio*. Plutarch's comparative method and his
interest in mysteries and enigmas impel him to take the problem
of defining a figurative or allegorical approach in his sources
more seriously than the Homeric allegorists.

One might almost say that Philo's problems were the
exact opposite of Plutarch's. Philo follows one text even more
closely than the Homeric allegorists and, unlike the Homeric
allegorists, he starts from the premise that there is nothing
mythical in Jewish law. Where the Homeric allegorists distinguish between the frivolous myths of the poets after Homer and
Homer himself and Plutarch distinguishes between fictional myths
and folk or religious myths as authorities, Philo has rejected
the idea of myth entirely and the greater flexibility of interpretation that goes along with it.[9] While Philo is capable of
going along for many pages of the type of unrhetorical allegorical exegesis performed by the Homeric allegorists, his
awareness of the problem of the author's intentions is evident
not only in certain programatic passages and asides, but even
in some of the formulae with which he introduces allegorical
interpretations. As a lawgiver, Moses has chosen the middle
way between a bald set of commandments and the myths and fic-
tions of the Greek poets (*Op.* I.1-3). In the law there is
nothing mythical or superstitious, nothing impious even in the
surface meaning, as Philo tries to prove through many a pains-
taking grammatical argument. Trivial or problematic elements
in the literal text are evidence for a deeper meaning, but
there are no combats, wanderings or bindings of the gods as in
Homer or Egyptian myth. In the law there is nothing to corrupt
or lead men astray and Plato's motives for banning the poets do
not apply. The main source of difficulty comes from passages
whose literal meaning seems to permit an inappropriate interpretation. Philo quarrels more with other interpreters than
with the surface meaning of his text, a contrast with the
Homeric allegorists.

In *De gigantibus* and *Quod Deus*, Philo makes a number of comments on Moses' intentions as an author. In *De gigantibus*, he twice makes the point that Moses does not use myths, once with a physical explanation of the supposedly mythical reference (*Gig.* 7-8) and again on Genesis vi.4, where he goes to some length to prove that the giants mentioned are not the giants of Greek mythology but the "earth-born" among men (58-61). In the latter passage there is an implicit comparison with Plato; both Plato and Moses banish the myths and representational art from their republics on the grounds that they are full of deception and lead men away from the truth. In this case an allegorical explanation of the problem passage is combined with the comparative method that Plutarch recommends in *De audiendis poetis*.[10] It would be contradictory of Moses to have introduced a myth, given his views on idols and the whole art of representation. One of Philo's most glaring *aporiai* in *Quod Deus* results from a similar conflict; on the one hand, Moses has clearly indicated that God is not like men, on the other hand, in Genesis, he seems to attribute mortal attributes to God in the course of his narrative. As in Plutarch, both his theology and his use of the comparative method told him that Moses could not have meant that God really had hands and feet, that God was really subject to mortal passions. For part of his solution to this difficulty, Philo appeals to Moses as teacher and law-giver, a Moses who speaks to all men, not only to the wise. Those who are more advanced in their rational and spiritual development will immediately see that God cannot literally be angry with his people, but Moses also wishes to persuade the dense and the ignorant to accept his laws. Moses sounds oddly like a Greek philosophical lawgiver or like Cicero in his *De legibus* and *De divinatione*, where superstition is refuted but permitted as a tool for the rulers who must legislate for the masses as well as for the wise.[11] He manipulates his two audiences through two types of emotional appeals, love of God for the wise and fear of punishment from an "angry" deity for the ignorant (*Deus* 60-68). Thus, the apparently inappropriate in the Genesis story is attributed to a calculated use of figurative language on Moses' part, aimed at a particular segment of his audience; this is a fairly sophisticated theory of how the allegories got into the text and there is nothing quite like it in the Homeric allegories. Homer is sometimes spoken of as "teaching" or "initiating" the Greeks,

but Moses not only teaches and reveals but also commands, warns,
advises and exhorts his hearers on various levels (*L.A.* I.96-
101).

      Philo also indicates his concern with this problem in
some of the formulae he uses to introduce allegorical interpretations. Philo accepts the term *allēgoria* from the Greeks and
the associated divisions of physical and ethical allegory, though
he uses these term far less often than Heraclitus. In contrast
to the Greeks, and above all in contrast to Plutarch, Philo
avoids *ainigma* terms in his Genesis commentary. These are
totally absent from *L.A.* I-II, and when they do occur in *L.A.*
III, it is in the context of an attack on the *ainigmatistai* and
Esebon, who represent for Philo speculative reason without divine
guidance. Riddles and probabilities are inherently untrustworthy
and Moses is warning us in Numbers 21.27-30 to trust in God
rather than in mortal guesswork (*L.A.* III.225-233). Elsewhere
Philo does make use of the *ainigma* terms, sometimes with an
expression of doubt about his own interpretation or when listing
alternative interpretations, sometimes quite casually, as in
some of the Homeric allegorists. In the Genesis commentary,
these terms are used rarely and often with a negative connotation, as in *Gig.* 58 and *Deus* 21, where *ainittomai* is used in
reference to hypothetical objectors who pose alternate and false
interpretations of the text. The casual use of *ainittomai* in
the sense of "allude" is more common in works like *De somniis*
and *De specialibus legibus*, but even in those texts the riddle
technique is not extolled as it is in Plutarch and some later
Platonists like Maximus Tyrius and Julian.

      For Philo, the riddle terminology simply does not fit
his conception of Moses as a divinely inspired lawgiver; Moses
is no Sphinx or Sibyl--his mode of prophecy and teaching is
quite different from that of the Egyptian priests and the Greek
oracles. The mysteries of Moses are approached through the
reason of those who are spiritually prepared and they are suggested through his legislation, not through enigmatic utterances.
In the law, the literal interpretation must also be valid; Moses
may speak to his audience on more than one level, but none of
the levels can be reduced to mere myth or riddle. Philo shows
a similar care in other formulae. He introduces divine speeches
from Genesis by saying that Moses speaks through the *persona* of
God; the words of God in the text are not literally transcribed

from a divine apparition, but spoken by the prophet, who translates from the *logos endiathetos* to the *logos prophorikos*.[12]
Philo repeatedly shows that he is aware of the rhetorical implications of an allegorical interpretation of Moses' words and,
unlike the Homeric allegorists, constantly keeps before us the
presence of Moses as an author speaking to an audience.

NOTES

[1]*Kronos* and *Khronos*: Heraclitus *Quaestiones Homericae*
41.6; Cicero *De natura deorum* II.25.64; Cornutus *De natura deorum*
II.142; Plutarch *De Iside* 363D.
        Gods and Giants: Heraclitus 52 ff.; Cicero II.28.70-71;
Cornutus XX.189.
        "Swift Night": Heraclitus 45.3-7; Plutarch *Moralia* 410D;
923B.
        The continuity of the Homeric allegory tradition is well
illustrated in F. Buffière, *Les Mythes d'Homère et la pensée
grecque*, Paris, 1956. There are occasional curious correspon-
dances of detail between Philo and pagan allegory. One of the
oddest is between Plutarch *De Iside* 364C and Philo *L.A.* II.67.
In both cases allegorical use is made of the observation that
the part of the eye that sees is black, a kind of physical paradox. In Plutarch it is the name of the land of Egypt, *Chemia*,
that is allegorized, while in Philo it is the Ethiopian woman,
whom Moses took to wife.

[2]Heraclitus 5.2, with illustrations in 5.3-11. Cf. the
definitions in Tryphon *On Tropes* 3 and Gregory of Corinth *On
Tropes* 1. In Latin, and of earlier date, see *Rhetorica ad
Herennium* 4.34.46 (*permutatio*) and Quintilian 8.6.44 ff.

[3]Phaedrus *Liber fabularum* III.1.33 ff.; Cicero *Ad Atticum* 2.19.5; 2.20.3; 7.13; Quintilian 6.3.69; 8.6.44-58.

[4]Dionysius of Halicarnassus *De Demosthene* 5-8; Cicero
De natura deorum II.8.22.

[5]Demetrius *On Style* 99-102, cf. 151, 241, 243; Hermogenes
De ideis I.6.

[6]Heraclitus 5.12-16.

[7]For Heraclitus' methods, see especially his account of
the battles of god with god and gods with giants in 52 ff. (cf.
Buffière, pp. 100-105 and 290 ff.). Cicero comments on a number
of aspects of allegorical method in *De natura deorum* Book II:
physical interpretation of myths (II.24.63 ff.), impiety and
inappropriateness as criteria for identifying allegories (II.
28.70-71), and systems of resemblances between mythical divisions
and the divisions of physics and ethics (II.23.60 ff.). For
comments on both pagan and Jewish allegory, see C. Siegfried,
Philo von Alexandria, Jena, 1875, pp. 160 ff., S. G. Sowers, *The
Hermeneutics of Philo and Hebrews*, Zurich, 1965, pp. 11-27, and
I. Christiansen, *Die Technik der allegorischen Auslegungswissenschaft bei Philon von Alexandrien* (Beiträge zur Geschichte
der biblischen Hermeneutik 7), Tübingen, 1969. The last is

interesting as an attempt to relate Philo's method to the
technique of division in Platonic dialectic.

[8]Plutarch *De Iside* 361D-E. For Plutarch as an allegorist, see A. B. Hersman, *Studies in Greek Allegorical Interpretation*, Chicago, 1906, esp. pp. 25-38.

[9]Philo's rejection of myth: *Op.* 1-3, 157; *Gig.* 7-8,
58-61.

[10]Plutarch's comparative method for ethical analysis of
poetry: *De audiendis poetis*, esp. 14E-17F and 19A-20E.

[11]Cicero *De legibus* I.43 (friendship and fellowship of
all rational beings as the motive for just actions), but II.16
(usefulness of the fear of divine punishment in enforcing the
laws) and II.27-31 (various primitive features of Roman religion
defended as deterrents to crime or examples of virtue). *De
divinatione* II.42-43, 54, 70-71 (political control through types
of divination that don't actually work).

[12]Philo *Op.* 72 (*eisagei gar ton patera ton holōn tauti
legonta*), *Deus* 23 and 109 (*ek prosōpou tou theou*). The first
is certainly a metaphor from drama; the second may be interpreted
differently, as in H. A. Wolfson, *Philo*, Camb., Mass., 1947, II, pp.
36-43. The whole question of prophecy in Philo is a very complex one; it seems to me that Philo is sometimes referring to
Moses as an author who introduces divine speeches in his own
words and sometimes attributing the words themselves miraculously to direct divine interference with the vocal cords of the
prophet (as at *Spec.* IV.49 and *Her.* 263-266). The need to distinguish the various types of utterance in the Law would be, at
any rate, an additional motive for Philo's awareness of Moses as
an author.

APPENDIX

Allegorical Terms in the Greek Tradition and Philo

This tabulation of the allegorical terms and characteristic phrases used by Heraclitus, Plutarch, and Philo is
intended to provide evidence for the consistency and continuity
of the tradition and also for the deviations from it in Plutarch
and Philo. Heraclitus represents the standard Stoic approach to
Homeric allegory, while Plutarch relies on Pythagorean and Platonic as well as Stoic methods and has a comparative approach to
mythology all his own. Philo uses much of the technical appar-
atus of the Homeric allegorists, but follows up a single text
more consistently and has a special view of the relationship
between the literal and the allegorical meanings in that text.
Like Plutarch, Philo makes specific reference to Pythagorean
allegory (*Op.* 100, cf. *L.A.* I.15) and uses numerological as well

as "physical" interpretations. Such numerological interpretations are common in Plutarch (*De Iside* 373F-374B, 376E-F, cf.
De E 387F-391E) and are also found in the Pseudo-Plutarchan *De
Vita et poesi Homeri*, but are rare or absent in Heraclitus,
Cicero *De natura deorum* II, and Cornutus. Both Philo and Plutarch are more eclectic in their modes of interpretation and
admit more controversy than the Homeric allegorists. *L.A.* I-II
has been chosen over *Gig.* and *Deus* for the comparison, since in
that work Philo is more consistently involved with allegorical
interpretations and has fewer axes to grind than in the works
covered by the commentary. Heraclitus, Plutarch's *De Iside*, and
Philo *L.A.* I-II are of approximately equal length and are comparable in the degree to which they pursue allegorical method.
Philo's allegorical terms in *Gig.* and *Deus* are listed at the
end of the comparative table.

        Philo's corpus is very extensive and his use of terms
changed with time and with his aims in the various works. Where
a term is absent from *L.A.* I-II, but occurs elsewhere in Philo,
I have marked the entry with an asterisk. The three works are
similar in scope and length, but Philo *L.A.* I-II is slightly
longer than Heraclitus and Plutarch *De Iside*.

        All three of our allegorists share a common terminology
for physical and ethical allegory, for the analysis of the meaning of proper names and epithets in their sources, and an interest in playing on the Greek terminology of mystery religion (con-
cealing and revealing) as a model for the process of allegorical
interpretation and the intentions of the author to be interpreted.
I think that, on the whole, the mechanics of allegorical interpretation are similar in all three authors, and that, so far as
they employ grammatical, etymological, physical, and ethical
interpretations, Philo and Plutarch are drawing upon the same
tradition as Heraclitus. There are, however, some important
divergences from this tradition in both Plutarch and Philo.
Plutarch and Philo make much more extensive use of the term
eikōn, the earthly, mythological or religious image of a form
or an idea, than the Stoic allegorists do. In Heraclitus, this
term is used only of the shield of Achilles, interpreted as an
image the universe, a legitimate use of the term for a Stoic;
in Philo and Plutarch, the term is used much more broadly, even
of the religious stories themselves as containing images or
representations of the Platonic forms. The terms *mimēma*,

	Heraclitus *Quaestiones Homericae*	Plutarch *De Iside*	Philo *Legum allegoriae I-II*
Terms for the essential activity of the author or interpreter of a text to be allegorized:			
ainigma	1	5	---*
ainigmatōdēs	1	1	---*
ainittomai	4	13	---*
proainittomai	1	---	---
hypainittomai	4	---	---*
allegoria	19	---	---*
allegorikos	15	---	---*
allegoreō	25	2	2
hyponoia	---	3	---*
hyponoeō	---	3	---*
The Levels of Allegory:			
physikos	23	2	10
ēthikos	2	1	5
psykhikos	---	---	9
Analysis of Proper Names and Epithets:			
onoma	9	42	24
onomazō	46	25	8
eponomazō	1	2	---*
eponymos	9	4	---*
prosrēma	---	1	---
homonymos	2	---	---*
paronymos	---	1	---
patronymikos	1	---	---
polyonymos	---	---	1
myrionymos	---	1	---
synonymos	---	---	1
prosēgoria	1	3	---*
prosagoreuō	18	13	---*

	Heraclitus *Quaestiones Homericae*	Plutarch *De Iside*	Philo *Legum allegoriae I-II*
Interpretation of Names, Words, and Images:			
hermēneuō	1	2	8
hermēneia	2	---	---*
hermēneus	3	---	1
hermēneutikos	---	1	1
methermēneuō	---	2	---
diermēneuō	---	1	---*
exermēneuō	---	2	---
katakhrēstikos	---	---	1
metalēptikos	2	---	---
metaphorikos	1	--- (but	---
tropikos	---	*metapherō* twice)	2
analogos	---	---	1
analogeō	---	---	2
eikōn	2	9	15
mimēma	---	6	5
symbolon	2	6	6
symbolikos	4	4	6
sēmainō	8	9	1
diasēmainō	1	---	---*
huposēmainō	10	---	---*
sēmeion	3	---	3
Myths:			
muthos	12	14	---*
muthikos	5	---	---*
muthōdēs	1	4	1
mutheuō	4	---	1
muthologia	---	3	---
muthologeō	---	10	---
muthopoiia	---	---	1
mutheuma	---	1	---
Mystery Language:			
aporretos	1	4	1
amuetos	1	---	1
epopteuō	1	---	---
epoptes	---	---	---*
epoptikos	---	1	---
hierophantēs	1	---	---*
hierophanteō	1	---	---*
mustagōgos	---	1	---*

	Heraclitus *Quaestiones Homericae*	Plutarch *De Iside*	Philo *Legum alle-goriae I-II*
Mystery Language:			
mustērion	---	---	1
musteriōdēs	---	1	---
mustēs	1	---	---*
mustikos	2	2	---*
orgia	1	---	---*
teletai	2	4	---*
hoi teloumenoi	1	2	---*
Revealing and Concealing:			
amudros	1	2	---*
anaptussō	---	---	---*
anaptuxis	---	1	1
apophainō	11	8	2
dēloō	17	7	13
prodēloō	---	1	---*
hupodēloō	---	4	---*
emphainō	---	12	5
emphanēs	2	3	1
emphasis	---	3	---*
enargēs	8	2	1
kalumma	---	---	1
kaluptō	---	---	---*
apokaluptō	---	1	1
epikaluptō	---	---	1
parakaluptō	---	3	---
perikaluptō	---	2	1
kruptō	---	3	1
epikruptō	---	1	1

aporroia, paradeigma (in its Platonic sense), and *huponoia* are found in close connection with *eikōn* in Plutarch, and these are specifically Platonic terms avoided by Heraclitus. Plutarch and Philo seem to be drawing upon Platonic and Pythagorean methods of interpretation as well as the Stoic tradition. A further distinction may be drawn between Philo on the one hand and the Greek allegorists on the other. Philo, at least in the Genesis commentary, seems to be hostile to the riddle terminology favored by Plutarch and common throughout the Greek tradition, and also rejects mythology, both literary and religious.

Allegorical Terms and Phrases in
  Gig. *and* Deus

        De gigantibus: *ainittomai* (58), *onoma* (16, 17, 62),
onomazō (6), *metonomazō* (50, 54, 62, 63), *homonymia* (56),*her-*
mēneuō (62 bis, 66), *sēmeion* (33), *muthos* (7, 60), *mutheuō* (58),
muthoplastein (58), *hierophantēs* (54), *mueisthai* (57), *mustēs*
(54), *orgia* (54), *teletai* (54), *anaptussō* (36), *apophainō* (2,
33), *dēloō* (19, 23, 34), *enargēs* (39), *katapetasma* (53 and *pro-*
kalumma), *apokaluptō* (32, 35, 39), *diaporeō* (1), *protrepei* (32),
hupographei (23, 66).

        Quod Deus: *ainittomai* (21), *huponoein* (104), *onoma*
(86, 103, 141), *hermēneuō* (5 bis, 137), *lexis* (141, 142), *ptōsis*
(141), *sumbolon* (96, 128), *sumbolikos* (96), *hierophantēs* (156),
hierophanteō (62), *mueisthai* (61), *mustēria* (61), *amudros* (43),
dēloō (45, 51, 103, 104, 128), *emphainei* (129), *emphanēs* (37),
enargēs (1, 4, 10, 14, 87), *diaporeō* (104), *epipherei* (124),
hupographei (79, 95).

Other Sources for Allegorical
  Terminology

        Cicero *De natura deorum* II.: *nomen* (II.61, 62, 64, 66
ter, 67 bis, 71, 72 bis), *nominare* (61, 62, 66 bis, 67 bis, 68,
69 bis), *appellare* (60, 61, 62, 64 bis, 72), *casus = ptōsis*
(II.25.64 quem conversis casibus appellamus a iuvando Iovem),
similitudo (38, 66, 70), *physicus* (23, 63, 64, 70), *fabula* (64,
66, 70, 71), *mysteria* (62), *id est = toutesti* (64 bis).

        Cornutus *De natura deorum*: *ainigma* (35), *ainittomai*
(1, 7, 17 bis, 18, 27, 28, 30, 32), *allēgoria* (2), *allēgorikos*
(2), *huponoia* (34), *huponoein* (18, 24, 31, 34, 35), *physikos*
(19 bis, 35), *onoma* (14, 16, etc. 11 times), *onomazō* (1 bis, 4,
5, etc., 34 times), *onomasia* (9, etc., 7 times), *eponomazō* (6,
20 bis, 22, 30, 34 bis), *exonomazō* (2), *prosonomazō* (32),
homonymia (14, 16), *prosēgoria* (1, 13, etc., 6 times), *pros-*
agoreuō (9, 11, etc., 21 times), *etymologia* (1), *etymologeō*
(1, 32), *dusetymologeō* (20), *kat'antiphrasin* (16, 35), *sumbolon*
(9, 14, 16 bis, 20, 30, 31, 33, 35), *sēmeion* (16, 33), *sēmainō*
and *episēmainō* (6, 16 bis), *muthos* (2, 6, etc., 10 times),
muthikos (17, 35), *mutheuō* (3, 6, etc., 14 times), *muthologia*
(8), *muthopoiia* (17), *aporrētos* (30), *epoptēs* (9, 34), *mustēria*

(28 bis), *orgia* (30), *emphainō* (16, 17, etc., 13 times), *em-phasis* (15, 34), *dia to* plus inf. (6, 12, 13, 14, etc., fre-quent), *apo* plus gen. (14, etc., very frequent in introducing an interpretation), *hoionei* (1, 6, 16, etc.), *toutesti* (14, 17, etc.), *hōsperei* (18, 20).

     Pseudo-Plutarch *De vita et poesi Homeri* 91-128: *ainigma* (92), *ainittomai* (100, 102, 126, 201), *allēgorikos* (102), *allē-goreō* (96), *huponoia* (92), *physikos* (92, 108, 109, 144, 218), *onoma* (103, 123, 127 bis, 128, 175 bis, 183), *onomazō* (133, 182), *prosagoreuō* (95, 99, 104, 107, 124, 126, 128, 131 bis, 148), *analogia* (99), *analogos* (102), *eikōn* (150, 182), *sumbolon* (212 bis), *sēmainō* (92, 93, 103, 114, 131, 200, 212), *sēmeion* (202), *muthos* (101), *muthikos* (92), *muthōdēs* (114), *apokaluptō* (214), *aporrētos* (187), *epikruptō* (213), *kruptō* (209), *apophainō* (123, 130, etc., 9 times), *dēloō* (94, 103, etc., 15 times), *diasaphei* (130, 138), *emphainō* (92, 102, 109, 110, 116, 131, 166, 169 bis, 217), *enargēs* (91, 118, 123, 182, 207), *epipherei* (142, 217), *toutesti* (96, 97, 102, 104, etc., 12 times).

     In addition to describing Homer as "teaching" the Greeks, an idea which is common to all of the Homeric allegorists and Philo's Moses, the author of this treatise describes Homer as bearing witness (*marturei* 138, 168, 172, 175), advising (*parai-nei* 129, 149, 165, 178, 198, 213), and exhorting (*protrepei* 168). This closely parallels Philo's terminology for Moses' intentions as an author of works requiring interpretation, but is not typi-cal of the other Greek allegorists. It indicates a greater awareness of Homer as an author addressing himself to an audience than is usual in this sort of interpretation (contrast Heracli-tus and the remains of Stoic allegory).

     Elsewhere in Plutarch: *De aud. poet.* 19E (*allēgoria* and *huponoia*); *De E ainigma* (389A), *ainittesthai* (389A), *hupo-noein* (386A, 391C), *physikos* (387B), *onoma* (386B, 388F, 391A, 393C, 394D), *onomazō* (385F, 388F, 389A, 393C), *eponomazō* (388A), *prosagoreuō* (392A), *prosagoreusis* (392A bis), *eikōn* (391C, 393D), *sumbolon* (386B, 391C), *sēmainō* (392A), *sēmeion* (387E), *apomimoumenon* (388D), *homoiotēs* (388A), *amudros* (391E), *apo-phainō* (391F), *dēloō* (386E), *emphasis* (393E), *kruptō* (388F), *mutheuma* (389A); *ainigma*, *allēgoreō*, *emphainō*, *prosēgoriai*, *sumbolikos*, etc., in fr. 157.

Scholia to Aratus (E. Maas, *Commentariorum in Aratum Reliquiae*, Berlin, 1968): *ainigmatōdēs* p. 356, *ainittesthai* pp. 335, 350, 359, 429, 541, *allēgorikos* p. 386, *sumbolon* pp. 343, 423, 494, 497, 533, 534.

Iamblichus *Protrepticus*: *ainittomai* (21 three times), *onoma* and *onomazō* (21), *hermēneia* (21), *eikōn* (21), *sumbolon* (20, 21, very frequent, in reference to the Pythagorean "*sumbola*"), *muthos* (17), *dēloō* (8, 10, 20), *emphainō* (20, 21).

Porphyry *Cave of the Nymphs*: *ainigma* (21, 32), *ainittomai* (1, 3, 5, 18, 23, 31, 36), *allēgoreō* (3, 4), *onoma* (28), *eponomazō* (6, 35), *episēmainō* (19), *eikōn* (6, 12, 21, 32, 34, 36), *sumbolon* (4, 5 bis, 6, 7, 9, 10, 13 ter, 14, 15, 16, 17 bis, 18, 19, 21, 27, 29, 31, 32 bis), *sumbolikos* (4).

Sallustius *On the Gods and the World*: *ainigma* (6.4), *ainittomai* (4.1, 8), *theologikos* (4.1), *physikos* (4.1, 2), *psykhikos* (4.1), *hylikos* (4.1), *miktos* (4.1), *mimēsis* (15.2), *mimeomai* (3.3 bis, 4.10, 7.3, 15.2), *homoiotēs* (3.1, 14.2, 15.2), *anomoiotēs* (3.1, 14.2), *sēmainō* (9.6), *muthos* (3.1 quater, 2 bis, 3 ter, 4 bis; 4.1 bis, 2, 4, 6, 7, 10, 11 bis), *muthologeō* (4.11), *teletai* (3.1, 12.6), *dēloō* (4.5), *kruptō* (3.3 bis), *phaneron* and *phainomenon* in opposition to the preceding (3.3), *epikruptō* (3.4), *prokalumma* (3.4).

J. Leopold

E. *Philo's Use of* Topoi

Given the intellectual and educational milieu in Philo's
Alexandria, it is hardly surprising to find *topoi* in his works,
particularly in works which are generally conceded to be "rhetorical," as is the case with, e.g., *Quod Omnis Probus Liber*.
However, *topoi* are found also in the allegorical works, including *Gig.* and *Deus*. Moreover, the presence of several distinct
kinds of *topoi* in those works and the various uses to which they
are put suggest, among other things, that current notions of the
nature of *topoi* may be in need of revision if we are ever to
understand properly Philo's exegetical and argumentative pro-
cedures.[1]

Topoi

The conception of *topos* as nothing more than a "motif,"
a fixed and established cliché, not only makes it impossible to
see how Philo used *topoi*; it also fails to do justice to the
rich rhetorical tradition concerning *topoi* as storehouses or
places for invention which had developed by his time.

In a superficial way, it is possible to distinguish two
senses of "*topos*" (or *locus*) in Hellenistic sources: (a) *topos/
locus* as *sedes argumentorum* or ἀφορμὴ πίστεως (or ἐπιχειρήματος);[2]
and (b) *topos/locus* as a standard "topic" on which an orator
might or should speak, given the appropriate opportunities or
circumstances.[3] The functions of the former sort might con-
veniently be characterized as "analytic"; those of the latter as
"cumulative."[4] A close examination of the sources reveals a
more complex picture yet, as, on the one side, the traditional
dialectical *topoi* seem to be the most purely analytic; and, on
the other, the stock epithets, exempla, and themes for amplification are the most purely cumulative and commonplace. Between
these extremes lie the so-called philosophical *topoi* (divided
into theoretical and practical),[5] and "stasiastic" *topoi* (which
can control the arrangement of a discussion as well as supply
special topics on which the orator may hold forth).[6] Instead of
a simple notion of *topos*, therefore, the tradition distinguishes

among a variety of "topical" types and uses, none of which could
fairly be called a cliché.

Topoi in Philo: A Conspectus

        An awareness of that variety enables us to approach the
topoi in *Gig.* and *Deus* in a more refined way than previous commentators have done. To that end, we may survey the *topoi* in
Gig. and *Deus* under three broad headings, beginning with that
which most closely corresponds to the notion of *topos* as a
stereotyped formula:

        I. *"Commonplaces"*. Philo makes extensive use of common-
place comparisons and similes, exempla, and themes in *Gig.* and
Deus. Of the comparisons and similes, we might note, for
example, the sea "imagery" (cf., e.g., *Gig.* 51; *Deus* 26, 98, 129,
177) which, though in places evidently traceable to passages in
Homer or Plato, is in fact to be found all over in Hellenistic
literature.[7] Light imagery (cf. *Deus* 3, 46, 78, 129, 135), the
image of the road (*Deus* 61, 142, 159f.), and athletics (*Deus*
36), all by Philo's time commonplace,[8] appear also. Secondly,
proverbs (e.g., *Deus* 75: μηδενὸς ἀνθρώπων τὸν ἀπὸ γενέσεως ἄχρι
τελευτῆς βίον ἄπταιστον ἐξ ἑαυτοῦ δραμόντος; and cp. *Deus* 90),
commonplace themes (e.g., *Gig.* 14 and 28 on the uncertainty of
ἀνθρώπινα πράγματα; *Deus* 27 ff. on the fickleness of man), and
chriai (*Gig.* 33 f., of Diogenes; and *Deus* 146, of Socrates) are
all used by Philo in the development of his argument.[9] Thirdly,
there are apparent "school cases" (e.g., *Deus* 101, on "deposits"
and perhaps *ibid.* 90, the tale of the farmer unexpectedly finding a treasure) and topical groupings (*Gig.* 51; *Deus* 58-9,
173 ff.) and lists: e.g., *Deus* 149 ff., which is reminiscent
of stock epideictic *topoi*,[10] and *ibid.* 17 f., a list which,
though perhaps "Stoic" in origin, is by Philo's time commonplace.[11] These latter are more or less "philosophical" in
origin usage and bring us to our second set of *topoi*.

        II. *Philosophical* topoi. These are generally traceable
to a philosopher or to a school but had become commonplace in
Philo's time. The idea that philosophy is a preparation for
death (cf. *Gig.* 14, *Deus* 159 f.) is common in Hellenistic writings, as are also the themes of the constancy of the sage (cf.
Deus 22) and that of the burden of the flesh (*Gig.* 31, *Deus*
143).[12] The theme of "the two ways" (*Deus* 49 f., 61, etc.),

the notion of virtue as a mean (*Deus* 164 ff.), of God needing
nothing (*Deus* 56), and of the kinds of *psychai* (*Deus* 35 ff.) may
also be considered not as transmissions of doctrine but as
instances of the use of philosophical commonplaces.[13] In at
least one case--*Deus* 30, the analogy between parent and offspring
and the craftsman and his product--we see a commonplace performing a distinct argumentative role, as Δῆλον μὲν οὖν . . . ἐπι-
στήμονα εἶναι δεῖ . . . supplies a major premise for Philo's
argument that οὖτε γὰρ ἄδηλον οὖτε μέλλον οὐδὲν θεῷ.

III. *"Dialectical"* topoi. These go back to the lists
of *topoi* collected by Aristotle in his *Topics* and in those parts
of the *Rhetoric* devoted to the so-called *koinoi topoi*.[14] In
Gig. and *Deus* there are three such dialectical *topoi* which are
noteworthy:

(a) "from etymology." Cf. *Deus* 42 (αἴσθησις from εἴσθεσις) and *ibid.* 103 (βίαιον from βαιόν). Etymology was not
only an instrument of allegorical exegesis but part and parcel
of the standard way of dealing with written texts in rhetorical
settings,[15] and a long-recognized source of arguments in the
rhetorical tradition. It is a common argumentative "move" in
Philo.[16]

(b) *ek to mallon kai hētton*. The argument "from the
greater and lesser" was also isolated by rhetoricians as a line
of argument, and appears frequently in the works of Philo and
his contemporaries.[17] Two good examples of the use of this
topos are: *Deus* 26: ὅπου γοῦν ἀνθρώπων ψυχὴ . . . εἴ τ' ἐν-
δοιάζεις, ὅτι ὁ ἄφθαρτος καὶ μακάριος . . . ; *ibid.* 78: ἢ
νομίζεις ἄκρατον μὲν τὴν ἡλίου φλόγα μὴ δύνασθαι θεαθῆναι . . .
τὰς δὲ ἀγενήτους ἄρα δυνάμεις ἐκείνας, . . . ἀκράτους περινοῆσαι
δύνασθαι; Cf. also *Deus* 8 where an argument for approaching
temples with purified minds is based upon the observation that
one may not enter a temple without cleansing one's body.

(c) *ex enantiōn*. This *topos*, too, is fairly common in
Philo and is of particular interest in *Gig.* and *Deus* since it
serves not only as an exegetical tool but also as an armature
for Philo's homily.[18]

(1) Philo grounds his explanation of the two parts
of *Gen* 6:1 (at *Gig.* 1-3, 4-5) on *topoi ex enantiōn*, chiefly τῷ
γὰρ ἐναντίῳ τὰ ἐναντία πέφυκέ πως μάλιστα γνωρίζεσθαι at §3 *fin.*

and ἀμήχανον γὰρ τὰ αὐτὰ πρὸς τῶν ἐναντίων, ἀλλὰ μὴ τὰ ἐναντία
πάλιν γενέσθαι at the end of §5.[19] In sec. 1-3, Philo manipulates the contrariety *topos* by juxtaposing different kinds of
contrariety: "rare" *vs.* "abundant" is a contrariety of a different order form "just" *vs.* "unjust," for instance. But the
differences in kinds of contrariety discussed by rhetoricians[20]
can be overlooked in view of the belief that the just are few
(cp. *Migr.* 59 f., citing *Deut.* 7:7), which may itself have been
a "philosophical" *topos.* As for sec. 4-5, the principle of
contrariety there is coherent.

          (2) *Deus* 122 ff. Probably inspired by his text of
Gen. 6:11 (ἐφθάρη ἡ γῆ ἐναντίον τοῦ θεοῦ), Philo introduces one
of the *topoi ex enantiōn*: ἐπειδὰν ἐν ψυχῇ τὸ ἄφθαρτον εἶδος ἀνατείλῃ, τὸ θνητὸν εὐθέως φθείρεται, κτλ. This topos is the
"backbone" of the curious exegesis of *Lev.* 13:14-15 which follows
in this part of *Deus.*[21]

          From the brief conspectus we have given, it is obvious
that, although Philo uses a number of "formulaic motifs" and
stereotyped schemes of rhetorical development, it is not the
case (as many scholars have been inclined to assume) that he
simply transmits those formulas. Philo's reliance on *topoi* is
understandable, and not only because he was a product of his
times, when rhetoric was nothing if not pervasive. He was,
after all, seeking both to communicate and support his interpretations and, moreover, to impress upon his audience both the
historical and ethical importance of the passages from the Pentateuch which are the subjects of his treatises. As common
"places," *topoi* served both as familiar references which rang
true without explicit argumentative support and as argumentative
premises which no audience could find easy to deny. Thus, the
interpretations Philo offers are rendered plausible by as much
as they are grounded on what his audience already knows and
accepts. Philo's intentions, in short, may have been in some
sense philosophical. But--as with many philosophers of his era--
his methods were thoroughly rhetorical.

NOTES

[1]The most firmly established (and hence most frequently
encountered) conception is that which understands by "*topos*" a
formulaic or stereotyped motif which remains constant as it is
transmitted from author to author. See, for example,

R. Volkmann, *Die Rhetorik der Griechen und Römer in systema-
tischer Übersicht* (Leipzig,[2] 1885) (esp. at pp. 266 ff. and
320 ff.); E. Pflugmacher, *Locorum communium specimen* (diss.
Greifswald, 1909); E. Norden, *Die germanische Urgeschichte in
Tacitus Germania* (Leipzig, 1920); J. Martin, *Zur Quellenfrage
in den Annalen und Historien* (*Würzburger Studien* 9 [1936]),
etc. In the last century--as indeed in the present--the discovery of *topoi* in Philo was an indispensable way of tracing
influences. Cf., above all, P. Wendland, *Philo und die kynische-
stoische Diatribe* (Berlin, 1895); H. von Arnim, *Quellenstudien
zu Philo von Alexandria* (*Philol. Unters.* XI: Berlin, 1888).
This notion of *topos*-as-cliché persists (cf., e.g., K. Thraede,
Grundzüge griechisch-römischer Brieftopik, Zetemata 48 [Munich,
1970]; H. Fischel, *Rabbinic Literature and Graeco-Roman Philosophy* [Leiden, 1973]) despite recent critiques: see E. Mertner,
"Topos und Commonplace," *Strena Anglica*: Otto Richter zum 80.
Geburtstag, ed. G. Dietrich and F. W. Schultze (Halle, 1956),
pp. 178-224 (repr. in P. John [ed.], *Toposforschung* [Frankfurt,
1972], pp. 20-68).

[2]Cf., e.g., Cicero, *Topica* ii.8; Alex. Numenius and
Neokles in *Anon. Seguer.*, pp. 448.23 ff., L. Spengel, *Rhetores
Graeci* I (Leipzig, 1853) (repr. Minerva GmbH, Frankfurt/Main,
1966).

[3]Cicero, *de Orat.* III.27.106 ff.; Aphthonius, *Progymn.*
7 (pp. II.32 Sp; I.80 ff. Walz); Theon, *Progymn.* 7: Τόπος ἐστὶ
λόγος αὐξητικὸς ὁμολογουμένου πράγματος ἤτοι ἁμαρτήματος ἢ
ἀνδραγαθήματος (p. II.106 Sp; I.222 Walz). Such *topoi* come
close to the modern sense of "commonplace" and are spoken of
disparagingly by Quintilian at, e.g., II.4.28 ff., where he says
that "they were trotted out so frequently that they became old
pieces of furniture which no one wanted to set eyes on again."
Such themes as "the fickleness of fortune" and the "degeneracy
of the present age," stock *loci* concerning envy, poison, and the
desire of criminal parents for innocent children, descriptions
of shipwrecks or of the torture inflicted upon a woman by a
tyrant apparently became too common. But the fact that some
loci appear so often in what remains of the literature of
Antiquity should not prompt us to imagine that their appearance
in a speech would have affected the audience the way it did
Quintilian. We have to bear in mind that the very "commonness"
of Hellenistic commonplaces was precisely what made them rhetorically effective. An oral culture such as the one in which
Philo flourished puts a premium on expected performances, looking for proficiency, not originality. Moreover, such λόγοι
αὐξητικοί do not really become hackneyed until they are separated
from any actual argumentative situation.

[4]For this distinction, see W. J. Ong, *The Presence of
the Word* (Yale, 1967), pp. 79 ff. The distinction is clear,
however, in Quintilian V.10.20 and X.5.12 (cf. I.11.12).

[5]Such *topoi* are frequently treated in connection with
theoretical and practical θέσεις. See Cicero, *de Orat.* III.
106 ff. (Crassus speaking); Theon *Progymn.* 12 (II.120 ff. Sp;
I.242 ff. Walz), where Hermagoras and Theodorus of Gadara are
also mentioned; *Anon. Seguer.*, *loc. cit.* for Neokles, etc.
That these *topoi* were recognized as part of rhetorical invention
is clear from, e.g., Seneca, *Controv.* I.7.17: Cicero, *Tusc.*
I.4.7, II.3.9; Tacitus *Dial.* 30, etc. On philosophical "theses"

in rhetorical schools, cf. G. Reichel, *Quaestiones Progymnas-maticae* (Leipzig, 1909), pp. 99 ff.

[6]This class of *topoi* was derived from the *status causae*: for the conjectural issue, for instance, there are *loci ex causa*, *ex persona*, and *ex facto* (Cicero, *de Inv.* II.5.16-12.38 f., for instance). Quintilian gives a rather more exhaustive list at V.10.53 ff. As these *loci* became formalized, they provided (as the authors of the handbooks intended) "check lists" and could be used as armatures upon which a speaker could shape his case. Hence, stock topics emerged for the διήγησις/*narratio* (cf., e.g., Quintilian IV.2.52 ff.), for encomium (cf. Hermogenes *Progymn.* 7 [pp. II.11 f. Sp; I.35 ff. Walz]; Menander Rhet. διαίρ. ἐπιδ. I.631 Walz), etc. The stock topics associated with the *status causae* were systematized by Hermagoras, whose authority prevails among Hellenistic rhetoricians; but the tradition of such stock topics goes back much further in time (cf., e.g., Aristotle, *Rhetoric* I.5 ff.; Anaximenes *Rhet. ad Alex.* 7.2, 1428a 17 ff.).

[7]Cf., e.g., Seneca *Controv.* 7.14, 8.6; *Suas.* 3.2; (Pseud. Dion.) *Technē* 10.17; Lucian *Tox.* 19, *Hermot.* 28; Lucan 5.597 ff.; Seneca *Ep. Mor.* 108.37. M. P. O. Morford surveys a great deal of storm-at-sea material in his *The Poet Lucan* (Oxford: Blackwell, 1967), chs. 3-4. For further citations, see commentary below.

[8]All of these similes were used by the Stoics (cf. K.-H. Rolke, *Die bildhaften Vergleiche in den Fragmenten der Stoiker von Zenon bis Panaitios*, Spudasmata 32 [Hildesheim, 1975], *passim*); but light "imagery" appears elsewhere, particularly in religious texts (cf. M. Nilsson *Acta Inst. Romani R. Sueciae* xv [1950] 96 ff. [= *Opuscula* III. 189 ff.]). Imagery of the road is to be found in Greek literature at least from Xenophon on; but it also appears in Jewish Wisdom literature (cf. J. Laporte, "Philo in the Tradition of Wisdom" in *Aspects of Wisdom in Judaism and Early Christianity*, ed. R. Wilken (Notre Dame, 1975), p. 132 ff., and B. Otzen, "Old Testament Wisdom Literature and Dualistic Thinking in Late Judaism" in *VT* Suppl. xxviii (Congress Volume, Edinburgh 1974) (Leiden, 1975), pp. 146-57). On the topical status of such similes and comparisons, see Rolke *op. cit.*, pp. 510 ff.

[9]Similar *topoi* find their way into the younger Seneca's *Epistles* (cf., e.g., 20.3-4; 45.6; 52.1-2; 95-57 f.; 120.19-22) and into Hellenistic consolation literature (e.g., Seneca *Vit. Beat.* I.1-3; *Ad Marc.* 26.2, etc.). A good survey can be found in E. Stemplinger, *Das Plagiat in der griechischen Literatur* (Leipzig, 1912), pp. 228-41. On *chriai*, see H. Fischel, "Studies in Cynicism and the Ancient Near East." *Religions in Antiquity* (ed. J. Neusner) (Leiden, 1970), esp. at pp. 372-85: 402 ff.; On Philo's handling of such a commonplace theme ("degeneracy of the present age"), see E. J. Barnes, "Petronius, Philo and Stoic Rhetoric," *Latomus* 32 (1973) pp. 787-98.

[10]The deposit case was a stock example in the schools. Cf. Cic. *Tusc.* III.8; *De fin.* III.17.58; *PLond* 256 (Ist C. A. D.: cf. F. Kenyon "Fragments d'exercice de rhétorique," *Mélanges Weil* [Paris, 1898], pp. 243-8), etc. Stock epideictic *topoi* (see above, Note 6) clearly inform Philo's *Life of Abraham*, for instance. Preissnig "Die literarische Form der Patriarchen Biographien des Philon von Alexandrien," *MGWJ* 73 [1929], pp.

143-55) has shown that the structure of *Abr.*, and that of the
other Lives, is dictated by rhetorical conventions of the period.

[11]The fortunes of, e.g., the commonplace lists of duties
that evidently originated with the Stoics are traced by J. E.
Crouch, *The Origin and Intention of the Colossian 'Haustafeln'*,
FRLANT 109 (Göttingen, 1972), pp. 57-101. See also P. Wendland,
Die hellenistische-römische Kultur (Tübingen, 1912), p. 86.

[12]These apparently originated, respectively, with the
Stoics and with Plato, but soon achieved commonplace status.
Cf. Reichel, *op. cit.* 99 ff. A. D. Nock is always valuable on
this matter. See his Introduction to Sallustius' *Concerning the
Gods and the Universe* (Cambridge, 1926) *passim*, for instance.
Some putative philosophical doctrines had, in fact, a
wider provenance. For instance, the connection Philo makes
between flesh and servitude, mind and freedom can be found in
Greek drama and hence perhaps can be considered a literary
commonplace. The disquisitions at *LA* iii.89, *Cher.* 71 ff., and
Agr. 57 ff. evidently draw upon Sophocles fr. 940 (cf. *TrGF* IV,
ed. S. Radt (Göttingen, 1977) (= fr. 854N): εἰ σῶμα δοῦλον,
ἀλλ' ὁ νοῦς ἐλεύθερος. To this we should compare Menander
fr. 722.7 f. (Korte): εἰ δ' ἡ τύχη τὸ σῶμα κατεδουλώσατο,/
ὅ γε νοῦς ὑπάρχει τοῖς τρόποις ἐλεύθερος. Both authors were,
of course, read in the schools.
Some "philosophical" issues were stock issues for dispute
in the schools of rhetoric, furthermore. See, e.g., Theon
Progymn. 12.1 (p. 244 Walz) on the question εἰ θεοὶ προνοοῦνται
τοῦ κόσμου, and, later (p. 250 ff. Walz), a list of stock arguments concerning the existence and powers of the gods. At
Prol. in (Hermogenes') *Peri staseōs* (VII. 43.21 ff. Walz), we
find a school exercise which consists of a prosecution of Epicurus.

[13]On God needing nothing, cp., e.g., *LA* iii.181: χρεῖος
γὰρ οὐδενός ἐστιν ὁ ὤν. See Nock, *op. cit.* p. xv. It is a
widespread notion in Hellenistic literature: cf., among others,
Plutarch *Comp. Arist. et Catonis* 4; *Stoic. Repugn.* 11(1034B)
41(1952E); Lucian *Cynicus* 12; Diogenes Laertius VI.105, etc.

[14]Cf. *Topics* I.13, 105a 22 ff., and *passim* in Bks. II-
VII; *Rhetoric* II.xviii, xxiii. Interest in these in Philo's
time was considerable: cf., e.g., Cicero, *Topica* I.1 ff.,
II.7 ff.; *de Orat.* II.163-73; Quintilian V.10.53 f.; and the
lists of Minoukianos (*Epich.* 3: pp. 419 ff. Sp; IX.604 ff.
Walz); Neokles *ap. Anon. Seguer.* 448-50 Sp; and Apsines *Rhet.*
10, I pp. 376 ff. Sp, etc. I have tried to describe the nature
and function of dialectical/rhetorical *koinoi topoi* in my
"'Logical Hylomorphism' and Aristotle's *koinoi topoi*," *Central
States Speech Journal* 29 (1978), pp. 92-97.

[15]Cf. Cicero, *Topica* ii.10; viii.35; *Acad.* i.32 (with
Reid's note); *Tusc.* 3.8.11.

[16]In Philo, see, e.g., *Plant.* 165: ἀπὸ διαφερούσης τῆς
πρὸς τὴν ἐτυμολογίαν πιθανότητος ἠρτημένος (μέθη from μέθεσις);
Op. 127, etc.

[17]See Cicero *Topica* iv.23; *de Orat.* II.40.172. In
Theon, this topos can be used in σύγκρισις (cf. Ip. 108.4 Sp):
τὸ γὰρ κατηγορούμενον ὑφ' ἡμῶν ἢ μείζονι ἑαυτοῦ συγκρίνομεν

ἢ ἐλάττονι ἢ ἴσῳ. Aristotle considers it one of the enthyme-
matic *topoi*: cf. *Rhetoric* II.xxiii, 1397b 12 ff. In Philo, see,
e.g., *Sobr.* 3, *Heres* 88 ff., *Somn.* II.145.

[18]In Philo, see, e.g., *Agr.* 118; *Heres* 242; *Somn.* II.134;
and *Mos* I.247 (to which Aristotle, *Rhet.* I.vi, 1362b 30 ff. may
be compared). It is of course in Aristotle's *Topics* and *Rhetoric* that we first find systematic discussions of this *topos*:
see *Topics* II. 112b ff., *Rhet.* II.xxiii, 1397a7 ff. Cf. also
Cicero, *Topica* xi.47; Quintilian V.10.73 f., etc.

[19]For the former, compare Aristotle *Topics* I.14, 105b
24 and 30 ff. and, perhaps, *Rhetoric* III.17, 1418b 5; and for
the latter, cp. *Topics* II.7, 113a23 and especially II.9, 114b
16 ff.

[20]Cf. Aristotle *Topics* II.7, 112b-113b 14; IV.4, 124b
15 ff.; Cicero *Topica* xi.47-50; Minoukianos *Epich.* 3, (Ipp.
422.6 ff. Sp.).

[21]See now the commentary below.

                                                    T. Conley

III. PHILOSOPHICAL THEMES IN THE *DE GIGANTIBUS*

AND *QUOD DEUS*

A. *Philo's Doctrine of Free Will* *

The much disputed question of free will owes much of its
notoriety to the cloud of semantic ambiguities which has envel-
oped it ever since it became an issue between competing philosophical schools. When Philo dealt with it, it already had had
a checkered career and a distinctive terminology attached to
it.[1] Most discussions of Philo's position, however, unfortunately have not taken adequate account of the philosophical
matrix out of which his analysis arises and either have mis-
construed his intentions or have accused him of contradictions
of which he was not guilty. We shall therefore seek to track
the relevant Philonic texts within their immediate philosophical
context in an effort to extract their true meaning.

Philo's ideal man would be one who most nearly approaches
the πρῶτος ἄνθρωπος described by him in *Op.* 136 ff. The latter
had a mind unalloyed (ἄκρατος) (150), able to receive sense impressions in their true reality and encased in a body which God
molded out of the purest and most subtly refined material available in order to serve as a "sacred dwelling-place or Temple of
the reasonable soul" (137). Such a mind was in complete control
of its sense-perceptions and thus guaranteed inner harmony and
wholeness to its possessor. No warring dualities disturbed the
stillness of this unperturbed being. "But since no created
thing is constant," continues Philo, "and mortal things are
necessarily liable to chances and reverses, it could not but be
that even the first man should experience some ill-fortune. And
woman becomes for him the beginning of the blameworthy life"
(*Op.* 151). Overcome by desire and pleasure, "the beginning of
wrongs and violation of the law," man chose "that fleeting and
mortal life, which is not life at all, but a period of time full
of misery" (*Op.* 152). Having abandoned the Creator for the
created, he forfeited his immortality, and became embroiled in
the war of the passions.

---

*This section reproduces D. Winston, "Freedom and
Determinism in Philo of Alexandria," *SP* 3 (1974-75) 47-70. The
notes, however, have been considerably curtailed.

Man before the "fall" thus represents for Philo an ideal
human type which unfortunately is theoretically precluded by the
actual conditions of earthly life. He therefore proceeds to
analyze man's present "fallen" condition while attempting to
lend to it an air of tragic grandeur. Though second best, it is
nevertheless a life far more elevated than that of the lower
animals. Endowed with mind, man possesses an unique, divine
gift which guarantees his relative preeminence in the scale of
being.[2]

> For it is the mind alone which the Father who begat it
> deemed worthy of freedom, and loosening the bonds of
> necessity, allowed it to range free, and of that power of
> volition which constitutes his most intimate and fitting
> possession presented it with such a portion as it was
> capable of receiving. For the other living creatures in
> whose souls the mind, the element earmarked for liberty,
> has no place, have been handed over to the service of man,
> as slaves to a master. But man who is possessed of spon-
> taneous and self-determined judgment and performs for the
> most part activities deliberately chosen, is rightly blamed
> for what he does with premeditation, praised when he acts
> correctly of his own will. In the others, the plants and
> animals, no praise is due if they are fruitful, nor blame
> if they fail to be productive: for they acquire their
> movements and changes in either direction through no
> deliberate choice or volition of their own. But the soul
> of man alone has received from God the faculty of voluntary
> movement, and in this way especially is assimilated to him,
> and thus being liberated, as far as possible, from that
> hard and grievous mistress, Necessity, may suitably be
> charged with guilt, in that it does not honor its Liberator.
> And therefore it will in all justice pay the inexorable
> penalty reserved for ungrateful freedmen. [Deus 47-48]

The first thing to be observed is Philo's emphatic
insistence on man's culpability and responsibility for his evil
actions, thereby explicitly absolving deity from any share in
the latter. The prime motivation of Philo in this passage is
thus very similar to that of Plato when he discusses the laws
of reincarnation both in Tim. 41E ff. and in Rep. 10.614 ff.
The dominant motif is there sounded by the oft-quoted phrase:
αἰτία ἑλομένου, θεὸς ἀναίτιος (617E; cf. 379B).[3] An analysis
of the Platonic passages may therefore help considerably in
unraveling the meaning of Philo. It has sometimes been assumed
that Plato was somehow attempting to reconcile the laws of
destiny with the absolute autonomy of human freedom. The fact
is, however, that in the very same dialogue in which Plato seeks
to clear the gods of blame for the individual soul's destiny
(Tim. 42D), he asserts that the soul may very well be plagued
by disease due to a defective bodily constitution coupled with

bad upbringing, and that this could lead to its being overcome
by the passions (*Tim.* 86B). In *Laws* 644DE, Plato speaks more
bluntly of the ultimately determined character of man's moral
nature:

> Let us suppose [says the Athenian] that each of us living
> creatures is an ingenious puppet of the gods, whether con-
> trived by way of a toy of theirs or for some serious pur-
> pose--for as to that we know nothing; but this we do know,
> that these inward affections of ours, like sinews or cords,
> drag us along and, being opposed to each other, pull one
> against the other to opposite actions. [Loeb ed., 1.69;
> cf. *Laws* 732E, 804B; also *Fug.* 46; *Op.* 117; *QG* 3.48]

It should be abundantly clear, then, that all Plato is
asserting by insisting that the blame is that of the soul that
chooses, is that the moral career of the latter is not a product
of fatality, but a result of its participation in the complex
process of choice.[4] That this process is itself ultimately
determined is part of the thorny problem of necessary evil which
Plato seeks to mitigate elsewhere (*Tim.* 48A, 56C; *Laws* 896-97;
Phaedr. 247) by pointing to an ineradicable residue of random
motion in the cosmos and an inherent ignorance within the human
soul.[5] In any case, the attribution of moral blame or responsibility to man is fully justified, as far as Plato is concerned,
as long as man's soul is not caught in the web of a fatality
which would constrain its actions arbitrarily. By participating
in the choice process, man becomes willy nilly a moral agent.
Thus, for Plato, a concept of *relative* free will is quite sufficient to allow for the notion of moral responsibility.[6]

Returning to Philo, it should now be clear that unless
an explicit statement of absolute free will can confidently be
extracted from the passage under consideration, the internal
logic of Philo's argumentation does not demand it and is fully
compatible with a relative free will concept. Though fully
cognizant of this fact, Wolfson has argued that

> when Philo says that God gave to the human mind a portion
> "of that free will which is His most peculiar possession
> and most worthy of His majesty" and that by this gift of
> free will the human mind "in this respect has been made
> to resemble Him," it is quite evident that by man's free
> will Philo means an absolutely undetermined freedom like
> that enjoyed by God, who by his power to work miracles
> can upset the laws of nature and the laws of causality
> which He himself has established. [*Philo* 1.436]

The fact is, however, that Philo is only adapting here for his
own use a characteristically Stoic notion. Epictetus, for
example, writes:

> But what says Zeus? "Epictetus, had it been possible I
> should have made both this paltry body and this small
> estate of thine free and unhampered. . . . Yet since
> I could not give thee this, we have given thee a certain
> portion of ourself, this faculty of choice and refusal."
> [*Diss.* 1.1.10][7]

Now the Stoics held a relative free will theory of the causal
type, and all they meant by saying that God has given us a portion of himself thereby enabling us to make choices is that
(as A. A. Long has neatly put it) "the logos, the causal principle, is inside the individual man as well as being an external
force constraining him. . . . This is but a fragment of the
whole, however, and its powers are naturally weak, so weak that
'following' rather than 'initiating' events is stressed as its
proper function."[8] For the Stoics, man is not a mechanical link
in the causal chain, but an active though subordinate partner of
God. It is this which allows them to shift the responsibility
for evil from God to man. Cleanthes says as much in his famous
Hymn to Zeus.[9] According to Long,

> Cleanthes is thinking of God as an absolute power, embracing
> all things and uniting good and evil. Yet evil actions are
> not planned by God in his identity as one omnipotent ruler.
> What he does is to unite all things in a harmonious whole.
> Can we say that evil actions are ones purposed by certain
> fragments of his logos? They would bear no more resemblance
> to God as such than does a brick to the house it helps to
> form.[10]

Philo's meaning, then, is that in so far as man shares
in God's Logos, he shares to some extent in God's freedom. That
this is only a relative freedom is actually emphasized by Philo
when he says that God gave man such a portion of his freedom
"as man was capable of receiving" and that he was liberated "as
far as might be." Yet this relative freedom, in Philo's view,
is sufficient for placing the onus of moral responsibility on
man and clearing God from any blame for man's sins. It is
impossible, then, to locate in our Philonic text an explicit
statement of absolute free will. For the sake of the argument,
however, let us follow up the logical consequences of an absolute free will doctrine and see how these would chime with
Philo's philosophical system as a whole. If absolute free will,
for Philo, means that man's will is completely autonomous and
independent of God, then he would be ascribing to God the ability
to do something involving a contradiction.[11] It seems, however,
highly unlikely that Philo's formula πάντα θεῷ δυνατά would
include the logically absurd. For Philo (as later for Saadia),

the latter would signify nothing and it would be meaningless
to ascribe it to God's omnipotence. Similarly Origen would
exclude from the general principle that all things are possible
to God, things that are contrary to reason (παράλογα) or to
God's own character (*Contra Celsum* 5.24).[12]

Moreover, if, as Wolfson believes, absolute free will
means that, contrary to the laws of nature, the mind by virtue
of its mysteriously free will can miraculously override the
effects of the warring potencies of two conflicting drives
(ὁρμαί), then we shall be ascribing to Philo the use of vacuous
terminology.[13] For the term "will" in this context cannot mean
(on the assumptions made)[14] either the predominance of the more
potent drive in man or some sort of rational process, but
remains a mysterious component never identified. But even if
we were to accept the existence of this mysterious entity, it
would be difficult to ascribe either merit or blame to man for
its inexplicable (or uncaused) inclinations now towards the
good, now towards evil. It were as if some alien force lodged
in our mind made decisions which we could not account for in
any rational manner. One could always argue, of course, that
Philo was unaware of these contradictions and difficulties,
but in the light of the fact that he was undoubtedly acquainted
with the subtle and detailed discussions of the Stoics and their
adversaries, it does not seem likely that this would be the
case.

Finally, Philo explicitly teaches that God "knoweth
well the different pieces of his own handiwork, even before he
has thoroughly chiselled and consummated them, and the faculties
which they are to display at a later time, in a word, their
deeds and experiences" (*LA* 3.88; Seneca, *Ben.* 4.32). It is
difficult to believe that Philo would be willing to involve himself in such a palpable contradiction (i.e., maintaining at the
same time both man's absolute freedom and God's complete foreknowledge of all man's future actions), when he had ready to
hand a relative free will theory which could serve all his needs
and which had probably already been accepted and adapted by some
Jewish Hellenistic and rabbinic writings.[15] Still, it would
be hazardous in the extreme to draw any conclusions from this
kind of argumentation. Much depends on how one reads the central
character of Philo's thought. Wolfson sees Philo as essentially
a pious Jew who rarely allows philosophic principle to override
the self-evident teachings of Scripture, and thus finds in him

a paradigm for much that was characteristic of medieval religious philosophy. It is becoming increasingly clear, however
(at least to this writer), that there are numerous hints in
Philo's writings that indicate an ambivalence in his manner of
philosophical exposition and which would seem to place him in
the ranks of those whose philosophical convictions run considerably deeper than their adhesion to religious dogma.[16] In
any case, our main line of argumentation is in no way involved
in the larger controversy concerning Philo's philosophical perspective.

Since many interpreters of Philo had taken his concept
of freedom in an absolute sense, they were somewhat puzzled by
the fragment from the lost fourth book of his *Legum Allegoria*,
which contains the following homily on Deuteronomy 30:15 and 19:

It is a happy thing for the soul to have the power to choose
the better of the two choices put forward by the Creator,
but it is happier not for the soul to choose, but for the
Creator to bring it over to himself and improve it. For,
strictly speaking, the human mind does not choose the good
through itself, but in accordance with the thoughtfulness
of God, since He bestows the fairest things upon the worthy.
For two main principles are with the Lawgiver, namely, that
on the one hand God does not govern all things as a man and
that on the other hand He trains, and educates us as a man
[cf. *Somn.* 1.237; *Deus* 53 ff.]. Accordingly, when he maintains the second principle, namely, that God acts as a man,
he introduces that which is in our power as the competence
to know something, will, choose, and avoid. But when he
affirms that first and better principle, namely, that God
acts not as man, he ascribes the powers and causes of all
things to God, leaving no work for a created being but
showing it to be inactive and passive.[17] He explains this
when he says in other words that "God has known those who
are His and those who are holy and he has brought them near
to himself" (Num 16:5). But if selections and rejections
are in strictness made by the one cause, why do you advise
me, legislator, to choose life or death, as though we were
autocrats of our choice?[18] But he would answer: Of such
things hear thou a rather elementary explanation, namely,
such things are said to those who have not yet been initiated in the great mysteries about the sovereignty and
authority of the Uncreated and the exceeding nothingness
of the created.[19]

Having committed himself to ascribing an absolute free will
doctrine to Philo, Wolfson is constrained virtually to transform
the simple meaning of the above fragment.[20] "In the first place,"
he writes, "the fragment deals only with man's choice of the good
but makes no mention at all of man's choice of evil." This omission, which "cannot be accidental," can be

accounted for only by the fact that the point which Philo
was going to make in this homily was that only the choice

of good was caused by God, but not choice of evil. In the
second place, with regard to the choice of good, we may say
at the very outset that such sweeping statements in this
passage about the "exceeding nothingness of the created"
. . . and about the unreality of the presentation of the
human mind as being "capable of knowing something, and
willing and choosing, and avoiding" do not in themselves
indicate that Philo denied of man the freedom to choose
good. Even with his belief in absolute human freedom he
could make these statements, in view of the fact that the
freedom, as he has said in his extant works, is a gift
bestowed upon man by God, a portion of his own proper
freedom, whereby he is made to resemble God. . . . Furthermore, God's direct causation of man's choice of good is
described as "the thoughtfulness of God, while he bestows
the fairest things upon the worthy." This quite obviously
implies that man must first do something to render himself
worthy of the bestowal upon him by God of the power to
choose good, and this must inevitably refer to some act
of free will.

Wolfson thus concludes:

The cumulative impression of all these statements then is
that, while a man is able to choose the better, he will
not have to rely upon his own power, that is to say, that
power of free will with which God will aid men, for, if
he proves himself worthy, God will aid him in making that
choice by bringing him to himself. The direct interven-
tion of God in man's choice of good dealt with in this
fragment must therefore be assumed to refer only to some
help lent by God to man in the choice of good, when man
proves himself worthy of such help.[21]

Now Wolfson's first argument is easily countered when
one remembers that it is a basic principle with Philo not to
ascribe evil to God, a principle which he shared both with Plato
and the Stoics. Our fragment is assessing man's actions from
the perspective of God, and since in that perspective evil does
not really exist, its focus can only be on man's choice of the
good. Wolfson's second argument that since man's absolute freedom is itself a gift of God it is proper to speak of his "exceeding nothingness," falls between two stools. For if God's gift
is real (or absolute), then man's will is truly sovereign and
independent and it would then be improper to speak of his
nothingness, and if on the other hand, it is somehow unreal (or
relative), then man does not indeed possess an absolute freedom
of the will. Finally, the third argument revolves around the
word "worthy," which according to Wolfson, must imply that man
already possesses some portion of free will. As a matter of
fact, however, it need imply no such thing. The "worthy," may
simply be those whom God in his infinite wisdom has predeter-
mined to be his chosen ones. Philo, for example, writes:

"God has not fashioned beforehand any deed of his, but produces
him [Melchizedek] to begin with as such a king, peaceable and
worthy of his own priesthood" (*LA* 3.79). Similarly, we read in
Ben Sira: "To fear the Lord is the beginning of wisdom, and
with the faithful was she created in the womb" (1:14).

        More decisive, however, for the interpretation of the
fragment from the *Legum Allegoria*, is that its plain meaning is
fully consonant with the rest of Philo's writings and is actually
reinforced by them. The theme of man's nothingness and utter
passivity runs through much of Philo's works.[22] In *Cher.* 77,
for example, he writes:

> What more hostile foe could there be for the soul than one
> who in his boastfulness claims for himself what is proper
> to God? For to act is the property of God, something which
> may not be ascribed to created beings whereas it is the
> property of creation to suffer. He who recognizes this in
> advance as something fitting and necessary, will readily
> endure what befalls him, however grievous it may be.[23]

Philo's language is occasionally almost identical with that of
the Stoics when he wishes to emphasize the relative passivity
of man's role in the cosmos. He writes, for example, in *Cher.*
128: "For we are the instruments, now tensed now slackened,
through which particular actions take place; and it is the
Artificer who effects the percussion of both our bodily and
psychic powers, he by whom all things are moved." (Cf. *Ebr.*
107). The Stoics similarly say: "The movements of our minds
are nothing more than instruments for carrying out determined
decisions since it is necessary that they be performed through
us by the agency of Fate."[24] More specifically, Philo insists
again and again that man's virtue is not really his own. "It is
necessary," he writes in *LA* 3.136, "that the soul should not
ascribe to itself its toil for virtue, but that it should take
it away from itself and refer it to God, confessing that not its
own strength or power acquired nobility, but He who freely
bestowed also the love of it." Indeed, in spite of the fact
that, according to Philo, God bestowed some of his own freedom
on man, only God, says Philo elsewhere, is ἑκούσιον in the
absolute sense of the word, since our own existence is ruled by
necessity (*Somn.* 2.253). Moreover, terms such as αὐτεξούσιος
or αὐτοκράτωρ are never used by Philo to designate man's freedom, but refer only to God's sovereign power.[25] Again, Philo's
constant use of medical figures in describing the various con-
digions of the soul and his insistence that at a certain stage

its diseased state becomes incurable clearly implies a deterministic scheme.[26] For if the soul were endowed with an absolute
freedom it should be able to overcome the natural forces attempting to enslave it. Nor does Philo assert in these frequently
recurring passages that God has withdrawn our absolute free will
in punishment for our previous choices. Finally, the Stoic terminology to which Philo consistently resorts in his definition
of the passions (ἄμετρος καὶ πλεονάζουσα ὁρμή: Spec. 4.79; cf.
1.305; 1.8), and his description of the diseased or healthy
state of the soul in terms equivalent to the Stoic ἀτονία and
εὐτονία[27] (Conf. 165-66; Virt. 13), lead us once again to a form
of ethical determinism.

It would thus appear that the general tone of Philo's
ethical thought is evidently deterministic, inasmuch as it seems
to be tied to the notion of an all-penetrating divine Logos which
reaches into each man's mind, thus converting it into an extension of the divine mind, albeit a very fragmentary one.[28] In
the light of this reading of man's psyche, it should be evident
that the relative free will doctrine which characterized much of
classical and Hellenistic Greek thought and had already left its
mark on some Jewish Hellenistic and rabbinic writings, was the
most natural option for Philo's thought to take. At any rate,
we have found nothing in Philo's writings sufficiently explicit
to warrant attributing to him an absolute free will doctrine,
and much that would seem to contradict it.

NOTES

[1]For a brief account of the history of this question in
Greek philosophy, see D. Winston, Wisdom of Solomon (N.Y. 1979)
51-55.

[2]Cf. Plotinus 3.2.9.30: "In this way man is a noble
creation, as far as he can be noble, and, being woven into the
All, has a part which is better than that of other living things,
of all, that is, which live on the earth" (cf. 3.1.8; Spec.
3.83; 4.14).

[3]Cf. Plotinus, 3.2.7; Corpus Hermeticum (ed. Nock,
Festugière) 1.52. According to Justin Martyr (Apologia 1.44.
1-8 [81B-E]), this dictum was taken by Plato directly from Moses.

[4]This process is clearly described in Laws 733B: "We
desire that pleasure should be ours, but pain we neither choose
nor desire; and the neutral state we do not desire in place of
pleasure, but we do desire it in exchange for pain; and we
desire less pain with more pleasure, but we do not desire less
pleasure with more pain; and when the two are evenly balanced,

we are unable to state any clear preference" (Loeb ed., 1.343;
cf. Aristotle, *De Caelo* 295b31). For the Socratic paradox that
no one voluntarily does what is wrong, and its distinctively
Platonic formulation (*Gorgias* 509E; *Laws* 731C, 860C ff.), see
the excellent discussion of Norman Gulley, *The Philosophy of
Socrates* (London 1968) 75-204. Plato's widening of the class
of involuntary actions by defining voluntary as that which one
"really" desires, i.e., what one rationally desires, involves
him only in a semantic dispute with both Socrates and Aristotle,
and as Plato himself notes (*Laws* 864B): ἡμῖν δὲ οὐκ ἔστι τὰ
νῦν ὀνομάτων πέρι δύσερις λόγος ("we are not now concerned with
a semantic dispute").

[5]Cf. H. Cherniss, "The Sources of Evil According to
Plato," *Plato: A Collection of Critical Essays*, ed. G. Vlastos
(Garden City 1971) 2.244-58. Plato, moreover, indicates (*Tim.*
41B-C) that mortal creatures came into being so that the Heaven
be not imperfect, which it would be if it did not contain all
the kinds of living being. Cf. *Conf.* 179; Spinoza, *Ethics* (New
York: Hafner, 1953) 1, Appendix, ad fin.: But to those who ask
why God has not created all men in such a manner that they might
be controlled by the dictates of reason alone, I give but this
answer: because to Him material was not wanting for the creation of everything down to the very lowest grade of perfection:
or to speak more properly, because the laws of His nature were
so ample that they sufficed for the production of everything
which can be conceived by an infinite intellect." Similarly,
Jalal al-Din Rumi writes: "Could He not evil make, He would
lack skill" (R. A. Nicholson, *The Mystics of Islam* [London 1963]
99).

[6]Plato, however, makes a sharp distinction between
ἄγνοια and ἀμαθία. The former designates a lack of ἐπιστήμη,
"a kind of emptiness of habit of the soul" (*Rep.* 585B), which
can be filled by νοῦς and τροφή (reason and training). The
latter, on the other hand, is a condition of fundamental ignorance produced by ἀπαίδευτος τροφή or improper training, and a
πονηρὰν ἕξιν τοῦ σώματος or a faulty habit of body due to a
physiological defect. It is a psychic disorder caused by a
pathological condition of the body, as, for example, when the
seed in the marrow is copious with overflowing moisture, it
causes states of frenzy in which one experiences excessive
pleasures and pains (e.g., a state of sexual licentiousness)
(*Tim.* 86B ff.). In short, Plato is referring here to biological
drives whose normal intensities have been rendered abnormal by
diseased neurophysiological conditions. In the *Sophist* (228 ff.)
Plato adds that a state of ἀμαθία can be produced by ἀμετρία by
which he apparently means a disproportion between the three
parts of the soul. In this case, we have an αἶσχος or deformity
(rather than a νόσος or disease), i.e., a structural defect in
the soul itself. Cf. Philo, *Virt.* 13 (in *Laws* 731E-732B, he
speaks of an excessive love of self as cause of ἀμαθία). Presumably this may be the result of either νόσος or αἶσχος. Dialectic is a useful treatment both for ἄγνοια and ἀμαθία, but is
obviously most effective in the former case, least effective in
the latter (*Sophist* 228 ff.). In any case, Plato would apply
punishment as a deterrent and rewards as positive reinforcement
in all cases that are judged to be curable to some extent (*Laws*
862D, 934A; cf. *Protagoras* 324B), but when neither dialectic,
nor deterrent punishment, nor the rewards of positive reinforcement prove effective (i.e., incurable conditions), then the
only recourse is execution. (Cf. *Protagoras* 325B; *Rep.* 410A,

Politicus 309A). Cf. E. R. Dodds, *The Greeks and the Irrational*
(Boston 1957) 207-35; J. J. Walsh, *Aristotle's Conception of
Moral Weakness* (New York 1963) 4-59; A. A. Long, "Freedom and
Determinism in the Stoic Theory of Human Action," *Problems in
Stoicism*, ed. A. A. Long; London 1971) 174; R. Hackforth, "Moral
Evil and Ignorance in Plato's Ethics," *Classical Quarterly* 40
(1946) 118-20; P. W. Gooch, "Vice is Ignorance: the Interpre-
tation of Sophist 226A-231B," *Phoenix* 25 (1971) 124-33; J.
Stenzel, "Das Problem der Willensfreiheit im Platonismus," *Die
Antike* 4 (1928) 293-313; F. Guglielmino, "Il problema del libero
arbitrio nel sistema platonico," *Archivio di Storia della Filo-
sofia Italiana* 4 (1935) 197-223; A. W. H. Adkins, *Merit and
Responsibility* (Oxford 1960) 302-8; I. M. Crombie, *An Examination
of Plato's Doctrines* (London 1962) 1.275-80. J. V. B. Gosling,
Plato (London 1973) 82-99.

[7] Cf. Epictetus, *Dissertationes* 1.17.27; 2.8.11 (Loeb
ed., 1.261): "But you are a being of primary importance; you
are a fragment (ἀπόσπασμα) of God; you have within you a part
of Him" (cf. *Her.* 283; *Op.* 146; *Somn.* 1.34).

[8] A. A. Long (cited n. 6) 178-79. Long also correctly
notes: "In fact, though he is not explicit on the point, Epictetus' freedom of the Logos seems to be subject to the same
qualifications as Chrysippus', and for the same reasons."

[9] Nothing occurs on the earth apart from you, O God,
    nor in the heavenly regions nor on the sea,
    except what bad men do in their folly;
    but you know how to make the odd even,
    and to harmonize what is dissonant; to you the alien
      is akin.
    And so you have wrought together into one all things
      that are good and bad,
    So that there arises one eternal "logos" of all
      things. . . .
The translation is that of A. A. Long in his *Hellenistic Philosophy* (London 1974) 181. For the Greek text, see J. U. Powell,
Collectanea Alexandrina (Oxford 1924) 227-31 (*SVF* 1.537). For
a detailed discussion, see A. J. Festugière, *La Révélation
d'Hermès Trismégiste* (Paris 1944-54) 2.310-30.

[10] Long (cited n. 6) 179. Cf. W. Theiler, "Tacitus und
die antike Schicksalslehre," *Phyllobolia für Peter von der Mühll*
(Basel 1946) 54-55 (reprinted in Theiler's *Forschungen zum Neu-
platonismus* (Berlin 1966) 46-103. Cf. Epictetus, *Dissertationes*
1.12.

[11] Briefly stated, the contradiction consists in asserting
that God, who alone is self-caused, can create a human will whose
moral choices are all self-caused. It is therefore equivalent
to saying that God can create another God. Maimonides' comment
on this was: "We do not attribute to God incapacity because he
is unable to corporify his essence or to create someone like him
or to create a square whose diagonal is commensurate with its
side" (*Guide* 1.75).

[12] See D. Winston, "The Book of Wisdom's Theory of Cosmogony," *History of Religions* 11 (1971) 197, n. 33; cf. Philo,
Abr. 268: "Though he can do all things, he wills only what is
best" (cf. *Op.* 46; *QG* IV 51).

[13]Epicurus had already cautioned against the use of
κενοὶ φθόγγοι or words devoid of meaning (*Epistula ad Herodotum*
1.38; *K.D.* 37; Cicero, *Fin.* 2.48; *Tusc.* 5.26.73) *Epict.* 2.6.19;
2.17.6. Cf. Aristotle, *Ethica Eudemia* 1.8.1217b, 22; Cicero,
Tusc. 1.10.21; Aristotle, *Metaphysica* 991a, 20 (κενολογεῖν);
Alexander Aphrodisiensis *De Fato* chap. 2; Philo, *Spec.* 1.327;
Seneca *Ben.* 5.12.4; *Corpus Hermeticum* 11.5.15; Plotinus 2.4.11;
Thomas Hobbes, *Leviathan* (ed. A. R. Waller; Cambridge 1935) pt.
1, 23-25: "And words whereby we conceive nothing but the sound,
are those we call *Absurd*, *Insignificant*, and *Non-sense*. And
therefore if a man should talk to me of a *round Quadrangle*, or
accidents of Bread in Cheese, or *Immateriall Substances*, or of
A free Subject; *A free-Will*; of any *Free*, but free from being
hindered by opposition, I should not say he were in an Errour;
but that his words were without meaning; that is to say, Absurd.
. . . The seventh [cause of absurd conclusions I ascribe] to
names that signifie nothing; but are taken up, and learned by
rote from the Schooles, as *hypostatical*, *transubstantiate*, *con-
substantiate*, *eternal-Now*, and the like canting of Schoolemen."
David Hume, *An Inquiry Concerning Human Understanding*, sect. 2,
in *English Philosophers of the Seventeenth and Eighteenth Centuries* (Harvard Classics 37; New York 1910) 320: "When we enter-
tain, therefore, any suspicion that a philosophical term is
employed without any meaning or idea (as is but too frequent),
we need but inquire, from what impression is that supposed idea
derived? And if it be impossible to assign any, this will serve
to confirm our suspicion."

[14]Wolfson (*Philo* 1.432) writes: "This power with which
the human mind was endowed to choose or not to choose refers not
only to the choice of good, but also to the choice of evil, even
though the mind is by its very nature rational, for, as says
Philo, there are in our mind 'voluntary inclinations (ἐκουσίους
τροπάς) to what is wrong.' *Det.* 122). The essential rationality
of the mind does not preclude the possibility of its acting, by
the mere power of its free will, against the dictates of reason."

[15]See Winston (cited n. 1).

[16]See D. Winston, "Philo's Theory of Cosmogony," in
Religious Syncretism in Antiquity, ed. B. A. Pearson; Missoula
1975) 157-71. Cf. Isaak Heinemann, *Philons griechische und
jüdische Bildung* (Breslau 1932) 542-74; S. Sandmel, *Philo's
Place in Judaism* (Cincinnati 1956) 1-29; Walther Völker,
Fortschritt und Vollendung bei Philo von Alexandrien (Leipzig
1938) 1-47; H. Thyen, "Die Probleme der neueren Philoforschung,"
Theologische Rundschau, N.F. 23 (1955-56) 230-46.

[17]Cf. R. Mordechai Joseph Leiner of Izbica (d. 1854; a
disciple of R. Menahem Mendel [Morgenstern] of Kotzk [1787-
1859], according to whose view the signal characteristic of the
future world is that in it the illusion of free choice will
vanish, and that acts will no longer be ascribed to their human
agents but to God, their true author. To substantiate his view,
he quotes the following passage from *BT Pesaḥim* 50a: "the
future world is unlike our present world, for in our present
world I (God) am written as YHWH but am called Adonai, but in
the future world, I shall both be written as YHWH and be called
YHWH" ([*Mei ha-Shiloaḥ*] pt. 1:14b). "Know and understand," he
writes elsewhere, "that everything you do is from God and save
for him, no one may lift hand or foot to do aught, and you should
not boast about your actions. . . . for all the good which you do

you may refer to God, but all the evil you must attribute to
yourselves" (55b). See Joseph Weiss "The Religious Determinism
of Joseph Mordecai Lerner [*sic*] of Izbica," *Yitzhak F. Baer
Jubilee Volume* (eds. S. W. Baron, S. Ettinger, et al.; Jerusalem
1960) 447-53.

[18]Cf. Plato, *Laws* 9.860E (Loeb ed., 2.223, 225): "If
this is the state of the case, Stranger (i.e., that all bad men
are in all respects unwillingly bad), what counsel do you give
us in regard to legislating for the Magnesian State? Shall we
legislate or shall we not?' 'Legislate by all means' I shall
reply."

[19]*Fragments of Philo Judaeus* (ed. James Rendel Harris;
Cambridge 1886) 8. (I have quoted the Drummond-Wolfson translation of this fragment, but have made a number of modifications.)
For the two principles "God is as a man, God is not as a man,"
cf. *Deus* 60-68.

[20]Drummond observes that this fragment "reduces the
belief in free will to a useful delusion of the less educated."
He concludes, however, that "if this passage has been correctly
preserved, it stands alone among Philo's utterances, though not
without important points of contact with them, and I must be
content to leave it without attempting a reconciliation" (James
Drummond, *Philo Judaeus* [reprint, Amsterdam 1969] 1.347, note).
E. Goodenough, on the other hand, has correctly understood
Philo's intent (see his *The Theology of Justin Martyr* [reprint,
Amsterdam 1968] 229).

[21]H. Wolfson, *Philo* 1.442-46 (I have somewhat abbrevi-
ated his remarks).

[22]Those commentators who find an inconsistency in Plato's
ethical determinism naturally find the same inconsistency in
Philo's. Billings, for example, writes: "Such passages (which
ascribe all human activity to God, including moral progress) are
in flat contradiction to the group in which man's freedom and
responsibility are asserted, but this inconsistency is one that
Philo shares with most determinists. It is in Plato. . . .
There is a similar inconsistency in Stoicism" (Thomas H. Billings,
The Platonism of Philo Judaeus [Chicago 1919] 71).

[23]Cf. Cleanthes, *SVF* 1.527: "Guide me, O Zeus, and thou
Fate, whither I have been appointed by you. For I will follow
freely; and if, grown evil, I prove unwilling I shall follow no
less." Chrysippus and Zeno illustrated this as follows: "Just
as a dog tied to a cart follows while being pulled, if it is
willing to follow, making its own self-determination comply with
necessity; yet it will be in all respects subject to compulsion
if it is unwilling to follow. So it is too with men" (*SVF*
2.975). Epictetus quotes Chrysippus: "As long as the consequences are unknown to me, I always hold fast to what is better-
adapted to secure preferred value, for God himself created me
with a faculty of choosing them. Yet if I really knew that it
was ordained for me now to be ill, I should wish to be ill; for
the foot too, if it had a mind, would wish to get muddy" (*SVF*
3.191). Cf. Epictetus, *Dissertationes* 2.10; 3.5.8 ff.; 4.1.
89 ff.; 4.7.19 ff.; Marcus Aurelius, *Meditationes* 5.8; 4.34;
6.39; 3.16; 7.57; 12.1; 4.23; "All that is in tune with thee,
O Universe, is in tune with me! Nothing that is in due time
for thee is too early or too late for me!" Seneca, *De Providentia*

5.4 ff.:   "Good men labor, spend, and are spent, and withall
willingly. Fortune does not drag them--they follow her, and
match her pace. If they had known how, they would have out-
stripped her. Here is another spirited utterance which, I
remember, I heard that most valiant man, Demetrius, make:
'Immortal gods,' he said, 'I have this one complaint to make
against you, that you did not earlier make known your will to
me; for I should have reached the sooner that condition in which
after being summoned, I now am. Do you wish to take my children?--it was for you that I fathered them. Do you wish to take
some member of my body?--take it; no great thing am I offering
you; very soon I shall leave the whole. . . . What, then, is
my trouble? I should have preferred to offer than to relin-
quish. What was the need to take it by force? You might have
had it as a gift. Yet even now you will not take it by force,
because nothing can be wrenched away from a man unless he with-
holds it.'"

[24]*SVF* 2.943: *Animorum vero nostrorum motus nihil aliud
esse, quam ministeria decretorum fatalium, siquidem necesse sit
agi per nos agente fato.* Cf. *Her.* 120; *Cher.* 64, 71: "But, if
you reform and obtain a portion of the wisdom that you need,
you will say that all are God's possessions and not yours, your
reflections, your knowledge of every kind, your arts, your conclusions, perceptions, in fact the activities of your soul,
whether carried on through the senses or without them." Cf. *LA*
2.46; 1.48 ff. ("when God sows and plants noble qualities in the
soul, the mind that says 'I plant' is guilty of impiety"); *Cher.*
40-52; *LA* 2.32; *Mos.* 2.147 (sin is congenital to every created
being); *Conf.* 125.

[25]See M. Harl, "Adam et les deux arbres de Paradis,"
Rech SR 50 (1962) 377. Cf. *Her.* 201; *Conf.* 125; *LA* 3.198; *Somn.*
2.293. αὐτεξούσιος, referring to man's freedom, does occur,
however, in a fragment printed in C. E. Richter's edition of
Philo (Leipzig, 1829) 6.219.

[26]See, for example, *Post.* 73; *Det.* 178; *Somn.* 2.195;
Abr. 115; *Ebr.* 140; *Mut.* 144; *Spec.* 1.281, 2.17, 3.11; *Virt.* 4;
Deus 89; *Spec.* 4.82; *Decal.* 142; *Virt.* 13; Billings, *Platonism*
(cited n. 22) 93-95; Völker, *Fortschritt* (cited n. 16) 47-95,
115-22.

[27]For the Stoic doctrine of ἀτονία see *SVF* 3.473, 2.531;
J. M. Rist, *Stoic Philosophy* (Cambridge 1969) 87-95. *Conf.* 166:
"For when the bonds of the soul which held it fast are loosened,
there follows the greatest of disasters, even to be abandoned by
God who has encircled all things with the adamantine chains of
His potencies and willed that thus bound tight and fast they
should never be unloosed." See Völker, *Fortschritt*, 93; cf.
Sacr. 81; *Ebr.* 95, 122 (here he implies that when the τόνος of
the soul is loosened, man can no longer act voluntarily).

[28]See, for example, *Det.* 90: "How, then, was it likely
that the mind of man being so small (cf. Aristotle, *EN* 10.7.7),
contained in such small bulks as a brain or a heart, should have
room for all the vastness of sky and universe, had it not been
an inseparable portion of that divine and blessed soul? For no
part of that which is divine cuts itself off and becomes separate, but does but extend itself. The mind, then, having
obtained a share of the perfection which is in the whole, when
it conceives of the universe, reaches out as widely as the bounds
of the whole, and undergoes no severance; for its force is

expansive (ὀλκός)." Cf. *Gig.* 27; *LA* 1.37; *Corpus Hermeticum* 12.1; Manilius 2.117 ff.; Plotinus 5.2; 1.7.1.25: "for the light is everywhere with it [the sun] and is not cut off from it": οὐκ ἀποτέτμηται; 5.3.12.

D. Winston

B. *Philo's Doctrine of Angels*

This essay will be confined largely to the discussion of
Philo's doctrine of angels as presented in the *De Gigantibus*,
which is, in fact, one of his main treatments of the topic,
though reference to other key passages will be inevitable. The
problems to be addressed are these: (1) Is Philo's angelology
essentially an adaptation of Greek, and more specifically,
Middle Platonic doctrine on daemons, or does it contain distinctly Jewish elements? (2) What is the status of the heavenly
bodies in Philo's theological scheme? (3) Does Philo recognise
the existence of evil daemons of any variety?

1. *Sources of Philo's Doctrine*

At *Gig.* 6, Philo declares, commenting on Gen 6:2:
"Those beings which other philosophers call 'daemons' Moses is
accustomed to term 'angels'. These are souls flying in the
air." The Greek ἄλλοι φιλόσοφοι conceals an ambiguity. Moses
may either be contrasted *exclusively* with "the (Greek) philosophers," or *inclusively*, with "the philosophers other than himself." Either interpretation would be possible grammatically,
but since Philo's basic position is that Moses himself is the
first and greatest of philosophers (e.g., *Opif.* 8, *Deus* 110,
etc. See Leisegang's Index s.v. Μωυσῆς), the latter interpretation seems the more natural. We may conclude from this that
Philo intends that Moses and "the rest of the philosophers" are
talking about the same beings, but that (as usual) Moses has a
somewhat more accurate conception of them, even to the extent of
propounding a more suitable name. Nevertheless, as we shall
see, "the others," whom I take to be a series of thinkers beginning with Plato himself (esp. *Symp.* 202E and *Phaedr.* 246 ff.),
through Xenocrates and the author of the *Epinomis* (984D ff.), to
Posidonius (in his work *On Daemons and Heroes*, perhaps), and
Eudorus of Alexandria, had preserved enough that was accurate
for Philo to feel justified in claiming it back. Philo's doctrine will therefore concord very largely with whatever else we
know of Middle Platonic daemonology, which is derivable chiefly

from Plutarch, Albinus, Apuleius and Maximus of Tyre, writing
from a century to a century and a half later.

Philo begins his theoretical exposition, at *Gig.* 7, from
a Platonist principle, derivable from the *Timaeus* (39E-40A), that
every part of the cosmos must be ensouled (ἐψυχῶσθαι), and
inhabited by beings proper to it. Plato actually expresses
himself somewhat ambiguously at this point in the *Timaeus*, with
the result that some of his later followers were led astray. He
distinguishes four *ideai* in the Essential Living Being, which
the Demiurge (here termed *nous*) resolves to implant in the physical cosmos--"one, the heavenly race of gods; second, winged
things whose path is the air; third, all that dwells in the
water; and fourth, all that goes on foot on dry land." It may
seem obvious to us that what Plato is intending to distinguish
here are, broadly, stars, birds, fish and land animals, but this
was by no means so obvious to later Platonists.

Proclus' commentary on the passage (*In Tim.* I 107,26 ff.
Diehl) notes that there are two schools of thought among earlier
commentators. One would take the four categories referred to as
being the heavenly gods and the various classes of (sublunar)
mortal being. The other--with a more thorough grasp of the
truth, in Proclus' view--would take them as referring to, first,
the gods, and then to the various classes of "beings superior
to us" (τὰ κρείττονα ἡμῶν γένη), daemons in the air, and demi-
gods (ἡμίθεοι) in the water, arguing that the creation of these
is described as preceding our own, and the Demiurge should proceed in proper order, not creating birds and fish before men.
Some from this school of thought, he adds, adduce the evidence
of the *Epinomis* (984D ff.) to strengthen their case.

This is, in fact, precisely what we find Albinus doing
in his account of Platonic daemonology in the *Didaskalikos*
(ch. 15), written about the middle of the 2nd cent. C.E. His
account is as follows:

> There are also other *daimones* (sc. than the planetary gods,
> which he has just dealt with), which one might also call
> "created" (γεννητοί, *Tim.* 40D) gods, throughout each of the
> elements, in aether and fire and air and water, in order
> that no part of the cosmos should be devoid of soul (cf.
> *Tim.* 41B), nor of a living being superior to mortal nature;
> and to these are made subject all things beneath the moon
> and upon the earth.

Here *Timaeus* 39E-40A is interpreted in the light of *Epinomis*
984D ff., aether being introduced from the *Epinomis*, between

celestial fire and air, to complete the picture, with its proper
inhabitants.

Philo himself vacillates somewhat on the subject of
aether, but he does distinguish between fire-animals and the
heavenly bodies, thus seeming to discriminate between sublunar
and heavenly fire. His interpretation falls between the two
later schools of thought, since he takes the proper inhabitants
of earth to be land-animals, and those of the sea and rivers to
be water-animals. Only on the question of the inhabitants of
air does he take a different line. Philo does not explicitly
disqualify birds as the proper inhabitants of air (indeed elsewhere, at *Plant.* 12, he identifies them as such), but he is here
plainly following a line represented later by Apuleius in the
De Deo Socratis, ch. 8. Apuleius, after laying down that each
of the four elements have animals proper to them (and he here
includes the animalcules in fiery furnaces mentioned by Aristotle), argues that birds cannot be considered the proper inhabitants of air, since they are really earthy, spending most of
their time in and around the earth. The proper inhabitants of
air must themselves be composed of air and invisible to us.
These are the race of daemons.

The argumentation so closely parallels Philo's as to
make it probable that they are two versions of the same source
(although in Apuleius' case the ultimate source is probably
mediated through Varro). Posidonius naturally comes to mind,
as being known both to have written a work *On Daemons and Heroes*
(Macr. *Sat.* I 23,7), and to have commented on the *Timaeus*. At
any rate, Philo's basic argument here is Middle Platonic.[1]

In his account of the role of angels, Philo also follows
closely Middle Platonic doctrine, based as it is on the well-
known passage of Plato's *Symposium* (202E). Certain souls, Philo
tells us (12), "have never deigned to be brought into union with
any of the parts of earth. These are consecrated and devoted to
the service of the Father, and the Demiurge is accustomed to
employ them as ministers and helpers for the overseeing of
mortals." They serve as "ambassadors backwards and forwards
between men and God." (16). Here one difference is noticeable.
Plato does not clarify the relationship between daemons and
souls, including human souls. Indeed, the implication is that
they are distinct species. Later Platonism, as we can see, for
instance, from Apuleius (*DDS*, chs. 15-16), made them just one

variety of soul, and that is what Philo does here. Since Philo
is not here primarily concerned with angels proper, but only
with fallen ones (who exactly these are we shall consider below),
he does not dwell much on them, though he has a good deal to say
elsewhere about their role in the universe (e.g. *Somn.* 1.141;
Plant. 14; *Abr.* 115; *QE* 2.13). However, enough is said here to
make clear that the *Symposium* passage is the ultimate source of
his doctrine, as it is for that of Plutarch, Albinus, Apuleius
or Maximus, though mediated through the *Epinomis* and later theo-
rising.

2. *The Heavenly Bodies*

If the angels are properly inhabitants of air, they are
not on the same level as the stars or planets, whose proper
realm and composition is that of pure fire. As to whether Philo
regarded the stars and planets as intelligent and divine, there
has been some dispute. At *Gig.* 8 he seems unequivocal enough:
"The stars are souls through and through immaculate (ἀκήρατοι)
and divine, wherefore also they move in a circle, which is the
motion most akin to intellect; for each is an intellect of the
purest type (ἀκραιφνέστατος)." The adjectives ἀκήρατος and
ἀκραιφνής certainly signify freedom from any admixture, and
since the stars are unmixed souls or intellects, one would suppose that, in Philo's view, they must be wholly immaterial and
imperceptible to sense. But this the stars and planets plainly
are not; they are visible as concentrations of fire.

H. A. Wolfson, in his great study of Philo (Vol. I,
p. 364), is made so uncomfortable by this that he seeks to deny
that this is Philo's true opinion, and cites in support of his
view certain other passages, to wit, *Plant.* 12, a parallel passage to *Gig.* 8, where Philo attributes this doctrine to "those
who have studied philosophy (οἱ φιλοσοφήσαντες), and *Opif.* 73,
where he says, rather vaguely, "these (sc. the stars) *are said
to be* not only living creatures but living creatures endowed
with mind (νοερά), or rather each of them a mind (νοῦς) in
itself." This seems a rather desperate suggestion. It is more
plausible, surely, that Philo in these other passages is being
somewhat more circumspect than at *Gig.* 8, attributing a view
which he actually held himself to the intelligentsia in general,
though not excluding himself--"those who have studied philosophy," after all, is not a class from which Philo can reasonably
exempt himself.[2]

The real problem is, rather, how something can be a pure
mind and yet visible, and this is a problem common to all the
passages concerned. Only a Stoic, surely, could think of a *nous*
as pure fire? Not necessarily, I would suggest; the position
is somewhat more complicated than that. One of the more curious
aspects of the revived dogmatic Platonism of Antiochus of
Ascalon is the degree to which he seems to have accepted Stoic
physics as a true interpretation of Platonism. In a significant
passage of Cicero's *De Finibus* IV (s. 36), which is clearly
dependent upon Antiochus, we find the statement, concerning the
mind, that it is "not an empty, impalpable something (a conception to me unintelligible), but belongs to a certain kind of
material substance" (*cum praesertim ipse quoque animus non inane
nescio quid sit (neque enim id possum intellegere), sed in quodam
genere corporis . . .*). This remark is made by Cicero in the
process of a criticism of the Stoics from an Antiochian perspective. Again, at *Acad. Post.* 39, Zeno is reported as maintaining, against Xenocrates (*not* Plato), that nothing incorporeal
is capable of acting or being acted upon. There is no suggestion
that Antiochus (represented by Varro) disagrees with Zeno on this.

The truth seems to be that Antiochus, Platonist though
he was, did not have any use for a concept of incorporeal substance. For him, mind and soul were the purest kind of fire;
"incorporeality" would mean simply freedom from the grosser,
sense-perceptible varieties of matter, being visible, perhaps,
only to the mind's eye. How exactly Antiochus got round the
sharp contrasts in Plato's written works between the realm of
true being and that of becoming we cannot be sure, but such a
passage as the discussion in *Sophist* 246A-248C (the dispute
between the "earth-born" and the "friends of the Forms"), culminating in the definition of true being as "the presence in a
thing of the power of being acted upon or acting in relation to
however insignificant a thing," which might inevitably seem to
involve materiality, must have been an encouragement for him,
as it may have been for Zeno before him. The terms ἀσώματος or
ἄυλος on Antiochus' lips need, then, mean no more than "uncon-
taminated by any of the four sublunar elements."

The stars and planets, however, are in a different
situation from minds or souls. The latter are not sense-
perceptible; these are. If the stars have, or are, minds, they
also, surely, have bodies. Later Platonists viewed them as
minds presiding effortlessly over bodies of pure fire (e.g.

Plot. *Enn.* II 1, 4), but the Stoics certainly made no such distinction, and Antiochus can hardly have done so either. Where
does Philo stand on this? He can use phraseology, as we see,
differing little from that of Zeno himself, who defined a
heavenly body as νοερὸν καὶ φρόνιμον, πύρινον πυρὸς τεχνικοῦ
(*SVF* I 120, from Stobaeus). The concept of πῦρ τεχνικόν holds
the key, perhaps, to the difficulty. This sort of "creative
fire" is so different from ordinary fire (πῦρ ἄτεχνον) and the
other elements as to be contrastable with them almost after the
manner of Platonic true being with the realm of generation. It
is preservative of beings that are made up of it, while ordinary
fire is destructive, and unchanging, while the other elements
are subject to constant change. Philo on numerous occasions
refers to *nous*, or the Logos, as a fiery substance, and is normally taken to be speaking metaphorically when he does so. But
there is really no reason to assume this. When, at *Fug.* 133,
he describes *nous* as ἔνθερμον καὶ πεπυρωμένον πνεῦμα, or in the
most revealing discussion of the nature of soul and mind at
Somn. I 30-33, where the mind is at once *pneuma*, and *asōmaton*
and *akatalēpton* to the senses, we have not, I suggest, a systematic ambiguity, or confusion of mind, on Philo's part, but
an acceptance that the divine substance, at least in so far as
it operates in the universe, is πῦρ τεχνικόν. While he does not
actually use this key expression, he shows his awareness of the
distinction of the two types of fire on various occasions (e.g.,
Mos. I 143; *Dec.* 48), and in a significant phrase at *Heres* 119,
describes the *theios logos* as ἀόρατος καὶ σπερματικὸς καὶ τεχ-
νικός. The problem of the stars' being visible is not, I think,
a great one. What we actually see, after all, is an *augē* given
off by a great concentration of *pyr tekhnikon*. We do not actually see the divine substance of the heavenly body as we would
see a physical object in the sublunar realm. We see, perhaps,
its most "material" aspect (the product, in Stoic doctrine, of
anathymiasis from the sublunar realm, but an *anathymiasis* which
distills only the purest aspects of the sublunar elements), not
the star-soul. Similarly, we can "see" lightning, but not the
electricity which causes the lightning. The Logos, or the *nous*,
or angels, we cannot see; they are too subtle, or fast-moving.
          Are we, then, to make Philo a materialist? Such an
appellation, I think, would be misleading, for two reasons.
First, Philo certainly envisages God, in his transcendent aspect,
as utterly beyond characterisation, and therefore devoid of any

attribute, material or otherwise. He is not even the purest
type of fire. Secondly, even the Logos, and pure souls, can be
described as *asōmatoi* and *aüloi*, despite their identification
as *pneuma*. At *Conf.* 176-7, for example, rational beings are
divided into two kinds, the mortal and the immortal, the latter
being τὸ ψυχῶν ἀσωμάτων (εἶδος), αἳ κατά τε ἀέρα καὶ οὐρανὸν
περιπολοῦσι. Those who go about in the air are the angels/
daemons with whom we are here concerned; those who go about in
heaven are necessarily the stars and planets. Their fiery
integuments do not prevent them from being *asōmatoi* in the sense
of being free from a mortal, changeable *sōma*, "that dwelling-
place of endless calamities," as he characterises it just below.
At *LA* I 82, similarly, the *nous* is described as *aülos kai asō-
matos* (symbolised by Judah), as opposed to Issachar, who has
need of *hylē sōmatikē*. Both the angels and the heavenly bodies,
then, are composed of *pyr tekhnikon*; they are not, however, for
that reason to be described as *sōmatika* or *hylika*. Those terms
have connotations of corruption and passivity which do not suit
these entities.

3. *Evil Daemons?*

          A third problem raised by the early sections of the *De
Gigantibus* is that of the existence and status of anything that
could be denominated an *evil* daemon or angel. We must distinguish here at the outset between angels whom God may use to
punish mortals for their own good, as agents of his Punitive
Power (*kolastērios dynamis*), and evil daemons in the strict
sense, beings whose nature is evil, and who, although perhaps
comprehended on the highest level within God's providence, are
immediately in the service of another master, Satan.

          As to the first category, there is no problem. Philo
repeatedly talks of God's *kolastērios dynamis* (e.g. *Sacr.* 132;
Conf. 171 ff.; *Spec. Leg.* 1. 307), and the beings that serve
as His agents in this area. At *Fug.* 66, Philo tells us that
"it is unbecoming to God to punish, seeing that He is the
original and perfect lawgiver; he punishes not by his own hands,
but by those of others who act as his ministers (ὑπηρετοῦντες)."
These ministers are connected in Philo's mind with the "Young
Gods" of Plato's *Timaeus*, whom the Demiurge uses to create the
lower parts of man's soul, his body, and irrational creation
in general (41A ff.), but the category is broader than this,

comprising angelic entities which would be much more particular
in their operation than the Young Gods, who by Philo's time were
generally equated with the planetary gods (and by Philo himself
at *Opif.* 46, for example). At any rate, all these entities are
essentially good, and we are not concerned with them in the
present connection.

What we seem to have a reference to at *Gig.* 16-18, on
the other hand, is a class of evil daemons, such as abound both
in Jewish apocalyptic literature, such as the Book of Enoch, and
in early Christianity, as well as in popular Greek belief. The
passage needs to be quoted *in extenso*:

> The common usage of men is to give the name of daemon to
> bad and good daemons alike, and the name of soul to good
> and bad souls. And so, too, you also will not go wrong
> if you reckon as angels, not only those who are worthy of
> the name, who are as ambassadors forwards and backwards
> between men and God and are rendered sacred and inviolate
> by reason of that glorious and blameless ministry, but
> also those who are unholy and unworthy of the title.
> (Colson's trans.)

Philo then quotes, to support his point, a passage of Psalm 77
(78):49, which goes in the LXX as follows:

ἐξαπέστειλεν εἰς αὐτοὺς ὀργὴν θυμοῦ αὐτοῦ,

θυμὸν καὶ ὀργὴν καὶ θλῖψιν,

ἀποστολὴν δι᾽ ἀγγέλων πονηρῶν.

These *angeloi ponēroi* Philo seeks to equate with the angels of
God of Gen 6:2 (in his version)--quite unsuitably, one would
think, since the context of Psalm 77 makes it clear that these
angels are agents of God, and thus *kolastērioi* rather than
ponēroi in the sense that Philo requires. At any rate, Philo's
point seems clear enough: the "angels" of Gen 6:2 are "unholy
and unworthy of the name of angel." Had Philo read I *Enoch*
6-21 (and he may well be acquainted with something of the tradition on which Enoch depends), he would have learned much about
these fallen angels, under their leaders Semjaza and Azazel, and
about their terrible punishment at the hands of God, through the
agency of the archangel Michael and others.

But is Philo really here talking about fallen angels?
For those who think he is, there is something strange about this
passage. Wolfson, who assumes that he is (*Philo*, I 383),
expresses the problem as follows: "But Philo speaks also (*Gig.*
17-18) of another class of angels whom he calls "evil angels,"
first referring to them as if they were real beings and then

treating them allegorically, without any formal transition from
one of these methods of treatment to the other." This would
certainly be the case, if Wolfson were right. Whatever Philo
is talking about in 16, by 18 he is talking about various types
of embodied souls, who pursue one sort of pleasure or another,
these latter being "the daughters of men"--as opposed to the
virtues, "the daughters of right reason."

　　　Now, however, Valentin Nikiprowetsky, in a most perceptive article,[3] has provided a persuasive solution to this
problem. Despite appearances, he argues, Philo is not here
envisaging a class of fallen angels at all, but is simply telling
of souls who fall into embodiment, as opposed to those who remain
pure from such contamination. It is we, in fact, in our unre-
formed state, who are the *angeloi ponēroi*, and it is in this
sense that Philo must be interpreting Psalm 77:49. I myself
had previously (*Middle Platonists*, p. 173) gone along with previous interpreters of Philo and seen a description of evil
angels in this passage, though, like Wolfson, I was disturbed
by the sudden "transition" in 18. I am persuaded now by Nikiprowetsky's exegesis. It clears up a bothersome anomaly in
Philo's doctrine. Whatever traces of dualism may be discernible
in odd corners of the Philonic corpus (and I continue to see
such a trace in *QE* 1.23, for example), there are not necessarily
any such here, though one could wish that Philo had made himself
clearer than he has done. Certainly, his remark in 16 about
"the common usage of men" (λέγουσιν οἱ πολλοί) not distinguishing
good and evil daemons in their terminology seems to imply his
acceptance of the fact that entities of both these varieties
exist; what follows, however, serves effectively to undercut
that assumption on the reader's part.

NOTES

　　　[1]Whether or not the argument in Philo (11), not reflected
in Apuleius, that the air is a source of life to others and thus
can hardly be devoid of life itself, is derived from Philo's
source or is an elaboration of his own, is not clear. On the
question of origins, see the useful survey of J. Beaujeu, in his
Budé edition of the *De Deo* (*Apulée, Opuscules Philosophiques et
Fragments*, pp. 219-22.

　　　[2]He repeats his view, after all, at *Gig.* 60.

　　　[3]"Sur une lecture démonologique de Philon d'Alexandrie,
De Gigantibus 6-18."

J. Dillon

C. *The Idea of Conscience in Philo of Alexandria*

In attempting to assess the significance and originality
of the notion of conscience in Philo, I find myself hampered by
the scarcity of contemporary evidence against which to evaluate
his doctrine. It is clearly fallacious of Wolfson[1] to treat
Philo as the source of any doctrine not attested in any earlier
philosopher; yet even this reflection does not express the full
measure of our difficulty. Our knowledge of Plotinus' philosophical predecessors is scarcely more detailed than our knowledge
of Philo's background; yet, even though we can rarely with certainty claim Plotinus as the source of a particular idea, we can
at least see that in his work we are dealing with doctrines
that have been fully thought out and thoroughly integrated into
his system. In Philo, on the other hand, we are faced with suggestions thrown out at need in order to explain particular biblical texts, which are not and do not claim to be part of a
fully formulated body of doctrine. And this is even more true
of a nebulous notion like conscience than of such more concrete
metaphysical doctrines as the negative theology or the Platonic
ideas as thoughts of God. What we can ask is, first, what is
the notion's significance for Philo himself and, secondly, what
do we find in him that is not present in preceding or near-
contemporary authors whose works survive. Even after formulat-
ing the problem in this way we shall still find certainty hard
to come by in a field where our comparisons must be based on
fine shades of meaning. In reaching my own highly tentative
conclusions I must express my great indebtedness to the well-
documented paper of Valentin Nikiprowetzky,[2] with whose main
conclusions I find myself in general agreement.

Clearly, as even Bréhier,[3] who stresses Philo's originality, admits, Philo was by no means the first to formulate the
notion of conscience. The Homeric notion of *aidōs*, for a start,
carries much of the undertones of what we understand by conscience. If we seek more exact parallels, as Bréhier and Nikiprowetzky[4] observe, they are to be found less in Plato, Aristotle
and the Old Stoa than in poets and popular moralists, such as
Euripides and Menander[5] and, above all, in the Epicureans'

constant stress on the pangs of conscience suffered by the
guilty sinner.[6] The closest verbal anticipation of Philo, as
has been noted, comes at Polybius 18.43.13, with its close fore-
shadowing of the language of Philo *Det.* 23.[7] It is true that
such passages stress the idea of a guilty conscience (or, conversely, the benefits of a clear conscience) and Philo might
therefore be thought to be original in his emphasis on the role
of conscience as a moral teacher and healer.[8] Yet such ideas are
by no means lacking in contemporary literature; one may especially note Seneca *De Ira* 3.36, where the positive role of conscience in moral self-examination is stressed.[9] The Polybius
passage at all events should warn us that closer parallels to
Philo may have existed in literature now lost. Does Philo's
originality then lie in his Jewish consciousness of man's weakness in the face of God and his need for divine help? There is
indeed likely to be much in this suggestion; yet we should
remember the stress laid by Euripides, in particular, on man's
moral imperfection and that the late Stoics, whom we cannot
reasonably suppose to be drawing on Philo, are no less emphatic
than he is in their stress on these themes and in the new dimension of inwardness which they give to man's moral life.[10] Pur-
suing such lines of thought we may be tempted to conclude that
Philo's originality lies in no more than his application of such
nonessential Jewish imagery as his comparison of conscience to
the High Priest.[11] It will therefore be best, before proceeding
further, to survey both the function and the metaphysical status
of conscience in Philo before returning to see what conclusions
regarding his originality can be drawn.

          We may first deal with Philo's vocabulary. To express
the concept of conscience he uses two main terms, either singly
or in combination,[12] *elegchos* and *to syneidos*. The latter, more
frequently in the form *synesis* or *syneidēsis* (or their cognates)
is the normal Greek term for conscience.[13] The former, on the
other hand, does not appear to be found in precisely this sense
in Greek authors before Philo. As a legal or philosophical term
(the latter applying particularly, of course, to the Socratic
method of argument), it connotes interrogation or cross-
examination and has sometimes the further sense of proof, refutation or conviction.[14] And while the parallel, and sometimes
the contrast, is drawn in contemporary philosophical literature
between conviction by an external court or accuser and by the
inner voice of conscience,[15] Philo's use of the term to mean

conscience as such still seems to be original. This seems
equally true of Philo's Hellenistic Jewish predecessors as of
Greek philosophy, despite the term's use, noted by Nikiprowetzky,
in the Wisdom of Solomon. Philo's use of the term to mean "conscience" as such does not seem to occur there. Professor J.
Milgrom, however, observes that the LXX version of Lev 5:24
anticipates him on this point.[16] To turn from Philo's terminology to the substance of his doctrine, the most complete description of the function of the *elegchos* comes at *Det.* 22-23, a passage already noted, in which conscience is described as the true
man, dwelling in each individual's soul, who at different times
performs the function of ruler and king, judge and umpire of
life's contests, or again of a silent internal witness or
accuser, who does not even suffer man to open his mouth, but
bridles his stubborn tongue by the reins of conscience (ταῖς τοῦ
συνειδότος ἡνίαις). The image of a judge or a law-court recurs
in several passages, notably *Fug.* 117-18, where *elegchos* is
identified with the most holy Logos, whose presence in the soul
prevents even involuntary sin from entering her. Therefore, it
is affirmed, we should pray that conscience should live in our
soul; for as both high-priest, king and judge, he obtains our
mind as his court and is put to shame by none of the sins brought
to him for judgment.[17] At *Virt.* 206 we learn that conscience is
the only court not swayed by artifices of words, while at *QE*
2.13 he is the only counsellor unswayed by fear or favor,[18] and
whose function, like that of the Socratic *elegchos*, is to convict the soul of its false conceit of wisdom. Similarly at
Deus 125 ff. the *elegchos* is represented by the "living color
upon the leper" (*Lev.* 13.11-13), who makes a catalogue of man's
sins, so that the soul, being convicted of her offences against
the *orthos logos*, recognizes her own impurity.[19] And, like the
Socratic *elegchos*, that of Philo has not just the negative role
of an accuser, but the positive function of a teacher. That the
criticisms of conscience are beneficial in themselves is stated
at *Det.* 146, where we are urged to pray for God to punish us,
as a mercy, to correct our sins and heal us by sending this
Logos, in the form of conscience, into our mind to reproach us
and put us to shame for our sins.[20] At *Deus* 138 conscience is
said to rouse in the soul a memory of her sins so that she may
turn away from them with weeping and loathing.[21] At *Decal.* 87
the *elegchos* is once again described as accuser and judge, who
by blaming and reproaching the soul puts her to shame, while in

the role of judge he teaches and admonishes her and exhorts her
to change; if the soul should prove recalcitrant, it is added,
he wages unceasing and merciless war on her by day and night
until he breaks the thread of her wretched life. Hence, it is
natural that *Op.* 128 should describe the Sabbath as having been
instituted so that man, by keeping away from external work,
should improve his character and attend to his conscience.[22]
The most positive passages, however, are *Deus* 182-83 and *Fug.*
5-6. In both these passages the *elegchos* is identified with the
angel of the Lord (in the former of them also with the Logos),
who guides man and keeps him from stumbling;[23] at *Fug.* 6 the
words *philos* and *symboulos*, are used of the *elegchos* without
qualification, while at *Deus* 182-83 we are exhorted by our
behavior to keep the internal judge kindly toward us, so as to
prevent our sins from becoming incurable.[24] It is passages like
these which bring us to the element in Philo, other than his
terminology, that seems most original. In his account of the
functions of conscience his difference from his contemporaries
would be at most one of greater emphasis on the role of conscience in man's moral life; as a transcendent gift of God to
the soul, or as a transcendent being, like the Logos or an angel.
And this in turn raises the most difficult problem in Philo's
account of conscience, that of whether such passages can be
reconciled with those which appear, in traditional Greek fashion,
to speak of conscience as immanent in the soul. To decide this
question we must first examine the most important relevant passages and secondly see what contemporary or near-contemporary
doctrines provide the closest parallels to this thought.

The most emphatic affirmation of the immanence of the
elegchos comes at *Decal.* 87, where it is described as ἑκάστῃ
ψυχῇ συμπεφυκὼς καὶ συνοικῶν. In similar vein come two passages
where the *elegchos* is identified with the true man within the
soul, *Fug.* 131,[25] and the already referred to *Det.* 23, where the
true man is said to dwell within each individual's soul and
admonish him invisibly from within, and is further identified
with ἠρθρωμένη καὶ λογικὴ διάνοια. Less definite, but still
pointing in the same direction is *Op.* 128, where the conscience
is described as seated in the soul like a judge (ἐνιδρυμένος τῇ
ψυχῇ, καθάπερ δικαστής). More numerous, however, are the passages where the transcendence of conscience is upheld. And even
the above passages are not entirely free from ambiguity regarding immanence versus transcendence, as the notion of Logos,

while the ἠρθρωμένη καὶ λογικὴ διάνοια could refer, not, like
the Stoic *orthos logos*, to a power innate in the human soul, but
to reason enlightened by divine grace. Other passages leave less
doubt. Thus at *Det.* 146 conscience is described as the divine
Logos sent by God into man's soul,[26] while at *Fug.* 117-18 the
elegchos, identified with the high priest, is said to die, not in
the sense of undergoing destruction, but of being separated from
our soul.[27] These passages, we may observe, come from the same
treatises from which the above "immanentist" texts were taken,
and it may therefore be that the latter texts, where we have
found them ambiguous, should be interpreted in the light of
those which more definitely point to the transcendence of conscience. Whether all contradiction could be removed in this way
is, however, more than doubtful. Two further texts identifying
conscience with the divine Logos or angel were quoted above
(*Fug.* 5-6, *Deus* 182-83), yet at the same time the latter passage
refers to conscience as the *interior* judge.[28] Other texts in
the same vein include *Fug.* 203 (conscience as an all-seeing
angel),[29] *QG* 4.62, where the divine Logos is said to enter man's
soul to examine and convict it, and *QE* 2.13, where it is identified with the divine Logos and with the subject of the text, "I
will send my angel before thy face" (Exod 23:20-21). Perhaps
most impressive of all is *Deus* 135-38, where conscience, identified with the High Priest, is described in quasi-mythical
terms as entering the soul like a pure ray of light, to reveal
our hidden sins in order to purify and heal us.[30] Later in the
section (*ibid.* 138) it is described as ὁ ἑρμηνεὺς τοῦ θεοῦ λόγος
καὶ προφήτης.

    Is there any hope of reconciling such transcendentalist
texts with the immanentist one quoted earlier? I think there
may be, though I am very doubtful whether Philo had consciously
worked out such a theory. It appears to me that the different
sides of Philo's thought here answer partly to a conflict between
his Greek and Jewish sides, partly perhaps to a conflict within
the Jewish tradition regarding man's capacity, but also largely
from a hesitation in Philo's own experience similar to that
which in more developed theologies has produced the nature-grace
controversy. One obvious and easy way to resolve the dilemma,
by supposing Philo to refer to a power innate in man's soul which
is yet ultimately a divine gift, is disproved by Philo's references to conscience as entering and withdrawing from the soul.
Nor, conversely, can we dismiss his portrayal of conscience as

a substantially existing entity by the argument that such a
picture follows from the need to allegorize individual biblical
characters. There are, in fact, two problems: (a) Is conscience
man's innate possession or a transcendent gift of God? (b) In
the latter case, is it given to man as a permanent gift, or one
that enters and leaves him? Plotinus is the first Platonist
whose extant works attempt to resolve the conflict. Man's *nous*
is regarded as a transcendent entity, sometimes equated with his
guardian daemon, by a minority of Middle Platonists, cf. Plutarch,
De Fac. 943A ff.; *Gen. Socr.* 591D ff.; *Corp. Hermet.* I 22, X
19-21. Further light may, perhaps, be thrown on the problem if
we consider the closest Greek parallels to Philo's doctrine. For
while, as we have observed, the idea of *conscience* as a transcendent force appears unparalleled in Greek thought,[31] there are
important resemblances to a closely related Greek notion, that of
man's guardian daemon.[32] We may briefly survey three such conceptions, those of Apuleius, Plotinus and the Late Stoa. The
distinctiveness of Philo's own position may then become apparent.

        We may first conveniently consider Apuleius, in whom, as
Nikiprowetzky observes, the moral role of the guardian daemon
receives greatest stress.[33] Yet while the operations of that
daemon, as described in chapter 16 of the *De Deo Socratis*, are
remarkably similar in many ways to those of conscience in Philo,
and while the daemon is said to operate in men's innermost minds
like conscience (*in ipsis penitissimis mentibus vice conscien-
tiae deversetur*), it appears to be conceived wholly as a transcendent being and in no sense as a force innate in and the
property of the human soul. Hence a full parallel to Philo is
lacking. Plotinus, on the other hand, in his discussion of the
guardian daemon in the treatise 3.4, is especially concerned to
resolve the immanence-transcendence dilemma. His solution rests
upon the principle that our soul contains the whole intelligible
world--that we are "each of us an intelligible cosmos,"[34]--and
that our guardian daemon is the level in the hierarchy of being
next above that on which we are habitually operative. Hence,
though immanent within us, it is yet transcendent to our normal
life.[35] Thus the apparent contradictions within Plato as to the
status of the daemon can be explained.[36] But here two obvious
differences from Philo reveal themselves. First, as we have
noted, Plotinus differs from Philo in his concern, in which on
the whole he succeeds, to produce a coherent theory on the

subject; secondly, and even more important, the daemon appears
to have no *moral* role in his system save insofar as it assumes
the leadership of good souls once their present life is through
and guides them to a place or state appropriate to their moral
condition.[37] Any notion of the daemon as watching over man's
moral life in the form of conscience appears to be wholly lacking in Plotinus, as does Philo's stress, in his transcendentalist passages, on man's weakness and his need for divine help.
Whether there is a place for grace in Plotinus' system is a
much-debated question; but certainly all his stress falls on
man's power to save himself by his own moral effort. He thus
seems further removed from Philo in these respects than either
Apuleius or the Late Stoa.

It is in the late Stoics, like Epictetus and Marcus
Aurelius, that the resemblance to Philo is closest. The moral
function of the guardian daemon for them is only too obvious.
The daemon is the *nous* and *logos*, which Zeus has given to each
man as his guide and is a particle of the divine substance, a
guardian of man's acts who never sleeps and is never beguiled,
who sees and hears all, and whom we should therefore keep
unsullied by upright speech and action.[38] At first sight,
indeed, the metaphysical status of the daemon seems to offer a
complete contrast with Philo's "transcendentalist" passages,
since, whereas he stresses man's total dependence on God, the
Stoic view involves the conception of the highest part of the
human soul as a particle of the divine substance.[39] Yet that
this is not the whole story can be seen from Marcus Aurelius
2.17, which stresses, no less than Philo, the weakness and
transience not just of man's body, but of his soul.[40] As we
have remarked, the feeling of human weakness becomes much more
pronounced in the Late Stoa than it had been in the founders
of the school and this, combined with the references to the
daemon as a gift of God,[41] suggests that in their emotional
attitude the Late Stoics are, at times at least, much closer to
Philo than their formal theory allows and as close as any contemporary or near-contemporary pagan author. Once again,
perhaps, we have the old theological conflict of human responsibility versus divine grace.

It seems, then, that the originality of Philo's conception of the moral role of conscience has been greatly exag-
gerated, and lies mainly, as compared with his predecessors
whose works survive, in his emphasis on its god-given nature.

Nor, as I have said, do I think he has achieved a consistent
metaphysical theory on the subject. If we ask how he could have
attained one, our best hope seems to be in a suggestion of
Professor David Winston, that "the divine Logos is ever present
to man, but its consummation in any particular case is condi-
tioned by the fitness of the subject."[42] Similarly, we may
recall, Aristotle's Passive *Nous* had been actualised by its
transcendent, Active, counterpart. With these suggestions in
mind, we can develop a theory which avoids the difficulties of
an exclusively immanentist or transcendentalist view and which
would, furthermore, anticipate the later Neoplatonists' desire
to preserve the transcendence of the divine *Nous*--a view which
ran counter to that of Plotinus, and one with which any orthodox theist would presumably feel considerable sympathy. For
Iamblichus and his followers, man's *nous* is only an irradiation
(ἔλλαμψις) from the transcendent Hypostasis (cf. Proclus, *E.T.*
props. 111, 175, 204; *In Tim.* 3.245, 18 ff.). Philo's doctrine
of conscience could similarly have postulated two entities, the
"irradiation" being man's inherent possession (as at *Dec.* 87),
but remaining a mere potentiality until actualised by the divine
Logos. Such, at least, whether he actually drew it or not, is
the logical conclusion of Philo's various pronouncements on
conscience.

NOTES

[1]H. A. Wolfson, *Philo*; 2 vols. (Cambridge, Mass. 1948),
passim.

[2]"La Doctrine de l'Elenchos chez Philon, ses Résonances
Philosophiques et sa Portée réligieuse," Colloques Nationaux du
Centre National de la Recherche Scientifique, Paris, 1967,
pp. 255-73.

[3]*Les Idées Philosophiques et Religieuses de Philon
d'Alexandrie*, 3rd ed., Paris, 1950, pp. 295 ff.

[4]Bréhier, *op. cit.* pp. 299-300; Nikiprowetzky, *op. cit.*
pp. 260-62.

[5]Euripides, *Or.* 396; Menander, *Monost.* 654; frs. 522
and 531 Körte; Plautus, *Most.* 544; Terence, *Eun.* 119, Ad. 348;
Cicero, *Pro Cluent.* 159, *ND* 3.85. Professor W. S. Anderson, to
whom I owe most of the above references also adduces the newly
discovered prologues to Menander's *Samia* and *Misoumenos*.

[6]Cf. e.g. Lucretius 3.1011 ff., Seneca *Ep.* 97.15, 105.7.

[7]Polyb. 18.43.13; Philo *Det*. 23. Bréhier further compares *Decal*. 87.

[8]Cf. Nikiprowetzky, *op. cit.* p. 256 n. 1.

[9]Cf. also Cicero *Tusc*. 4.45 (*Morderi est melius conscientia*) and Seneca *Ep*. 28.9 (*initium est salutis notitia peccati*, a quotation from Epicurus). From Philo cf. *Det*. 146, *Congr*. 157-58, 179.

[10]Cf. e.g. Marcus Aurelius 2.17, discussed later in this paper.

[11]*Fug*. 118, *Deus* 135.

[12]For the terms in combination cf. e.g. *Op*. 128, *Ebr*. 125, 149; cf. also *Det*. 146, *Jos*. 47-48, etc.

[13]Cf. the passages in Stobaeus *Anth*. 24 (cited above in n. 5). The term *to syneidos* is used there only in passage 8, ascribed to Pythagoras, but certainly of later, probably much later origin, and passage 15, from Plutarch, a post-Philonic author.

[14]Cf. the article in LSJ and Nikiprowetzky *op. cit.*, pp. 255 n. 1, 274.

[15]In Philo cf. e.g. *Virt*. 206, *Jos*. 47-48; from contemporary literature cf. e.g. Cicero *Leg*. 1.40.

[16]Cf. J. Milgrom, "On the Origins of Philo's Doctrine of Conscience," *Studia Philonica* 3, (1974-75) pp. 41-45. As Nikiprowetzky observes (*op. cit.* pp. 267-73), the word occurs frequently in Wisdom of Solomon though apparently not in the sense of "conscience." It is used five times, for instance, in the book's first two chapters.

[17]*Fug*. 117-18.

[18]*Virt*. 206, with *QE* 2.13; cf. *QG* 4.62.

[19]*Deus* 126.

[20]*Det*. 146. Cf. *QG* 3.28.

[21]*Deus* 138.

[22]*Op*. 128.

[23]*Deus* 182.

[24]*Ibid*., 183.

[25]*Fug*. 131.

[26]Cf. above n. 21.

[27]*Fug*. 117.

[28]Cf. above n. 24.

[29]*Fug*. 203.

[30] *Deus* 135.

[31] Though the *elegchos* is personified at Menander fr. 145 (quoted by Lucian, *Pseudol.* ch. 4); cf. also Menander *Monost.* 654: βροτοῖς ἅπασιν ἡ συνείδησις θεός.

[32] Cf. Nikiprowetzky *op. cit.* pp. 263-66.

[33] Cf. *ibid.* p. 265 n. 3.

[34] *Enn.* 3.4.3.22.

[35] *Ibid.* 3.4.3.3 ff.

[36] The contrast is between *Phaedo* 107D (where the daemon is represented as an individual entity) and *Timaeus* 90A (where it is identified with the highest part of the human soul).

[37] *Enn.* 3.4.3.8 ff.

[38] For late Stoic views on the daemon cf. Posidonius, fr. 187 Edelstein-Kidd (quoted by Galen, *de Placitis Hippocratis et Platonis*, p. 448.4 ff.); Epictetus 1.14.11-14, Marcus Aurelius 3.6.2. For *nous* as the daemon cf. Marcus Aurelius 5.27; for the need to keep the daemon unsullied cf. Epictetus 2.8.13-14, Marcus Aurelius 2.17, 3.16.2-4.

[39] For the human soul as an *apospasma* from the divine substance cf. Epictetus 2.8.11; for the term as applied to the daemon cf. Marcus Aurelius 5.27, cf. also Epictetus 1.14.11: τοῦτο δέ σοι καὶ λέγει τις, ὅτι ἴσην ἔχεις δύναμιν τῷ Διί;

[40] A particularly striking passage is the first section of Marcus Aurelius 2.17.

[41] For Daemon as a gift of God cf. Epictetus 2.14.12, Marcus Aurelius 5.27.

[42] An observation made in a comment on a first draft of this essay. As he observes, we have here a fundamental Neo-platonic principle, most concisely expressed at Proclus, *E.T.*, prop. 142.

                                                        R. Wallis

D. *The Nature of God in the* 'Quod Deus'

In his theology, Philo follows a system in which the Supreme Principle is a Monad, though for him it is also, of course, the personal God of Judaism. He frequently calls God "one" (e.g. *Op.* 171; *LA* 2.1-3; *Cher.* 87, etc.), the Monad (*LA* 2.3; *Her.* 183; *Deus* 11), or "the really existent" (*Op.* 172; *Decal.* 8; *Spec.* 1.28). At *Spec.* 2.176, however, the Monad is said to be "the incorporeal image of God," whom it resembles because it also stands alone, and in a remarkable passage at *Praem.* 40 God is described as ἀγαθοῦ κρεῖττον καὶ μονάδος πρεσβύτερον καὶ ἑνὸς εἰλικρινέστερον, but even this flight of negative theology can be taken as meaning only that God does not have goodness as a *quality*, and that he is not a *countable* unit. Along with the "normal" epithets for God, such as "eternal," "unchanging" and "imperishable," Philo produces others for which he is our earliest authority. At *Somn.* 1.67, for example, God is described as "unnameable" (*akatonomastos*) and "unutterable" (*arrhêtos*), and "incomprehensible under any form," none of which terms are applied to God before his time in any surviving source.

The question thus arises as to whether Philo is responsible for introducing the concept of an "unknowable" God into Greek thought. H. A. Wolfson, in *Philo*, Vol. II, pp. 110-26, argues (against Eduard Norden, in *Agnostos Theos*[1]) that he did, and, though it is not strictly relevant to our present theme, it seems worth discussing this claim, since a decision on it will throw some light on the sources of Philo's theology in general.

Wolfson points out correctly that neither Plato nor Aristotle declares God to be unknowable. Indeed, Plato regards the realm of Ideas in which the Demiurge of the *Timaeus* and even the Good of the *Republic* are included, as "comprehensible by intellect with the aid of reason" (*Tim.* 28A). Aristotle, however, provides at least the seeds of later negative theology by declaring God to be "simple and indivisible" (*Phys.* VIII 10, 267b25-6, *Met.* XII 7, 1072a32-3), which makes God by Aristotle's own rules of logic undefinable and unknowable, since knowledge

is dependent upon definition, and definition involves the distinction of genus, species and differentiae, which is not
possible in the case of God. However, as Wolfson says, Aristotle does not explicitly draw this conclusion in the case of
God. The question is, therefore, whether anyone else in the
Greek philosophical tradition could have done so, or whether
the idea of the unknowability of God is altogether alien to
Greek thought until Philo introduced it.

          It does not seem to me that the concept of the unknow-
ability of God's essence, as opposed to his attributes or activities, is one that is alien to Greek thought. The difficulty of
naming Zeus adequately is, after all, familiar enough to Greeks
on the poetic level. But there is, admittedly, a dearth of
explicit philosophical statements of this before Philo's time.
In claiming this for a Philonic contribution, however, Wolfson
does not take proper account of all that has perished in the
Hellenistic period--the writings of Speusippus and Xenocrates,
all of the early Stoics, Panaetius, Posidonius, Antiochus of
Ascalon, Eudorus of Alexandria. We have fragmentary reports of
these people's views, but there is inevitably much that is lost
to us. What we do find is, on the one hand, an important statement of later Platonic doctrine on the nature of God in Albinus'
Didaskalikos, ch. 10, and an interesting Pythagorean pseudepig-
raphon, an extract from "Archytas," *On First Principles* (*Peri
Archôn*), preserved by Stobaeus (*Anth.* I, 41.2).[2] Wolfson quotes
this on p. 115, but actually misinterprets it against himself.
It is not God that "Archytas" denominates as "pertaining to an
irrational (*alogos*) and ineffable (*arrhêtos*) nature," but simply
the second of his pair of principles, Substance or Matter (*ôsia*),
as opposed to Form (*morphô*), which is *rhêtos* and *logon echoisa*.
"Archytas" does, however, introduce God as a third principle
above these two, as "not only *nous*, but something superior to
nous." It is plain that "Archytas" wishes to make God a principle above the opposition of *logikos-rhêtos/alogos-arrhêtos*,
though he stops short of saying that. The passage is not, therefore, quite as troublesome for Wolfson as he thought it was, but
it is significant none the less. Wolfson was driven to what
seems the desperate expedient of assuming that "Archytas" must
be dependent on Philo. These treatises are, of course, not
exactly datable, but, if anything, it is more likely that Philo
is influenced by *Pythagorica* (he does, after all, know works
of "Philolaus" (*Opif.* 100), and of "Ocellus Lucanus " (*Aet.* 12)).

The connection of "Archytas" with Eudorus of Alexandria is more
interesting to pursue, especially since Eudorus seems to have
known "Archytas" *On the Categories* (the purported original of
Aristotle's *Categories*).[3] Eudorus also follows a system, which
he attributes to "the Pythagoreans," which involves a supreme
principle, called the One, above a pair of opposites, a Monad
and a Dyad, the Monad representing Form, the Dyad Matter (Simpl.
In Phys. p. 181,10 ff. Diels). Whether or not Eudorus knew
"Archytas," he certainly seems to have known a Pythagorean tradition representing the same doctrine, and this indicates that
a doctrine of a One above all attributes (i.e. all members of
the Pythagorean Table of Opposites) was a part of the Pythagorean
tradition at least by the first century B.C.E. It seems more
reasonable, then, to assume that Philo is influenced by the tradition of which "Archytas" is a representative than that
"Archytas" is influenced by Philo.

Still less plausible is Wolfson's suggestion that
Albinus[4] is influenced by Philo. There is no indication that
anyone within the Platonic tradition, with the possible exception of Numenius, had ever heard of Philo, and one would
require much more compelling evidence than this before conceding
such a possibility.[5]

Albinus begins ch. 10 of his work with the remark that
Plato considers his supreme principle, God, to be "all but
indescribable" (μικροῦ δεῖν καὶ ἄρρητον). After this significant initial qualification, however, he has no hesitation twice
later in the chapter about giving God the epithet ἄρρητος *tout
court*. On the second occasion, though, he expands on this in
an enlightening way. "God," he says, "is ineffable, and comprehensible only by the intellect (cf. *Rep*. 7.529D), since
there is neither genus nor species nor differentia predicable
of him." He is, in fact, neither qualified (*poios*) nor unqualified (*apoios*), since he is above qualification. We have here,
surely, the missing link which Wolfson sought, though a few
hundred years later than one would wish. On the other hand,
there is small likelihood that Albinus is indulging in bold
innovation here: his concern is to present the consensus of
Platonic doctrine as it appears to him. This formulation, if
not produced already in the Old Academy, is at any rate a good
deal older than Albinus, and, based on good Aristotelian principles as it is, there is nothing "unhellenic" about it.[6]

All this, however, by way of background to the proper
subject of this essay, which is the doctrine of the immutability
and impassivity of God, and the consequences of that doctrine
for the more religious side of Philo's thought. It was the arguments for this contained in this treatise which made it particularly popular, among Philo's works, with the Church Fathers,
both Greek and Roman, from Clement and Origen on, and sects. 51-
68 in particular constitute one of the most comprehensive attacks
on anthropomorphism, and explanations of anthropomorphic terminology, surviving from antiquity (Cicero's *De Natura Deorum*
II 45-72 being another, from a Stoic perspective).

Philo begins, in 52, by asserting, against certain
literal interpreters (or perhaps just the uneducated believer),
that the Existent (*to on*) is neither subject to "the irrational
passions of the soul," nor does he possess bodily parts or
limbs.[7] Despite this, Moses frequently uses expressions which
suggest that God is subject to passions and has bodily parts.
This constitutes a problem to be solved. The solution, of
course, lies in the very crudeness of Moses' expressions in
their literal interpretation. The real meaning lies beneath.

Philo's doctrine is based on the juxtaposition of two
passages of Scripture, in their LXX version, Num 23:19 (God is
not as a man--οὐχ ὡς ἄνθρωπος ὁ θεός), and Deut 8:5 (The Lord
your God will discipline you as a father disciplines his son--
ὡς εἴ τις παιδεύσαι τὸν υἱὸν αὐτοῦ οὕτως κύριος ὁ θεός σου παιδεύσει σε). Num 23:19 is actually an inspired utterance by
Balaam, which allows it to qualify, with Deut 8:5, as a "summa-
tion" (*kephalaion*, 53) of Moses' laws about the proper way to
refer to God.[8] The verb *paideuô* in Deut 8:5, which the LXX is
using in a "vulgar" sense, to translate the Hebrew *yassēr*,
meaning "to punish, discipline," Philo takes in the Classical
sense of "educate," which enables him to see this passage as
alluding to the educational purpose of Moses' anthropomorphic
references.

Such paideia, however, is only necessary for those whom
Philo calls "the Friends of the Body," the non-intellectual man
in the street. The Friends of the Soul, on the other hand, have
a true concept of the Deity. They do not compare Him with anything created, but see Him as free of all qualification (*poio-
tēs*), only apprehensible in respect of His bare existence (*kata
to einai*; *psilē hyparxis*). Later, at 62, this is reiterated.
God cannot be equated with the cosmos or the heavens, as the

Stoics would have him, since these are *poia eidê*, qualified
forms; He cannot be apprehended even by the mind, except as
regards His bare existence: "It is only His existence (*hyparxis*)
that we can apprehend (*katalambanomen*)."

This distinction between *hyparxis* and *poiotês*, borrowed
from the Stoics (not necessarily by Philo, however; very possibly by a Platonist intermediary) is of great importance for
Philo's doctrine. The connection with Albinus, in the passage
of *Did.* ch. 10 quoted above, is clear enough, and Wolfson's suggestion that Albinus is here influenced by Philo is, as I have
already suggested, implausible. Elsewhere, at *LA* 3.206, for
example, Philo comes even closer to Albinus' formulations: "Who
can assert of the First Cause," he says, "either that it is
without body or that it is a body, or that it is qualified
(*poion*) or unqualified (*apoion*)? In a word, who can make any
positive assertion concerning its essence (*ousia*) or quality
(*poiotês*) or state or movement?" It should be plain enough from
this that Philo is able to draw on a tradition of scholastic
discussion as to the apprehensibility of God which Albinus is
also reflecting, The precise identity of this source is beyond
our knowledge (to talk of "Neopythagorean sources" is only to
give our ignorance a name), but the admixture of Aristotelian
and Stoic terminology with Platonist doctrine points to figures
such as Antiochus of Ascalon, Eudorus of Alexandria or Arius
Didymus.

The argument, at any rate, is conducted entirely in
terms of Greek philosophy. Our concept of God involves His
transcending any genus or species, since these are divisions of
created things, and involve having other things similar to Him,
and thus in some sense equal to Him. This is not possible for
God. Philo does on occasion describe God and His Logos, in
terms of Stoic logic, as "the most generic (*genikôtaton*) of
entities, the 'something' (*ti*)" (*LA* 2.86; 3.175; *Det.* 118), but
it is plain from the consensus of these passages that it is
really the Logos that is the primary genus. When God himself
is described as *genikôtatos*, this must be taken to mean that
there is no genus which comprehends Him. The most general Stoic
category, "*ti*," is in any case designed to cover both bodies
and incorporeal entities (*asômata*), such as Space, Time, and
lekta (*SVF* II 329-332), so that it asserts bare existence, and
does not categorise or describe an entity.

Such being God's nature, it is impossible that He be
subject to passion or affection of any kind. This conclusion,
however, though philosophically excellent, could prove to be
subversive of all religion. In what sense, Philo must ask himself, can our actions be open to praise or blame, if God is not
moved by them (71)? Is there any sense in which God takes note
of our activities, to punish or reward them? To deny this
would eliminate the doctrine of divine providence, to which
Philo is certainly committed, and would really sever all connection between the Creator and His creation.

Philo's solution to the problem is the following.
Although God cannot be known or described as to His essence, He
can be characterised variously in His relation to man and the
world. First of all, he is "good," he possesses "perfect goodness in all respects" (ἡ περὶ πάντα τέλεια ἀγαθότης, 73; but
cf. *Praem.* 40, quoted above). But this need mean no more than
that, like the Demiurge of the *Timaeus*, He works to bring all
things to their best form. His task is complicated, by His own
decision, in the case of man, because He has granted him, alone
of all beings, free will (47), and that means that He has to
put up with many short-term frustrations of His purpose.

In this context, what can be the meaning (other than
mere propaganda for the "friends of the body") of Moses' talk
of God's "wrath" (*thymos*)? Philo's answer is somewhat obscure,
and involves some rather desperate juggling of the LXX text:
ἐθυμώθην ὅτι ἐποίησα αὐτούς (see notes to 70, and introductory
notes to Sect. VII). What he seems to want to say, however, is
that *thymos*, action prompted by irrational impulses, is an
essential component of our mode of existence, leading to what
will be denominated in normal parlance "sinful" or "wicked"
behavior, which in turn draws down upon it, not God's wrath,
but its own natural consequences. Such behavior is balanced
and emended by *logismos*, rational calculation and repentance
(taken from the *dienoēthē* of the lemma), which God's general
agathotēs works to promote. In all this process no actual passion of God is involved; yet His benevolent *pronoia* is exercised
throughout. The administration of the world is the function of
God's two chief Powers (expressed by his two LXX epithets "god"
(*theos*) and "lord" (*kyrios*)), his creative Power, by which he
brings the world into being, and his sovereign or governing
Power, by which he administers the world, once created.[9]

This, it seems to me, has to be Philo's philosophical
position, based on his doctrine of God's transcendence. But it
is notable that, immediately following on this exposition (ss.
74-81), he enters upon a distinctly theological discussion of
God's tempering of his justice with mercy, since the human race
would not otherwise be able to survive the just consequences of
their wickedness and folly. This disquisition, which is typical
of many others in Philo's works, must either be taken as being
presented on the popular level, but translatable into philosophic
terms, or as being simply inconsistent with his philosophical
position. The religious nature of Philo's thought makes the
latter alternative more likely; he cannot really abandon the personal aspect of Jahweh's relations with his creation without
rejecting his ancestral faith altogether.

There is, certainly, an interesting passage at 80, where
he says:

> The Creator, then, knowing His own surpassing excellence and
> the natural weakness of His creatures, however loud they
> boast, wills not to dispense benefit or punishment according
> to His power, but according to the measure of capacity (ὡς
> ἔχοντας . . . δυνάμεως) which he sees in those who are to
> participate in either of these dispensations. (Colson's
> trans.)

This, transposed into philosophical terms, seems to be a version
of the later Neoplatonic doctrine of "suitability for reception"
(ἐπιτηδειότης πρὸς ὑποδοχήν),[10] according to which God, or the
gods, are constantly benevolent in their bestowal of benefits
and wisdom, but creatures can only receive as much as they are
constitutionally able to absorb (cf. *Post.* 143-5). The purpose
of prayer and ascetic exercises, therefore, is to increase one's
receptivity, not to produce changes in the attitude of the deity.
However, one must admit that that is not how the doctrine comes
across in this passage. To all appearances we are back with the
personal God of Judaism, albeit a much more benevolent figure
than Jahweh appears in the tradition. Philo perhaps reconciled
his philosophy with his religion in the privacy of his study,
but, if so, he has covered his tracks pretty well.

There is, however, one line which Philo could have taken
in attempting to reconcile his philosophical with his religious
convictions, and I do not see that any scholarly attention has
so far been paid to it.[11] God is free from passions, but might
he not enjoy the rational equivalent of passions in Stoic
theory, *eupatheiai* or "equable states"? In terms of Stoic

theory, the attribution of *eupatheiai* to God would make no sense,
since God is not a person but an impersonal force, and there is
naturally no evidence of any such attribution in the sources,
but for Philo the case is different, and a creative extension of
the Stoic concept might well be in order.

For Philo, the Sage, as exemplified by the Patriarchs
and Moses, is a man very much in the image of God. He enjoys
eupatheia, and this passionless *eupatheia* of his is to be seen
as a mortal reflection of an equivalent state in the divine
nature.   There are two passages of particular interest in this
connection, *Abr.* 202-3 and *Spec.* 2.54-5.   Again and again, when
mentioning *eupatheia* or *eupatheiai*, Philo makes it clear that
for him the chief *eupatheia* is Joy (*chara*), exemplified particularly by Isaac, whose name he translates into Greek as "laughter"
(e.g. *LA* 3.86; *Migr.* 157; *Congr.* 36; *Mut.* 167).   The other two
eupatheiai recognised by the Stoics, Caution (*eulabeia*) and Will
(*boulēsis*), are very much in the background, though they are
implied in the repeated mention of "the *eupatheiai*."[12]   At *Abr.*
202-4, in connection with Abraham's sacrifice of Isaac, which
is interpreted as the Sage's offering of his *chara* to God as
being its source, we find the following:

> The nature of God is without grief or fear and wholly
> exempt from passion of any kind, and alone partakes of
> perfect happiness and bliss. The frame of mind which has
> made this true acknowledgement God, who has banished jeal-
> ousy (*phthonos*, cf. Plat. *Phaedr.* 247A) from His presence
> in His kindness and love for mankind, fitly rewards by
> returning the gift in so far as the recipient's capacity
> allows. And indeed we may almost hear His voice saying:
> "All joy (*chara*) and rejoicing I know well is the possession
> of none other save Me alone, the Father of All. Yet I do
> not grudge that this My possession should be used by such
> as are worthy, and who should be worthy save one who should
> follow Me and My will, for he will prove to be most exempt
> from distress and fear if he travels by this road which
> passion and vice cannot tread, but good feelings (*eupa-
> theiai*) and virtues can walk therein." (Colson's trans.)

Here God himself, in spite of His freedom from *pathē*, is made
to acknowledge his peculiar possession of *chara*, which is characterised as a *eupatheia*. One cannot reasonably argue that
while God dispenses *chara*, He does not actually possess it Himself, since it is described as his particular possession (*ktēma*).
This doctrine is repeated at *Spec.* 2.54-5, where the subject is
Sarah and her laughing to herself (Gen 18:12):

> And so it was that in the days of old a certain mind of
> rich intelligence (sc. Sarah), her passions now calmed

> within her, smiled because joy (*chara*) lay within her and
> filled her womb. And when, as she considered the matter,
> it seemed to her that joy might well be the peculiar
> property of God alone, and that she herself was sinning in
> taking for her own conditions of well-being (*eupatheiai*)
> above human capacity, she was afraid, and denied the
> laughter of her soul until her doubts were set at rest.
> (Colson's trans.)

Just below, Philo declares that the unmixed and pure form of
Joy is "especially characteristic" (*exairetos*) of God, so that
God possesses at least one *eupatheia*, or better, *eupatheia* in
at least one aspect, since in Stoic doctrine the *eupatheiai*,
like the virtues, are mutually implied. We may note also the
notion, expressed in Sarah's fear of going beyond her station,
that there is a level of *eupatheia* above human capacity. Philo
seems here to imply, then, a divine level of *eupatheia*. It is
notable, though, that Philo makes no effort to attribute either
eulabeia or *boulēsis* to God. Perhaps he felt some danger of
falling into absurdity here. Of what could God be cautious?
Or what could He wish for that He had not got? But one would
have thought that it would not be beyond Philo's ingenuity to
work out a divine equivalent of these *eupatheiai*. Indeed, such
seems to stand ready to hand in the form of God's two chief
Powers. The ruling power could, after all, be characterised as
a form of *eulabeia* (as also could God's *pronoia*), while His
creative power could be seen as *boulēsis*. Certainly Philo
talks much of God's *boulēma* (e.g. *LA* 3.239; *Post.* 73; *Her.* 272,
and *Abr.* 204 above), so that recognition of His *boulēsis* should
not be a problem. But, for whatever reason, Philo does not
explicitly credit God with any *eupatheia* other than *chara*.

This doctrine of divine *eupatheia* is, of course, non-
sense in Stoic terms, and is liable to the accusation of inco-
herence on any terms. Joy, for instance, is defined as "rational
elevation of the soul" (ψυχῆς εὔλογος ἔπαρσις). Now even if God
may be said to have a soul (and Cleanthes and Diogenes of Babylon (*SVF* I 532), at least described God as "the soul of the
cosmos"), it would not be proper for his soul to suffer periodic
"elevation," even of a rational nature. The term *eparsis*,
after all, implies alteration of some sort in the soul. Sometimes the Sage is in a more elevated mood than at other times.
Not that the Sage is ever sad; it is just that he may normally
be taken to be in a state of psychic equilibrium, with occasional
rational rufflings of joy, caution or anticipation. Such changes
do not seem to me to be suitable to God, and indeed Philo makes

it clear that God's *chara* is His permanent state. He equates
it with His *eudaimonia* (*Abr*. 202). So this is Stoic doctrine
used for non-Stoic purposes, and with the meaning of the terms
somewhat altered. But Philo need not apologise for that. He
is not claiming to be a Stoic. Platonists had been borrowing
Stoic formulations, and investing them with varying degrees of
new meaning, ever since Antiochus, and Philo is quite entitled
to do the same.

Whether this doctrine (if he really holds it) solves all
his problems is, however, another question. It does not seem to
solve the problem of God's wrath or God's mercy, both of which
we are concerned with in the *Quod Deus* (and throughout the
Philonic corpus). The Stoics recognised no rational form of
either anger or grief. The Peripatetics did, however, and it
may be that Philo is able to profit from Antiochus of Ascalon's
juggling of Stoic and Peripatetic ethics[13] to attribute rational
forms of these emotions to God. At any rate, such language used
of God requires "translation" before it can concord satisfactorily with Philo's philosophical doctrine of the divine nature,
and Philo makes it less than clear that he intends such translation.

NOTES

[1]Wolfson manages to dispose of all of Norden's alleged
counter-examples quite satisfactorily, but this does not leave
the way clear to his own solution, as we shall see.

[2]Collected in H. Thesleff, *The Pythagorean Texts of the
Hellenistic Period*, Abo, 1965, pp. 19-20.

[3]Simpl. *In Cat.* 206, 10 ff. Kalbfleisch, etc. See my
discussion in *Middle Platonists*, pp. 134-35. It is also possible, of course, that "Archytas" was acquainted with Eudorus,
and that the influence goes in the other direction.

[4]If it is indeed Albinus who composed the *Didaskalikos*.
John Whittaker has recently given persuasive arguments for
resuscitating the Alcinous of the mss. (*Phoenix* 28, 1974). For
our present purpose the question is fortunately not crucial.

[5]Wolfson carried his speculations further in an article
in the *Harvard Theological Review* for 1952, "Albinus and Plotinus on Divine Attributes" (now included in his *Studies in the
History of Philosophy and Religion*, Vol. I), but without adding
anything substantial to his arguments. See also his "Answers to
Criticisms of my Discussions of the Ineffability of God," *HTR*
67 (1974) 186-90 (included in vol. 2 of *Studies*).

[6]Also, when a man like Clement of Alexandria (*Strom.* V.12)--quoted by Wolfson in *Philo*, Vol. II, pp. 113 and 154-- declares that God is "neither genus nor differentia, nor species, nor individual, nor number," it is much more likely, *pace* Wolfson, that he has derived this from some handbook of Platonism very like that of Albinus than from the works of Philo, familiar though he was with the latter.

[7]The phrase "τὰ ψυχῆς ἄλογα πάθη" might seem to leave open the possibility that God might experience rational *eupatheiai*, though that does not seem to be in Philo's mind at the moment. On this question, though, I shall have more to say at the end of the essay.

[8]This pair of precepts is employed again by Philo at *Somn.* 1.237, to make the same point, and at *Sacr.* 101 Philo refers to Deut. 1:31, in which ὡς ἄνθρωπος is also used of God ("You saw there how the Lord your God carried you all the way to this place, as a father carries his son"--ὡς εἴ τις τροφο- φορήσει ἄνθρωπος τὸν υἱὸν αὐτοῦ. This passage Wolfson strangely appears to confuse with Deut. 8:5, *Philo* II, p. 129 (apparently following Cohn-Wendland's false reference; see Leisegang's note to *Deus* 54).

[9]These powers, and others, are discussed extensively elsewhere, e.g., *Cher.* 27-28, *Abr.* 120-30, *QE* 2. 61-62, but do not enter into the exegesis here. On the powers, see Wolfson, *Philo* I, pp. 217-226.

[10]E.g. Proclus, *In Tim.* I, p. 51, 25 ff., 139, 20 ff. Diehl; *Elem. Theol.* 71, 79.

[11]I am indebted to Prof. David Winston for pointing this out to me.

[12]Only in one passage, I think, *QG* 2.57 (where the Armenian translator has in fact obscured the subject-matter; see Dillon and Terian, "Philo and the Stoic Doctrine of *Eupa- theiai*," *Studia Philonica* 4, 1976-77, pp. 17-24) are all the *eupatheiai* mentioned together, and there Philo has added a fourth, non-Stoic one, *dēgmos*, as a rational equivalent of Grief! Philo also calls the virtues *eupatheiai*, or at least links them closely together, another non-Stoic development; see Wolfson, *Philo* II, pp. 275-79.

[13]See Dillon, *The Middle Platonists*, pp. 75-78 for a fuller discussion of this.

J. Dillon

COMMENTARY

I

Gig. 1-5

Commentary on Gen 6:1: καὶ δὴ ἐγένετο, ἡνίκα ἤρξαντο
οἱ ἄντρωποι πολλοὶ γίνεσθαι ἐπὶ τῆς γῆς, καὶ θυγατέρες ἐγεννήθησαν αὐτοῖς.

δὴ add. Philo; πολλοὶ γίνεσθαι LXX, cett.cod. Philonis,
πληθύνεσθαι U.

A. *General Comments*

In Philo's great scheme, the pair of commentaries *De
Gigantibus--Quod Deus sit Immutabilis* resume the exegesis of
Genesis after a brief gap, occasioned by the rather intractable
material, genealogical in nature, which comprises Genesis,
chap. 5. The previous treatise, *On the Posterity and Exile of
Cain*, took us to the end of chap. 4, the birth of Seth. The
treatise *On the Giants* thus constitutes a new beginning to a
rather greater extent than most of the treatises. Equally
clearly, it is closely connected, structurally and thematically,
to the treatise which follows it. Between them they constitute
a commentary on that part of Genesis covering the period from
the birth of the sons of Noah (and the multiplication of the
human race) to the Flood (Gen 6:1-12).

Philo's exegesis of Gen 6:1 is at first sight surprising.
Why should the growth of population and the birth of daughters
in itself be a bad thing? This can partly be explained, perhaps,
by the nature of the preceding chapter, "The Book of the Generations of Adam," where each of the patriarchs is described as producing both sons and daughters, culminating with Noah (v. 32),
who engenders only sons (cf. *BR* 26.4, T-A 246); and partly also
because the concepts of multiplicity and the female had definite
negative connotations in contemporary Platonism (particularly in
the Pythagorean wing of it) to which Philo was fully alive. The
juxtaposition of the fewness and maleness of Noah's progeny, with
the pullulating anonymous femininity of what follows him was
something too striking for Philo to miss.

Overriding themes, therefore, in this pair of treatises,
are the duality and tension between the spirit and the flesh,
virtue and pleasure, self-abnegation (or God-centeredness) and
self-centeredness; the nature of God's providential care for us,
not governed by any passion, as a superficial reading of the
inspired text might suggest, but purely by reason; and, as a
corollary, our responsibility for our actions, our freedom of
will, and the role within us of the Logos, acting as a conscience.

In this introductory passage, a comment on Gen 6:1 ("When
men began to increase on earth and daughters were born to them
. . ."), Philo begins by establishing a contrast between the
rarity of excellence and the frequency of its opposite, such that
the excellence concerned actually makes clear the existence and
nature of its opposite (this notion takes on great importance in
relation to the doctrine of Conscience, below, *Deus* 122 ff.).
Εὐφυΐα is thus contrasted with ἀφυΐα; the scarceness of excellence in arts and sciences with the ubiquity of its contrary
manifestations; and, with the adducing of one of his favorite
images (cf. F. N. Klein, *Die Lichtterminologie bei Philon von
Alexandrien und in den Hermetischen Schriften* [Leiden 1962]),
the singleness of the sun as opposed to the vast multiplicity
of darkness. The fewness of Noah and his sons brings us to a
consideration of the multitude of wicked men--opposites are best
illustrated by the use of opposites. We may note here how Noah
returns as a point of contrast in *Deus* 122-23, this time his
virtue being contrasted with the wickedness of the generality
of men, which it makes manifest, thereby bringing on the Flood.

Next, we are presented with a contrast between Male and
Female, another of Philo's favorite images (cf. R. A. Baer,
Philo's Use of the Categories Male and Female [Leiden 1970]).
The wicked man does not generate anything "male" (virtuous) in
his soul, but rather produces multitudinous "female" offspring
(wicked), and this is the meaning of the statement that they
produced daughters, but no son. Noah, by contrast, produced
only male offspring (τέλειος καὶ ὀρθὸς λόγος), thus revealing
the wickedness of the Many--for opposites produce opposites.

It is instructive to consider how Philo treats this
verse of Genesis in the corresponding section of his other great
project of the commentary, the *Questions and Answers on Genesis
and Exodus* (the sections parallel to *De Gig.* and *Quod Deus* as a
whole are *QG* 1.89-100, i.e., the end of Book I). Section 89
raises the question, "Why, from the time when the great flood

drew near, is the human race said to have increased into a multitude?". A remarkable contrast is immediately apparent. For
Philo in the *Quaestiones*, the πολυανθρωπία, like all abundance,
is essentially a good thing. It simply in this case presages
disaster:

> Divine favours always precede His judgements, for His
> activity is first to do good, while punishment is sec-
> ondary. It is then normal, when great evils are about
> to take place, that an abundance of great and numerous
> good things should come about first. In this same manner,
> when the seven years' barrenness was about to come, as the
> prophet says (Gen 41:25ff.), Egypt became fruitful for the
> same number of years in succession, through the beneficent
> and preserving power of the universe.

The second part of the section introduces a moral element:

> In the same way as He does good, He teaches men to refrain
> and keep themselves from sins, lest they change the good
> into the opposite. Because of this now too cities grow to
> excellence through freedom of customs, so that if after-
> wards disaster arises, they may blame their own immeasur-
> able and irremediable wrongdoing, and not make the Deity
> responsible, for He is innocent of evil and evil deeds,
> since His proper activity is to bestow only the good in a
> primary way.

Philo is presumably saying that men learn through their misuse
of God's blessings to blame, not Him, but themselves, for such
disasters as may follow. The reference to contemporary luxury
seems to confirm this interpretation. (Cf. the comment on the
prosperity of the Sodomites at *Abr.* 134 ff.) If so, it is easy
to see that Philo's understanding of the meaning of "multiply-
ing" and abundance in *De Gigantibus* is more sophisticated than
that in the *Quaestiones*. Here it is a sign of decadence and
inferiority in itself, not at all a blessing or benefit. The
exegesis is enriched by the contrast between the oneness or
simplicity of the Divine or the Good, and the variety and mul-
tifariousness of evil and of the human or earthly condition in
general, a contrast characteristic of Greek philosophy, and of
Platonism in particular.

B. *Detailed Commentary*

1   Ἄξιον . . . διαπορῆσαι. A common Philonic formula for
introducing an aporia, cf. *LA* 1.85; *Det.* 57; *Post.* 33; *Cong.* 73.
Closely analogous to the formulae of Neoplatonic exegesis, e.g.
Procl. *In Tim.* 1.325.14 ff.: ἀποροῦσι δέ τινες; *In Parm.*

1184,9 ff., Cousin: ἴσως δ᾿ ἄν τις ἀπορήσειε . . . suggesting
a common source, perhaps, in Stoic-influenced exegesis of Homer.

    ἀεὶ γὰρ ἐπειδὰν τὸ σπάνιον φανῇ. Doctrine of symmetri-
cal contrast: "good/bad," "few/many." (Mss. reading τὸ σπάνιον;
the conjecture of Cohn, τι σπάνιον, is unnecessary. For the
rarity of the good, cf. LA 1.102; Ebr. 26; Mig. 59, 61, 63, 123;
Mut. 34-56; Abr. 19; Prob. 63, 72; Agr. 180; Plato, Phaedo 90A;
Rep. 6.503D; Arist. EN 2.1109a29; 7.1145a27, etc; Seneca, De Ira
2.6; De Const. 7.1; Ep. 105.3; SVF 3.658: σπανιώτερον τοῦ φοί-
νικος.

2   εὐφυΐα/ἀφυΐα. Contrasted also at Her. 212. εὐφυΐα is
not a Platonic term, but Aristotelian (EN 3.5.1114b12); ἀφυΐα
also (Arist. PA 659a29), but not contrasted. Cf. Fug. 27.

3   ἐν τῷ παντὶ ἥλιος. Contrast of ἥλιος/φῶς and σκότος
very popular with Philo (see Leisegang's Index s.v. σκότος).
Cf. e.g. Virt. 164: καθάπερ γὰρ ἀνατείλαντος ἡλίου τὸ μὲν
σκότος ἀφανίζεται, φωτὸς δὲ πληροῦται τὰ πάντα. The contrast
between ἥλιος as εἷς and σκότος as μύριος is not found elsewhere. n.b. Philo vacillates between σκότος, -ου m. and σκότος,
-ους n. Always neuter in LXX. Philo always uses g. σκότους,
but d. σκότῳ

    τῷ γὰρ ἐναντίῳ . . . γνωρίζεται. The principle that
opposites are most easily recognized by opposites is perhaps a
development of the principle τῶν ἐναντίων ἡ αὐτὴ ἐπιστήμη (Arist.
Topics 1.105b25), but its immediate ancestry is not clear. Cf.,
however, Plato, Phaedo 70E (opposites generated by opposites);
Ep. 7.344B (opposites must be learned simultaneously); Chrysippus
ap. Gellius NA 7.1 (SVF 2.1169): opposites can only be known
through opposites; Chrysippus ap. Plut. Stoic. Rep. 35.1050F:
vice is not useless, for otherwise there could not be any good
(there is a hint of this already in Plat. Theaet. 176A). Cf.
discussion of Philo's views on origin of evil in M. Hadas-Lebel,
De Providentia pp. 112-14; and Plot. 4.8.7.14-16.

    This principle seems to be operative at Deus 122, where
the point is that only at the appearance of a sense of good (or
of conscience, τὸ συνειδός) does evil become recognizable. The
imagery of light and darkness is used there too: γένεσις γὰρ
τῶν καλῶν θάνατος αἰσχρῶν ἐπιτηδευμάτων ἐστίν. ἐπεὶ καὶ φωτὸς
ἐπιλάμψαντος ἀφανίζεται τὸ σκότος. Cf. LA 1.46; 3.73; Ebr.

186; (6th trope of Aenesidemus); *Fug.* 27; *Her.* 213:   "For the
two opposites together form a single whole, by the division of
which the opposites are known."   (Philo attributes this principle to Heraclitus, but insists that Moses had already discovered it; cf. *QG* 3.5)

     This figurative use of θηλυγονέω is unique, but the
equation of the female with the lower parts of our nature, the
passions or the irrational soul, is a basic Philonic image,
e.g. *Sacr.* 103: θῆλυ μὲν οὖν ἔγγονον ψυχῆς ἐστι κακία καὶ πάθος,
οἷς καθ᾿ ἕκαστον τῶν ἐπιτηδευμάτων ἐκθηλυνόμεθα, ἄρρεν δὲ εὐπάθεια καὶ ἀρετή, ὑφ᾿ ὧν ἐγειρόμεθα καὶ ῥωννύμεθα.   (It may be
noted that Philo here ignores Ham, who in *QG* 1.88 [cf. 2.71] is
designated as symbolizing evil.)   θηλυτοκέω is used in the same
way in *Mig.* 206 (commenting on Num 27:3).   Cf. also the description of Lot as θυγατροποιός at *Ebr.* 135.   For the male-female
contrast, see R. Baer, *Philo's Use of the Categories Male and
Female* (Leiden 1970).

     δένδρον ἀρετῆς.   This image takes its origin from the
allegorization of the trees in the Garden of Eden, e.g. *LA* 1.56
(on Gen 2:9): ἃ φυτεύει ἐν τῇ ψυχῇ δένδρα ἀρετῆς, νῦν ὑπογράφει·
ἔστι δὲ ταῦτα αἵ τε κατὰ μέρος ἀρεταὶ καὶ αἱ κατ᾿ αὐτὰς ἐνέργειαι,
καὶ τὰ κατορθώματα, καὶ τὰ λεγόμενα παρὰ τοῖς φιλοσοφοῦσι καθή-
κοντα· ταῦτά ἐστι τοῦ παραδείσου τὰ φυτά.   Cf. also *Op.* 153-54.

     ἀμήχανον γὰρ τὰ αὐτὰ πρὸς τῶν ἐναντίων.   For the prin-
ciple that opposites arise from opposites, see Arist. *Phys.*
188b21 ff., *De Caelo* 310a23 ff., *Gen.Corr.* 331a14, and G. E. R.
Lloyd, *Polarity and Analogy* (Cambridge 1966) 15-171.

     ἐπεὶ γὰρ ὁ δίκαιος.   Note the use which Philo makes of
the δίκαιος-ἄδικος contrast throughout §§3-5: ἡ τοῦ δικαίου
Νῶε γένεσις--τοὺς ἀδίκους; ἄδικος δὲ οὐδείς; ὁ δίκαιος Νῶε--
ἀδικία.

     ἀρρενογονεῖ.   A biological term, used by Aristotle and
Theophrastus.   Philo's exegesis here takes account only of the
masculinity of Noah's progeny, taking no account of the per-
sonalities of his sons.   At *QG* 1.88, by contrast, we read: "who
are the three sons of Noah--Shem, Ham and Japheth?"   "These
names are symbols of three things in nature--of the good, the
evil and the indifferent.   Shem is distinguished for good, Ham
for evil, and Japheth for the indifferent."

II

Gig. 6-18

Commentary on Gen 6:2: ᾿Ιδόντες δὲ οἱ ἄγγελοι τοῦ θεοῦ
τὰς θυγατέρας τῶν ἀνθρώπων ὅτι καλαί εἰσιν, ἔλαβον ἑαυτοῖς
γυναῖκας ἀπὸ πασῶν, ὧν ἐξελέξαντο.

ἄγγελοι] υἱοί LXX (ἄγγελοι A^r).

A. *General Comments*

For a fuller discussion of Philo's theory of angels/
daemons, see the essay on the subject in the Intro. pp. 197-206.
The present section shows both that the Middle Platonic theory
of daemons was well developed by Philo's time, and that he was
well acquainted with it. The analysis of the true relation
between the terms "daemon," "angel" and "soul" is for Philo a
matter of some importance. The relation is indeed obscure.
Plato, in an influential passage of the *Timaeus* (90A), had identified the rational part of the soul as the *daimon* of each man,
and later Platonism made no very clear distinction between
daemons and angels (ὀνόματα μὲν διαφέροντα, ἓν δὲ καὶ ταὐτὸν
ὑποκείμενον). What "other philosophers" (the Greeks) call
daemons, he says in sect. 6, Moses is accustomed to term
"angels."

But does Moses in this passage refer to angels at all?
This is one of Philo's more interesting departures from the LXX
text as we have it (apart from a corrector of the *Codex Alexandrinus*). In place of οἱ υἱοί τοῦ θεοῦ of Gen 6:2, Philo reads
οἱ ἄγγελοι τοῦ θεοῦ. This must have been the tradition available to him. He makes the interesting remark at *QG* 1.92 that
Moses "sometimes calls the angels 'sons of God,' because they
are made incorporeal." Since here too he seems to read ἄγγελοι
at Gen 6:2 and 4, the reference may be to some other passage,
such as Deut 32:8, where, however, most manuscripts of our LXX
text also have ἀγγέλων θεοῦ, but one, 848, from the first century B.C.E., gives υἱῶν (see J. W. Wevers, *Text History of the
Greek Deuteronomy* [Göttingen, 1978] 85). He is certainly not
making his own translation from the Hebrew, which speaks also
of "sons." It seems as if someone in the Alexandrian tradition
was offended, as well he might be, by the idea of God having
sons, and glossed "sons" by the less offensive term ἄγγελοι

(cf. P. Katz, *Philo's Bible* [Cambridge 1950] 20-21). On the
question of Jewish angelology, see further D. S. Russell, *The
Method and Message of Jewish Apocalyptic* (Philadelphia 1964)
235-62; J. Z. Smith, "The Prayer of Joseph," *Religions in
Antiquity*, ed. J. Neusner (Leiden, 1968) 253-94; J. Strugnell,
"The Angelic Liturgy at Qumran," VT Supp. 7 (Leiden 1960) 318-
45; Urbach, *The Sages* 115-60; M. Margoliot, *Sefer Ha-Razim*
(Hebrew) (Jerusalem, 1966); I. Gruenwald, *Apocalyptic and Merkavah
Mysticism* (Leiden/Köln, 1980); *IDB*, s.v. angel.

The discussion of angels here starts from the argument
that every element, every part of the universe, must contain
forms of life proper to it (7). Therefore air too, contrary to
appearances, must have its proper forms of life. These will be
souls (cf. *Plant.* 14). Philo does not make the point, made
later by Apuleius in a parallel argument in the *De Deo Socratis*,
ch. 8, that birds are not the proper inhabitants of air, being
earthy. On the other hand he produces an argument not used by
Apuleius, that the air is actually the element which gives life
to the inhabitants of earth and water. Must it not, then, *a
fortiori* support living beings itself? Further, when the air
is corrupted, plagues of various sorts are liable to break out
among earth-creatures, and clean air is eminently conducive to
health (9-10).

Souls, then, are what we are talking about. "Angel"
and "daemon" are simply terms for souls performing certain roles.
Philo proceeds (12) to make a distinction between two classes of
souls. The one class descend into bodies and become human souls
(the reason for this he leaves aside for the moment); the other
scorn all contact with the earthly realm, and remain above, to
serve God as his agents for the supervision of mortals.

Among the former class, there are some who succeed in
rising above the torrent of earthly existence (see note *ad loc.*)
sufficiently to rise again, after one (?) incarnation, to whence
they came. Others sink beneath the waves, becoming fascinated
by bodily or external goods (15). It is not at all clear here
how far Philo is subscribing to the Platonic theory of reincarnation on which this whole distinction is based. We are left in
some uncertainty as to what happens to those who "sink." Certainly elsewhere he envisages reincarnation, e.g. *Somn.* 1.139.

Philo now feels he has cleared up the confusion in some
quarters about souls, daemons and angels, and about the problem
of good and evil daemons or angels. Evil angels (κακοὶ ἄγγελοι),

so-called, are simply souls which have descended into cor-
poreality, and have become fascinated by the pleasures associated with it (17-18). Whatever about his doctrine elsewhere
(e.g. *QE* 1.23), Philo does not here seem to recognize any such
thing as an evil daemon. κακοί ἄγγελοι are souls which have
become enamoured of "the daughters of men," which he allegorizes
here as the pleasures of the flesh, in contradistinction to
"the daughters of right reason (ὀρθὸς λόγος)," the branches of
scientific knowledge and the virtues, which are presumably the
"brides" both of those souls who preserve a correct attitude to
incarnation (i.e. οἱ ἀνόθως φιλοσοφοῦντες), and of those who do
not descend at all.

B. *Detailed Commentary*

6   ψυχαί . . . πετόμεναι. The other passage in which Philo
sets out his daemonology (or angelology) is *Somn.* 1.135-43, in
connection with the exegesis of Jacob's Ladder (Gen 28:12). The
Ladder symbolizes the element of Air, which is the abode of
souls. The argument there is parallel to this (see Intro.
p. 199). *BR* 26.5, T-A 247 reflects a similar motivation to deny
that the biblical passage is literally referring to fallen
angels. R. Simeon b. Yoḥai says the reference is to the sons
of judges, and curses those who insist that it refers to the
sons of God. Cf. Justin, *Dial.* 79. "From allusions in the
Talmud (*BT Yoma* 67b) it is clear that also in authoritative
Jewish circles they were formerly of the opinion that it was
actually to angels that the passage referred " (U. Cassuto,
Biblical and Oriental Studies [Jerusalem 1973] 1.20).

7   μῦθον. For Philo, a word of negative connotation, connected with Greek traditions, e.g. *Her.* 228: Stoic theory of
ἐκπύρωσις and a void a μυθευομένη τερατολογία. At *Conf.* 2 ff.,
certain ill-intentioned persons (disloyal Jews, presumably) are
said to assert that there are μῦθοι in the Pentateuch, and compare the Tower of Babel story to that of the Aloeadae. At the
outset of *Op.* Moses is praised for not tricking out his law-
giving with μυθικὰ πλάσματα, such as obscure the truth. Cf.
also *Op.* 157, 170; *Det.* 125; *Gig.* 58; and *Prov.* 2.109, where
the Cyclopes are described as πλάσμα μύθου; *LA* 2.19, 1.43; *Deus*
59; *Agr.* 96-97; *Sacr.* 13.

ἀνάγκη γάρ . . . A parallel argument to this is given
by Apuleius, *De Deo Socratis*, ch. 8, showing it to be part of
the Platonic tradition. Apuleius' source may well be Varro (*ap.*
Aug. *CD* 7.6), whose source in turn might be Posidonius, though
possibly also Antiochus of Ascalon. Cf. Plato, *Epin.* 984BC, Ar.
Gen.An. 3.762a18 ff.; Cic. *ND* 2.42; Sext. *Math.* 9.86; D. L.
8.32 (attributed to Pythagoras); Plotinus 3.2.3.26. See also
J. Beaujeu in the commentary of his Budé ed. of Apuleius, ad
loc.; Bréhier: 126-28; W. Bousset, *Jüdisch-christlicher Schul-
betrieb in Alexandria und Rom* (Göttingen, 1915) 14-22; H. Leisegang, *Der heilige Geist* (Leipzig, 1919) 51 ff.

ἐψυχῶσθαι. For the doctrine, cf. Plat. *Tim.* 40A and
41BC, where it is laid down that all varieties of living things
must exist, in order that the cosmos may be complete. Philo
states the doctrine clearly at *Prov.* 2.110: ἀναγκαῖον μὲν γὰρ
ἦν εἰς τὴν τοῦ ὅλου συμπλήρωσιν, ἵνα γένηται κόσμος, ἐν ἑκάστῳ
μέρει φῦναι ζῴων ἰδέας ἁπάντας. Cf. *Conf.* 179; Plotinus 6.7.11.
For the idea of the apportionment of living beings among the
different elements, cf. *Det.* 151: τοῖς ζῴοις ἡ φύσις διαφέ-
ροντας καὶ οὐχὶ τοὺς αὐτοὺς τόπους πρὸς διαμονὴν ἐδωρήσαντο,
θάλατταν . . . γῆν. . . . For the actual verb ψυχόω Philo
seems to be our earliest extant source. In fact he is not using
it here in a fully Platonic sense, since ὅλον δι' ὅλων τὸν
κόσμον ἐψυχῶσθαι should mean that the cosmos is ensouled *as a
whole*, whereas all that Philo means is that every part of it is
full of souls.

οἰκεῖα καὶ πρόσφορα. Philo employs these two terms also
at *Mut.* 230, as a seeming *variatio*: οὐ τὰ αὐτά, ἀλλὰ τοῖς μὲν τὰ
πρόσφορα ἵνα μηδ' ὅλως νοσήσωσι, τοῖς δὲ τὰ οἰκεῖα, ὅπως πρὸς
τὸ ὑγιεινότερον μεταβάλωσι. Cf. *Det.* 151: τὰς οἰκείους χώρας;
same collocution in Epicurus, Fr. 250, Usener. The argument for
air having its proper creatures is a development of Aristotle's
argument, apparently in the lost Περὶ Φιλοσοφίας (Fr. 21 Ross),
in support of fire or aether having their proper creatures. Who
extended the argument to air is not clear. Aristotle must have
said something about air, but it seems likely that he claimed
birds, not souls, as its proper inhabitants. We may note that
at *Plant.* 12, where Philo is following Aristotle's argument more
faithfully, and is not concerned with proofs of the existence
of angels, he accepts birds as the proper inhabitants of air
(τὰ δὲ πτηνὰ ἀέρι). This is presumably, then, the original form

of the argument. Just below, however, in 14, Philo amplifies
it to include pure souls, declaring now that the air supports
two classes of being. We seem here to catch the argument at an
intermediate, and rather incoherent, stage. The affinity of
various types of creatures for different elements was already
taught by Empedocles, A.72, and adopted by Plato, *Tim.* 39E ff.;
cf. Diod. 1.75.

    τὰ πυρίγονα. Cf. *Aet.* 45; *QE* 2.28. Philo is the first
attested user of this word, but the "fire-born creatures" are
introduced first by Aristotle, at *HA* 5.19, 552b. The connection
with Macedonia, which Philo makes again at *Plant.* 12, is not
derivable from Aristotle's account, which described the creatures as appearing in copper-smelting furnaces in Cyprus, and
is of mysterious provenance. Cicero knows the argument (*ND*
1.103), but talks of the little animals as appearing *in ardenti-
bus fornacibus*, which assumes A.'s account in the *HA*. It may be
that Aristotle spoke of these creatures also in the Περὶ Φιλοσοφίας, which Cicero also knows (*ND* 1.33, 2.42; cf. *BT* Ḥulin
127a [the salamander lives in fire]). There is also the possibility of Posidonius as an intermediary. In ch. 13 of Achilles'
Commentary on Aratus (p. 41,10 Maass), we have a context where
Posidonius has just been quoted on the subject of the stars'
being alive, and the statement is then made, 'καὶ ὅτι πάντα τὰ
στοιχεῖα ζῷα ἔχει,' but it is not quite clear that Posidonius
is still being quoted, or that, if he is, he understands the air
as being inhabited by daemons, though this is probable. Cf.
Cic. *Divinat.* 1.64; Aelian *NA* 2.2.

8   ψυχαὶ . . . ἀκήρατοί τε καὶ θεῖαι. For the doctrine of
stars and planets as pure souls, see Intro, p.200. It takes its
origin from *Timaeus* 40A-D. Cf. also *Op.* 27, 73, 144; *LA* 2.10;
Cher. 23; *Deus* 46; *Somn.* 1.135; *Spec.* 1.19; *QG* 4.157; *Plant.* 12.
See Zeller, *Stoics* 206; Wolfson, *Philo*, 1.363 ff., 417 ff.

    κινοῦνται . . . κίνησιν. Cf. *Tim.* 34A: κίνησιν γὰρ
ἀπένειμεν αὐτῷ τὴν τοῦ σώματος οἰκείαν τῶν ἑπτὰ τὴν περὶ νοῦν
καὶ φρόνησιν μάλιστα οὖσαν, and the discussion of *Laws* X 897C-
898B, esp. 898A.

    νοῦς . . . ἀκραιφνέστατος. ἀκραιφνής not a Platonic
word, nor found in Classical Attic prose, except Thuc. (1.19
and 52). Ps.-Plat. *Axiochus* uses it, however, at 366A. A
popular word with Philo.

9   φαντασιωθῆναι. Philo is the first attested user of this
word, which is plainly, however, to judge from its use by Sextus
Empiricus (e.g. *Math.* 8.506) and Plutarch (*Soll.An.* 960D), a
technical term in later Greek philosophy.

      ἐπεὶ καὶ τί φήσομεν; . . . τί δέ; . . . τί δε; For dis-
cussion of Philo's use of rhetorical apostrophe, see Intro, p.
141.

10   οὐκ ἀέρι καὶ πνεύματι ζῇ. Cf. Diogenes of Apollonia B.4
and 5.

      ἀέρος κακωθέντος. Cf. *Prov.* 2.24: καὶ γὰρ εἰ ἐν ἀέρι
γεγενῆντο λοιμικῷ, πάντως ὤφειλον νοσῆσαι; 1.18; 2.67, 102;
Prob. 76; *Aet.* 126. On the origins of the physical theory
envisaged here, cf. *Leg.* 125-26, and Smallwood's commentary
ad loc. On the importance of the quality of the air, cf. *Prov.*
2.109; Cic. *ND* 2.17 and 42; Sextus *Math.* 9.79.86. Philistion,
Fr. 4, Wellmann (the air that is breathed is vital for the
entire body).

11   ζῳοτοκέω. In sense of "producing living things," this
verb seems peculiar to Philo, cf. ζῳογονεῖν, *Prov.* 2.104, and
Somn. 1.136: καὶ μὴν εἰκός γε ἀέρα γῆς μᾶλλον καὶ ὕδατος ζῳο-
τροφεῖν.

12   τῶν οὖν ψυχῶν . . . Theory of pure souls, again,
Platonic. Their being consecrated to the service of the Demiurge is a development of Plato's statements in *Symp.* 202E and
Polit. 271DE. Philo seems to be the first prose author to use
the word ἀφιερόω (isolated instance in Aesch. *Eum.* 451).

      ὑπηρέτισι καὶ διακόνοις. Collocution of διακονεῖν and
ὑπηρετεῖν at Plato, *Rep.* 5.466E. ὑπηρέτης and ὑποδιάκονος are
combined at *Spec.* 3.201.

13   ὥσπερ εἰς πόταμον . . . Cf. *Somn.* 1.147. Plainly
borrowed from *Tim.* 43A: αἱ δὲ εἰς ποταμὸν ἐνδεθεῖσαι; with
overtones of the *Phaedrus* myth (248A ff.), but with Philonic
elaborations. συρμός is not a Platonic word, nor even a Classical one, but one that Philo likes in nautical metaphors
referring to human affairs in general, or to human desires, cf.
Deus 177; *Sacr.* 61; *Det.* 144; *Mut.* 214-15; *Spec.* 3.1-6; 4.50;
Prob. 38 (the adjective ἀνερμάτιστος, which occurs frequently

in these passages, shows the influence also of *Theaet*. 144A).
Δίνη is used by Plato once metaphorically, at *Crat*. 439C: εἴς
τινα δίνην ἐμπεσόντες κυκῶνται but we may also recognize the
influence of Stoic allegorical interpretation of Odysseus' ship-
wreck in *Odyssey* V; ἀνενήξαντο in particular is reminiscent of
the repeated use of νήχειν in the passage. Cf. *Mut*. 107. There
may also have been allegorization of the Scylla and Charybdis
episode. ἀνέπτησεν is, again, reminiscent of the *Phaedrus* myth
(*Phaedr*. 249D). For various types of souls, see Plut. *De Gen.
Soc*. 591D ff.

14   τῶν ἀνόθως φιλοσοφησάντων. ἄνοθος/ἀνόθως is to all
appearances a Philonic term, but there is a reference here to
Phaedrus 249A: τοῦ φιλοσοφήσαντος ἀδόλως. Cf. *Prov*. 2.22:
ἄνοθος φιλοσοφία.

     μελετῶσαι . . . βίον. A ref. to *Phaedo* 67DE.

15   αἱ δὲ καταποντωθεῖσαι . . .   καταποντίζω/-όω in metaphorical usage is post-Classical. This is only semi-metaphorical,
however, being part of the extended sea-imagery. Reminiscent of
language of *Phaedrus* 248A: ὑποβρύχιαι συμπεριφέρονται. Cf. *LA*
2.103-4.

     ἀστάτοις καὶ τυχηροῖς πράγμασιν. Philo likes ἄστατος,
and associates it in various places with sea imagery. A good
passage is *Post*. 22, with extended nautical imagery. Also *LA*
3.53.

     τὸν συμφυᾶ νεκρόν. A reference here, perhaps, to
Aristotle's story in the *Protrepticus* (Fr. 10b Ross), of Etrus-
can pirates tying living prisoners to corpses, used by him as an
image of the linking of the soul to the body. Admittedly here
the corpse is συμφυής. Cf. *LA* 3.69, 74; *Agr*. 25; *Migr*. 21;
Somn. 2.237; *Flac*. 159.

     τὰ ἀψυχότερα τούτου. Distinction of three grades of
good, in normal Middle Platonic manner.

     τῶν μὴ τεθεαμένων τὰ πρὸς ἀλήθειαν καλά. *Phaedrus* myth
again, 248BC.

     ἀναπλάττεται καὶ ζωγραφεῖται. Similar collocution at
Plant. 27, in ref. to Bezalel who, in contrast to Moses, τὰς
σκίας πλάττει καθάπερ οἱ ζωγραφοῦντες, οἷς οὐ θέμις οὐδὲν

ἔμψυχον δημιουργῆσαι, which has a clearer reference than this to
the Platonic theory of art in *Rep.* X. Cf. comm. on *Gig.* 59.

16   δεισιδαιμονία. It is of some interest to work out what
Philo means by this term. At *Deus* 164, it is seen as one of the
(Aristotelian) vices--ἀσέβεια being the other--between which
εὐσέβεια is set as a mean, but Aristotle does not include these
at *EN* 2.6-7. The term first appears in a bad sense only in
Theophrastus, *Char.* 16. Plutarch assumes this development of
Aristotelian doctrine in his essay *On Superstition*, making it
explicit in the very last sentence (171F): οὕτω γὰρ ἔνιοι φεύ-
γοντες τὴν δεισιδαιμονίαν ἐμπίπτουσιν εἰς ἀθεότητα τραχεῖαν καὶ
ἀντίτυπον, ὑπερπηδήσαντες ἐν μέσῳ κειμένην τὴν εὐσέβειαν--though
he uses ἀθεότης as the other extreme instead of ἀσέβεια. But
this shows that it is part of the Platonic-Peripatetic tradition,
rather than anything original to Philo. The same scheme appears
at *Spec.* 4.147. At *Sacr.* 15 δεισιδαιμονία is a πάθος, fostered
in children by nurses and *paidagōgoi*. An example is given at
Plant. 107-8: thinking to escape blame for one's transgressions
by sacrificing oxen and suchlike expensive things is δεισιδαιμονία. Cf. also the definition of δεισιδαιμονία at *Prov.* 2.81
as "metus malorum daemonum." At *Cher.* 42, δεισιδαιμονία is
connected with the use of "the birdlime of verbiage and preten-
tious clap-trap of ceremonial."

17   μαρτυρεῖ δέ μου. Philo here quotes a passage of the
Psalms (77:49), where bad angels surely *are* being referred to,
but he enlists it, allegorically understood, to support his
position that "bad angels" are no angels at all (cf. *Conf.* 17).
Philo, it may be noted, very rarely moves outside the Pentateuch
in his quotations. There are only 19 instances in his works
preserved in Greek where he quotes the Psalms.

        τὸ ἀγγέλων ὄνομα ὑποδυόμενοι. The verb ὑποδύομαι here
does not imply any activity of disguise on the part of these
souls. Philo is here thinking of *Gorgias* 464C ff., where Plato
describes ἡ κολακευτική as ὑποδῦσα ὑπὸ ἕκαστον τῶν μορίων (sc.
of the virtues), and pretending to be that ὅπερ ὑπέδυ.

        τὰς μὲν ὀρθοῦ λόγου θυγατέρας. For Philo, ὀρθὸς λόγος
is both a cosmic principle and an aspect of the human soul, cf.
Op. 143, *Jos.* 31, etc., as against *LA* 3.106, *Sacr.* 51, etc.
Contrast between immortal/mortal and γνήσιος/νόθος frequent in

Philo, and thoroughly Platonic, cf. *Deus* 151-52. For mortal
and immortal goods, cf. Plato *Laws* 1.631BC. For γνήσιος/νόθος,
Rep. 6.496A, 7.535C-536A, 9.587B.

   ἀλλ' ἔνιοι ἐνίας ἐκ μυρίων. For an analogy to the notion
of being controlled by one or another consuming passion, cf.
Plato, *Rep.* 9.573AB. The worst condition of all is that of the
"tyrannical" man, in whom a single desire is dominant.

18   ποικίλαι γάρ . . . The variation of desires is curiously
arranged, initially by senses, then by parts of the body, in
degree of distance from the head, seat of the *logos*. The phrase
τὰς μηκίστας ἐν ἑαυτοῖς τείνοντες ἐπιθυμίας calls for comment.
There are textual difficulties here, addressed by Wendland, but
they do not greatly affect the sense, which appears to be that
some fallen souls extend themselves to the ultimate, stretching
like the longest string in a lyre, for instance, in their pursuit of recherché and contradictory pleasures.
   The whole of §18 is concerned with explaining the ἀπὸ
πασῶν of the lemma.

III

Gig. 19-57

   Commentary on Gen 6:3: εἶπε κύριος ὁ θεός· οὐ καταμενεῖ τὸ πνεῦμά μου ἐν τοῖς ἀνθρώποις εἰς τὸν αἰῶνα διὰ τὸ εἶναι
αὐτοὺς σάρκας, ἔσονται δὲ αἱ ἡμέραι αὐτῶν ἑκατὸν εἴκοσι ἔτη.
   Textual variants: οὐ μὴ καταμείνη U. οὐ μὴ καταμείνῃ
LXX. ἐν τοῖς ἀνθρώποις τούτοις LXX. Heb. *yādôn* obscure. Usually rendered "shall not abide in" or "strive with"; new JPS
trans.: "shall not shield." Heb. *bĕšagām* equally obscure. New
JPS: "Since he is but flesh" (another translation: "by reason
of their going astray they are flesh").

A. *General Comments*

   We move now to an exegesis of Gen 6:3, closely linked
by Philo to his preceding exposition by the introductory

sentence 'ἐν δὴ τοῖς τοιούτοις . . .' The theme of this passage
is the dealings of the spirit with the flesh, and the imperfections attendant thereon. Philo departs from the obvious meaning
of the LXX here, in which πνεῦμα means only "the breath of life,"
and the sense is simply that men will not live for ever. He
takes up a position concordant with Stoicism and Stoicizing Platonism as against a more "broad-minded" Peripateticism. These
positions were liable to be confused if one did not clearly grasp
the contrasting psychological doctrines on which they were based.
What the Aristotelians meant by moderation of the passions might
in practice be little different from what the Stoics meant by
their extirpation, so that Aristotelian *metriopatheia* might
result in what the Stoics would accept as *eupatheiai*, but the
Peripatetic ideal did not theoretically demand complete elimination of irrational emotions, only their moderation and control.
The moderated passion of the Peripatetic would thus not be
properly equivalent to the Stoic *eupatheia*, which is a completely
rational feeling from the very first, and requires no moderation.
The soul for the Stoics is a unitary entity. The Stoic sage,
guided by an infallible process of reasoning, engenders within
his psyche only rational emotions, since they are the result of
perfectly rational ideas as to what is best for the human organ-
ism in its drive to increase its power to persevere in its own
existence. (See on this J. M. Rist, *Stoic Philosophy*, ch. 3,
with the refs. there given.)

     The Peripatetic, who recognized an irrational "part" of
the soul, would thus presumably moderate his fear or his grief
to the point where he could feel adequate self-control, whereas
the Stoic wise man would never experience fear in the first
place, but only a completely rational feeling of caution or
wariness which requires no further moderation or modification.
Grief, on the other hand, he would never be subject to at all,
experiencing at the most a mental sting or minor soul contrac-
tions, which are morally neutral and betray not the slightest
trace of irrationality. Their Peripatetic opponents undoubtedly
argued that such a psychic state was an impossible ideal and
untrue to the human condition, but, in any case, the chasm
dividing the two schools was a deep one and due to substantive
philosophical differences, cf. Cic. *Fin.* 3.41.

     Philo in fact vacillates a good deal between these two
positions (cf. *Abr.* 257). His predominant position, however, is

Stoicizing, reflecting the dominant trend in Alexandrian Platonism in his time (see on this Dillon, *Middle Platonists*, ch. 3).

        In this passage Philo's position is relatively austere,
although in §34 it becomes clear that what are to be avoided are
τὰ περιττά, not τὰ ἐπιτήδεια. This is reinforced by an allegorical misinterpretation of πρὸς πάντα οἰκεῖον σαρκὸς αὐτοῦ οὐ
προσελεύσεται in Lev 18:6, the οὐ being taken closely with πάντα
(see comment on text), which produces an injunction "not to
approach *all* properties of one's flesh," and thus allows moderate use of the good things of life. This is Philo's basic position, as is evident from many other passages (e.g. *Her.* 285-86;
Virt. 78-126; *QG* 3.16; *Spec.* 4.168).

        We have in this passage a good example of his exegetical
method. First, in 23 and 24, he brings in parallel texts from
Exodus (31:2-3)--adduced also in the parallel passage *QG* 1.90--
and Numbers (11:17) to support his allegorical interpretation of
πνεῦμα in Gen 6:3 as ἡ ἀκήρατος ἐπιστήμη. 25-27 expand on the
exegesis of Num 11:17 on a point relevant to the main subject,
to wit, that ἀφαίρεσις of an intellectual quality like ἐπιστήμη
entails no diminution of the original source--a commonplace of
Platonic teaching. In 28 we return to the main point, that the
divine πνεῦμα cannot remain permanently in the human soul, bound
as it is to the flesh. Then in 32 a passage from Leviticus
(18:6) is introduced which on its literal level prohibits incest,
but which Philo takes as an exhortation against indiscriminate
yielding to the desires of the flesh. From this point until 51
we are involved in a detailed exegesis of this supporting text,
with a number of small digressions, only at 52 returning to Gen
6:3, with which we continue until 57.

        At 40, Philo turns to comment on the last two words of
Lev 18:6: ἐγὼ κύριος, which he seems to take first as meaning,
not so much "I am the Lord," as "I am the real thing" or "I am
in the truest sense," implying "I am the true ἀγαθόν" (cf. sect.
45). He finds here an allusion to the great chasm dividing God
from created being, a recurring theme in the Philonic corpus.
Man must turn away from pleasure's lure and fix his gaze instead
on the genuine beauty of virtue. It is the paradoxical nature
of pleasure that she harms when she gives and benefits when she
takes away. The words "I am the Lord," continues Philo (45 ff.),
are especially addressed to those who need to be threatened by
God's sovereign power of chastisement. The wise man, on the
other hand, lives in unperturbed tranquillity by the side of

God. The worldly-wise vanity called Jethro, however, stands
dumbfounded in amazement before this phenomenal serenity. Indeed, contemplative reason alone can attain the high spiritual
state of perfect stability, since the two-fold nature of uttered
speech robs it of constancy. Philo thus returns to one of his
favorite themes (53 ff.), namely, that only the celestial type
of soul which has abandoned the earthly regions and has disrobed
itself of all concern with externals can enter into the "darkness" of divine being and become privy to its holy mysteries.

        Ss. 55-57 contain a brief exegesis of the superficially
troublesome remark at Gen 6:3: ἔσονται δὲ αἱ ἡμέραι αὐτῶν
ἑκατὸν εἴκοσι ἔτη, which, as Philo notes, would make the god-
forsaken of equal age with Moses himself (cf. Deut 34:7).
Herein must surely lie some hidden meaning. In fact, however,
Philo begs off explaining this for the present, simply taking
refuge in the suggestion that the two 120's may be homonymous,
and thus not strictly comparable (not having the same λόγος τῆς
οὐσίας, Ar. *Cat.* 1a1). He promises to discuss the problem in
more detail elsewhere, in his examination of the προφητικὸς βίος
as a whole (the prophetic life in general, or that of the
Prophet [Moses] in particular?), a promise not, so far as we
can see, fulfilled (see note *ad loc.*). In the parallel passage
QG I.91, we find an elaborate arithmological excursus on the
virtues of the number 120 (on which see further K. Staehle, *Die
Zahlenmystik bei Philon von Alexandreia* [Leipzig-Berlin 1931]),
but no suggestion that there is any problem about the equality
of age between Moses and the many.

B. *Detailed Commentary*

19   διαιωνίσαι. First attested in Philo, and used by him
frequently (*Plant.* 93; *Congr.* 38; *Mut.* 209, etc.). Presumably
provoked by εἰς τὸν αἰῶνα in the lemma.

20   τίς γὰρ οὕτως ἄλογος . . . ; Cf. *LA* 1.33-35. Every
being possessed of a human soul has some ἔννοια of the good at
some time. This can be seen as an application of the Stoic concept of κοιναὶ ἔννοιαι, which are imprinted on human reason. In
the writings of Epictetus we find the Natural Law grounded in
the προλήψεις or preconceptions which the Stoics believed were
common to all men (1.22.1; 2.11; 4.1.41), cf. Arist. *EN* 6.114b5;
Cic. *Fin.* 5.4.3. [*virtutum quasi scintillas*]; *Tusc.* 3.2 [*semina
innata virtutum*]; Sen. *Ben.* 4.17.4: "Of all the benefits that

we have from Nature, this is the greatest, the fact that Virtue
causes her light to penetrate into the minds of all; even those
who do not follow her, see her"; 7.19.5; *Ep.* 108.8; *Stob.* 2.7.5b8;
cf. *LA* 1.34-35, 38; *Det.* 86; Musonius, 2.14 Lutz: σπέρμα ἀρετῆς
ἑκάστῳ ἡμῶν ἐνεῖναι. We may also note Plato's doctrine in the
Phaedrus (249B) that no soul that has ever had a vision of the
truth will rise from brutish into human shape. Conversely, then,
any human soul must have seen something of truth at some time--
in terms of Plato's myth, during the Heavenly Ride.

     ἐπιποτᾶται. Poetical word--Aeschylean (*Pers.* 668, *Eum.*
378)--though Herodotus uses ἐπιπέτομαι, of a dream, at 7.15.
Philo uses this verb also at *LA* 2.11, of the passions fluttering
about over the mind like birds; and at *Somn.* 2.212.

21   οἰκήτορας. The image of visiting and leaving houses
recurs in connection with conscience at *Deus* 131 ff., influenced
by Lev 14:34-36.

     ἐκδεδιῃτημένους. ἐκδιαιτάομαι with accusative is Hellen-
istic, cf. Dion. Hal. *Ant.* 5.74.

     εἰ μὴ τοῦ διελέγξαι. Cf. *LA* 1:35: "One, then, into
whom real life had not been breathed, but who was without experience of virtue, when punished for his transgressions, would have
said that he is unjustly punished, for that it was through inexperience of good that he failed in respect of it, and that the
blame lay with Him who had failed to breathe into him any conception of it."

22   λέγεται δὲ θεοῦ πνεῦμα . . . ὁ ῥέων ἀὴρ ἀπὸ γῆς. Cf.
Ps.-Arist. *De Mundo* 394b8: οὐδὲν γάρ ἐστιν οὗτος πλὴν ἀὴρ πολὺς
ῥέων καὶ ἀθρόος· ὅστις ἅμα καὶ πνεῦμα λέγεται; *QG* 1.90; *Det.*
83: ἡ δὲ [sc. δύναμις] ἐκ τῆς λογικῆς ἀπορρυεῖσα πηγῆς τὸ
πνεῦμα, οὐκ ἀέρα κινούμενον, ἀλλὰ τύπον τινὰ καὶ χαρακτῆρα θείας
δυνάμεως; Emped. DK, B.100, 13-15; Plat. *Crat.* 410B; *SVF* 2.471;
Dox. 374a,19; Heron, *Pneum.* 6.5. See O. Gilbert, *Die meteorolo-
gischen Theorien des griechischen Altertums* (Leipzig 1907) 512 ff.;
H. Leisegang, *Der heilige Geist* (Leipzig-Berlin 1919) 15-75.

     ἡ ἀκήρατος ἐπιστήμη. Cf. *QG* 1.90: "For the divine
spirit is not a movement of air, but intelligence and wisdom";
Det. 83-90; Plato, *Phaedrus* 247D: ἐπιστήμῃ ἀκηράτῳ τρεφομένη
(θεοῦ διάνοια); *Laws* 735C; *Congr.* 25; *Mut.* 219; *Jos.* 146; *Virt.*
55. A completely different allegorical interpretation of Gen 1:2
is given by Numenius, Fr. 30 Des Places = Porph. *Antr.* 10.

23   ἐπὶ τοῦ τῶν ἁγίων ἔργων δημιουργοῦ. For Bezalel, cf.
LA 3.96-103; *Plant.* 27; *BT Ber.* 55a (cf. note on *Gig.* 15). No
contrast is made here, however, between Bezalel and Moses in
respect of the nature of their knowledge of God.

        ὁρικῶς. Adverb first extant in Philo; cf. *Deus* 167;
Sextus, *Math.* 7.426; D.L. 9.71; Hermog. *Stat.* 8.

25   κατὰ ἀποκοπὴν καὶ διάζευξιν. Platonic doctrine of the
imparting of spiritual qualities, without loss to the source.
Cf. *Det.* 90: τέμνεται γὰρ οὐδὲν τοῦ θείου κατ' ἀπάρτησιν, ἀλλὰ
μόνον ἐκτείνεται . . . ὁλκὸς γὰρ δύναμις αὐτοῦ; *Spec.* 1.47;
Wisd. 7:27: καὶ μένουσα ἐν αὐτῇ τὰ πάντα καινίζεται. For the
concept, see Ennius, quoted by Cicero, *Off.* 1.51; Ps.-Ar. *De
Mundo* 398b10 ff.; Sen. *Ep.* 41; M. Aurel. 8.57; 7.59; Numenius,
Fr. 14 Des Places (a torch lighting another does not lose anything of its own light, nor is the teacher's learning diminished
when he imparts it to his pupil [cf. Plot. 6.5.8; 4.9.5]).
There is an analogy in Persian tradition, Ormuzd's creation of
the Bounteous Immortals being compared to the lighting of a
torch from a torch (*Ayadgar I Jamaspiq*, ed. G. Messina [Rome
1939] 3.3-7). In the Indian tradition, cf. *The Questions of
King Milinda*, trans. T. W. Rhys Davids (Dover rep. N.Y., 1963)
1.111 [3.5.5]: "'Suppose a man, O king, were to light a lamp
from another lamp, can it be said that the one transmigrates
from, or to, the other? 'Certainly not.' 'Just so, great king,
is rebirth without transmigration.'" Also, *Shir HaShirim R.* on
Cant 3:10; *BT Sanh.* 39a; *B.R.* 68.9; *Tanhuma*, ed. Buber,
Behaᶜalotkha 22 (torch image); Plot. 1.7.1; 5.3.12; 5.4.2;
3.8.10; Justin, *Dial.* 128 *ad fin.*; Tert. *Apol.* 21.10-13; Lac-
tantius, *Div.Inst.* 4.29.4-5; Aug. *Conf.* 9.5.1.

        ὥσπερ φασὶ τὰς ἀπαντλουμένας πηγάς. A piece of agricul-
tural lore, to the effect that the more water one draws off from
a spring, the sweeter it becomes. Clement uses this image also,
at *Strom.* 1.12, but he may simply be borrowing from Philo.

26   μελέτην καὶ ἄσκησιν. A frequent collocution: *Sacr.* 85;
Agr. 91; *Conf.* 110; *Mig.* 31; *Mos.* 2.27; *Ebr.* 21, etc.

27   τὸ ἀστεῖον. For Moses as ἀστεῖος, cf. *Conf.* 106.

28   διὸ δή. We return to the main theme: the divine *pneuma*
cannot remain permanently in the soul of man.

ἀντιρρεπόντων καὶ πρὸς ἑκάτερα ταλαντευόντων. Same
notion emphasized in *Somn.* 1.153-56 (for this theme applied to
nations, see Gen.Comm. on *Deus* 140-83, *ad fin.*). Cf. also *LA*
2.83; *Post.* 22, 100; *Plant.* 111, etc.

29   ἡ πρὸς σάρκα οἰκείωσις. Cf. *Post.* 157; *Her.* 154. For
that *oikeiosis* by means of which we become well-disposed not just
to ourselves but to other people, see Cic. *Fin.* 3.62-68, 5.65;
and S. G. Pembroke, "Oikeiosis," in *Problems in Stoicism*, ed.
A. A. Long (London 1971) 114-49. οἰκείωσις is probably an antic-
ipatory reference to Lev 18:6, πρὸς πάντα οἰκεῖον σαρκὸς αὐτοῦ,
which he turns to in §32.

γάμος καὶ παιδοτροφία. The Stoic attitude towards the
practical life was not unambiguous: cf. *SVF* 3.691, 693-94, 698
with 703, and Epict. 3.22, 67. (See E. Zeller, *Stoics, Epicureans and Sceptics* [repr. New York 1962] 321-26; J. M. Rist,
Stoic Philosophy [Cambridge 1969] ch. 1; J. Gould, *The Philosophy of Chrysippus* [New York, 1970] 172-73; and the excellent
discussion of Seneca's position on this matter in M. T. Griffin,
Seneca, A Philosopher in Politics (Oxford, 1976) 315-66. Philo's
attitude is similarly not free from ambiguity. Philo never
loses track of the body's legitimate needs and functions, though
he is keenly aware of its capacity to entrap and entice the
higher self. He believes that most men must wean themselves
from the physical aspect of things only very gradually, and with
the expenditure of much effort and toil, though he is aware of
the psychological contamination which may result from too
extended an exposure to bodily concerns (cf. *Cont.* 18-20; *Praem.*
17-19; *Spec.* 2.44-46; *QG* 4.47). He is convinced, however, that
some, though not many, may ultimately succeed in focussing their
minds much of the time on the eternal realities, while yet going
through the motions of somatic activity which will have finally
faded into insignificance.

πρὶν . . . ἀνθῆσαι, κατεμάραναν. Same image and phraseology in Plut. *Mor.* 804E: διὸ πολλοὶ πρὶν ἀνθῆσαι περὶ τὸ βῆμα
κατεμαράνθησαν, so a common source is indicated. Cf. *Prov.* 2.21:
πρὶν ἐπὶ μήκιστον ἀνθῆσαι . . . ἀμαυρώσας; *Post.* 112; *Jos.* 130:
πρὶν ἀνθῆσαι μαραινόμενον; *Spec.* 1.311 (μαραινόμενα . . . πρὶν
ἀνθῆσαι βεβαίως). καταμαραίνω is only found once in Philo.

30   καθάπερ τις θεμέλιος . . . ὑποβέβληται, ᾧ . . . ἐποικο-
δομεῖται. Cf. *Mut.* 211; *Cher.* 101; *Somn.* 2.8.

31   ψυχαὶ . . . ἄσαρκοι καὶ ἀσώματοι. Cf. *Fug.* 58: ἔρωτι
καὶ φιλίᾳ θεοῦ ἀσάρκῳ καὶ ἀσωμάτῳ κατεσχῆσθαι; *Ebr.* 87. At *Spec.*
2.44-46, the wise are described as the closest observers of
Nature, who, "while their bodies are firmly planted on the land
provide their souls with wings, so that they may traverse the
upper air and gain full contemplation of the powers which dwell
there." Cf. also *Deus* 151; *Mos.* 1.190.

        ἐν τῷ τοῦ παντὸς θεάτρῳ. The "theater of the universe"
is a striking image, and one which was very influential in the
Renaissance (see Frances Yates, *The Art of Memory* [1966] 129 ff.,
149, 302, 330; and E. Curtius, *European Literature and the Latin
Middle Ages* [1953] 138 ff.). The soul, when freed from its
fleshly envelope and worldly concerns, will be a spectator of
the divine sights and sounds which are denied to mortal men;
they will be able to see the world from above and observe the
divine order of the universe directly, and they will be able to
hear the music of the spheres. In *Somnium Scipionis* (Cic. *Rep.*
6.15), the universe as perceived from above is compared to a
temple; Plato does not refer to the universe as either a temple
or a theater, but the joy experienced by souls free to observe
the symmetry of the world and the harmony of the stars and
planets is a recurrent theme in the *Phaedo*, *Phaedrus*, *Republic*,
and *Timaeus*. Plato usually uses θεωρία or θεάομαι (esp. *Phaedo*
109B-110E: θεωροῦσα, 109E: εἴ τις ἄνωθεν θεῷτο, 110B). For
Philo, cf. *Op.* 53-54, 77-78; *Spec.* 3.1-6. In *Op.* 77-78, the
souls are invited as to a banquet or a spectacle (θέατρον-θέαμα)
where the entertainment is, again, Platonic.

        ἄπληστος . . . ἔρως. ἄπληστος a good Attic word in
Plato and the Orators. Usually refers to excessive or uncon-
trollable desires, especially greed. In Plato, *Rep.* 562B,
ἀπληστία is desire for a good, but still excessive and dangerous.

        μηδενὸς κωλυσιεργοῦντος. κωλυσιεργέω a Hellenistic for-
mation, first attested in Polybius (6.15.5).

        τὸν σαρκῶν φόρτον ἀχθοφοροῦσι. ἀχθοφορέω also first
attested in Polybius (4.32.7).

        βαρυνόμεναι καὶ πιεζόμεναι. A frequent collocution in
Philo, *Deus* 14; *Det.* 16; *Ebr.* 104, 214; cf. *LA* 3.152; *Spec.*
4.114. A reminiscence of *Phaedo* 81C: ψυχὴ βαρύνεται, cf. Wisd.
9:15: φθαρτὸν γὰρ σῶμα βαρύνει ψυχήν; Jos. *BJ.* 7.346. A fragment of the Pythagorean Onatas states that "the earthly mixture
of the body defiles the purity of the soul: (Thesleff, p. 140,

9 f.) and Ecphantus taught that on earth man is "weighed down
by a large portion of earth" (Thesleff, p. 79, 3 ff.; L. Delatte,
Les traités de la royauté d'Ecphante, Diotogène, et Sthénides
[Liège 1942] 189). See also Plutarch, *Isis and Osiris* 353A:
"But they want their bodies to be compact and light around their
souls and not to oppress or weigh down the divine part with a
mortal element"; Epict. 1.1.15; *CH Asclep*. 1.9; Sen. *Ep*. 65, 16;
Plot. 6.9.8,16.

ἄνω μὲν βλέπειν. Cf. *Plant*. 16-27; *Det*. 85; *QG* 4.46;
Xen. *Mem*. 1.4.11; Plato, *Tim*. 90A-D; Cic. *ND* 2.140. See A.
Wlosok, *Laktanz u. die philosophische Gnosis* (Heidelberg 1960)
8-69.

προσερρίζωνται. Verb first attested in Philo. Also at
Det. 85, in a similar context.

32   ἐκνόμους καὶ ἐκθέσμους. Cf. *Praem*. 126; *Spec*. II 50;
Mos. II 198. ἔκνομος an Aeschylean word (*Eum*. 92; adverb, *Ag*.
1473); ἐκθεσμος first attested in Philodemus, *Sto*. 339, 18.

προοιμιάζεται. Cf. *Op*. 1-3; Plato *Laws* 11.926E; Cic.
Leg. 2.14. It was similarly characteristic of the Book of
Deuteronomy, which was profoundly influenced by ancient Near
Eastern wisdom literature, to counsel and persuade. Its legis-
lation is never in the lapidary style, as in the Book of the
Covenant, but is invariably accompanied by explanatory clauses
which address the heart and mind of man. See G. von Rad, *Studies
in Deuteronomy* (London 1953) 8-9; M. Weinfeld, "Zikato shel Sefer
Devarim la-Hokhma," *Kaufmann Jub. Vol.*, ed. M. Haran (Jerusalem
1961).

ἄνθρωπος ἄνθρωπος . . . Philo recognizes the literal
meaning of Lev 18:6, but his interest is in the allegorical
meaning.

33   καίτοι οὐκ ἀποτρέπει μόνον. Treatise from here until
51 now becomes an exegesis of Lev 18:6.

παγίως. Possibly a *vox Platonica* for Philo (cf. *Rep*.
434D; *Theaet*. 157A; *Tim*. 49D).

ὁ πρὸς ἀλήθειαν ἄνθρωπος. Theme of the "real Man" very
common in Philo and in Greek literature. See *Her*. 231; *Fug*. 71;
Somn. 1.215, 124-25, 2.167; *Det*. 23; *Fug*. 131; *Jos*. 71; *Spec*.
1.303; *Congr*. 97 (the man within the man; cf. Plato, *Rep*. 589B:

ὁ ἐντὸς ἄνθρωπος; *Hipp. Maj.* 304D; *Excerpta ex Theodoto* 51.1);
Plant. 42; *Prob.* 111; Arist. *EN* 1166a; Cic. *Somn.Scip.* [*Rep.* 6]
26; *Tusc.* 1.52; *Alcibiades I* 130C (Plato, *Phaedo* 115C; *Rep.* 469D;
Laws 959B). For a detailed discussion see Jean Pépin, *Idées
grecques sur l'Homme et sur Dieu* (Paris 1971) 71-86. Cf. also
Plot. 1.1.7.20.

  ἀλλοτρίωσιν. Opposite of οἰκείωσις; cf. *Plant.* 25; *Post.*
135: ἡ πρὸς τὸ γενητὸν ἀλλοτρίωσις πρὸς θεὸν οἰκείωσιν εἰργάσατο;
Cher. 41, 74; *Conf.* 82.

  τὸ μὲν οὖν μὴ ἅπαξ ἀλλὰ δὶς φάναι. Note Philo's indifference to the Hebraism here, as so often. Rabbinic exegesis,
attuned to the slightest superfluity of expression in Scripture,
derives an additional legal ruling (i.e., that Gentiles are
included in the prohibition) from the ἐπαναδίπλωσις or doubling
of the word ᾽iš (*Sifra, Aḥarê* 9-13; *BT Sanh.* 57b). Here the
doubling simply indicates for Philo ὁ πρὸς ἀλήθειαν ἄνθρωπος.

  τῶν παλαιῶν . . . τις. Use of the famous story of
Diogenes and the Lamp (cf. D.L. 6.41). See Intro. p. 171 on
Philo's use of Greek anecdotal tradition.

34   πρὸς πάντα οἰκεῖον. A strained interpretation of πάντα
as distributive rather than inclusive. Since this interpretation
really makes nonsense of the literal meaning of the passage,
which forbids all intercourse with any member of one's family,
it is plain that Philo's rules of allegory allow of this.

  ἔνια γὰρ προσετέον. Distinction between ἐπιτήδεια and
περιττά. At *Deus* 162-65, Philo espouses the Aristotelian mean,
identifying the μέση ὁδός with the βασιλικὴ ὁδός leading to God,
and at *Spec.* 4.101-2 he says that "Moses opened up a path midway
between Spartan austerity and Sybarite luxury." Those who need-
lessly fast, or refuse the bath and oil, or are careless about
their clothing and lodging, thinking that they are thereby practising self-control, are to be pitied for their error (*Det.* 19-
21). Even the wise man will indulge in heavy drinking, although
in the more moderate manner of the ancients rather than in the
style of the moderns who drink "till body and soul are unstrung"
(*Plant.* 167-68. In *Cont.* 73 and *QG* 2.67, however, Philo suggests that the use of wine is superfluous). Frequently, however,
as here, he emphasizes the need to be content with little (ὀλι-
γοδεία), for the less one needs the closer one is to God (*Virt.*
8-9). Cf. Xen. *Mem.* 1.6.10 ("to have no wants is divine; to
have as few as possible comes next to the divine"); *Praem.* 99-100;

Somn. 1.97; *Virt.* 6-7; *Prob.* 77, 84; *Op.* 164; *Somn.* 1.124-25,
2.195, 2.40, 64; *Ebr.* 58, 214-15; *Mos.* 2.185 ("But in very truth
that most holy company, justice, temperance, courage, wisdom,
follow in the train of the practisers and all who devote themselves to a life of austerity and hardship, that is to continence
and self-restraint, together with simplicity and frugal content-
ment"); *Cont.* 37-39; *Spec.* 1.9 ("thus making circumcision the
figure of the excision of excessive and superfluous pleasure"),
173-74, 2.159-60; *QG* 3.48; *LA* 2.17, 3.140-43, 147, 154, 236;
Sacr. 59 (Jethro is the man of superfluity; cf. *Gig.* 50; *Mut.*
103); *Det.* 101; Xen. *Mem.* 1.3.5-6; Musonius (in Stob. 751, 526.16,
173). Wendland has pointed out the parallels between numerous
passages in Philo and Musonius, and argues that they must have
had a common origin in Cynic-Stoic diatribe. See P. Wendland,
Philo und die Kynisch-Stoische Diatribe (Beiträge zur Gesch. d.
griechischen Philosophie) (Berlin 1895); and D. R. Dudley, *A
History of Cynicism* (London 1937) 186, 32, 67, 189-201.

        Although the Epicurean distinction between necessary and
unnecessary desires was already anticipated by Plato (*Rep.*
558D ff.; cf. *Tim.* 70E; *Phileb.* 62E; Arist. *EN* 1147b24), Philo's
contrast of the gifts of nature with those of κενὴ δόξα (*Praem.*
100; *Virt.* 7; *QG* 3.47; *Somn.* 1.255) in addition to his contrast
between necessary and unnecessary desires points to his dependence on an Epicurean source. (See Usener, *Epicurea* 456. *Schol.
in Arist. EN*: αἱ δὲ [sc. ἐπιθυμίαι] οὔτε ἀναγκαῖαι οὔτε φυσικαὶ
ἀλλὰ κατὰ κενὴν γενόμεναι δόξαν; Cic. *Tusc.* 5.93: *tertias, quod
essent plane inanes neque necessitatem modo.* Plut. *Grylli* 989B:
τὸ δὲ τῶν μήτ' ἀναγκαίων μήτε φυσικῶν ἀλλ' ἔξωθεν ὑπὸ δόξης κενῆς.
D.L. 10.149: αἱ δὲ οὔτε φυσικαὶ οὔτε ἀναγκαῖαι ἀλλὰ παρὰ κενὴν
δόξαν γιγνόμεναι; *K.D.* 30.) For other possible Epicurean echoes
in Philo, see Bréhier 263-64.

        σκορακιστέον. σκορακίζω rather a slang word, formed
from "ἐς κόρακας" and found first in Philo, except once in Ps.-
Demosthenes (11.11). σκορακισμός in LXX (Sir 41:19), so that
may be the relevant influence. See Intro, p. 137 for discussion
of Philo's vocabulary. Vulgar elements appearing in LXX had
considerable effect on him, paralleled later by that of NT on
Church Fathers. However, we know that vulgar diction was to be
found in Comedy, and in some of the orators (Hyperides and the
author of Dem. 17), so the word may have been more common than
we would suppose in Classical Attic authors.

ὑφ᾽ ὧν ἐξαπτόμεναι . . . ῥύμῃ μίᾳ καταφλέγουσι. For
image of passions as a consuming fire, cf. *Virt.* 9: ἀπλήστου
καὶ ἀκορέστου . . . ἐπιθυμίας, ἣν πυρὸς τρόπον ἀναρριπίζων καὶ
ἀναφλέγων ἐπὶ πάντα μικρά τε αὖ καὶ μεγάλα τείνει.

35   ἡδοναὶ γὰρ ἀτίθασοι. Comparison of the passions to wild
beasts very frequent in Philo: *LA* 1.69 (desire compared to a
tiger, animal least capable of being tamed) (ἀτιθασωτάτῳ ζῴῳ);
ib. 2.9-11, 92; ib. 3.156; *Sacr.* 62; *Plant.* 43; *Conf.* 24, 110;
Mig. 219; *Abr.* 32; *Spec.* 1.148; 2.9; 4.94; *Praem.* 59, 88 (the
wild beasts within the soul must be tamed); *Cont.* 74. The image
is Platonic (*Tim.* 70E; *Rep.* 588C). Cf. Plot. 1.1.7.21. ἀτίθα-
σος (aside from a dubious reading in Hdn. 5.6.9) found only in
Philo, who uses it frequently.

    ὅταν κυνῶν τρόπον προσσαίνωσιν . . . ἀνίατα ἔδακον.
Philo is fond of the image of rabid dogs whose bite is irremedi-
able. See *Prob.* 90: κυνῶν ἰοβόλων τρόπον προσσαίνοντες, ἀνι-
άτων γενόμενοι κακῶν αἴτιοι; *Cont.* 40: κράζουσι καὶ λυττῶσι
τρόπον κυνῶν ἀτιθάσων καὶ ἀπανιστάμενοι δάκνουσιν ἀλλήλους.
"During the early stages of the disease a rabid animal is most
dangerous because it appears to be healthy and may seem friendly
but will bite at the slightest provocation" (*Encycl. Brit.* s.v.
Rabies) (1963, v. 18, p. 863a). For the signs of a mad dog
(κυνὸς λυσσῶντος σημεῖα), see Philumenus, *De venenatis animali-*
bus 1.1.1 ff.; Paulus Aegineta 5.3, ed. Heiberg in *CMG* 9, p. 8;
Theophanes Nonnus, *Epitome de curatione morborum* 271, ed. Bernard
(1795), p. 324; *PT Yoma* 8.5 (*BT* ib. 83b); *Shir Hashirim Zuta* 6.6
(discussed by S. Lieberman, *Hellenism in Jewish Palestine* [New
York 1950] 188-89). See also J. Dillon and A. Terian's note on
the four *eupatheiai* in *QG* 2.57 in *Studia Philonica* 4 (1976-77).
(At *Decal.* 115, the dog is called τοῦ θηρίων θρασυτάτου.) ὑπο-
στροφή found in Philo only here.

    ἀνήνυτον. Possibly here *vox Platonica*, containing
reminiscence of *Gorgias* 507E: οὐκ ἐπιθυμίας ἐῶντα ἀκολάστους
εἶναι καὶ ταύτας ἐπιχειροῦντα πληροῦν, ἀνήνυτον κακόν, a sentiment which parallels Philo's thought here.

    ὀλιγοδεΐαν. Seems to be first used by Philo (later
found in Gregory of Nazianzus, Nilus of Ancyra, and Isidore of
Pelusium). For frequency of usage in Philo, see references in
note on ἔνια γὰρ προσετέον above. (At *Sacr.* 27 it appears as

part of a long list of similar virtues. For connection between
ὀλιγόδεια and intelligence, cf. *Prov.* 2.110.)

36   ἄξιον ἀναπτύξαι. ἀναπτύσσω seems to be only poetical in
this sense in Classical period. Cf. *Agr.* 136: τὰς διπλᾶς καὶ
ἀμφιβόλους λέξας ἀναπτύσσων; *Cont.* 78: τὰ μὲν σύμβολα διαπτύ-
ξασα καὶ διακαλύψασα; *Spec.* 3.6; Porphyry, *Antr.* 4; Iambl. *Protr.*
21.

      πολλάκις οὐ γενόμενοί τινες πορισταὶ χρημάτων. The idea
of the danger of having wealth, fame, and physical excellence
thrust upon one Philo may, at least in the case of the first two,
be applying to himself, although three different sets of people
are mentioned.

      εὐτονία. εὐτονέω, εὔτονος, εὐτονία seem to occur earli-
est in the Hippocratic writings (*Ep.* 16,17; 15; *Aph.* 3.17),
though how early these are is not clear. τὸ εὔτονον at least is
used by Plato in *Laws* 815A, in a context of prescribing suitable
physical exercise.

      μαθέτωσαν δὴ . . . For a parallel to the admonitory
phrase, cf. *Prov.* 2.2.

37   προσέρχεσθαι. As Moses says (comm. *ad loc.* p. 38),
Philo invests this word (taken from οὐ προσελεύσεται of Lev
18:6) with much significance, making it a theme-word for his
homily. It connotes here assent to the trio of "human goods,"
wealth, fame and health. It is taken up by πρόσοδος and οὐ
προσερχόμενοι further down, and finally by the Homeric-Platonic
phrase κατ᾽ ἴχνος βαίνειν (see below).

      φιλάθλοις. First attested in Philo. Used here to
buttress φιλογυμνασταῖς and balance φιλαργύροις and φιλοδόξοις.
(For the collocation of φίλαθλος and φιλογυμναστής, see *Congr.*
25 and *Somn.* 1.251.) Note his triadic construction, with the
third colon of the triad suitably amplified. Cf. 27 above, and
Longinus, *Subl.* 9.6, 10.3. A good parallel, which also involves
a series of qualities, is Demosthenes 3.26. The amplification
of the final clause is very common with three or more cola.

      τὸ γὰρ ἄμεινον. The theme of submitting soul, which
should naturally rule, to the soulless, which should naturally
be ruled (cf. *Phaedr.* 246B: ψυχὴ πᾶσα παντὸς ἐπιμελεῖται τοῦ
ἀψύχου), is trite enough. Cf. *Decal.* 76 μηδεὶς οὖν τῶν ἐχόντων
ψυχὴν ἀψύχῳ τινὶ προσκυνείτω; *LA* 2.50; *Cont.* 9; Wisd 15:17.

38   ὡς ἡγεμόνι τῷ νῷ. νοῦς as ἡγεμών is a popular turn of
phrase with Philo, of obvious Stoic provenance, cf. *Ebr.* 60;
Heres 186; *Spec.* 2.61, etc., but it is noteworthy that the actual
phrase is nowhere in Old Stoic sources. It may be that Philo is
being original here, giving a Platonist tone to the Stoic ἡγεμονικόν.

   ὡς καὶ δίχα αὐτῶν. Definite rejection here of Peripatetic ethics. Happiness is independent of any material advantages.
Cf. *LA* 2.16-18, a good exposition of Philo's views.

39   κατ' ἴχνος βαίνειν. Echo here of Homeric phrase: ὁ δ'
ἔπειτα μετ' ἴχνια βαῖνε θεοῖο (*Od.* 2.406; 3.30, of Telemachus
following Athena in the guise of Mentor, and 5.193, of Odysseus
following Calypso, allegorized as the initial leading of the
soul forth to begin its journey through life). Cf. *Mig.* 128.

   αἰσχρᾶς ἀναπίμπλησι δόξης φιλοσοφίαν. The translations
of Colson ("with the baseness of men's opinion") and Mosès
("d'une opinion déshonorante") are unsatisfactory, Colson "over-
translating," Mosès being indefinite. The meaning surely is
"gives philosophy a bad name."

   πωλούντων . . . καὶ ἐπευωνιζόντων. Cf. *Mos.* 2.212;
Cher. 123. Latter word Demosthenic (23.201). A Demosthenic
echo, direct or indirect, is possible, but cf. also Plato, *Prot.*
313CD (Sophists as crooked market traders); *Soph.* 231D. Also
Lucian, *Bion Prasis* (cut-rate sale of philosophies).

   τοτὲ μὲν μικροῦ λήμματος. All these genitives presumably
refer to the various pitches which the hawkers are making. Cf.
Plato, *Soph.* 234A: πάνυ σμικροῦ νομίσματος ἀποδίδοται.

   εὐπαραγώγου. A theme-word of Philo's (cf. 59 below; *Agr.*
16, 96; *Ebr.* 46; *Fug.* 22; *Spec.* 1.28, etc.). May be a *vox Platonica*, echo of *Tim.* 69D: ἐλπίδα δ' εὐπαράγωγον, though Philo
uses it in the active sense here, as "seductive" (Philo uses
ἐλπίδος just after this). The Platonic image of the sophist as
huckster is elaborated in typical Philonic fashion.

40   ὦ γενναῖε. The homiletical formula employing direct
address in a very personal manner, as here, is very frequent in
Philo. Cf. *LA* 3.75; *Det.* 150; *Agr.* 86, 167; *Her.* 91; *Mut.* 177,
187; *Somn.* 1.93, 2.253; *Decal.* 73; *Spec.* 2.84; *Prov.* 2.31.
(Equally common is ὦ ψυχή or ὦ διάνοια: *Gig.* 44; *Cher.* 29; *Deus*

4, 114; *LA* 1.49; *Somn.* 2.68, 76; *Sacr.* 20; *Prov.* 2.16; etc.)
See H. Thyen, *Der Stil der jüdisch-hellenistischen Homilie*
(Göttingen 1955) 94-100. It is also common, as a slightly
ironical address, in Plato's dialogues, e.g. *Alc.* 1.135E; *Hipp.*
Maj. 298A; *Gorg.* 521B.

παγκάλως καὶ σφόδρα παιδευτικῶς. Same formula occurs
at *Spec.* 4.39; cf. *Mig.* 14; *Spec.* 4.66 (σφόδρα π.); *Virt.* 165
(ἄγαν π.); *Sacr.* 42 (δογματικῶς καὶ π.).

ὁ νοῦς τῶν ὅλων, ὁ θεός. This Stoic formula (*SVF* 1.157:
νοῦν κόσμου πύρινον) appears frequently in Philo: *Mig.* 4, 192-93;
Op. 8; *LA* 3.29; *Spec.* 1.18; *Fug.* 46. θεός here should properly
refer to God's *logos*, however, rather than to God himself.

41   ἐφάμιλλός γε ἡ ἀσύγκριτος σύγκρισις. Cf. *Ebr.* 43: ὅταν
συγκρίνῃς τὰ ἀσύγκριτα; *Somn.* 2.284: συμφωνία . . . ἀσύμφωνος.
Some corruption seems to have crept in here. Wendland conjec-
tured ἡ ἀσυγκρίτων σύγκρισις. Colson suggests the following
reconstruction: οὔκουν <εἰ> τὸ μὲν σαρκός ἐστιν ἄλογος ἡδονή,
τὸ δὲ ψυχῆς καὶ τοῦ παντὸς ὁ νοῦς τῶν ὅλων, ὁ θεὸς ἐφάμιλλός
<τε> ἢ <ἀ>συγκρίτων ἡ σύγκρισις, εἰ μὴ . . . i.e., "then if the
first is . . . , and the second is . . . , the comparison is not
an evenly balanced one or between two really comparables, unless
we are prepared to admit . . . ," etc. But Wendland's emendation makes good enough sense, if we assume Philo to be speaking
ironically, i.e., "the comparison of the (essentially) incomparable is, forsooth, a serious context, . . .". The reading of
H, which omits μή after εἰ, seems to give a rather easier sense:
"that is, if one is also prepared to say that" all opposites are
really the same.

42   τὸ μὲν γέγονέ τε καὶ πείσεται, ὁ δ᾽ ἐστὶν ἀγένητός τε
καὶ ποιῶν ἀεί. A development on Plato, *Tim.* 38AB, with a Stoic-
influenced contrast between τὸ ποιοῦν and τὸ πάσχον (*SVF* 1.85).

43   μὴ λιποτακτῆσαι μὲν τῆς τοῦ θεοῦ τάξεως. Cf. Plato,
Apol. 28E-29A: τοῦ δὲ θεοῦ τάττοντος . . . φιλοσοφοῦντα με δεῖν
ζῆν . . . λίποιμι τὴν τάξιν. *Deus* 34; *Ebr.* 145; *Cher.* 32; *Det.*
142; *Aet.* 65; *Cont.* 11: καὶ μηδέποτε τὴν τάξιν ταύτην λειπέτω;
Decal. 104, 178; also Epict. 1.16-21; 1.9.16; 4 Macc 9:23.

καινοτάτη . . . ἡ φύσις. This remark on the paradoxical
quality of pleasure, that its bestowals do good and its

deprivations harm, is a notable conceit, a development of the comparison with mad dogs at 35.

44   ἡδονῆς φίλτρων. A frequent collocution in Philo. *Post.* 135; *Deus* 170; *Agr.* 98; *Sobr.* 23; *Spec.* 1.9; *Cont.* 69; *Op.* 165.

μετάκλινε. First in Philo. Cf. *Post.* 100, 111; *Deus* 180; *Conf.* 129; *Mig.* 184 (generally refers to a shift away from an erroneous path).

ἀντιπεριάγουσα. Cf. *Agr.* 70 (where it refers to pulling the horse's neck around the other way). A reminiscence of Plato, *Rep.* 518B ff., where true education is spoken of as a περιαγωγή (518D) of the ὄψις of the soul.

ἵμερος ἐντακῇ σοι. In earlier usage (Soph. *El.* 1311; Plato, *Menex.* 245D; Lucian, *Peregr.* 22) ἐντήκω leans to a bad sense (cf. *Post.* 165). Philo, however, uses it mostly in a good sense: *Ebr.* 159; *Mig.* 157 (ὁ θεῖος ἐντακεὶς ἵμερος); *Her.* 310; *Congr.* 64; *Mut.* 174; *Prob.* 117; cf. Julian 130C: ἀνέτηκέ μοι δεινὸς τοῦ θεοῦ πόθος.

καὶ ὡς σιδηρῖτις λίθος ἐπισπάσηταί σε . . . καὶ ἐξαρτήσῃ. Cf. *Praem.* 58; Plato, *Ion* 536A: καὶ ὥσπερ ἐκ τῆς λίθου ἐκείνης ὁρμαθὸς πάμπολυς ἐξήρτηται χορευτῶν. (See *Sacr.* 20 ff. where both virtue and vice are personified; cf. Xen. *Mem.* 2.1. See Méasson's introduction to *Sacr.*, pp. 28-35.) There is a good description of the lodestone in Pliny, *NH* 36.126-27. Cf. Plut. *Is. et Os.* 376BC; *Platon. Quaest.* 7, 1005CD.

45   ἐγὼ ὁ ἄρχων καὶ βασιλεὺς καὶ δεσπότης. The rabbis interpreted Lev 18:6 in a similar manner. *Sifra, Aḥarê* 9.1: "'I am the Lord, (Lev 18:6). I am the judge who punishes, and faithful to reward." Cf. *Wayyikra R.* 23.9.

47   πάντα γὰρ πεπληρωκὼς ὁ θεὸς ἐγγύς ἐστιν, ὥστε ἐφορῶντος. Cf. *LA* 3.4; *Sacr.* 67; *Det.* 153; *Post.* 14, 30; *Deus* 57; *Conf.* 136; *Somn.* 1.62, 2.221; Sen. *Ep.* 41.1-2, 83.2; Epict. 1.14; 2.8.9-14: "You are bearing God about with you, you poor wretch, and know it not . . . But when God himself is present within you, seeing and hearing everything. . . ."

κολαστηρίῳ δυνάμει. Philo explains God's designation as κύριος as a reference to his ἐξουσία or sovereignty, and his designation θεός as a reference to his ἀγαθότης or goodness.

To the former he applies the adjectives βασιλική, ἀρχική, νομοθετική, and κολαστήριος, whereas for the latter he employs the adjectives ποιητική, εὐεργετική, χαριστική, δωρητική, and ἵλεως. On the powers of God, see Wolfson, *Philo* I pp. 217-26.

ἠρεμήσωμεν. ἠρεμέω c. part. or inf. in the sense of refraining from doing is apparently first attested in Philo (and only once at that). Cf. Lucian, *Jud. Voc.* 4.

τὸ σοφίας πνεῦμα θεῖον. Σοφία is here identified with the πνεῦμα or λόγος of God pervading the universe, as a force both cosmological and ethical. For the relationship of σοφία to λόγος, see U. Früchtel, *Die kosmologischen Vorstellungen bei Philo von Alexandrien* (Leiden 1968) 172-83. Cf. esp. *Fug.* 97 and 109.

48   ὁ σοφὸς ἀχώριστος ἀρετῆς. According to the Stoics, whom Philo is following, the Wise Man is no longer separated from virtue, whereas the προκόπτοντες are still liable to reverse course and slip back into their former habits. "For many, after beginning to practise virtue, have changed at the last: but on the man to whom God affords secure knowledge, he bestows both advantages, both that of tilling the virtues, and also that of never desisting from them" (*LA* 1.89). At *Agr.* 160, Philo is apparently reproducing Seneca's three-fold classification of the προκόπτοντες (*Ep.* 75). He speaks there of beginners, those making progress, and those who have reached perfection but are still unpractised in virtue. In describing the latter, he uses the Stoic expression διαλεληθότες σοφοί (unwitting wise men). Seneca describes this group as men who have already laid aside all passions and vices, but whose assurance has not yet been tested. They have already arrived at a point from which there is no slipping back, though they are not yet aware of the fact (cf. *SVF* 3.539-42). Philo also seems to be referring to this stage at *Somn.* 2.270, where he says that the "destruction and removal of passion is a good, yet it is not a perfect good, but the discovery of wisdom is a thing of transcendent excellence." Although both Chrysippus and Philo agree that once a man achieves wisdom his actions acquire a firm consistency and he is no longer liable to slip back into vice (*SVF* 3.510), they nevertheless insist that the onset of a diseased physiological condition, such as melancholia, lethargy or various drug-induced stages, could temporarily interrupt the sage's virtue (D.L. 7.127-28; *Abr.* 207).

ὀρθοῦ λόγου βεβαιότητι ἱδρυμένον. Cf. *SVF* 3.510: ὅταν αἱ μέσαι πράξεις αὗται προσλάβωσι τὸ βέβαιον καὶ ἑκτικὸν καὶ ἰδίαν πῆξιν τινὰ λάβωσι. For πῆξιν cf. *Agr.* 160, where Philo employs the same image; *LA* 2.55; ἡ φιλόθεος ψυχὴ ἐκδῦσα τὸ σῶμα . . . πῆξιν καὶ βεβαίωσιν καὶ ἵδρυσιν ἐν τοῖς τελείοις ἀρετῆς δόγμασι λαμβάνει.

49 "σὺ δὲ αὐτοῦ στῆθι μετ' ἐμοῦ". (Deut 5:31) (v. 28 in Heb.) The rabbis deduced from this verse that Moses separated himself from his wife, and that God gave his approval to this act (*BT Shab.* 87a. cf. *Mos.* 2.68-69; *Sifre* on Num 12:1 [99], ed. H. S. Horovitz 98). The ideal of εὐστάθεια or inner calm and stability is a central theme running through Philo's writings. At *Post.* 23 Philo writes: "Proximity to a stable object (τῷ ἑστῶτι) produces a desire to be like it and a longing for quiescence (ἠρεμίας). Now that which is unwaveringly stable (ἀκλινῶς ἑστώς) is God, and that which is subject to movement is creation. He therefore that draws nigh to God longs for stability . . ."; ib. 27: "Abraham the wise, being one who stands, draws near to God the standing One (τῷ ἑστῶτι θεῷ), for it says, 'he was standing before the Lord' (Gen 18:22). For only a truly unchanging soul has access to the unchanging God (ἄτρεπτον θεόν) . . . But what shows in the clearest light the firm steadfastness of the man of worth is the oracle communicated to the all-wise Moses which runs thus: 'But as for thee stand thou here by Me' (Deut 5:31). This oracle proves two things, one that the Existent Being who moves and turns all else is Himself exempt from movement and turning; and secondly that he makes the worthy man sharer of his own nature, which is repose (ἠρεμίας);" *ibid.* 29: ὅτι θεοῦ μὲν ἴδιον ἠρεμία καὶ στάσις. Cf. *Cher.* 19; *Somn.* 1.158, 2.219: "to be unswerving and stable belongs only to God and to such as are the friends of God" (for the last phrase see Plato, *Tim.* 53D: ὃς ἂν ἐκείνῳ φίλος ᾖ); *Virt.* 32; *Legat.* 113; *Conf.* 130-32; *Fug.* 174; *Abr.* 27; *Ebr.* 100, 76; *Sacr.* 8; *Flac.* 135. For the earliest application of the term εὐσταθής to the human soul, see Democritus, D-K B. 191: αἱ δ' ἐκ μεγάλων διαστημάτων κινούμεναι τῶν ψυχέων οὔτε εὐσταθέες εἰσὶν οὔτε εὔθυμοι. Cf. also Epicurus, fr. 11 (Bailey); Epict. 1.29; *SVF* 3.280, 264; Muson. Ruf., fr. 38; Ps.-Aristeas 261 (ψυχῆς εὐστάθεια); Aristobulus, *FPG* 224; Wisd. 8:16: προσαναπαύσομαι αὐτῇ (sc. Sophia); *Corp.Her.* 13.20: βουλῇ τῇ σῇ ἀναπέπαυμαι; *Excerp. ex Theod.* 63.1; *Gosp. of Philip* 119.13-15;

Plot. 6.9.11, 6.9.8, 4.8.1, 4.8.5; Plat. *Rep*. 532E. See
H. Gomoll, *Der stoische Philosoph Hekaton* (Bonn 1933) 21 ff.;
Y. Amir, "A Religious Interpretation of a Philosophical Concept
in Philo," (Heb.), *Memorial Vol. for Prof. Benzion Katz* (Tel-
Aviv 1970) 112-17; P. Vielhauer, *Aufsätze zum Neuen Testament*
(München 1965) 215-34; O. Hofius, *Katapausis* (Tübingen 1970)
75-90. (It may be noted that Clement of Alexandria, after citing Deut 5:31, writes: "The Adherents of Simon want to be like
in conduct to the 'standing one' whom they worship" [*Strom*. 2.
52.2].) See H. Leisegang, *Die Gnosis* (Stuttgart, 1955) 62 ff.

στάσις. Stability or στάσις is one of the five categories (the μέγιστα γένη of the *Sophist*) applied by Plotinus to
the Intellectual Principle. For ἀκλινής cf. Plato, *Phaed*. 109A;
Aet. 116. The adv. ἀκλινῶς appears to be first attested in
Philo. Stability, as opposed to regular, eternal motion, is
the characteristic which Numenius discerns in his First God or
Father, as opposed to the Second or Demiurge (fr. 15 Des Places).

ὑγιεῖ κανόνι. Cf. *LA* 3.233; *Aet*. 116.

50   ὁ περισσὸς τύφος, ἐπίκλησιν ᾿Ιοθόρ. In two other places
Philo explains the name Jethro, ᾿Ιοθόρ in Greek, by περισσός:
Mut. 103; *Agr*. 43. "Amir pointed out," writes Rokeah, "that in
all other cases Philo uses the Attic form περιττός. Moreover
in the same sentences, after using the form περισσός, he reverts
to the Attic style and uses περιττός in his own syntactical construction. He does this also when he gives the meaning of the
Hebrew without stating that it is a translation (*Sacr*. 50).
Amir argued that this interchange of dialects in a writer who
took pains to write in a pure style can only be explained on the
assumption that there was in front of Philo, in writing, the
form περισσός as a translation of ᾿Ιοθόρ, and that, as Philo
wrote, he did not think himself privileged to change it. Amir
added that he did not dare say whether this was a bare list of
biblical names and their Greek equivalents, or a literary essay
which contained etymological explanations. In any case, it is
difficult to suppose that this document contained only the
explanation of the name Jethro, and not also explanations of
other names that Philo needed. Therefore, said Amir, whoever
wishes to attribute to Philo a knowledge of the original language of the Bible will no longer be able to make use of Philo's
explanations of Hebrew names as evidence. Amir omitted a third

example of translation of a sort by Philo, where he therefore
had 'Ιοθόρ-περισσός, i.e., our passage. Now three cases of
περισσός as over against about seventy cases of περιττός is very
telling, even if there were no strict distinction between the
Attic and the κοινή as argued by H. D. Mantel. Indeed, I cannot
see any other satisfactory explanation of this phenomenon than
the above suggested. In fact we have at our disposal part of
this compilation in the Greek onomastica, the Oxyrhynchus papy-
rus, and Hieronymus' Onomasticum (Ox. AB 15 reads Ιεθερ περισσος).
With their help we can solve almost all the problems that the
Philonian etymologies pose." (David Rokeah, "A New Onomasticon
Fragment from Oxyrhynchus and Philo's Etymologies," *JThS* N.S.
19 [1968] 76-77; Y. Amir, "Explanation of Hebrew Names in Philo,"
Tarbiz 31 [1962-63] 98-99 [Heb.]; Y. Kohen-Yashar, "Did Philo of
Alexandria know Hebrew?", *Tarbiz* 34 [1964-65] 337-45. [Heb.])

There is no need, however, to say with Amir that Philo did not
"think himself privileged" to change περισσός into περιττός.
What is clear is that Philo did not bother to change it, and
this is sufficient to establish Amir's basic point.

τὴν ἀρρεπῆ . . . καὶ κατὰ τὰ αὐτὰ καὶ ὡσαύτως ἔχουσαν
προαίρεσιν. Cf. *Deus* 23; *Conf.* 30, 32; *Mut.* 87, 183; *Somn.*
2.220, 227; *Abr.* 170; *Prob.* 29. ἀρρεπής apparently first
extant in Philo (also common in later Platonism). κατὰ τὰ αὐτὰ
καὶ ὡσαύτως ἔχουσαν is a basic Platonic phrase, e.g. *Phaedo* 78D.
The use of προαίρεσις to mean something like "character" is
common in later Stoicism, particularly Epictetus (*Diss.* 1.8.16,
1.29.1, 2.10.25, etc.; cf. J. M. Rist, *Stoic Philosophy* 228-31),
but can be discerned also in Philo, e.g. *Leg.* 230; *Cont.* 2; *Deus*
102, 114 (π. βίου).

51   τὸν ἐν εἰρήνῃ συνεχῆ πόλεμον ἀνθρώπων. Cf. *Conf.* 46:
"For all the deeds of war are done in peace. Men plunder, rob,
kidnap, spoil, sack, outrage, maltreat, violate, dishonor and
commit murder sometimes by treachery, or if they be stronger
without disguise." This war-in-peace antithesis was a common
theme in the Cynic-Stoic diatribe literature of the first
century C.E. Cf. Ps.-Heraclit. *Ep.* 7: "In peace you make war
with words; in war you deliberate with iron . . . Give me an
opportunity for laughter in peacetime, when you do not do battle
in the lawcourts with weapons on your tongues, after committing
frauds, seducing women, poisoning friends, spoiling temples,

procuring, being found faithless in your oaths." See H. W.
Attridge, *First-Century Cynicism in the Epistles of Heraclitus*
(Missoula 1976) 73 line 17, 69 lines 21-25. Cf. Ps.-Diog. *Ep.*
28 (Hercher, *Epistol.Gr.* [Paris 1873] 242); Wisd 14:22.

τὸν ἐν ταῖς ψυχαῖς . . . βαρὺν χειμῶνα. For image of
storm in soul, cf. *Congr.* 60 (βαρὺν χειμῶνα).

52   ὁ ἀρχιερεὺς λόγος. The equation of the High Priest with
the Logos is a common one in Philo (cf. *Fug.* 108 ff.; *Mig.* 102;
Somn. 1.215), but here it plainly cannot be the Logos of God
which only attains union with God once a year; it must refer
simply to human reason, but it is a human reason which is able
to function only rarely on a level of reflection without words
(λόγος ἐνδιάθετος).

κατὰ προφοράν. Cf. *Mig.* 71-81; *Mos.* 2.121-30; *Anim.* 12.
The Stoic distinction between λόγος ἐνδιάθετος and λόγος προ-
φορικός goes back to Plato (*Theaet.* 190A, 206D; *Soph.* 263E) and
Aristotle (*Anal.Post.* 1.10.76b24), though, of course, without
the cosmic dimensions which Philo here presupposes. See
Heraclit. *Quaest.Hom.* 72.14-15; Sext. *Math.* 8.275; Plut. *Prin.*
Phil. 777B; *Sollert.Anim.* 973; cf. Plot. 1.2.3, 27-31; E. Zeller,
Stoics, Epicureans and Sceptics (rep. New York 1972) 73 n. 2;
M. Pohlenz, *Die Stoa* (Göttingen 1959) 1.39; K. Otte, *Das Sprach-
verständnis bei Philo von Alexandrien* (Tübingen 1968) 131-42.

ὅτι κατὰ τὴν ἀδιαίρετον ἵσταται μονάδα. Cf. *Deus* 83-84:
μονάδας μὲν οὖν ἀκράτους ὁ θεὸς λαλεῖ. Mention of the dyad,
though ostensibly only referring to the duality of speaker and
hearer produced by utterance, also has reference to the dyadic
aspect of the Logos in the universe, and of Sophia. Some Neo-
pythagorean influence is manifest here.

53   γυμνῇ τῇ διανοίᾳ. Cf. *LA* 2.59-60; *Cher.* 31; *Sacr.* 84;
Ebr. 34; *Mig.* 90, 192; *Mut.* 199; *Somn.* 1.43; *Abr.* 236; *Spec.*
1.63, 4.71; *Prob.* 43. The image of stripping goes back to some
extent to the myth of the *Gorgias* 523A ff. Cf. Plot. 1.6.7.5-7;
Proclus, *Comment. on Alcib.* 138.16-18, p. 63, Westerink; *Excerp.*
ex Theodoto 27; Emped. B.127: σαρκῶν ἀλλογνῶτι περιστέλλουσα
χιτῶνι; Plato, *Phaed.* 87E. It is also common in Gnostic texts.
In the *Poimandres*, for example, "the ascent of the knower's soul
after death is described as a series of progressive subtractions
which leave the 'naked' true self free to enter the divine realm

and to become one again with God (cf. Plot. 1.6.7). Similarly,
the Mysteries of Mithras had for their initiates the ceremonial
of passing through seven gates arranged in ascending steps
representing the seven planets (the so-called κλῖμαξ ἑπτάπυλος,
Orig. *C.Cels*. 6.22); in those of Isis we find a successive put-
ting on and off of seven (or twelve) garments or animal dis-
guises" (H. Jonas, *The Gnostic Religion* [2nd ed. Boston 1963]
166. See also W. Bousset, *Die Himmelreise der Seele* [Darmstadt
1960]; Dodds, *Proclus* 307; Rist, *Plotinus* 188-91; P. Wendland,
"Das Gewand der Eitelheit," *Hermes* 51 [1916] 481-85; Dodds,
Pagan and Christian 94-95).

54   εἰς τὸν γνόφον. A reference to Exodus 20:21; cf. *Post.*
14; *Mut.* 7; *Mos.* 1.158; εἰς τε τὸν γνόφον . . . εἰσελθεῖν λέγεται, τουτέστιν εἰς τὴν ἀειδῆ καὶ ἀόρατον καὶ ἀσώματον τῶν ὄντων
παραδειγματικὴν οὐσίαν. Clement borrows from Philo, e.g. *Strom.*
2.6.1. For the use of this image in Gregory of Nyssa, see
J. Daniélou, "Mystique de la Ténèbre chez Grégoire de Nysse,"
Dict. de la spiritualité, ed. M. Viller (Paris 1932 ff.) 1872-85.

    ἱεροφάντης ὀργίων. Philo uses this designation for
Moses frequently. See *LA* 3. 173; *Sacr.* 94; *Post.* 16, 164, 173;
Cher. 49 (of Jeremiah); *Deus* 156; etc. On the whole question
of the correct evaluation of mystery imagery in Philo, see
V. Nikiprowetsky, *CEP* 17-28. Useful discussion also in Salva-
tore Lilla, *Clement of Alexandria* 148 ff.

55   The rabbis had already connected this verse with Moses.
BT Ḥulin 139b: "Where is Moses indicated in the Torah (i.e.,
where is his coming foretold)? In the verse *'Beshagam hu basar'*
(the numerical value of *'beshagam'* is equivalent to the name
'Mosheh.' Moreover this verse adds, 'Therefore shall his days
be 120 years, which corresponds with the years of the life of
Moses).'" Cf. *BR* 26.6, T-A 253; *Midrash Tannaim, Deut.* 34.7.
Cf. 2 Baruch 17.1-4: "With the Most High account is not taken
of much time nor of a few years. For what did it profit Adam
that he lived 930 years, and transgressed that which he was
commanded . . . Or wherein did Moses suffer loss in that he lived
only 120 years, and, inasmuch as he was subject to Him who
formed him, brought the law to the seed of Jacob, and lighted
a lamp for the nation of Israel?" A detailed arithmological
discussion is given by Philo at *QG* 1.91.

56   τὰ ὁμώνυμα. See Arist. *Cat.* 1a1. Two things are
homonymous, according to Aristotle, if the same name applies to
both but not in the same sense. Thus, for example, both a man
and a picture are animals (ζῷον had come to be used also of
pictures or other artistic representations, whether of animals
or not). Cf. *Plant.* 150 ff.; frag. from *QE*, R. Marcus' *Supplement to Philo II* (LCL) no. 5, p. 259.

        δίδυμον εἰσάγεται. Cf. *Praem.* 63: ἅμα τῇ γενέσει κυο-
φορεῖ δίδυμα ἡ ψυχή, κακόν . . . καὶ ἀγαθόν. Colson and Whittaker have suggested that we have here an echo of Socrates' remark
concerning pleasure and pain to the effect that if a man "pursues
the one and captures it, he is generally obliged to take the
other also, as if the two were joined together in one head"
(Plato, *Phaed.* 60B); cf. Heraclit. B.111. Mosès suggests that
Philo is here alluding to the births of Cain and Abel which are
allegorized at the beginning of *Sacr.* There are two opposite
views of life, says Philo, one which ascribes all things to
man's own mind, the other which follows God. The first is
figured by Cain, the other by Abel. "Now both these views lie
in the womb of the single soul. But when they are brought to
birth they must needs be separated." Neither of these analogies
is persuasive. It is probable that Philo's point is a more
general one.

57   τὸν δὲ ἀκριβῆ λόγον. This corresponds to nothing in
Philo's existing *Life of Moses*, so that it seems to be a promise
unfulfilled. If it refers to an intention connected with the
Life of Moses, this would be interesting for the chronology of
his writings.

IV

Gig. 58-67

Commentary on Gen 6:4:   οἱ δὲ γίγαντες ἦσαν ἐπὶ τῆς γῆς
ἐν ταῖς ἡμέραις ἐκείναις.

A. *General Comments*

This section is concerned with the contrast between the
"giants" of Gen 6:4, denominated by Philo "the Men of Earth,"
and "the Men of God," a class of whom Moses is the paradigm case,
but which includes "priests and prophets," and all those who
have "risen above the whole universe of the senses and transferred themselves to the intelligible world" (61). The doctrine
here is largely based on the Stoic theory of the Sage, though
with the important difference that Philo's sage transcends the
material world in the precise Platonic sense of partaking of a
separate incorporeal and truly real realm of being, a process
which is in contrast to the Stoic conception of the active
rational divine nature as immanent within the physical universe,
though logically transcending it.

We have also in this section a most interesting threefold distinction (60-61) between the Men of Earth, the Men of
Heaven, and the Men of God. (There is no comparable distinction
in the parallel passage of the *Questions and Answers*: *QG* 1.92.)
It is the middle category here that requires comment, and the
idea of a threefold distinction. A simple antithesis between
the sensual and the godly is trite enough, derivable from, among
other sources, Plato *Sophist* 246A ff. (where, however, the contrast is between physical rather than ethical doctrines), but
the antecedents of this schema are obscure (see comment. on 60).

Once again, we may note Philo's adducing of parallel
passages. In 62, he brings in Abraham as the prime example of
the mind which progresses from a "Chaldaean" or intracosmic
state of mind to a higher, transcendent one. This leads him to
quote Gen 17:1: ἐγώ εἰμι ὁ θεός σου· εὐαρέστει ἐναντίον ἐμοῦ,
καὶ γίνου ἄμεμπτος, in connection with Abraham's change of
name (63). In 65 he transfers his attention to the γῆς παῖδες,
which leads him first to quote Gen 2:24: ἐγένοντο γὰρ οἱ δύο
εἰς σάρκα μίαν, and then to bring in Nimrod (Gen 10:8), as a
prime example of a giant.

B. *Detailed Commentary*

58   'οἱ δὲ γίγαντες . . .' According to *BR* 26.7, T-A 254,
the "nefilim" were so called "because they caused the world to
fall (Heb. *nfl*), and fell from the world, and filled the world
with abortions through their sexual promiscuity."

       τὰ παρὰ τοῖς ποιηταῖς μεμυθευμένα . . . μυθοπλαστεῖν.
Philo is plainly sensitive about apparent analogies between the
Pentateuch and Greek mythology (cf. note on sect. 7; *Fug.* 121;
Mig. 76; *Sacr.* 28, 76; *Aet.* 56; *Cont.* 63). See Wolfson, *Philo*,
1.22-26. Aristobulus had already taught that if men are to
understand the philosophical or real (φυσικῶς) meaning of the
Torah, they should not "fall victim to mythological and human
conceptions" (*FPG* 217, 22-27). Cf. *Fug.* 130; *Mig.* 128; *Op.* 144.

       τοῖς ἀληθείας ἴχνεσιν . . . ἐπιβαίνειν. A further
reminiscence of *Od.* 5.193. (Cf. note on sect. 39).

59   παρὸ . . . ἐξήλασεν. Moses, like Plato, is a stern
censor of the arts. Philo is thinking of the Second Commandment
(Exod 20:3). Cf. *Ebr.* 109; *Decal.* 66, 156; *Spec.* 1.28-29; *Her.*
169; Wisd. 14:18-21; Cic. *ND* 1.42: *ipsa suavitate nocuerunt* (of
the poets); ib. 77 (these are Epicurean arguments); Sen. *Ep.*
88.18: "For I do not consent to admit painting into the list of
liberal arts, any more than sculpture, marble-working and other
helps toward luxury" (unlike Seneca, however, Philo condemns
sculpture and painting as aids to myth-fabrication, not luxury);
Clem. Alex. *Protr.* 4: "In Rome, the historian Varro says that
in ancient times the *Xoanon* of Mars--the idol by which he was
worshiped--was a spear, artists not having yet applied themselves to this specious pernicious art; but when art flourished,
error increased." See J. Gutmann, "The Second Commandment and
the Image in Judaism," *No Graven Images* (New York 1971) 12-14:
"Philo's strictures bore little relation to the Temple cult,
which in its own day was known far and wide for its artistically
wrought appurtenances, but were expressed in terms of how one
might best attain the goals established by a philosophic system
. . . His statements cannot be used to establish an antagonism
toward images on the part of Judaism; nor do they indicate a
strict enforcement of the second commandment during the Hellenistic period." There is an obvious parallel here to Plato's
"driving out" of the poets in *Republic* III. The talk of Moses'
πολιτεία is also significant.

60   οἱ μὲν γῆς . . . γίγας is taken etymologically as
γηγενής. This threefold division of classes is most interesting.
There is a possible parallel to Philo's triadic distinction of
Men of Earth, Men of Heaven and Men of God in Plato's enumera-
tion of three classes of men at *Rep.* 9.581C: the philosopher
or lover of wisdom, the lover of victory, and the lover of gain
(cf. *Phaedo* 68BC); and in Aristotle's distinction of three types
of life in the *Nicomachean Ethics* (1.3, 1095b17 ff.), the Life
of Enjoyment, the Life of Action, and the Life of Contemplation.
(Cf. *EE* 1215a25; *QG* 4.47; *Fug.* 36; *Decal.* 100-101. See Wolfson,
Philo 2.262-66.) This doctrine of the three lives may even be
seen as going back to Pythagoras, who is said to have compared
human life to a festival celebrated with magnificent games, at
which three classes of men appear: those who come to compete,
those who come to buy and sell, and those who come to contem-
plate the spectacle (Cic. *Tusc.* 5.3.8; cf. Iambl. *VP* 58.). For
a similar Stoic distinction of lives, see D.L. 7.130; Plut. *Mor.*
8A; Sen. *De Otio* 7.1. A detailed treatment of this theme may
be found in R. Joly, "Le Thème philosophique des genres de vie
dans l'antiquité classique," *Académie Royale de Belgique*,
Mémoires, Classe des Lettres et des Sciences Morales et Poli-
tiques, 51 (Brussels, 1956).

On the other hand, this threefold distinction, in the
particular form Philo gives it, seems to prefigure to some
extent the later Christian and Gnostic distinction between
σαρκικοί (or χοϊκοί) ψυχικοί, and πνευματικοί (see Iren. I.1.14;
Exc. ex Theod. 54.1). The Men of Earth, as one would expect,
are devoted to pleasure and material things. The Men of Heaven
are very much like the ψυχικοί of later systems, intellectuals
(φιλομαθεῖς) and skilled craftsmen, but lacking the light of
higher wisdom (they are portrayed here, however, as acting not
according to *psychê* but to *nous*.) They are the masters of *ta
enkyklia*, developing their *nous* and contemplating the *noêta*--
whatever Philo means by that in the present context.

τὸ γὰρ οὐράνιον τῶν ἐν ἡμῖν ὁ νοῦς. By itself this is
a thoroughly Stoic remark.

παραθήγων καὶ ἀκονῶν. Cf. *Fug.* 125; *Congr.* 25; *Ebr.*
159. For the image, cf. Isoc. *Antid.* 261 ff.

γυμνάζων καὶ συγκροτῶν. Cf. *Fug.* 5; *Mut.* 85; *Somn.*
2.263. (Another frequent collocution is ἀλείφω καὶ συγκροτέω:
Legat. 39, 178; *Somn.* 1.251.)

61   θεοῦ δὲ ἄνθρωποι. The actual phrase Philo may derive
from LXX. Cf. Deut 33:1. Among the men of God Philo here
classes priests and prophets, but plainly the class is larger,
including, in Platonic terms, οἱ φιλοσοφοῦντες ὀρθῶς. These
rise above purely human, or even cosmic, wisdom, and disdain
even the ideal of becoming κοσμοπολῖται (a dig here at the
Stoics--cf. D.L. 7.87--we may note, however, that elsewhere
κοσμοπολίτης is a term of commendation for Philo, e.g., Op. 3,
142; Spec. 2.45).

        τὸ δὲ αἰσθητὸν πᾶν ὑπερκύψαντες. There is a conscious
reminiscence here of the Phaedrus myth (esp. 249C: ἀνακύψασα
εἰς τὸ ὂν ὄντως). Philo also uses the term noētos kosmos, of
which he is actually the first extant user (Op. 16, 25; Mos.
2.127; Deus 31; etc.), though the concept may be regarded as
present in the noētos topos of the Phaedrus, as well as implied
in the Paradigm of the Timaeus. The idea is further developed,
by way of contrast with the Stoic concept, in the phrase ἀφθάρ-
των καὶ ἀσωμάτων ἰδεῶν πολιτεία. For the realm of Ideas as the
home of truly philosophic souls, cf. Her. 280.

62   Ὁ γοῦν Ἀβραάμ. For Philo, Abraham is a paradigm of
conversion--specifically from the state of an οὐράνιος, a cosmos-
bound intellectual, who (coming as he does from Chaldaea) is one
of those who worships the heavenly bodies (τὰ μετέωρα) rather
than their Creator--a reference here surely to the Stoics, and
in particular to the heliolatrous tendencies developed a generation or so before Philo by Posidonius (F 17, 20, Kidd). (Cf.
Sandbach, The Stoics [London 1975] 72-75.) For Abraham's practice of astrology, see G. Vermes, Scripture and Tradition in
Judaism (Leiden 1973) 76-83.

        τήν τε μετάρσιος . . . φύσιν. μετάρσιος is slightly
post-Classical in prose (first in Theophrastus Ign. 3), but its
technical use here, as opposed to αἰθέριος, to signify the
intermediate realm of the upper air, is only found later, in
Achilles In Aratum 32, probably deriving from Posidonius. That
Philo knows this usage is made plain by his employment of it
elsewhere (Plant. 3).

        Ἀβρὰμ γὰρ ἑρμηνευθεὶς πατήρ ἐστι μετέωρος. Hebrew:
ʾāb = "father," and rām = "lofty." Cf. Cher. 7; Mut. 66, 69-76;
Abr. 81-84; LA 3.83-84, where "Abram" is given a favorable interpretation.

πατὴρ δὲ τοῦ συγκρίματος ὁ νοῦς. Father-mother antithesis between *nous* and *psyche* (or *alogos psyche*) common in Philo,
especially in relation to Adam and Eve in *LA* 2.5 ff., 38-45,
68-70; 3.56-58, 220-24. Eve here is regularly αἴσθησις, sense-
perception. (See Baer, *Categories*.)

64   καλεῖται γὰρ πατὴρ ἐκλεκτὸς ἠχοῦς. According to A.
Hanson, this derivation is apparently from the three Hebrew
words: *ʾāb*, *bōr*, and *hôm* or *hāmô*. In the LXX *bōr* and *bārôr*
are occasionally rendered by ἐκλεκτός, and ἠχεῖν is a frequent
translation of *hôm* and *hāmô* (*JTS* N.S. 18 [1967] 128-39).
Another possibility is that it derives from *ʾab* and *raʾam*. See
E. Stein, *Exegese des Philo aus Alexandria* (Giessen 1929) 58.

ᾗ συνηχοῦμεν. συνηχέω here presumably means "sound
together," in the sense of making mutually comprehensible
sounds.

προσκεκλήρωται. Verb, in passive, first extant in
Philo. Cf. *Spec.* 1.114; 4.159; *Leg.* 279; *Post.* 41; *Virt.* 34.
(In active not before Lucian.)

ὀπαδός. Perhaps a *vox Platonica* for Philo; cf. *Phaedr.*
252C: τῶν Διὸς ὀπαδῶν; *Phileb.* 63E: θεοῦ ὀπαδοί.

βασιλικῇ τῷ ὄντι χρώμενος ὁδῷ. The allegorization of
the Royal Road of Num 20:17-20 is a favorite of Philo's; cf.
Deus 140-66, and notes ad loc.

παντοκράτορος. παντοκράτωρ is very frequent in LXX for
Heb. *ṣebāôt* and *šaddai*.

65   οἱ δὲ γῆς παῖδες. The γίγαντες of 6:4 seem here to be
interpreted in the light of the "earth-born" of *Sophist* 246A ff.

μεταλλοιώσαντες. This is actually Wendland's conjecture
for μεταλλεύσαντες/μεταλλεύοντες of mss (with an apparent emendation or gloss μεταβάλλοντες in A). Wendland may be right,
but there is a possibility that Philo may be using μεταλλεύω in
the sense of "alter for the worse," "pervert." We find such a
curious usage in Wisd. 4:12; 16:25.

'Ἐγένοντο γὰρ οἱ δύο εἰς σάρκα μίαν'. Gen 2:24; cf. *LA*
2.49 ff., where the text is quoted more accurately: "ἔσονται
οἱ δύο . . . ."

τὸ ἄριστον ἐκιβδήλευσαν νόμισμα. The image of adulter-
ating the coinage is common in Philo: *Post.* 89, 98; *Congr.* 159;

etc. Its remote origin, presumably lies in the story told of
himself by Diogenes the Cynic, as to why he was expelled from
his native city (D.L. 6.20).

66   ἑρμηνεύεται δὲ Νεβρὼδ αὐτομόλησις. The rabbis deduced
from Gen 10:9 that Nimrod knew his Master and intentionally
rebelled (marad) against him (Sifra, Beḥuqqotay 2.2). Cf. BT
Pesaḥ 94b (Nimrod caused the whole world to rebel [himrid]
against God); Ps-Jonath., ad loc. The association of Nimrod
with rebellion against God may be rooted in the fact that Gen
10:8 says of him "he was the first man of power (gibbōr) on
earth," which in the LXX is translated, "he began to be a giant
(gigas) upon the earth." Since the rebellious nefilim were also
designated as gibbōrîm (translated as gigantes in LXX) (Gen
6:4), Nimrod was placed in their bad company. Ps-Eupolemus,
who probably wrote in Palestine in the first half of the first
century B.C.E., had already identified Nimrod with Bel and
Kronos, considering him as the only one of the "giants" to have
been rescued from the great Flood, after which he founded Babylon and built the famous Tower (according to BT A.Z. 53b, he
built the Tower for idol worship). (FGH 724, F 1 and 2. Ps-
Eupolemus thus combined Gen 6:4 and 10:8, LXX with the account
of Berossus about the foundation of Babylon by the creator God
Bel and the myth of the revolt of the Titans in Hesiod. Philo,
at Conf. 2, also assimilates the building of the Tower to the
Greek legend of the Aloadae in Od. 3.310 ff. See Freudenthal,
Hell.St. 35-82; Hengel, Judaism and Hellenism 1.89; Wacholder,
Eupolemus 104-5; Ginzberg, Legends 1.177, 5.198-204.) In QG
2.82, Philo interprets Nimrod to mean "Ethiopian." Marcus says
that he is confusing the etymology of Nimrod with that of his
father Cush, but according to BR 41.4, T-A 408, Cush is only
another name for Nimrod. Ginzberg suggests that Philo is con-
necting Nimrod with nmr "spotted." Moreover, Philo, following
Jewish tradition, condemns Nimrod's hunting as something that
is "as far removed as possible from the rational nature," for
"he who is among beasts seeks to equal the bestial habits of
animals through evil passions"; cf. Virt. 140. (The rabbis
interpreted Gen 10:9, "he was a mighty hunter," to mean that
Nimrod caught people through their own mouths [BR 37.2, T-A
345].)

τῇ παναθλίᾳ ψυχῇ. Πανάθλιος, a poetic word, is found
in all the Attic Tragedians. Cf. *Det.* 109; *Post.* 53; *Congr.* 159.

μετάθεσις δὲ καλεῖται βαβυλών. Gen 11:9 connects Babylon
with Heb. *balal* "confound" (a play on *Babel*).

67   κατὰ τὸν ἱερώτατον Μωυσέα ὁ μὲν φαῦλος . . .   Moses
seems here to be adding to the usual Stoic paradoxes about the
phaulos and the *spoudaios*.

τοσαῦτα . . . εἰρηκότες. Common formula of transition
also in Neoplatonic commentaries. Here we see the essential
unity, or continuity, of these two treatises.

V

Deus 1-19

Commentary on Gen 6:4: καὶ μετ᾽ ἐκεῖνο, ὡς ἂν εἰσεπορεύοντο οἱ ἄγγελοι τοῦ θεοῦ πρὸς τὰς θυγατέρας τῶν ἀνθρώπων, καὶ
ἐγέννων αὐτοῖς.

Textual variants: οἱ υἱοὶ τοῦ θεοῦ . . . καὶ ἐγέννωσαν
ἑαυτοῖς, LXX; αὐτοῖς mss. Philon., exc. A. (Philo's ἐγέννων is
a "correction," rather than a variant.) New JPS translation
reads: "It was in those days, and later, that the Nephilim
appeared on earth--after the divine beings had consorted with
the daughters of man, who bore them sons." The Hebrew is ambiguous; *weyāldû lahem* might mean either "they (the Giants) begot for
themselves" of "they (the daughters of men) generated for them
(the Giants)." It is quite possible that Philo's LXX text
actually read αὐτοῖς, taking the latter interpretation, but it
is clear that he understands αὐτοῖς, something that it would be
quite easy for him to do, since the rough breathing was not
operative by his time, and may not even have been written in the
manuscript. It is also noteworthy that Philo is either ignorant
of the last phrase of 6:4: ἐκεῖνοι ἦσαν . . . οἱ ὀνομαστοί, or
deliberately ignores it. This is a troublesome statement for
his interpretation, and would surely have deserved comment.

A. *General Comments*

This whole first section (§§1-19) follows on directly
from *De Gigantibus*, being still concerned with "the sons of god"
and their commerce with "the daughters of men." The theme of
God's immutability is not broached until §20, making it plain
that for Philo there is no sharp break between the two treatises.
It is, indeed, not quite clear why the break is made here.

The Hebrew of Gen 6:4 reads awkwardly. It is unclear
whether the divine beings continued to consort with the
daughters of men even afterwards, or whether the union with the
daughters of men was a one-time occurrence, as a result of which
were born the giants, who continued to beget after their own
kind. The rabbis understood the vague phrase "and also afterward" to signify that "the latter did not learn from the former,
the generation of the Flood did not learn a moral lesson from
the generation of Enoš, nor did the generation of the Tower
(lit. "of Division") learn from the generation of the Flood"
(*BR* 26.4, T-A 254). Philo, as is often the case, takes advantage of the lack of clarity in the verse and explains the phrase
"and also afterward" as referring to the spiritual fact that it
is only after the departure of the divine spirit from man, when
the light of wisdom ceases to illumine the soul, that the forces
of darkness and falsehood take over, and, mating with the emas-
culated passions, beget offspring not for God but for themselves,
thus producing vices instead of virtues. The ἄγγελοι are plainly
here not evil spirits of any sort, but represent the irrational
impulses, which "mate" with the passions to produce evil actions.
(At *QG* 1.92, the angels are not treated as blameworthy, but the
exegesis takes quite a different turn.)

"Begetting for oneself" is the central theme of the
passage, interpreted as φιλαυτία, "self-love" (18). The principal axis of development is an opposition between "begetting
for God," i.e. manifesting the virtues. Philo proceeds to
introduce the perfect Abraham as the paradigm of those who beget
for God, inasmuch as he had offered up Isaac, or self-learned
wisdom, as a thank-offering to the deity, which signifies either
that he had abandoned mortal concerns in his single-minded devo-
tion to the divine, or that he wishes to give a firm basis to
his knowledge of the sense-world. Here we are again confronted
with one of Philo's central religious themes, namely, that it is
due to God's singular gift of grace that man is bidden to render

Him what is His own, since it is in this way that man is enabled
to purify his soul.

This leads Philo to an exegesis of I Samuel 1:11 (5-7)
where we are presented with Hannah, who is interpreted as "the
gift of divine wisdom." Hannah is a soul which receives the
logos of God, and produces offspring which she dedicates to God,
i.e., a virtuous disposition. Philo's interpretation of the LXX
δίδωμί σοι αὐτὸν δοτόν, as "I give him (back) to you as something given (to me)," allows him, by adducing Num 28:2, to emphasise the point that the truly virtuous soul knows that all things
are from God, and so on offering things to Him one is only
returning to Him what is His own. Cf. *Her.* 124.

He next embarks on a digression, in diatribe style, contrasting men's concern with bodily purity when entering temples,
with their indifference to spiritual impurity in the same circumstances (8-9). He then turns from this to an exegesis of
Hannah's utterance, in the course of her psalm, at I Sam 2:5:
"The barren has borne seven, but she who has many children has
languished" in which he returns to one of his favorite numerological principles, the identity of the hebdomad with the monad,
and so back to his starting-point, the rejection of those who
are characterised by self-love and a self-centered cosmic perspective, and therefore beget only for themselves (16-19). Of
these the type is Onan (Gen 38:9), who meets with (spiritual)
death through recognising no loyalty except to himself. Onan,
we may note, is depicted as sinning not only against piety, but
against philanthropy, through neglecting his duties to his
relations and to the community.

B. *Detailed Commentary*

2   πολυσχιδεῖ. First attested in Philo in general sense
of "much-divided," and only here in an unfavorable sense. Later
in Sextus Emp. *Math.* 7.349; Iambl. *VP* 29.161. Cf. *Op.* 69; *Mos.*
1.117: τῷ πολυτρόπῳ καὶ πολυσχιδεῖ τῶν ἐπιστημονικῶν ἔργων;
Spec. 2.63. For the doctrine of the division of the soul when
joined to the body, see V. Nikiprowetzky, "Στεῖρα, Στερρά, Πολλὴ
et l'exégèse de I Sam. II 5," *SILENO*, Roma, 1979, pp. 27-28.

βαρύτατον ἄχθος. See comment. on *Gig.* 31.

δύσεργος. First used in Plb. 28.8.3 in the sense of
"hard to effect," "difficult."

ἐλλάμπουσι . . . καθαραὶ φρονήσεως αὐγαί. Cf. *Praem.*
37: "For a beam purer than ether and incorporeal suddenly shone
upon him and revealed the conceptual world ruled by its chari-
oteer." The phrase αὐγὴ καθαρά derives from the striking passage,
Phaedr. 250BC. Philo uses the phrase repeatedly. Cf. *Deus* 29
and note.

3   ψευδαγγελούντων. Only found here. (ψευδάγγελος appears
in Il. 15.159.)

π— περιρραντηρίων. Cf. *Cher.* 96: ἔξω περιρραντηρίων ἀπε-
λαύνεται, βωμοῖς οὐκ ἐώμενον προσαχθῆναι. For Philo's use of
temple and mystery imagery, see Intro. p. 150.

ἀμυδρωθὲν. ἀμυδρόω is first attested in Philo (later in
Proclus and Olympiodorus). Cf. *Deus* 78; *Praem.* 28. Reminiscence
of δι' ἀμυδρῶν ὀργάνων in *Phaedr.* 250B.

οἱ τοῦ σκότους ἑταῖροι. Analogous expressions at *LA*
3.22; *Somn.* 2.64, 205; *Deus* 143; etc.

παρευημερήσαντες. In active sense of "flourish,"
"abound," first attested in Philo, who uses it frequently.
(Passive sense, "be surpassed," found in D.S. 20.79.) Found
again in Patristic Greek.

ἐπισκιασθῇ. ἐπισκιάζω in the metaphorical sense of
"conceal," "obscure," first attested in Philo. Cf. *LA* 2.30, 58,
3.7; *Gig.* 2; *Deus* 103; etc. Cf. συσκιάζεται, *Deus* 30.

κατεαγόσι καὶ τεθηλυμμένοις. Cf. *Gig.* 4: καὶ κατεαγό-
τες καὶ θηλυδρίαι.

4   ὁλόκληροι ἀρεταί . . . ἀνάρμοστοι κακίαι. ὁλόκληρος is
used at *Phaedr.* 250C. ἀνάρμοστος is also a Platonic word associated with vice in the soul, *Gorg.* 482B; *Phaedo* 93C; cf. *Phaedo*
93E6: ἡ μὲν κακία ἀναρμοστία. Note that this whole sentence is
a commentary, in chiastic form, on the previous clause, καὶ
γεννῶσιν ἑαυτοῖς, οὐ θεῷ.

μάθε δ' . . . ὦ διάνοια. For Philo's use of rhetorical
apostrophe, see Intro. p. 141. This is probably best understood,
however, as directed, not to Philo's own mind, but to his audience.

τὸ ἀγαπητὸν καὶ μόνον . . . (ἔγγονον). Cf. *Ebr.* 30;
Abr. 196, 168; *Mos.* 1.13.

αὐτομαθοῦς σοφίας. For Isaac as αὐτομαθής, cf. *Sac.* 6;
Det. 30; *Post.* 78; *Plant.* 168; *Ebr.* 60, 94; *Sob.* 65; *Conf.* 74,
81; *Mig.* 29 ff., 101, 125, 140, 166-67; *Congr.* 34-38, 111; *Fug.*
166; *Mut.* 1, 12, 88, 137, 255, 263; *Somn.* 1.68, 160, 168 ff.,
194, 2.10; *Praem.* 27, 59.

συμποδίσας. In fact, Abraham is here "binding his own
feet" (Isaac being an aspect of himself), either, as Philo says,
as an indication that he wishes to have no more to do with mortal things, or that he recognises the instability of the realm of
generation. In the one case, presumably, he is "tying up" his
αὐτομαθής σοφία; in the second case he is "tying it down."

παρόσον. παρόσον with indic. for ὡς with participle is
post-Classical. Cf. *Gig.* 9 (where, however, ὅτι with indic.
seems the more exact equivalent); and Sextus, *Math.* 7.419.

ἀνίδρυτον. Classical, but not used metaphorically
before Philo. Cf. *Gig.* 67; *Ebr.* 170; *Congr.* 58; *Abr.* 85; *Mos.*
1.196; *Virt.* 40; etc. For the collocution ἀνίδρυτον καὶ ἄστα-
τον, cf. *Det.* 12; *Post.* 22; *Somn.* 1.156. For ἀβέβαιος καὶ ἀνί-
δρυτος, cf. *Op.* 156; *Abr.* 84; *Spec.* 1.29, 4.88, 139, 153.
(ἄστατος is a word favored by Epicureans, cf. Epicur. *Ep.* 3,
p. 65 U.; Diog. Oen. 18.)

ἀνενδοίαστον. First attested in Philo, cf. *Det.* 148.

μαθητρίς. Feminine form found only here. Use of terms
μαθητής καὶ διάδοχος borrowed from terminology of succession in
philosophical schools.

Ἄννα . . . χάρις αὐτῆς. Ḥannâh = ḥinnâh. Cf. *Ebr.*
145 ff.; *Mut.* 143 ff.; *Somn.* 1.254. χάρις can have the sense
of "free gift."

τελεσφόροις . . . ὠδῖσι. A development on I Sam 1:20:
καὶ ἐγενήθη τῷ καιρῷ τῶν ἡμερῶν καὶ ἔτεκεν υἱόν. τελεσφορέω is
used in later Greek for "bearing perfect offspring." Artem.
1.16; Dsc. *Eup.* 2.97, but Philo may also not be oblivious to the
fact that τελεσφόρος (like καιρός) is a Pythagorean term for the
number "seven" (cf. *Op.* 102), which as it turns out (11), Samuel
represents. [Such an interpretation seems arbitrary, V.N.]

Σαμουήλ . . . τεταγμένος θεῷ. Cf. *Somn.* 1.254; *Mig.*
196; *Ebr.* 144. Samuel is here derived from šôm, šîm = set,
appoint + ʾēl.

μηδὲν ἴδιον ἑαυτῆς κρίνουσα ἀγαθόν. A basic motif in
Philo. Cf. *LA* 3.209, 1.82; *Her.* 85, 103-8, 111; *Ebr.* 106-7;
Det. 56: "To God men can bring nothing except a disposition full
of love to their Master." Cf. Epict. 1.16.15-21. See Jean
Laporte, *La doctrine eucharistique chez Philon d'Alexandrie*
(Paris 1972). Laporte shows that Philo interpreted the whole
liturgical practice of Judaism eucharistically. A parallel to
the doctrine may be found in Plutarch, *Consol. ad Apoll.* 116AB:
all good things are only loaned to us by the Gods, so that we
should not take it ill when they ask for them back (Euripides,
Phoen. 555-56 is quoted in this connection). As a biblical
parallel cf. Job 1:21.

6   "δίδωμί σοι αὐτὸν δοτόν". Philo is following the LXX on
I Sam 1:11, which may either be translating a Hebrew text different from ours, i.e., ûnetattîw la'adonoy mattānā (although
mattānā is elsewhere rendered in the LXX as δόμα, e.g., Ez 46:17),
or else represents a slight expansion of the Hebrew text as we
have it.

        τὸν δεδομένον δίδωμι. Cf. I Chr 29:14: "For all things
come from thee, and of thy own have we given thee." Cf. *LAB*
32:2: "Lo, now my son, I offer thee for a burnt offering and
deliver thee unto his hands who gave thee unto me."

        τὰ δῶρα . . . δόματα . . . καρπώματα. Cf. *LA* 3. 196,
and *Cher.* 84, where a distinction is in fact made between these
three terms. Here they are taken as equivalents, since the idea
is that one is offering back to God his own gifts.

7   χρεῖος. In prose, only Hellenistic. Not attested
before Philo in this sense. Cf. *Deus* 37.

7-8   εὐχαριστητικῶς. Adverb only here. The adjective εὐχα-
ριστητικός is found thrice in Philo and nowhere else: *Sacr.* 74;
Ebr. 94, 105. τιμητικῶς also, in this sense, only found in
Philo. Adjective not before Jos. *Ant.* 19.8 and Plutarch *Consol.
ad Apoll.* 120A.

        καθαρεύσομεν ἀδικημάτων ἐκνιψάμενοι τὰ καταρρυπαίνοντα
τὸν βίον . . . ὃς ἂν μὴ πρότερον λουσάμενος φαιδρύνηται τὸ σῶμα,
εὔχεσθαι . . . ἐπιχειρεῖν ἔτι κεκηλιδωμένῃ καὶ πεφυρμένῃ διανοίᾳ. We have here a conceit and a family of words of which
Philo is particularly fond. Cf. *Her.* 112-13: ᾧ καθαρθησόμεθα
ἐκνιψάμενοι . . . τὰ καταρρυπαίνοντα ἡμῶν τὸν ἄθλιον . . . βίον;

Cher. 94-97: τὰ μὲν σώματα λουτροῖς καὶ καθαρσίοις ἀπορρύπτονται,
τὰ δὲ ψυχῆς ἐκνίψασθαι πάθη, οἷς καταρρυπαίνεται ὁ βίος, οὔτε
βούλονται . . . ἀκηλιδώτους ἐσθῆτας ἀμπεχόμενοι διάνοιαν δὲ κεκη-
λιδωμένην . . . ; *Fug.* 41; *Mut.* 49, 124.

8   εἰς τὰ ἱερὰ μὴ ἐξεῖναι βαδίζειν.   See Maim. *M.T.*, Laws
of Temple Entry, chs. 3-5. On the dialectical *topos* ἐκ τοῦ
μᾶλλον καὶ ἧττον, see Intro, p. 171.

κεκηλιδωμένη. Cf. Ecphantus, p. 80.17 Thesleff: καθὸ
καὶ τὼς ἁγιωτάτως τόπως ἐκαλίδωσάν τινες. (For ἀκηλίδωτος, cf.
Wisd. 4:9, 7:26; *Apoc. Abr.* 17, where "spotless" is one of God's
attributes.)

ἀκάθαρτος ὤν. Cf. *Spec.* 1.283; *Plant.* 164; *Her.* 82; *LA*
1.62. Cf. *Agr.* 130, and the similar argumentation used by the
rabbis in *MRS*, Epst-Mel.: 157; *Tosef. B.Q.* 7.6; *Mek. Bahodesh*
11, Lauterbach, 2.290. For an analogous use of the trope ἐκ τοῦ
μᾶλλον καὶ ἧττον, cf. *Semahot* 8.16, Higger: 165: "Similarly,
it is written: Thou shalt build the altar of the Lord thy God
of perfect stones (Deut. 27.6)--of stones that establish peace
in the world. Let us reason *a minori ad majus*: If of stones
that neither see, nor hear, nor speak, nor eat, nor drink, but
because they establish peace between Israel and their Father in
heaven, the Holy One, blessed be He, said, 'Let them be perfect
before me'--in the case of students of Torah, who effect atone-
ment for the world, how much more necessary is it that they be
perfect before the Holy One, blessed be He." Cf. *Spec.* 1.89.
See J. Neusner, *A Life of Yoḥanan Ben Zakkai* (Leiden 1970) 128-
36; 24-42.

μετανοήσειν. For Philo's doctrine of repentance see
TDNT 4.993-94; Wolfson, *Philo* 2.252-59; Völker 105-15, and
Winston's forthcoming study "The Limits of Jewish Piety and Greek
Philosophy in Philo's Thought," in *Jewish and Christian Self-
Definition*, v. 3: *Hellenistic Judaism in the Diaspora*.

9   δυσκάθαρτος. First attested in Philo. Cf. *Det.* 144;
Post. 75; *Deus* 183; *Plant.* 107; etc. Found, however, in a
slightly different sense, in Soph. *Ant.* 1284, and Ar. *Peace* 1250.

ἐμπεριπατοῦντα. Cf. LXX Lev 26:12; *Det.* 4; *Post.* 122.

10   Philo here returns to the discussion of Ḥannah. Commentary on I Sam 2:5: στεῖρα ἔτεκεν ἑπτά, ἡ δὲ πολλὴ ἐν τέκνοις
ἠσθένησε. (Textual variants: καὶ ἡ πολλὴ ἐν τέκνοις ἠσθένησεν.)

11   μονάδα ἑβδομάδι τὴν αὐτὴν . . . νομίζει. Cf. *Op.* 100;
Post. 64; *Decal.* 102; *Spec.* 2.59; *LA* 1.15.

        ἐναρέτου. Cf. *SVF* 3.295; Plot. 1.3.3; Jos. *B.* 6.1.8.
Only here in Philo.

12   ἀναπαυομένης ἐν θεῷ . . . καὶ περὶ μηδὲν τῶν θνητῶν
ἔργων ἔτι πονουμένης. Cf. *LA* 1.16: "whenever there comes upon
the soul the holy Logos of which Seven is the keynote, six
together with all mortal things that the soul seems to make
therewith comes to a stop"; *Spec.* 2.59. The identification of
seven with both light and Logos was already made by Aristobulus:
"God created the world and, because life is troublesome to all,
gave us for rest the seventh day, which in reality (φυσικῶς)
could also be called the prime source of light, in which all
things are comprehended. The latter could also be transferred
metaphorically to wisdom, for all light comes from her" (*Fragm.
Pseudepig. Graeca*, ed. A. M. Denis [Leiden 1970] 224). See also
N. Walter, *Der Thoraausleger Aristobulos* (Berlin 1964) 65 ff.
For the rest of the soul in God, cf. *Post.* 28; *Somn.* 2.228; *Fug.*
174; *LA* 1.6; Philolaus, DK A.12.

        ἑβδομάδος . . . κατὰ ἀπόλειψιν ἑξάδος. ἑξάς is first
attested in Philo, and used frequently by him. For a Pythagorean exposition of the hexad cf. Anatolius, ap. *Theol. Ar.* p. 42,
19 De Falco; Theo Smyrn. p. 102,4 ff. Hiller. Cf. *Op.* 13; *LA*
1.4, 16; *Post.* 64; *Spec.* 2.58-59, 64. Ḥannah has transcended
the βίος πρακτικός symbolised by the hexad, to attain to the
βίος θεωρητικός, symbolised by the hebdomad, the number proper
to the Logos, and to God himself. For the notion of moving up
the scale of being described in terms of numbers, cf. *The Eighth
Reveals the Ninth* (Tractate 6, Nag Hammadi Codex 6): "O Lord,
grant us wisdom from thy power extended unto us, that we may tell
ourselves the vision of the eighth and the ninth. We have
already advanced to the Seventh, practising piety and being
citizens in thy Law" (L. S. Keizer: 97-98); *Congr.* 103-5: "for
they have learned to rise above the ninth, the seeming deity,
the world of sense, and to worship Him who is truly tenth and
alone" (referring to the mystical identity of the Ten and the
One).

13   στεῖραν . . . στερράν. Is this a piece of "creative
etymology," or simply an instance of paronomasia? The former
view gains support from the confusion that seems to have taken
place, at least in later antiquity, between the two words, e.g.
in mss of Eur. *Andr*. 711, where a scholiast on V notes that
στεῖρος is "Attic" for στερρός (meaning "barren," not "firm").
But cf. also στερρός meaning "barren" in Arist. *GA* 773b27 ff.
For a similar exegesis in Philo based on this verbal connection,
cf. Philo, LCL Supplement, II p. 273, line 9 (on Gen 26:32):
stabilitatem non sterilitatem, presumably representing στερεό-
της, οὐ στερρότης. A passage in Plutarch's *Isis and Osiris*
(366E) tends to confirm the possibility of such an eytmological
word-play. Here, Nephthys is described as being at first στεῖρα
after her marriage to Typhon. Plutarch wishes to interpret this
as referring to τὸ παντελῶς τῆς γῆς ἄγονον καὶ ἄκαρπον ὑπὸ
στερρότητος, that is, the barrenness of the earth due to its
sun-baked hardness. Wyttenbach's emendation στειρότητος is
quite misguided. Admittedly, Plutarch is here using στερρότης
to mean "hardness," whereas Philo, if our rendering is correct,
is using it to mean "barrenness," but it is the connection
between the two meanings that is the important factor. Philo
elsewhere does recognise a "positive" meaning for στεῖρος, in
the sense of "barren, unreceptive, to vice." At *Congr*. 3, we
find this stated as a startling paradox, yet true. Virtue
(Sarah) is "barren" (ἐστείρωται) as regards all that is bad,
but shows herself a fruitful mother of the good (εὐτοκίᾳ χρῆται).
At *Praem*. 159, the soul is described as "many" (πολλή), full,
that is, of passions and vices, which makes her feeble and sick.
But when she has become "barren" (στειρωθεῖσα), and ceases to
produce these children, she is transformed into a pure virgin.
Cf. also *Mut*. 143, where I Sam 2:5 is explicitly quoted, and
explained in the same way as in the present passage. In none
of these places, however, is any connection made between στεῖρος
and στερρός. [For a persuasive argument against any etymological intention on Philo's part, however, see V. Nikiprowetzky,
"Στεῖρα, Στερρά, Πολλή et l'exégèse de I Sam. 2:5 chez Philon
d'Alexandrie," *SILENO*, Roma, 1979.]

         Ḥannah is "barren" as regards the realm of Generation
and particularly as regards Vice, but this involves firm estab-
lishment in the realm of Being and Virtue. For a similar contrast between sterility and fecundity, cf. Wisd. 3:13-15, where
we are told that sterility, if pure, is redeemed by a spiritual

fertility; Sir. 16:3: "For better is one than a thousand, and
to die childless than to have a presumptuous posterity." For
other etymologizing by Philo, see Intro. p. 173.

14   τὴν δὲ πολλὴν ἀσθενεῖν ἐν τέκνοις. Cf. *Praem.* 159.
This word-order makes it plain that Philo has deliberately construed the LXX text to suit his allegorical purposes, by taking
ἐν τέκνοις with ἠσθένησε. While this makes no significant difference to the meaning, it is worth noting as another example of
Philo's troubles in construing the "translatorese" of the LXX.
It does, however, enable him to take πολλή by itself as meaning
"multiple" or "multifarious," in a bad sense.

    ἀψευδῶς καὶ σφόδρα ἐναργῶς. One of Philo's favored ways
of introducing an allegorial interpretation. Cf. σφόδρα ὀρθῶς
καὶ προσηκόντως, 16; *Praem.* 17: αἰνίττεται δὲ ἐναργῶς.

    πολλὰ ὠδίνη τοῦ ἑνὸς ἀποστᾶσα. Platonic-Pythagorean
contrast of One and Many. The sensible and the flesh imply
plurality. The soul diversifies itself into various potencies
in the process of becoming linked to matter.

    ἀμβλωθρίδια. In the sense of "abortive child" only in
Philo (although frequent later in Patristic Greek). Cf. *LA* 1.76;
Mig. 33: ἀμβλωθρίδια, ἠλιτόμηνα. Contrast here with τελεσφό-
ροις ὠδῖσι of 5, above.

    βαρυνομένη καὶ πιεζομένη. See comment. to *Gig.* 31.

15   τῶν ὑπ᾽ αὐτήν. I.e., sexual lusts. Cf. *Cher.* 93: καὶ
τοῖς μετὰ γαστέρα ἀπολέγεται; LXX Jonah 4:8.

    ὅσοι . . . ἑαυτοῖς . . . γεννῶσιν. Note how here, as
well as with the ref. to Gen 38:9 in 16, αὐτῶν ἕνεκα in 17 and
οἱ γεννῶντες αὐτοῖς in 19, Philo keeps recalling the lemma
ἐγέννων αὐτοῖς.

16   φιλαυτία. For bad sense, cf. *UPZ* 42.10 (ii B.C.E.).
Abraham's faith (πίστις) in God is paradigmatic for Philo of the
"unswerving and firm assumption" that is attained when the mind
has a vision of the First Cause, the truly Existent. The opposite of *pistis* is called by Philo οἴησις, τῦφος, κενὴ δόξα,
ἀφροσύνη, ἀλαζονεία, τὸ ὑπέραυχον, and φιλαυτία (*Mut.* 176; *Spec.*
1.10; *Somn.* 2.48-66, 162, 192; *Her.* 106; *Mig.* 147; *Ebr.* 111;
Sob. 57). It consists in giving to the senses or to the thought

based on them that trust which should be bestowed on God alone.
Cf. *Sacr.* 58; *Post.* 52, 180-81 (contains a long list of duties
similar to the one in *Deus* 19); *Her.* 106-111; *Congr.* 130; *Spec.*
1.334-45, 4.131; *Praem.* 12.

ὁ γοῦν Αὐνάν. Cf. *Post.* 180, where Onan is similarly
depicted as the type of φιλαυτία, with a very similar string of
clauses.

17   μὴ γονέων τιμῆς . . . ἐπιστρεφόμενοι. ἐπιστρεφόμενοι
with genitive not in classical prose. Note the impressive
sequence of *eight* parallel cola, one of them actually double
(μὴ ἰδίων μὴ κοινῶν).

ἐκφύλου. Late Greek prose. Cf. Strabo 4.4.5; Plut.
Brut. 36; *Caes.* 69; *Det.* 61; *Fug.* 144; *Abr.* 137.

19   μὴ τὰ πάντα προσθήκην ἑαυτοῦ . . . νομίζοντα. Cf. *Somn.*
2.115-16; *Prov.* 2.84; M. Aurel. 9.39: "the part ought not to
grumble at what is done in the interests of the whole"; 10.6:
"as I am a part, I shall not be displeased with anything allotted
me from the whole"; Epict. 2.5.25; Plato, *Laws* 903 BD; Plot.
2.9.9.75.

πατρί, μητρί . . . καὶ ἡγεμόνι τῶν συμπάντων. A Middle
Stoic concept which is found also in Antiochus. According to
the latter, friendship is seen extending outwards from the family until it includes even the gods (Aug. *CD* 19.3). "This affection comes into being right from our birth, in that children are
loved by their parents and the whole family is held together by
the bond of marriage and parenthood. From there it gradually
spreads beyond the home, first through ties of blood, then
through marital relationships, then through friendships, later
by association with neighbors, afterwards to fellow-citizens and
to partners and friends in public life, and finally by embracing
the whole human race" (Cic. *Fin.* 5.65). Cf. also Apuleius, *De
Plat.* 2.2.222, for the doctrine in later Middle Platonism. For
Philo's doctrine of φιλανθρωπία and its Stoic antecedents, see
Winston, "Philo's Ethical Theory," forthcoming in *ANRW*.

VI A

Deus 20-32

Commentary on Gen 6:5-7: Ἰδὼν οὖν, φησί, κύριος ὁ θεὸς ὅτι ἐπληθύνθησαν αἱ κακίαι τῶν ἀνθρώπων ἐπὶ τῆς γῆς, καὶ πᾶς τις διανοεῖται ἐν τῇ καρδίᾳ ἐπιμελῶς τὰ πονηρὰ πάσας τὰς ἡμέρας, ἐνεθυμήθη ὁ θεὸς ὅτι ἐποίησε τὸν ἄνθρωπον ἐπὶ τῆς γῆς, καὶ διενοήθη. καὶ εἶπεν ὁ θεός· Ἀπαλείψω τὸν ἄνθρωπον ὃν ἐποίησα ἀπὸ προσώπου τῆς γῆς.

Textual variants: ἰδὼν δὲ κύριος . . . καὶ ἐνεθυμήθη.

Hebrew: By translating ἐνεθυμήθη and διενοήθη the LXX has expunged all reference to God's repenting and its attendant sadness which is found in the Hebrew text. It should be noted, however, that when the biblical context deals with God's love for man, and his compassion and forgiveness for those who repent or those who have been punished and are in need of his merciful love, the LXX translators do not deviate too sharply from the Hebrew text. Cf. Deut 32:36; Exod 32:12 and 14, where the Hebrew words *wĕhinnāḥēm, wayyinnāḥem, yitneḥām*, are translated as if the verb meant in the *nipᶜal* "have compassion," or in the *hitpaᶜel* "be comforted." (See Gutman, 2.127-28.)

A. *General Comments*

The whole passage from 20-69 constitutes in fact a single commentary on Gen 6:5-7, but, following A. Mosès, we have thought it best to divide it into three parts, for ease of exposition.

In the first passage Philo turns to the question which gives this treatise its name. He engages first in a well-wrought polemic in diatribe style against those who would base themselves on this passage of Genesis to argue that God is subject to change, even change of mind. His position here is based ultimately on Plato's "second canon of theology" in *Republic* II (380D-383B), that God suffers no change either from any external force or from his own volition (cf. Sen. *Ben.* 23.1). His first argument proceeds from a Stoic base; we assume that the true philosopher is superior to the changes of fortune (μὴ τοῖς πράγμασι συμμεταβάλλειν), and maintains an undeviating single-ness of purpose. (Cic. *Tusc.* 5.81; *Pro Murena* 61; *SVF* 3.548; Sen. *Ben.* 4.34.3). Moses also holds this to be the ideal of the Sage; Deut 5:31 (a popular passage with Philo, who uses it for various purposes) is brought in to support this point (23).

This prompts Philo to celebrate the harmony of the soul, or at least of the well-tempered soul, which, if itself correctly tuned, can impose calm upon the storms suddenly whipped up by κακία. The train of thought is not difficult to follow. Deut 5:31 is interpreted as an exhortation to the sage to achieve ἠρεμία. In 26 we come back to the point that God (ὁ ἄφθαρτος καὶ μακάριος) can hardly be supposed to be less stable than the well-tempered human soul.

From 27-29 a contrast is then made between the uncertainties and inconsistencies of human life and the constancy of God's existence. This develops, in 30-32, into a contrast between the conditions of temporality and eternity, which owes much to the discussion of Time and Eternity in *Timaeus* 37C-39D. This passage is of particular interest, both for its importance in the debate about divine "foreknowledge," and as suggesting a possible link between Philo and Plotinus via Numenius. Note the ideas that God knows temporal events (a) in a timeless eternity, and (b) as their cause. Both ideas recur in Plotinus as regards the knowledge possessed by the World-Soul 4.4.12), and *a fortiori* by Nous (e.g., 6.7.1). That they are of Stoic inspiration is shown by Cicero, *Div.* 1.82 (divine causal knowledge) and 1.125-27 (simultaneous knowledge of events divided by time). Cicero's immediate source is stated in the passage to be Posidonius.

In 31-32, the notion of God as Father is developed remarkably; if God is father of the cosmos (*Tim.* 28C), then the cosmos is plainly his son: cf. *Ebr.* 30; *Mos.* 2.134; *Spec.* 1.96; Plut. *Quaest. Plat.* 1001B; *Is. et Os.* 373A (Horus, begotten by Isis, is the perceptible world, an image of what is spiritually intelligible); the idea of sonship of the cosmos is no doubt helped by the description in *Rep.* 6.509E, etc., of the Sun as ἔκγονος of the Good. But Time is the measure of the motion of the cosmos (*Tim.* 38B ff.), and is therefore produced by it, and is therefore its son; so Time will be the *grandson* of God. (Cf. Dante, *Inferno* 11.105, where Virgil describes human art as the "grandchild of God," since art is said to copy nature, and nature is the child of God.") Further, the intelligible cosmos is prior to the physical cosmos, so that this latter is the younger son of God as opposed to his elder son, the intelligible cosmos. The contrast between the elder son who stays at home with his father, and the younger son who wanders abroad, finds an interesting parallel in Plotinus 5.8.12-13 and 5.5.3 (originally

parts of a single work, cf. R. Harder, *Hermes* 1936, pp. 1-10;
V. Cilento, *Plotino: Paideia Antignostica*, Florence, 1971).
For Plotinus the sensible world is God's youngest son Zeus (5.
8.13.1), who alone appears "without," whereas his elder brothers
remain with their Father (Nous-Kronos), who "abides bound in
identity" (5.8.13.1), and gives the sense-world to his son (now
apparently regarded as the World-Soul) to rule. Note also in
5.8.13 and 5.5.3 the genealogical language used of the three
Plotinian hypostases, of which the highest (the One) is the
grandfather of the World-Soul (5.5.3.23). We may note also the
possibly Hebraising phrase "King of Kings," *ibid.* 20, and the
more mythological expression of the genealogical relation at
5.1.7.

Of course in Philo's less elaborate scheme, God is the
grandfather of *Time*, not of the World-Soul. If there is any
connection between Philo's language and that of Plotinus, it
will almost certainly be an indirect one, through Numenius of
Apamea. Numenius does use genealogical language about his
three gods (Procl. *In Tim.* 1.303.27 ff. = Fr. 21, Des Places;
cf. Dillon, *Middle Platonists*: 366-67).

B. *Detailed Comments*

20   τούτων μὲν δὴ ἅλις. Compare other phrases of transition,
e.g. *Gig.* 67; *Deus* 33, 51, 70.

τὰ δ᾽ ἀκόλουθα. For Philo, ἀκόλουθος implies not just
"following next after," but "following logically upon" (cf. the
use in Stoic logic of ἀκολουθία). We find it, throughout his
works, in various usages:

(1) *used absolutely*: *LA* 3.150; *Det.* 81; *Decal.* 32
(συνυφαίνειν . . . τὰ ἀκόλουθα); *Agr.* 124, etc.

(2) *followed by a dative*: *Decal.* 128; *Agr.* 32; *Ebr.*
206 (ἐπὶ τὰ ἀκόλουθα τῷ λόγῳ τρεψώμεθα), etc.

(3) *followed by a genitive*: *Gig.* 67 (ἐπὶ τὰ ἀκόλουθα
τοῦ λόγου τρεψώμεθα). For the use of συνυφαίνω here, cf. *Post.*
14, *Cher.* 171 (τούτου δὴ προδιομολογηθέντος, ἀκόλουθον ἂν εἴη
συνυφαίνειν τὰ ἁρμόζοντα); *Fug.* 119. Since this verb can be
construed both with a direct object only, and with an indirect
object, also, in the dative, τῷ λόγῳ could be taken either with
ἀκόλουθα or with συνυφαίνωμεν. In the former case, it would
refer to the text of Scripture; in the latter to Philo's own

discourse. For similar use of προσυφαίνω, cf. *Her.* 17, *Congr.*
122.

In fact there is a logical link between *De Gig.*-*Deus*
1-19, and the present section. After having described and commented upon the multiplication of evil on the earth, Philo
embarks on the subject of the reaction of God to the spectacle
of evil.

21   τινὲς τῶν ἀνεξετάστων. Compare with other phrases of
referring to superficial or literalist critics and commentators.
Cf. below, 52. These literalists are in this case not to be
taken as literal-minded exegetes, but rather "the man in the
street." The term ἀνεξέταστος is no doubt derived ultimately
from Plato *Apol.* 38A. Cf. *Spec.* 2.244; *Somn.* 1.39, 102, 301;
Cher. 42; Origen *C. Cels.* 6.54; A. von Harnock, *Marcion* (rep.
Darmstadt, 1960) 279*.

ἐπελαφρίζουσι καὶ ἐπικουφίζουσι. For collocution cf.
Spec. 4.171; *Legat.* 27. ἐπελαφρίζω first recorded in Philo
(ἐπελαφρύνω in Plut. *Superst.* 165F, Dio Chrys. 56C).

ἀθεότητος. Parallels for ἀθεότης as a term for the
holding of false views about God; *Conf.* 114; *Decal.* 90; *Ebr.*
110; *Mos.* 2.193; *Aet.* 10; *Legat.* 163.

22   τοὺς ἀδόλως καὶ καθαρῶς φ. A reference to philosophers
of the type of the Stoic sage, but couched in language reminiscent of *Phaedrus* 249A (τοῦ φιλοσοφήσαντος ἀδόλως). Cf. *Decal.*
58, where this appellation serves to characterise the disciples
of Moses.

τὸ μὴ τοῖς πράγμασι συμμεταβάλλειν. Cf. *SVF* 3.548,
23-24: οὐδὲ μεταβάλλεσθαι δὲ κατ' οὐδένα τρόπον οὐδὲ μετατί-
θεσθαι οὐδὲ σφάλλεσθαι. συμμεταβάλλειν in this sense ("change
along with") an Aristotelian term, e.g. *EN* I 10, 1100a28.

23   "σὺ δὲ αὐτοῦ στῆθι μετ' ἐμοῦ". Philo gets a good deal
of value from this passage. See list of parallels in note on
Gig. 49, where he uses it in connection with Moses' εὐστάθεια
and ἠρεμία. To capture Philo's meaning, one must render the
text "remain immobile here with me."

τὸ ἀκλινὲς καὶ ἀρρεπὲς τῆς γνώμης. Neither ἀρρεπής,
nor ἀκλινής in the sense of "steadfast, unwavering," is attested

before Philo. Ἀρρεπής is used by Plutarch (*Proc. An.* 1015A) as
an epithet of Matter. Both adjectives are common in Philo, being
used in a parallel context in *Gig.* 49-50, and *Conf.* 30: ἀκλινεῖ
καὶ ἀρρεπεῖ; *Mut.* 87: ἀκλινοῦς καὶ ἀρρεποῦς; ib.183; *Somn.* 2.220,
227; *Abr.* 170; *Prob.* 29. The collocution is found also in Proclus, *In Tim.* 2.313.5: ἡ πρώτη πληρουμένη γνῶσις ἀπὸ τῶν νοητῶν,
ἀκλινὴς καὶ ἀρρεπὴς καὶ ἀμετάπτωτος ὑπάρχουσα.

24   ὥσπερ τινὰ λύραν. As usual, when Philo fixes upon a
metaphor, he exploits it to the full. (For other uses of the
metaphor cf. *Sacr.* 37 and *Ebr.* 116). Here the figure of the
soul as a harmony is elaborated upon variously. The notion that
it is harmonised by ἐπιστήμη τῶν ἐναντίων, playing the role of
high and low notes, is peculiar. The Platonic theory that knowledge is of opposites is never elsewhere connected with the
notion that knowledge harmonizes the soul. The image is continued with ἐπιτείνει and ἀνεῖναι, reflecting ultimately the
precepts of *Rep.* III, esp. 412A, where the effects of a good
blending of gymnastic and music are being summed up: ὅπως ἂν
ἀλλήλοιν ξυναρμοσθῆτον ἐπιτεινομένω καὶ ἀνιεμένω μεχρὶ τοῦ προσή-
κοντος; and then with κροτεῖν and ἐπιψάλλειν, the latter a rare
word, found before Philo only in a fragment of Sophocles (fr.
60).

        προσυπερβάλλοντα. Verb not found before Philo.

        τῶν φύσει καλῶν. It is not quite clear to what this
phrase refers. Mosès (trans. *ad loc.*) seems to take it as
referring to natural good parts ("les merites naturels"); but
it may just be a synonym for the virtues.

25   ὄργανον γὰρ τελεώτατον. The image is continued further
with the description of the soul as a perfect instrument fashioned by Nature (cf. *Sacr.* 37; Stoic influence here, surely,
overlaying that of the *Timaeus*) as an archetype of those (musical instruments) fashioned by human skill. Its perfect tuning
consists in the ὁμολογία of all its actions with each other, the
Stoic ideal. This is its τέλος. Perfect tuning is connected
here with the notion of perfect stability, ἠρεμία, with which
we began in §23.

        ἀρχέτυπον τῶν χειροκμήτων. Cf. Sen. *Ep.* 90.22-24.

        συμφωνίαν. Cf. *SVF* 1.179: καθ' ἕνα λόγον καὶ σύμφωνον
ζῆν.

26   τὸν πολὺν κλύδωνα καὶ σάλον. His thought moves effortlessly now to another of his favourite images, the storm at sea.
(Cf. *LA* 2.90; *Cher.* 12-13, 38; *Sacr.* 13, 90, etc.) The sudden
blasts of evil break upon the soul, rousing up a raging sea,
which the well-tempered soul reduces to calm.

        γαληνιάζει. The verb is found before Philo only in the
Hippocratic corpus, *Vict.* 2, though γαληνιάω is used by Epicurus
[Fr. 425 Usener], but γαλήνη in the metaphorical sense is to be
found in Plato (*Phaed.* 84A, *Laws* VII.791A), as well as elsewhere
in Philo (e.g., *Sacr.* 16, 90; *Somn.* 2.229).

        εἶτ᾽ ἐνδοιάζεις. We arrive at the point to which all
this has been building up. If the soul of the philosopher is so
steadfast, how can we doubt that God himself, who is not subject
to corruption, and is the origin of all the virtues and excel-
lencies of the Sage, could be any less steadfast? The whole
passage 24-26 constitutes a good example of Philo's rhetorical
style (cf. Intro. p. 141).

        ἀνημμένος τὸ κράτος. Better to render this, with
Colson, "who has taken as his own the sovereignty of the virtues," than with Mosès, "qui a attaché sa puissance aux vertus."

27   ἀνθρώποις μὲν οὖν τὸ εὐμετάβολον. Men have two sources
of ἀβεβαιότης, an internal and an external. On the first, Philo
makes the interesting psychological observation that we sometimes change our friendships into indifference, or even enmity,
for no very positive reason, showing in this a κούφη εὐχέρεια.
The combination of εὐμετάβολον and ἀβεβαιότης may own something
to a reminiscence of *Rep.* VI.503C: τὰ βέβαια αὖ ἤθη καὶ οὐκ
εὐμετάβολα, where Plato is analysing the various types of character which must be possessed by candidates for guardianship.

28   κραταίως. A poetic adjective. Adverb found before
Philo only in LXX (Judges 8:1).

        ὁ δὲ θεὸς οὐχ ἀψίκορος. Is a certain degree of sarcasm
discernible in the use of this adjective? In the Platonic
corpus, it is found only in the *Axiochus* (369A), which Philo
would have accepted as genuine, as an epithet of the δῆμος. It
is frequently used by Plutarch (*Mor.* 7B, 20A, 93D, 752B, etc.),
of greed and of the bad sort of democracy, and Dio Chrysostom,
33.369C (also of the bad sort of democracy).

καὶ μὴν ἔστιν ὅτε. The second source of human variabil-
ity is external, but here Philo specifies rather the inconstancy
of other individuals (our partners, perhaps, in some enterprise),
than inanimate causes. This may be because in fact it is easier
for the wise man to remain constant in face of the vagaries of
nature than of those of his associates.

29   προϊδέσθαι γάρ. A chief cause of our inconstancy is our
inability to foresee the future, whereas to God all things are
plain. This involves Philo indirectly in the problem of human
free will (a problem that will recur later, §§47-48). God can
see all things ἐν αὐγῇ καθαρᾷ (a Platonic echo, Phaedr. 250C4),
and administers all things προμηθείᾳ καὶ προνοίᾳ. This means he
allows nothing ἀπελευθεριάζειν (a word not found before Philo),
or to stray outside of his κατάληψις. The statement οὐδὲ ἡ τῶν
μελλόντων ἀδηλότης αὐτῷ συμβατή could be taken to imply that the
contingency of future events can have no substance from God's
point of view; therefore future events are not ultimately con-
tingent. This might seem in turn to involve strict determinism,
but we may postpone discussion of this question to the commentary on 47-48. Philo's concern here, however, is simply to
emphasise God's omniscience and omnipotence.

ἀρίδηλα. Apart from Herod. 8.65, a poetic word.

τηλαυγῶς. Poetic word in Classical times; found in
Hellenistic prose, e.g. Diod. Sic. 1.50; Mark 8:25.

30   τῶν δημιουργηθέντων. Cf. LA 3.88: ὁ γὰρ ζῳοπλάστης
θεὸς ἐπίσταται τὰ ἑαυτοῦ καλῶς δημιουργήματα.

ὁ δὲ θεὸς πατὴρ καὶ τεχνίτης καὶ ἐπίτροπος. The first
two epithets of God are a variation of the πατὴρ καὶ ποιητής of
Tim. 28C, and the title of ἐπίτροπος arises naturally out of his
πρόνοια of the universe. Cf. Op. 7 ff. for discussion of God's
relation to the world; Post. 68-69; Congr. 118: ὁ τῶν ὅλων
ἐπίτροπος.

31   Δημιουργὸς δὲ καὶ χρόνου θεός. The familial relationships here listed have been noted already in the General Comments. The definition of Time as the measure of the motion of
the cosmos (Chrysippus' formalisation of Plato's doctrine in
the Timaeus, SVF 2.509-16) is general in Middle Platonism, e.g.

Albinus *Did.* ch. 14, p. 170,21 Hermann: τῆς κινήσεως τοῦ κόσμου
διάστημα.

32   οὐδὲν παρὰ θεῷ μέλλον . . . ἀλλὰ μόνον ὑφέστηκεν. For
Philo's concept of time, cf. *Fug.* 57; *Jos.* 146; *LA* 3.25; *Mut.*
11; *Sacr.* 76; *Mig.* 139; *Ebr.* 48. See J. Whittaker, *God Time
Being* (Oslo 1971); S. Lauer, "Philo's Concept of Time," *Journ.
of Jew. St.* 9 (1958) 39-46.

ὑφέστηκεν. Chrysippus makes a distinction (*SVF* 2.509,
518) between past and future time, which ὑφεστάναι μέν, ὑπάρχειν
δὲ οὐδαμῶς, and present time, which μόνον ὑπάρχει. Philo here
makes use of this distinction to assert that αἰὼν μόνον ὑφέστηκεν. See H. Dörrie, "*Hypostasis*, Wort- und Bedeutungsgeschichte,"
Nachrichten der Akad. d. Wiss. z. Göttingen, phil.-hist. Klasse,
1955, 3, pp. 35-92; reprinted in Dörrie's *Platonica Minora*
(München, 1976) 13-69, esp. p. 31.

VI B

Deus 33-50

        Commentary on Gen 6:6:   ἐνεθυμήθη ὁ θεὸς ὅτι ἐποίησε τὸν
ἄνθρωπον ἐπὶ τῆς γῆς καὶ διενοήθη.

A.   *General Comments*

        After having dismissed, on grounds of general principle,
the possibility that God can be subject to change of mind, Philo
here returns to the solution of the problem raised by the expressions ἐνεθυμήθη ὁ θεὸς . . . καὶ διενοήθη. To explain the meaning of the LXX rendering of Gen 6:6, Philo provides us with an
analysis of the hierarchic structure of being and man's place in
it, in accordance with Stoic theory. He begins with an attempt
to distinguish between ἔννοια and διάνοια, corresponding to LXX
ἐνεθυμήθη and διενοήθη respectively. The former, he says,
employing a Stoic usage, is "thought stored up" or quiescent
(ἐναποκειμένη νόησις: *SVF* 2.89), whereas the latter is thought
in its [all-traversing] course (νοήσεως διέξοδον) (cf. *Det.* 90;

Gig. 27; D.L. 7.138-39: "Reason [νοῦς] pervades every part of
the cosmos just as does the soul in us. Only there is a difference in degree; in some parts there is more of it, in others
less. . . ." Philo's use of διανόησις here instead of νοῦς is
undoubtedly dictated by the διενοήθη of his text, but it corresponds with Stoic usage. See Plut. *Soll. An.* 961D [referring
to the Stoics]: ὥσπερ ἀμέλει τὰ περὶ τὰς νοήσεις, ἃς ἐναποκει-
μένας μὲν "ἐννοίας" καλοῦσιν, κινουμένας δὲ "διανοήσεις." As
Philo explains in *QG* 2.54, only God employs διάνοια in the strict
sense (κυρίως) of that term, since his firm and unvacillating
thought "is extended (ἐκτείνεσθαι) and passes completely and
effortlessly among all things." (He explains elsewhere that
God's thinking is simultaneous with his acting or creating and
there never was a time when he did not act. See *Prov.* 1.7; cf.
Sacr. 65-68; *LA* 1.5; *Mos.* 1.283: "God cannot repent or fail to
abide by what He has once said. He will utter nothing at all
which shall not certainly be performed, for His word is His
deed." Strictly speaking, then, God's ἔννοια is not distinct
from his διάνοια. Only in man do they constitute two distinct
phases.) For the analogy between the twofold Logos in God and
the twofold logos in man, see *Mos.* 2.127-29; *LA* 2.23; cf. *Deus*
31. See M. Heinze, *Die Lehre vom Logos in der heidnischen
Philosophie* (Oldenburg, 1872) 231-35. Scripture is thus empha-
sizing that it was part of the unchanging divine plan to deal
with man in accordance with his essential nature, which involves
the responsibility of choosing between good and evil. Hence God
is constantly praising those who do not leave their posts in
life, and punishing those who depart from it.

          In order to explain man's exalted and unique position
among earth creatures, Philo now proceeds with a detailed
account of the scale of being, beginning with ἕξις, or cohesion
which holds the cosmos together and prevents its disintegration
in the void (*SVF* 2.540, 552-53). This ἕξις operates not only
in inanimate objects, such as wood and stones, but also in parts
of animals, such as the bones and sinews (*SVF* 2.634). It is
identified by the Stoics with the active cause, the source of
qualities, and is effected through pneumatic motion (*SVF* 2.449).
In describing the next level, that of φύσις (growth or nature),
exemplified by the plant world, Philo characteristically employs
vivid imagery. His anthropomorphizing of nature is very effective for his purpose, which is presumably to contribute to the
notion of the συμπάθεια of all creation (cf. D.L. 2.140). He

then continues with the level of ψυχή (life), which is characterized by αἴσθησις (sensation), φαντασία (impression) and ὁρμή
(impulse), all of which are lacking in plants (cf. Arist. *De
An.* 2.2, 413b2; 3.3, 427b15-16; 3.10, 433b28-29). Finally he
turns to a description of man's unique superiority over the
animals, and provides us with a eulogistic account of the human
intellect (νοῦς), which emphasizes its indestructibility and its
freedom. (For the orderly progression in creation, cf. *Op.*
65-68). [For a detailed analysis of Philo's conception of human
freedom, see Introduction p. 181.] It is man's unique freedom
to choose between good and evil which constitutes him a moral
agent who is responsible for his actions. Philo has thus
arrived at his goal, which was to explain God's continuous and
unchanging contemplation of man's nature, through which he holds
him accountable for his various actions.

B. *Detailed Commentary*

33   "ἐνεθυμήθη". ἐνθυμοῦμαι in the meaning of "be irri-
tated" is already a Classical usage, e.g. Thuc. 7.18, Dem.
1.43. In the parallel passage of *QG* (1.93), Philo seems to be
taking the verb in its more normal sense of "be concerned,"
"take thought for," and his exegesis is accordingly different.

34   ἐναποκειμένην. First attested in Philo, but only here
in a technical sense. Cf. Plut. *Aem.* 14; Plot. 3.6.2.40; *SVF*
2.89 (ap. Galen): ἐπίνοιά ἐστιν ἐναποκειμένη νόησις.

       διέξοδον. Cf. *Det.* 130; *Post.* 79; *Agr.* 145; *Plant.* 49;
etc. Also Plot. 6.7.13.48: "Since it does not change, Nous
ever pursues the same course (τὴν αὐτὴν διέξοδον) through things
that are not the same."

       μὴ λείποντα τὴν τάξιν. Cf. comment. on *Gig.* 43.

35   τὰ μὲν ἐνεδήσατο ἕξει . . . φύσει . . . ψυχῇ . . .
λογικῇ ψυχῇ. ἐνεδήσατο should be taken as middle rather than
passive, "he bound down." Possibly a reminiscence of *Tim.* 43A
ἐνέδουν, though the verb there is active. The cosmic pneuma,
according to the Stoics, has a fourfold function. In the form
of ἕξις it provides unity and quality; in the form of φύσις,
nutrition and growth, in the form of ψυχή, sensation and movement; and in the form of νοῦς or λόγος, it provides rationality.
Inanimate objects possess only ἕξις; plants possess, in addition,

φύσις; irrational animals possess ψυχή; and man and the cosmos
possess also reason (*SVF* 2.473, 460, 634, 714-16, 804, 1013; cf.
LA 2.22-23; *Her.* 137; *Aet.* 75 [where there is a further elaboration: "mind and reason in men and the perfection of virtue in
the good" (*SVF* 458-59)]). Whereas Cleanthes had followed Aristotle in distinguishing three psychic functions (θρεπτικόν;
αἰσθητικόν; διανοητικόν, λογιστικόν: Cic. *ND* 2.23-24; 30-31;
Arist. *De An.* 2.2-3.8; *EN* 1097b33 ff.; *GA.* 736a32), Chrysippus
added a fourth, ἕξις, the distinctively Stoic contribution. See
S. Sambursky, *Physics of the Stoics* (London 1959) 7-11; David E.
Hahm, *The Origins of Stoic Cosmology* (Ohio State U.P. 1977)
136-74. The Stoic scale of beings is obviously indebted to
Aristotle's scale, in which plants possess only the nutritive
soul, animals also possess the perceptive soul, and man possesses
mind in addition to the two lower forms of soul. For the background of Aristotle's scale, see F. Solmsen, "Antecedents of
Aristotle's Psychology and Scale of Beings," *AJP* 76 (1955) 148-
64, reprinted in his *Kleine Schriften* (Hildesheim 1968) 588-604.
Cf. also J. Moreau, *L'âme du monde de Platon aux Stoiciens*
(Paris 1939).

συμφυΐας. First found in Philo (though *cognatio* in Cic.
ND 2.19 may be a translation) and used by him fairly frequently.
Cf. *Flac.* 71; *Cont.* 7. The pneuma makes the cosmos a living,
organic whole, with each part grown together (συμφυές: *SVF*
2.550) in living sympathy with all the rest (*SVF* 2.473, 912).
Plutarch uses the word in *Mor.* 923C, 1080F, 1112A-C.

πνεῦμα ἀναστρέφον ἐφ' ἑαυτό. Pneumatic motion has two
phases, a movement into itself (πρός or εἰς ἑαυτό) and a movement out of itself (ἐξ αὐτοῦ), or movements back and forth
(πρόσω καὶ ὀπίσω), either from the center of the cosmos to its
extreme boundaries, or from the center of any given entity to
its surface (*SVF* 2.442, 471, 551). The inward movement toward
the center holds the body together and produces cohesion
(συνέχεια), unity (ἕνωσις), and being (οὐσία); the outward
movement causes dimensions and qualities (*SVF* 2.451-52, 551).
According to some sources, tensional motion (τονικὴ κίνησις)
is a simultaneous motion in opposite directions (Alex. *De Mixt.*
10.224.25; *Mant.* 131.10, 16, 19-20). Both these texts are
polemical "and the notion of simultaneous motion," writes
Robert B. Todd, "may have been an accretion to the description
that we find in the doxography. It is only reported elsewhere

by Nemesius" (*SVF* 2.451) (*Alexander of Aphrodisias on Stoic Physics* [Leiden 1976] 37 n. 86). The exact nature of this motion is by no means clear. Hahm believes that "the image of compressed air gives, on the whole, the most satisfactory explanation of the pneumatic motion and its effects. Such pressure has no local motion and the fact that it acts simultaneously in opposite directions could have given rise to the notion that it comprises a simultaneous motion toward the center and toward the periphery" (*Origins* 167). Sambursky's interpretation of this motion as something akin to wave motion, according to Hahm, is an interesting thesis which goes beyond the texts. Cf. *Conf.* 136; *Plant.* 9; *Mig.* 181. It is odd that although διὰ πάντων διῆκον is an almost formulaic description of pneuma's motion (*SVF* 2.416, 1035, 1021; Alex. *De Mixt.* 216.15; D.L. 7.139), Philo never uses the verb διήκω in this context. (It is used, however, by the author of Wisdom [7:24].) On the other hand, Philo does consistently use the verb τείνω to indicate the tensional character of pneumatic motion. (The Stoic concept of τόνος is first met with in the fragments of Cleanthes, who said that it was a "stroke of fire" [πληγὴ πυρός]: *SVF* 1.563. For the origin of the concept of τόνος, see Hahm, *Origins* 155.)

36   δίαυλος. Philo is rather fond of this image. Cf. *Mut.* 117; *Spec.* 1.338; 2.246; *Plant.* 9, 76, 125; *Aet.* 58; *Op.* 44, 47. Aristotle (*GA* 741b21) compares nature to a runner covering a double course (διαυλοδρομούσης) and retracing her steps toward the starting-point whence she set out. Pausanias (5.17.6) uses this comparison to illustrate Boustrophedon writing. The main point of the comparison here is simply to emphasize that the motion is one that returns on itself and need not indicate that it is necessarily sequential. (According to F. H. Sandbach, Philo "must intend a continuous stream of which at any moment part is moving outward, part turning, part coming back": *The Stoics* [London 1975] 77-78.)

37   μεταβλητικῆς. This is the only occurrence of this word in Philo. Cf. Arist. *Met.* 1020a5.

τεκμήριον δέ. Characteristic rubric for introducing supporting evidence, cf. *Deus* 148, 181.

αὐξητικῆς. Cf. *Her.* 137: αὐξητικῶς κινούμενα, in the course of a similar contrast between ἕξις and φύσις.

38   It is not surprising that Philo's imagery here is primarily of vines (cf. *Mut.* 162; *Anim.* 78) and that he seems well
acquainted with them (for his acquaintance with the cultivation
of trees, cf. *Det.* 107), for "one of the earliest steps taken by
the Ptolemies to satisfy the ever-growing demand of the Greek
inhabitants for wine was an extensive planting of vines of
various kinds. There is evidence of this in many documents.
Our fullest information relates to the Arsinoite nome. This
nome in the time of Philadelphus was covered with vineyards
large and small, some planted by the kings, but most by immi-
grants, not by natives. Vines were planted with feverish activity on the *doreai* (gift-estates) of Apollonius the *dioicetes*.
Many sorts of vine were tried. In 256 B.C.E. Apollonius sends
messengers to a certain Lysimachus to get cuttings of vines and
fruit trees from him. Nicias, Lysimachus' manager, replies to
the message from Apollonius and attaches a list of cuttings.
Eleven varieties of vine are named, among them Cilician, Mendean,
Maronean, Phoenician, and Alexandrian, and some others, all
famous for their quality. In one letter, Apollonius speaks of
10,000 vine plants (φυτὰ ἀμπέλινα) and 1,700 shoots (μοσχεύ-
ματα)" (M. Rostovtzeff, *Social and Economic History of the
Hellenistic World* [Oxford 1941] 1:353-54; cf. P. M. Fraser,
Ptolemaic Alexandria [Oxford 1972] 1.166-67; 2.282, for further
bibliography). In this regard we may also compare Seneca, who
was a prosperous vine grower and who often resorts in his
Letters to figures dealing with the vine. (*Ep.* 112.1; 104.6;
86.14 ff.; 12.2; 83.16; *NQ* 3.7.1). See M. T. Griffin, *Seneca,
A Philosopher in Politics* (Oxford, 1976) 290; C. Magenta,
"Riflessi di agronomia et economia agricola in Seneca Filosofo,"
RIL 73 (1940) 244 ff.

        ἀθλητής. Athletic imagery is extremely frequent in
Philo. Cf. *LA* 1.98; 2.21; 3.14, 70, 72, 201; *Cher.* 80; *Sacr.*
160; *Det.* 49; et al. See V. C. Pfitzner, *Paul and the Agon
Motif* (Leiden 1967) 16-75; and H. A. Harris, *Greek Athletics
and the Jews*, ed. I. A. Barton and A. J. Brothers (Cardiff 1976)
51-95.

39   περιαναστᾶσα. First found in Philo. Cf. *LA* 2.26;
Cher. 62: ἐκ βαθέος ὕπνου περιαναστάς; *Somn.* 2.106.

        οἱ τοῖς ἐν γυναιξὶ μαστοῖς ἀναλογοῦσι. Note how Philo
keeps before our minds the unity of nature, by such analogies
as this. The βαθὺς ὕπνος image serves the same purpose.

41   ἄόρμητα, ἀφάνταστα, αἰσθήσεως ἀμέτοχα. All three negative adjectives found first in Philo (except for one doubtful
use of ἀμέτοχος in *Thuc.* 1.39).

42   εἴσθεσις. First found here and not used again by Philo.
(See also Damasc. *Dub. et Sol.* 102 p. 265,11 Ruelle, opposed to
ἀφαίρεσις). αἴσθησις/εἴσθεσις is apparently an attempt to understand Plato's etymologizing at *Tim.* 43A5-6. Proclus and the
Platonic tradition took this as a derivation from ἀἴσσειν (*In
Tim.* 332,5 ff.), but knowing Plato's powers at etymologizing,
εἴσθεσις is not too bad a suggestion as to what he might have
intended. If it *is* Stoic, it may nevertheless derive ultimately
from *Tim.* 43C. (Modern linguists prefer to derive αἴσθησις from
ἀἴω, "hear, perceive," cf. Skt. *āvíḥ*, "evidently," OCS *avě*, Lat.
audio.)

       ταμεῖον . . . ἐναποθησαυρίζεται. Cf. *SVF* 2.56: μνήμη,
θησαυρισμὸς οὖσα φαντασιῶν; *LA* 3.36: τί γὰρ τὰς φαύλας δόξας
. . . ταμιεύεις καὶ θησαυρίζεις, ὦ διάνοια, ἐν σαυτῇ; *Post.* 57;
Plato, *Phaedr.* 276D. Also Cic. *Acad.Pr.* 30 (representing
Antiochus' doctrine). For νοῦς as ταμεῖον, cf. *Det.* 68. For
πανδεχές, cf. *Tim.* 51A, where Plato speaks of the Receptacle as
πανδεχές (though Philo must here be thinking of a πανδοκεῖον).
Cf. *LA* 1.61; *Sacr.* 135; *Det.* 34. Cf. also Iamb. *V.P.* 29.162.
Philo's preference for νοῦς over ἡγεμονικόν or διάνοια in reference to man's reason is a mark of his essential Platonism.

43   φαντασία δέ ἐστι τύπωσις. Cf. *LA* 1.30. Philo is influenced by the *Theaetetus* account, as were later Platonists in
general (Ar. Didymus, *ap.* Euseb. *PE* 11.23.36-; Plut. *Is. et Os.*
373B), but also by Stoic doctrine. Cf. *SVF* 2.55-56.

       ὥσπερ δακτύλιός τις ἢ σφραγίς. Cf. *SVF* 1.484.

       ἐναπεμάξατο. A characteristically Stoic term, used in
the definition of the καταληπτικὴ φαντασία; D.L. 7.46: ἐναπε-
σφραγισμένην καὶ ἐναπομεμαγμένην; *SVF* 1.59 (Zeno, ap. Sext.);
cf. *Op.* 151; *LA* 1.79; *Post.* 165. etc.; [Plut.] *De Lib. Ed.* 3F:
καθάπερ γὰρ σφραγῖδες τοῖς ἀπαλοῖς ἐναπομάττονται κηροῖς.

       κηρῷ δέ ἐοικὼς ὁ νοῦς. This description of the process
by which the mind acquires concepts is peculiar, in that it seems
to revert to the more primitive doctrine of the Old Stoa (Zeno,
Cleanthes), disregarding the more sophisticated model proposed
by Chrysippus, according to which each new image introduces a

"modification" (ἐτεροίωσις) into the ἡγεμονικόν (Sext. Emp.
Math. 7.227, 372 = *SVF* 2.56), rather than impressing anything
upon it. Philo is perhaps influenced by what he (or some intermediate source?) takes to be the doctrine adumbrated in the
Theaetetus. The manner in which λήθη "smooths out" and "effaces"
the imprints of memory is, also, far from clear. It is perhaps
fair to say that Philo is not vitally interested in the techni-
calities of epistemological theory. Cf. *Op.* 166, where he
accepts the same doctrine.

44   τοτὲ μὲν οἰκείως τοτὲ δὲ ὡς ἑτέρως διέθηκε τὴν ψυχήν.
A reference to the Stoic doctrine of ὁρμή (resulting in οἰκείωσις), and ἀφορμή (resulting in ἀλλοτρίωσις), arising from the
reaction of the Soul to the impressions it receives (*SVF* 3.169-
77), though Philo here uses ὁρμή for both types of impulse. The
subject of ἔφασαν in the next sentence is left vague by Philo,
but since "they" define ὁρμή as πρώτη ψυχῆς κίνησις, the subject
is inevitably the Stoics.

45   σωμάτων τε ὁμοῦ καὶ πραγμάτων. What contrast is
intended here? Neither Mosès nor Colson in their translations
("aussi bien les corps vivants que les choses," "both of all
material objects and of things in general") seem quite adequate.
The contrast σώματα-πράγματα is a very common one with Philo
(see Leisegang's Index, s.v. πρᾶγμα), and in many cases it seems
to be simply between animate and inanimate objects (e.g. *Op.*
150, *Det.* 165, *Conf.* 21), though sometimes πράγματα could be
taken as meaning intelligible objects (*Post.* 57; *Ebr.* 167).
When Philo wants to make this latter contrast, he usually says
so, *Somn.* 2.134: τοῖς κατὰ ψυχὴν πράγμασιν; *Mut.* 56: τὴν τῶν
ἀσωμάτων θέαν πραγμάτων; but at *Her.* 130 we find σώματα and
πράγματα contrasted in a way which, as becomes clear in 131,
involves their reference to sensibles and intelligibles respectively; and so it seems to be in the present passage. (Cf. also
Somn. 2.101: πραγμάτων οὐ σωμάτων.) This curious usage must
derive from the Stoic use of πρᾶγμα to mean λεκτόν, as attested
in *SVF* 2.173, and especially Diog. Laert. 7.59: προφέρονται
μὲν αἱ φωναί, λέγεται δὲ τὰ πράγματα, ἃ δὴ καὶ λεκτὰ τυγχάνει.
Also Sextus, *Math.* 8.11-12, cf. [Plut.] *Plac.* 1.6.13.

46   ψυχῆς γὰρ ὄψις οὗτος. See Plato *Rep.* 7.518BC. So, too,
Arist. *Top.* 1.17, 108a: ὡς ὄψις ἐν ὀφθαλμῷ νοῦς ἐν ψυχῇ. Cf.

EN 1.6.1096b28. In *Art of Rhetoric* 3.10.7, 1411b, Aristotle quotes from an unknown writer the following example of a metaphor: "reason is a light that God has kindled in the soul." Also, Cicero *ND* 1.19: *oculis animi*, in a reference to Plato.

οἰκείαις περιλαμπόμενος αὐγαῖς. Cf. *Spec.* 1.42; *Praem.* 45; *SVF* 2.54, 63.

βαθὺς ζόφος. ζόφος is a Homeric term and carries with it the connotation of the ζόφος ἠερόεις which Hades has for his portion (*Il.* 15.191), though by Philo's time this connotation may not have much force. Cf., however, Plut. *Mor.* 48C. τὸν δ' ἐντὸς εὑρῶτα τῆς ψυχῆς καὶ ζόφον is reminiscent of the ζόφος εὐρώεις of Hades mentioned in *Hom. Hymn to Demeter* 488. Philo likes the word, cf. *Praem.* 82: ὥσπερ ἐκ ζόφου βαθέος εἰς φῶς ἀναχθέντα; *LA* 3.171, etc.

καθαρωτέρας δὲ καὶ ἀμείνονος ἔλαχε τῆς οὐσίας. The reference could be taken to be to Aristotle's πέμπτη οὐσία. Cf. Cic. *Acad.* 26; *Her.* 283; *QG* 3.6. At *Plant.* 18, however, Philo seems to reject the αἰθήρ as the source of the mind, which he assigns instead to the divine pneuma, which is immaterial, and this seems to be rather his meaning here. Cf. *Det.* 86; *LA* 1. 37-38. Elsewhere Philo tells us that the mind is incapable of knowing itself (*LA* 1.91; *Somn.* 1.30-33, where he insists that the soul is incorporeal). Moreover, at *Somn.* 1.21, he shows himself agnostic as to whether *aithēr* is "a fifth substance, circular in movement, with no part in the four elements," and concludes that "one may confidently take one's oath that the day will never come when any mortal shall be competent to arrive at a clear solution of these problems" (*ibid.* 24). Billings has suggested that Philo's materialistic language in regard to the rational soul is "merely metaphorical." (See T. Billings, *The Platonism of Philo Judaeus* [Chicago 1919] 53-59.) It might be more correct to say that Philo feels himself able to use materialistic terminology borrowed from the Aristotelians and Stoics with systematic ambiguity.

47   ἄφετον εἴασε. The term ἄφετος seems to give a clue to Philo's conception of the mind's conditional freedom. This word is properly used of animals allowed to roam free (often in sacred enclosures, and sometimes preparatory to being sacrificed), instead of being bound in stalls and employed for specific tasks.

τοῦ πρεπωδεστάτου καὶ οἰκείου κτήματος. A characteristically Stoic notion. Cf. Epict. 1.1.10: "We have given thee
a certain portion of ourself, this faculty of choice and refusal";
cf. 2.8.11.

μοῖραν, ἣν ἠδύνατο δέξασθαι. Philo is clearly emphasiz-
ing the limited character of the freedom bestowed by God on man.
Cf. *Tim.* 38B: [Time] was made after the pattern of the Eternal
Nature, to the end that it might be as like thereto as possible
(κατὰ δύναμιν); *Theaet.* 176B: φυγὴ δὲ ὁμοίωσις θεῷ κατὰ τὸ
δυνατόν; Plot. 3.2.3.32-33; Philo, *Abr.* 203, where God bestows
χαρά on Isaac only "in so far as the recipient's capacity allows";
Virt. 203; *Op.* 23, where God confers benefits "in proportion to
the capacities of the recipients"; *Deus* 48: ὡς οἷον ἦν ἐλευθε-
ρωθεῖσα.

ἐγχαλινωθέντα. In its metaphorical sense, first used by
Philo. Cf. Plut. *Lys.* 21; *LA* 3.155, 195; *Cher.* 19; *Det.* 53.

ἐθελουργοῦ καὶ αὐτοκελεύστου γνώμης. Philo seems deliberately to be avoiding Stoic terminology here, since neither
ἐθελουργός nor αὐτοκέλευστος appear to have been used by the
latter. It may well be that in those passages where he is
anxious to emphasize man's freedom, relative though it be, he
prefers to dissociate himself from the Stoic formulae which were
under heavy attack by those who accused the Stoics of trying to
camouflage their deterministic position by coating it with innocuous but meaningless phrases that suggested some sort of human
freedom. (The Cynic Oenomaus called the lot accorded to man by
Chrysippus "semi-slavery." Euseb. *PE* 6.7.2 and 14; cf. Nemes.
De Nat. Hom. 35; and Plotinus 3.1.7.15.) On the other hand,
when writing for the "initiated" and wishing to indicate the
very limited nature of human freedom, he does employ the Aris-
totelian/Stoic formula ἐφ' ἡμῖν (fragment from the lost fourth
book of the *LA*; Harris, *Fragments* 8). It is also interesting to
note when ἐθελουργός and αὐτοκέλευστος are first used. In both
cases, by Xenophon (*Eq.* 10.17; *Anab.* 3.4.5 respectively), in the
former case in the context of "animals" (horses) doing things
willingly and spontaneously; in the latter of soldiers doing
something without command from above. We may be relatively
free, but we are still chattels of God. Moreover, ἐθελουργὸς
καὶ αὐτοκέλευστος is a very frequent collocution in Philo, and
it is illuminating to examine the various contexts in which this
phrase occurs. They all refer to that kind of human action that

is spontaneous and not the result of external compulsion, i.e., precisely what is ordinarily meant in Greek philosophy by the term ἑκούσιον. At *Conf.* 59, for example, it refers to the Israelites' readiness to perform God's will even before learning and understanding its nature, whereas at *Mut.* 270, it refers to the relative independence of the pupil in the absence of his teacher's presence. Cf. *Det.* 11; *Mos.* 1.6.3; *Spec.* 1.57; 2.146; 3.127; *Prob.* 22. Cf. also *Anth. Pal.* 5.22: "Love gave me to thee, Boöpis, for a servant, yoking the steer that came himself to bend his neck to Desire, all of his own free will, at his own bidding, an abject slave (ταῦρον ὑποζεύξας εἰς πόθον αὐτόμολον, / αὐτοθελῆ, πάνδουλον, ἑκούσιον, αὐτοκέλευστον) who will never ask for bitter freedom, never, my dear, till he grows grey and old."

εἰκότως ψόγον μὲν ἔσχεν. The prime motivation of Philo in this passage, to show that man is responsible for all his actions, is very similar to that of Plato in the *Timaeus* (42D) and *Republic* (10.614 ff.). The dominant motif is there sounded by the oft-quoted phrase: αἰτία ἑλομένου, θεὸς ἀναίτιος (*Rep.* 617E; cf. *Plot.* 3.2.7.20; *CH*, Nock-Festug., 1:52. According to Justin Martyr [*Ap.* 1.44.108], this dictum was taken by Plato directly from Moses.) The attribution of moral responsibility to man is fully justified, as far as Plato is concerned, as long as man's soul is not caught in the web of a fatality which would constrain its actions arbitrarily, and thus bypass its normal choice-process.

48   εὐφορίαι. Cf. Chrysippus, *SVF* 2.1174; Hp. *Epid.* 6.7.2.

κακοπραγίαι. This may mean either (1) "misfortune" or "bad condition," in which sense it is applicable also to plants and animals, or (2) "evil deed," in which sense it is properly applicable to man. Philo's use of the word here amounts almost to a pun.

τὴν κατ᾽ ἀπελευθέρων ἀχαρίστων . . . δίκην. These words constitute an implicit commentary on the last words of the lemma quoted in 20: ἀπαλείψω τὸν ἄνθρωπον ὃν ἐποίησα ἀπὸ προσώπου τῆς γῆς. The Roman law on the subject of the respect due by freedmen to their masters is better reported than the Greek. Ulpian, in *Digest* 47.10.7.2, advises judges not to admit actions for insult and the like from freedmen against their former masters.

49   παγίως καὶ βεβαίως. For this collocution, cf. *Cher.* 83.
There are also many passages where these two words occur in very
close proximity: *Cher.* 26; *Agr.* 160; *Plant.* 84; *Conf.* 106; *Deus*
22. Philo is here concerned to emphasize that the use of the
aorists in the lemma does not imply any temporal activity on the
part of God.

50   "'Ιδοὺ δέδωκα . . . ἔκλεξα τὴν ζωήν". This juxtaposition of Deut 30:15 and 19 occurs only here, and in a fragment of
LA 4 (*Fr.* 8, Harris), though there is an interesting use of Deut
30:15 in *Fug.* 58, in a different connection.

      λογισμὸν ἔχοντες ἐν ἑαυτοῖς. For Philo's concept of
conscience, and of the relation of our λογισμός to the ὀρθὸς
λόγος in the universe, see Introduction, p. 207.

                              VI C

                          Deus 51-69

      Commentary on Gen 6:7: ᾿Απαλείψω τὸν ἄνθρωπον ὃν ἐποί-
ησα ἀπὸ προσώπου τῆς γῆς, ἀπὸ ἀνθρώπου ἕως κτήνους, ἀπὸ ἑρπετῶν
ἕως πετεινῶν τοῦ οὐρανοῦ, ὅτι ἐθυμώθην ὅτι ἐποίησα αὐτόν.

A.   *General Comments*

      Philo moves on now to the next sentence of Genesis,
giving particular attention to the bothersome phrase "ὅτι ἐθυμώθην ὅτι ἐποίησα αὐτόν." This apparently unequivocal attribution of θυμός to God provokes him to what becomes an important
statement both of his theology and of his theory of exegesis.
      Philo accepted the Platonic-Aristotelian concept of the
deity, as an entity which could be subject to no passion, nor
even change. The previous section, commenting on Gen 6:6, concerns God's changelessness; we are here concerned with his freedom from passions. Contrary to the view of literal exegetes,
God is totally free from any attributes which are proper to the
irrational portion of the soul (52). Why, then, does Moses
talk of his θυμός?

Philo's answer is that he does this only for the purpose
of εἰσαγωγή, the leading to the truth--or, at least, the keeping
in order (νουθετῆσαι)--of those who are not susceptible to any
higher type of teaching. Philo takes as his key texts two passages which he also employs in the parallel passage *Somn*. 1.231-
37 (cf. also *QG* 2.54, a comment on Gen 8:21, where the same discussion takes place, with the use of the same pair of texts),
(1) Num 23:19: "God is not as Man," and (2) Deut 8:5: "Like a
man, he will chastise his son." (54) This juxtaposition of
apparently contradictory passages has the mark of a rabbinic
aporia. For Philo it is the starting-point for a comprehensive
theory of levels of exegesis, a theory much favored later by the
Alexandrian school of Christian exegetes, in particular Clement
and Origen (who in fact particularly valued this Philonic treatise). It is plain, after all, that only the former of these
passages is literally true. Why, then, does Moses present us
with the other?

The answer is, for the purpose of παιδεία and νουθεσία.
Men, says Philo (55), are divided into two classes, the Friends
of the Soul and the Friends of the Body. The friends of the
soul, being familiar with the truths of the intelligible world,
are not tempted to attribute to τὸ ὄν (note the neuter here) any
of the attributes proper to things of generation, but free it
from all ποιότης, comprehending it as pure ὕπαρξις, endowing it
with no character or form at all (cf. also 62). This is a clear
statement of the necessity of negative theology, at least to the
extent of denying of God all attributes other than pure existence. At *Somn*. 1.231-37 we find also a comprehensive denial to
God of anything but simple ὕπαρξις, and an explanation of Moses'
attribution to him of physical characteristics more or less
identical to what we have here.

The criticism of the friends of the body leads Philo into
a tirade (56-59), in diatribe style, against the absurdities of
anthropomorphism, which reproduces the criticism that Greek
philosophers had been making against popular Greek religion from
Xenophanes on, but which is also applicable to certain tendencies within the rabbinic tradition. Anthropomorphism is closely
connected, for Philo, with superstitious fear, because of the
tissue of myths to which it gives rise.

To explain why Moses uses such terminology in regard to
God, Philo makes use of an elaborately worked-out medical comparison (65-68). This in itself, the setting up of an analogy
between the care of the mind and the care of the body, the

Philosopher as Doctor of Souls, is trite enough, being a favorite of Plato's, and is used repeatedly elsewhere by Philo, but
his use of the analogy here has a slightly unexpected twist--at
first sight illogical, but in fact sound enough. The good doctor, he says, conceals the truth about the seriousness of the
disease from his patient in order not to cause mental distress
within him which would be fully as serious as the disease
itself. Even thus, Moses conceals the truth about God's nature
from the friends of the body, attributing to him human passions
such as anger, in order to protect them from sinfulness and
ruin, consequent on the recklessness they would give way to if
they knew God to be incapable of such passions. The circum-
stance that the good doctor is minimizing the seriousness of the
situation, while Moses, so to speak, is exaggerating it, is
irrelevant to the point of the comparison. In each case what
we have is a benevolent concealment of the truth. (Cf. Origen,
C. Cels. 4.71.)

        He ends the discussion (69) with the reflection that the
two opposed sayings previously quoted may be associated with two
attitudes to the deity, Love (ἀγάπη) and Fear (φόβος). Those
who attach no anthropomorphic characteristics to God approach
him with love; the others must approach him with fear.

B. *Detailed Commentary*

  51   <u>Δεδηλωκότες ἀποχρώντως περὶ τούτων, τὰ ἑξῆς ἴδωμεν</u>. Cf.
formula of transition at end of *Gig.* (67): τοσαῦτα ἀρκούντως
εἰρηκότες, ἐπὶ τὰ ἀκόλουθα τοῦ λόγου τρεψώμεθα. The connotation
of τὰ ἑξῆς, as opposed to τὰ ἀκόλουθα, is presumably that of
purely physical, as opposed to logical, sequence.

  52   τινές. Criticism of literal interpreters, probably, as
above, 21, simply "the man in the street." On the question of
Philo's criticism of literalist interpretation, see Intro. p.
77 and M. J. Shroyer, "Alexandrian Jewish Literalists," *JBL* 55
(1936) 261-84 and D. M. Hay, "Philo's References to Other Allegorists," *SP* 6 (1979-80) 41-75.

        τὸ ὄν. Here, τὸ ὄν, as opposed to ὁ ὤν, seems to lay
emphasis upon the abstractness of the divinity (cf. 55). A
study of Philo's use of τὸ ὄν/ὁ ὤν in relation to God is much
to be desired.

κηραίνειν. A poetical verb in Classical times, first
attested in prose with Philo. Also Plut. *Mor.* 886E. The verb
seems to mean for Philo "be subject to passions" in general,
rather than simply "be sick at heart, anxious" (LSJ). Presumably this is a result of πάσχειν having lost much of its force.

μέχρι τινὸς εἰσαγωγῆς. Εἰσαγωγή is the normal term for
an introductory handbook, e.g. Albinus' *Isagoge* to the dialogues
of Plato. Here the μέχρι is restrictive, "as a sort of introduction." Cf. *Her.* 102: ἀπὸ στοιχειώδους εἰσαγωγῆς.

53   τῶν γὰρ ἐν ταῖς προστάξεσι καὶ ἀπαγορεύσεσι νόμων. See
LA 1.93 for distinction between πρόσταξις, ἀπαγόρευσις, ἐντολή
and παραίνεσις. Cf. *Praem.* 55; *Congr.* 120; *Mos.* 2.46.

"οὐχ ὡς ἄνθρωπος ὁ θεός." "ὡς ἄνθρωπος παιδεύσει τὸν
υἱὸν αὐτοῦ." These texts are used again in just the same way
at *Somn.* 1.237. Cf. *Sac.* 94; *Conf.* 98; *QE* 2.54; Fragments,
Harris, pp. 8, 15, 23. Note here that Philo's interpretation
is only validated by the LXX. The Hebrew does not say "God is
not *as a man*," but "God is not a man."

54   "παιδεύσει"--παιδεία. Use of παιδεύω in sense of
"chastise" vulgar Greek, only in LXX and NT (e.g. Pontius
Pilate's statement in Luke 23:16: παιδεύσας οὖν αὐτὸν ἀπολύσω).
It is not quite clear that Philo understands the usage here,
since he glosses παιδεία by νουθεσία, but both these words can
have overtones of "punishment" in Classical Greek; cf. e.g.
Plato, *Prot.* 325CD, *Laws* III 700C.

55   οἱ μὲν ψυχῆς, οἱ δὲ σώματος . . . φίλοι. Cf. Plato,
Soph. 248: τῶν εἰδῶν φίλους.

ἐνομιλεῖν. Verb first attested in Philo. (Used in different sense by the Epicurean Polystratos [p. 32 Wilke], in
third century B.C.E.)

ἐκβιβάσαντες αὐτὸ πάσης ποιότητος. See the comprehensive discussion of H. A. Wolfson, *Philo* 2.101-10, on the meaning
of the denial of "quality" to God by Philo. Here Philo is simply
denying any physical quality or accident of God. Cf. Intro, p.
217.

τὴν ὕπαρξιν καταλαμβάνεσθαι. On the grasping of the
simple existence of God, as opposed to any attributes, cf.
Intro, p. 217.

56   ἀπαμφιάσασθαι τὸ σαρκῶν περίβλημα. Verb first found in
prose, in Philo. The imagery presumably originates in the myth
of the *Gorgias* (523A ff.), but is influenced also by Gen 3:21.
Cf. Philo's exegesis of "the garments of skin" at *QG* 1.53.

ἐκ πλειόνων συνόδου δυνάμεων. No reference here to the
doctrine of Powers. The simplicity of the essence of God is a
basic principle of Philo's theology; cf. Intro. p. 217.

57   εἰ κέχρηται τοῖς ὀργανικοῖς μέρεσι. For the rabbinic
attitude to anthropomorphism, see Wolfson, *Philo* 1.135 ff.;
M. Kadushin, *The Rabbinic Mind* (New York 1965) 273-87; A. Mar-
morstein, *The Old Rabbinic Doctrine of God II. Essays in Anthropomorphism* (New York, 1937, rep. 1968 Ktav); S. Maybaum, *Die
Anthropomorphien und Anthropopathien bei Onkelos und den späteren
Targumim* (Breslau 1870); C. T. Fritsch, *The Anti-Anthropomor-
phisms of the Greek Pentateuch* (Princeton 1943).

οὐ γὰρ ὑγείας φροντίζων. Cf. Arist. *Phys.* 2.3.194b32.

λόγῳ χρώμενος ὑπηρέτῃ δωρεῶν. At *LA* 3.177-78, however,
we are told that God gives the principal boons in his own person, whereas the secondary ones, i.e., those involving riddance
from ills, are bestowed by his Angels and Words; cf. also *Fug.*
67; *Conf.* 181. For the Logos as God's ὄργανον in creating the
world, cf. *LA* 3.96; *Mig.* 6. Here, Philo is concerned primarily
with freeing God from all direct activity upon the world, so
such distinctions are not to his purpose.

58   φωτὶ χρώμενος ἑαυτῷ. A curious notion. God "sees,"
but not with eyes as instruments, and using as "light," in
place of the sun, which is necessary for physical seeing, himself. Perhaps the Sun Simile of *Rep.* VI is an influence here.
The Good there, the intelligible archetype of the sun, would,
in the Middle Platonic tradition, as Philo would have known it,
be identified with God himself.

59   ἀποπαύεται. Some mss. (MAHP) read ἀποπατεῖ, and this
was accepted by Wendland. It is certainly more in accord with
diatribe style, and is tempting, but (a) there is the following
παυσάμενος, which sounds as if it picks up ἀποπαύεται, the
simple form of the verb picking up the compound, a good stylistic flourish; and (b) the notion of excretion seems to be covered more tactfully by Philo with the phrase τἄλλα ὅσα τούτοις

ἀκόλουθα οὐκ ἂν εἴποιμι. But if Philo did not write ἀποπατεῖ,
it is interesting that some lively-minded scribe should have
substituted it for the rather tame ἀποπαύεται.

   ἀνθρωπόμορφον . . . ἀνθρωποπαθές. The former of these
compounds is attested first in Epicur. *Frag.* 353 (cf. Hecataeus
of Abdera, ap. Diod. 40.3.4); the latter seems to be a coinage
of Philo himself. He makes the contrast again at *Sacr.* 95. Cf.
also *Post.* 4: ἀκολουθεῖ δ᾽ ἐξ ἀνάγκης τῷ ἀνθρωπομόρφῳ τὸ ἀνθρωποπαθές, *SVF* 2.1021, 1076; Cicero *ND* 2.70.

60   Ξιφηφοροῦντα γὰρ <εἰσάγει> κ.τ.λ. Ξιφηφορέω first
attested in Philo (though adj. ξιφηφόρος in Aeschylus and
Euripides). (Wendland's addition of εἰσάγει seems necessary.)
Cf. Exod 15:3; Deut 32:23, 41-42; Gen 19:24; Ps 104:4-7; II Sam
22:13-16.

   φθοροποιῷ πυρί. Presumably a reference here to Sodom
and Gomorrah. φθοροποιός first attested in Philo, but also in
[Plut.] *Plac.* 5.911A: φθοροποιὸν γὰρ ἑκατέρου μοναρχία, where
the doctrine of Alcmaeon is being given.

   καταιγίδα καὶ κεραυνόν. Interpreting accounts of divine
warlike activity as descriptions of natural phenomena is a type
of exegesis that goes back at least to the fifth century (e.g.
Socrates' explanation of Boreas' rape of Oreithyia at the beginning of the *Phaedrus*), and was popular with Stoic commentators
on Homer (cf. Heraclitus, *All. Hom.* 6-8, the explanation of
Apollo's sending of the plague on the Achaeans in *Iliad* I).
Philo, however, is not here saying that Moses is indulging in
the same sort of allegorizing; Moses is simply concerned, in
using this sort of language, to produce a salutary effect in the
minds of the duller-witted or corrupted hearers (cf. 63).

   ἀνθρωπολογῶν. Verb first attested in Philo, though adj.
ἀνθρωπόλογος in Aristotle, *EN* 4.3.31.1125a. Cf. *Sacr.* 94; *Conf.*
135.

61   πάντας ὠφελῆσαι τοὺς ἐντυγχάνοντας. The notion that the
aim of a good lawgiver should be to benefit all those who come
in contact with his laws, by so framing them that they are comprehensible on some level by even the meanest intelligence, does
not seem to occur elsewhere in so many words. This sentiment
serves here as an introduction to the doctrine of various levels

of understanding of scripture, a doctrine also developed at
Somn. 1.191.

εὐμοίρου φύσεως . . . καὶ ἀγωγῆς . . . ἀνυπαιτίου. A
reference to at least the first two of the three components
declared, in the Platonist-Aristotelian tradition, to be necessary to the attainment of perfect virtue, φύσις, ἄσκησις and
μάθησις. This goes back at least to Protagoras (80 B 3, DK:
"φύσεως καὶ ἀσκήσεως διδασκαλία δεῖται"), is alluded to by Plato
at the beginning of the *Meno* (70A), and is formalized by Aristotle (*EN* 10.9.1179b 20 ff.; *Pol*. 8.13.1332a 40; *EE* 1.1.1214a16
ff. Cf. Diog. Laert. 5.18); it turns up in the Pythagorica
(e.g. "Archytas" *De Educ.* 3, p. 41, 20 ff. Thesleff), and is
found in Albinus *Did.* ch. 28. Philo knows the formulation well,
cf. *Abr.* 52-54.

The adjective ἀνυπαίτιος is not found before Philo.

ὁδὸν τοῦ βίου λεωφόρον καὶ εὐθεῖαν εὑρίσκοντες. The
figure of life as a road is common in Philo. Cf. *LA* 3.253;
Post. 31, 102, 154; *Deus* 143, 165, 182; etc. As usual, Philo
elaborates his image. Truth becomes a fellow-traveller (συν-
οδοίπορος), in the form of a goddess, who initiates one into
the mysteries of True Being. Mystery imagery thus obtrudes
itself, for a judicious discussion of which see Nikiprowetzky,
CEP pp. 17-28.

παρ' ἧς μυηθέντες. Truth here performs the role of
δᾳδοῦχος, and of hierophant. Cf. *Ebr.* 168, where παιδεία plays
the same role as ἀλήθεια does here. In *Her.* 311, it is God who
is the δᾳδοῦχος.

προσαναπλάττουσιν. This compound first attested in
Philo. Also, "Longinus," 7.1. The sense of the verb seems to
be "to attribute imaginary qualities to," cf. *Post.* 3; *Sacr.* 96;
Dec. 54, 74.

62   ἀλλ' οὐδ' ὡς οὐρανὸς οὐδ' ὡς κόσμος. No doubt, as
Colson suggests (App. p. 485), aimed at least partly at the
Stoics, who held the cosmos and/or the heavens to be the οὐσία
θεοῦ (*SVF* 1.164). Here, however, what seems at issue is God's
form. For the unknowability of God, cf. *Mut.* 7; *Spec.* 1.20; *QE*
2.45.

ὕπαρξις. ὑπάρχειν/ὕπαρξις as term for God's mode of
existence has its roots in the Stoic distinction, taken up by

the Neoplatonists, between ὑπάρχειν and εἶναι. Cf. Arist. *Cael.* 297b22; *Met.* 1045b10; *SVF* 2.65.

63   νωθεστέρᾳ μὲν καὶ ἀμβλείᾳ . . . τῇ φύσει. Cf. *Somn.* 1.237, which also employs the passages Num 23:19 and Deut 8:5.

περὶ δὲ τὰς ἐν παισὶ τροφὰς πλημμεληθέντες. Perhaps a reference to the Stoic concept of διαστροφή or κατήχησις, wrong instruction acquired in childhood that stands in the way of the attainment of wisdom (*SVF* 3.228-236). Cf. Plato, *Tim.* 87B, and *Rep.* II 377A-383C, where fables and myths are linked to the education received in infancy from the mouths of mothers and nurses.

ἰατρῶν . . . νουθετητῶν. νουθετητής first attested in Philo. Here in fact it is an emendation of Wendland's, for νομοθετῶν, but a convincing one, cf. *Her.* 77; *Flac.* 15; *Legat.* 53. Introduction of medical parallel, to be developed in 65-68.

64   ἐπεὶ καὶ . . . ὠφέλιμος. Introduction of doctrine of φόβος as proper guide for the foolish, to be picked up in 69. The notion of the advantage for a foolish slave of having a stern master seems to owe something to the doctrine of Plato's *Gorgias* (479B). Philo expresses this thought again at *Conf.* 165, and *Prob.* 57, with reference to Esau's enslavement to Jacob. The concept of the Noble Lie is also introduced, with τὰ ψευδῆ, δι᾽ ὧν ὠφεληθήσονται.

ἐπανάτασις. First attested in this sense in Philo. The idea is that of a stick raised and stretched out against someone (= ἀπειλή). Cf. *Deus* 167; *Conf.* 165; *Somn.* 2.7, 96.

οἱ δοκιμώτατοι τῶν ἰατρῶν. Mss. read νομιμώτατοι, which gives a difficult sense (perhaps "legitimate"?). But Mangey's emendation is persuasive, unless we render νομιμώτατοι, "the most truly concerned with legality." This, however, is rather strained.

65   τἀληθῆ λαλεῖν οὐχ ὑπομένουσιν. Cf. *Cher.* 15. The same notion is expressed by Plato in *Rep.* 389B. Cf. *SVF* 3.554-55; 2.132.

καὶ [οὐ] ῥωσθησομένην τὴν νόσον. Cohn seems right to suppress οὐ. Otherwise ῥώννυμι would have to mean "get better," instead of "become stronger," which is the proper meaning,

contrasting with λωφῆσον below. Diseases, properly speaking,
do not "get better"; people do (but cf. *Jos*. 110, where λιμός
is described as ῥωσθεῖσα). It is undeniable that someone took
ῥωσθησομένην in this sense, and added οὐ. Colson keeps οὐ,
translating "and will bring no recovery from the malady," but
this rather glosses over the problem, surely.

66   τλητικῶς. Adverb first attested in Philo.

        ἄσμενος. Slight textual problem here. Mss. read ἄσμενος
ἐκ δέ, which connects ἄσμενος with ἀπερεῖ, giving a difficult
sense, "will be glad to decline the treatment (?)." Colson proposes transposing δε to before ἐκ, giving an easier sense.
Wendland proposed moving ἄσμενος to line 15, but that is more
complicated.

67   τῶν τῆς ψυχῆς παθῶν καὶ νοσημάτων ἄριστος ἰατρός. For
the concept of Moses, or the philosopher in general, as Doctor
of Souls in Philo, cf. *Decal*. 12; *Mos*. 1.42. Here the notion
of removing the diseases of the soul αὐταῖς ῥίζαις is Stoic
rather than Peripatetic. Cf. *LA* 3.129-31, an exegesis of Lev
8:29.

        βλαστὴν ἀρρωστήματος . . . δυσιάτου. ἀρρώστημα here,
as above in 65, is no doubt used by way of *variatio* for νόσος,
but it is also worth noting that ἀρρώστημα is a technical term
in Stoicism for the imperfection that attends all but philosophers, cf. Cic. *Tusc*. 4.10.

68   ἀμυντηρίοις ὅπλοις. Perhaps *vox Platonica* here, and at
Somn. 1.235, cf. Plato *Laws* 944D: τὴν τῶν ἀμυντηρίων ὅπλων
δύναμιν. The context in Plato concerns the proper punishment
of army deserters, but Plato has said just above: τὸν γὰρ κακὸν
ἀεὶ δεῖ κολάζειν, ἵν' ἀμείνων ᾖ, οὐ τὸν δυστυχῆ, which may have
attracted Philo's attention to the passage (cf. *Decal*. 178,
where the question of punishing λιποτάκται also arises).

69   ἢ πρὸς τὸ ἀγαπᾶν ἢ πρὸς τὸ φοβεῖσθαι. Cf. *Somn*. 1.237,
where, however, the contrast between Love and Fear is not explicitly made, but rather between τὸ ἀληθές and τὸ λυσιτελές.

        τὸν ὄντα. Note use of masculine here, as opposed to
neuter elsewhere in the passage (including περὶ τὸ ὄν just

below). God is here thought of as having relationship to Man,
and this makes the masculine more suitable.

VII

Deus 70-85

Commentary on Gen 6:7: ὅτι ἐθυμώθην, ὅτι ἐποίησα
αὐτούς (Heb. "for I regret that I made them").

A. *General Comments*

Philo now finally comes to grips with the biblical words
which have caused grave difficulties to most Jewish commentators,
who were hard put to reconcile God's eternal and unchanging
nature with the very human attribute of a sudden change of mind
or heart. Through a type of mental acrobatics to which he had
become accustomed in the course of his long struggle to reinter-
pret Scripture in accordance with the principles of Platonism,
Philo boldly transforms the simple meaning of the biblical
verse. He suggests that perhaps the intent of the verse is to
indicate that the wicked are so through God's wrath i.e.,
through the wrath that comes from God, and the righteous by his
grace, since the next words are "but Noah found grace with Him"
(Gen 6:8). He then squeezes out of the fact that the word-order
is "I was wroth in that I made them," rather than the reverse,
"because I made them, I was wroth," the notion that these words
are only a figure to convey the meaning that it was through wrath
that God made or caused their blameworthy actions. Scripture's
meaning, then, is that those human actions which result from any
of the four primary passions or their derivatives are blameworthy, whereas those which are the product of right reason are
worthy of praise.[1]

---

[1]Cf. the rather more straightforward exegesis of *QG* 1.95,
where the possibilities of juggling the ὅτι clause have not yet
occurred to Philo. For similar deductions from word-order, see
LA 2.78; *Mig.* 140; *Conf.* 103. Bréhier (p. 151) sees a possible
connection here with Philo's assignment of the creation of the
sublunary world of growth and decay to God's Regent Power, whereas
the aetherial world is assigned to his Creative Power (*QG* 4.8).

Having thus rendered innocuous a most troublesome set
of words, Philo proceeds to the statement that Noah had found
grace with God, and finds in it a pointed teaching concerning
God's saving mercy.[2] Were the divine judgment not tempered by
mercy, we should find, he says, that the human race could not
endure, since sin is unavoidable. In this connection, he makes
use of Psalm 100 (101):1: "I will sing of pity and of judgment,"
in which he sees a statement of God's mixture of these two elements in his administration of the human race. This leads into
a discussion of the nature of God's powers, which, according to
Philo, are unmixed in respect of God himself, but mixed to
created beings. He here brings in Ps 74 (75):9: "a drinking
cup in the hand of the Lord, of unmixed wine full of mixture,"
where he bases his exegesis on giving full weight to the apparent contradiction between ἀκράτου and κεράσματος (see note ad
loc.). Man is incapable of looking even upon the sun's flame
untempered, much less upon the unmixed splendor of God's potencies, though the diluted draught he does receive should prove to
be an ample source of joy. The same notion, continues Philo,
may be extracted from Ps 61 (62):12: "One thing God has spoken;
two things have I heard."[3] "One" refers to the unmixed, which
is a monad, whereas "twice" is like the mixed, since it admits
both combination and separation. God thus speaks in unmixed
monads or unities, for his work constitutes a naked disembodied
unity, whereas man's hearing is a product of two factors, i.e.,
pneuma in concussion with air (and the consonance of a high and
low pitch). In conclusion, Philo remarks that Moses did well to
oppose to the multitude of unjust thoughts the single just man
(Gen 6:8), since the righteous few more than counterbalance the
wicked many.

---

[2]This leads him away from the topic of God's "anger" and
immutability, a topic to which he does not, in fact, return. It
is notable, thus, that only the sections 20-72 justify the title
of the treatise, ὅτι ἄτρεπτον τὸ θεῖον.

[3]It is noteworthy that Philo quotes from the Psalms
three times in the course of this section (74, 77, 82), and
bases his exegesis in large part on these quotations. Such a
concentration seems to be matched only at *Somn.* 2.242-46, where
he passes from Ps 36 (37):4 to 64 (65):10 to 45 (46):5.

B. *Detailed Commentary*

70   ἐπανιτέον . . . σκέψιν. Philo here indicates that he is
returning to the question originally raised in 52, "how is anger
predicable of God?" The section from 52 to 69 has been a preliminary discussion.

ἐθυμώθην ὅτι ἐποίησα αὐτούς. Although some rabbis take
God's regret literally, others connect Heb. *niḥamti* with *neḥamā*,
"consolation." Cf. *BR* 27.6, T-A 258: "R. Judah said: [God
said] 'I regret that I created him from the elements below, for
had I created him from those above, he would not have rebelled
against me.' R. Nehemiah said: 'There is some consolation in
my having created man from the elements below, for had I created
him from those above, then just as he had caused those below to
rebel against me, so would he have done with those above.'" It
is noticeable that in the rejected hypothetical order of the
clauses, Philo uses διότι (= "because"), whereas in the Biblical
order he uses ὅτι. He presumably wants to take ὅτι *not* as meaning "because" (i.e. the divine anger *caused by* having made man),
but in the sense "as is proved or shown by the fact that." Cf.
LSJ s.v. ὅτι, B2. διότι is not normally used in this sense;
hence Philo's use of it in the re-ordered phrase which he rejects.

ὅτι οἱ μὲν φαῦλοι θυμῷ γεγόνασι θεοῦ, οἱ δ' ἀγαθοὶ χάριτι.
In the Jewish Wisdom literature it is similarly assumed that not
all men are capable of obtaining wisdom, that some men are wise
and others foolish (Prov 1:7, 32, 22; 9:7; 14:6; 17:16). Ben
Sira, for example, spells out God's polar plan of creation which
provides for two antithetical categories of people: "Likewise
also all men are made from the clay, and Adam was created of
earth. In his great wisdom God distinguished them, and differ-
entiated their ways. Some he blessed and exalted, and others he
hallowed and brought nigh to himself. Some he cursed and abased,
and overthrew them from their place. As clay is in the power of
the potter, to fashion it according to his good pleasure; so is
man in the power of his creator, to make him according to his
ordinance. Over against evil stands the good, and against death
life; likewise over against the godly the sinner. Even thus
look upon all the works of God, each different, one the opposite
of the other" (Sir 33:10-15). See D. Winston, *The Wisdom of
Solomon* (N.Y., 1979) 48-49.

71   κυριολογούμενον. First attested in Philo. Cf. *Sacr.*
101; *Det.* 58; *Post.* 7, 168; *Somn.* 2.245; *Abr.* 120; *Mos.* 1.75.
(κυριολογία in Philodemus *Rhet.* 1.1745, "Longinus," 28.1.)
τροπικός in sense of "figurative" not attested before the rhetoricians of the first century B.C.E., Dionysius of Halicarnassus, Philodemus and "Longinus." Philo uses the term frequently, e.g. *LA* 2.14 and *Jos.* 125 (ἡ τροπικὴ ἀπόδοσις, opposed
to ῥητῇ), *LA* 1.45 (τροπικῶς εἴρηται); *Det.* 167 (τροπικώτερον καὶ
δι' ὑπονοιῶν). At *Post.* 53 ff. it is used interchangeably with
συμβολικῶς. At *Conf.* 190, à propos the Tower of Babel (Gen
11:7), we find the term used in the context of a (respectful)
criticism of literal interpreters: ταῦτα μὲν ἡμεῖς· οἱ δὲ
τοῖς ἐμφανέσι, καὶ προχείροις μόνον ἐπακολουθοῦντες οἴονται
νυνὶ γένεσιν διαλέκτων 'Ελληνικῶν τε καὶ βαρβάρων ὑπογράφεσθαι·
οὓς οὐκ ἄν αἰτιασάμενος--ἴσως γὰρ ἀληθεῖ καὶ αὐτοὶ χρῶνται λόγῳ--
παρακαλέσαιμ' ἄν μὴ ἐπὶ τούτων στῆναι, μετελθεῖν δὲ ἐπὶ τὰς
τροπικὰς ἀποδόσεις, νομίσαντας τὰ μὲν ῥητὰ τῶν χρησμῶν σκιάς
τινας ὡσανεὶ σωμάτων εἶναι, τὰς δ' ἐμφαινομένας δυνάμεις τὰ
ὑφεστῶτα ἀληθείᾳ πράγματα. Nowhere else does it seem to be
used in conjunction with κυριολογεῖν.

     εὐθυβόλως. Adverb first attested in Philo. Cf. *Cher.*
1: κυρίως καὶ εὐθυβόλως; *Det.* 22; *Flac.* 132; *Spec.* 4.51; *Mig.*
79. There is some uncertainty among the translators as to how
this is to be taken, but it seems best to understand: "the
term 'anger' . . . is *accurately* applied in a metaphorical sense
to the Existent." εὐθυβόλως does not go comfortably in close
connection with κυριολογούμενον.

     δι' ὀργήν. ὀργή in Stoic ethical theory is a species
of ἐπιθυμία, and is defined as a desire for revenge against
someone who appears to have wronged us (*SVF* 3.394-98). For the
four primary passions, see *SVF* 3.391-93.

     ἐπίληπτος. In sense of "culpable," first attested in
Philo.

72   προφορά. Hellenistic term, attested in Philodemus,
Rhet. 1.159.5, Dionysius Thrax, *On Grammar* 2, D.H. *Dem.* 22.

     κατ' ἀναστροφήν. In sense of "inversion of natural
order," first attested in Apollonius Dyscolus, *Synt.* 71.18;
cf. Athenaeus, *Deipn.* 11.493d; Lieberman, *Hellenism*: 65-67.
The verb ἀναστρέφω ("invert order of words or statements" and
equivalent to Hebrew s̄ar̄ēs) is found in Demetr. *Eloc.* 11.

προφυλακή. In sense of "caution," first in Philo. Cf. *Mos*. 2.145; *Decal*. 98; *Spec*. 3.166; 4.104, 196. Also Plut. *Soll. An*. 978A.

"ὅτι ἐθυμώθην, ὅτι ἐποίησα αὐτούς" εἰπών. The first ὅτι, as Colson remarks, may either introduce the quotation or be a part of it, but the former seems more likely, in view of the form of the quotation in 70.

μετανοοῦντος. Cf. *Aet*. 40, where he calls μετάνοια, πάθος καὶ νόσημα ψυχῆς.

τὰ πάντα προμηθουμένη θεοῦ φύσις. Cf. *LA* 3.88; Seneca, *Ben*. 4.32.

συνεκτικώτατον. In the sense of "most essential" first attested in Philo. Cf. *Op*. 8, 101, 162; *LA* 1.59; 3.5, 145; *Cher*. 88, etc.

πηγὴ μὲν ἁμαρτημάτων θυμός. In Stoic usage, θυμός refers specifically to the πάθη or irrational emotions. For the distinction between καθήκοντα and κατορθώματα, see *SVF* 3.516-17. Cf. Cic. *Off*. 1.3.8; 3.3.14; *LA* 1.56.

73   τὴν δεξιὰν καὶ σωτήριον χεῖρα ὀρέγων. Cf. *Sifre Numbers Pinḥas* 134, where it is said that God's "right hand," representing the attribute of mercy which is extended to all, is also called "the mighty hand," inasmuch as it has to repress the attribute of strict justice.

74   ἀνακεράσηται. Thus is introduced the theme of "mixture" which occupies the rest of the passage, to 85.

"ἔλεον καὶ κρίσιν ἄσομαι σοι". Ps 100 (101):1. Philo quotes accurately here, though reading ἔλεον for ἔλεος with the Codex Alexandrinus, which is the Classical form.

75   μηδενὸς ἀνθρώπων . . . ἄπταιστον. Cf. *Mos*. 2.147: παντὶ γενητῷ . . . συμφυὲς τὸ ἁμαρτάνειν ἐστίν. Even Noah's justice, we may note, is a relative thing. Without God's mercy, he too would perish.

ὀλισθήμασιν. In moral sense first attested in Philo and found only in this passage. For life as "one long slipping," cf. *Mut*. 55-56, 185. Cf. Plut. *Mor*. 49C.

εἰδικῶν. εἰδικός really seems to mean "individual"
here. Cf. note on 95.

76   βύθια. First attested in Philo. Cf. *Det.* 15, 100;
Post. 153; *Somn.* 1.122; *Mos.* 1.175; *Spec.* 3.6; *Legat.* 357. Also
Plut. *Crass.* 23. Some suggestion of the Flood seems present
here.

τὸν ἔλεον ἀνακίρνησιν. On God's mercy, cf. *Sacr.* 42;
Spec. 1.308; *Praem.* 163; Ps 103:7-13; 78:38; Jonah 3:8; 4:3;
Sir 17:29; 18:11-14; Wisd 11:23-26; 12:16-21; Test.Abr. A.10;
BT R.H. 17b; Ber. 7a; *M.Q.* 16b; *PT Peah* 1.1; 16b. R. Berechiah
[Amora of the 4th cent.] presents a similar view concerning
God's tempering his judgment with mercy: "When the Holy One,
blessed be He, came to create the first man, He foresaw that
righteous and wicked persons would descend from him. He said:
'If I create him, wicked people will descend from him; if I do
not create him, how shall righteous people issue from him?'
What did the Holy One, blessed be He, do? He removed the way
of the wicked from before him; made the attribute of compassion
a partner in His action, and created man." A Scriptural basis
for the idea of this partnership is to be found in the wording
of the verse, 'In the day that Y. Elohim made heaven and earth.'
The juxtaposition of the two Names was expounded by an anonymous
homilist, under the influence of R. Samuel bar Naḥmani, as
follows: "It is like the case of a king who had empty cups.
The king thought: If I put hot water in them, they will crack;
cold water, they will become warped. What did the king do? He
mixed hot with cold water and put it in them, and they remained
undamaged. Even so the Holy One, blessed be He, argued: 'If
I create the world with the attribute of compassion, there will
be many sinners; if I do so with the attribute of justice, the
world will not endure. Therefore I shall create it with both
the attribute of justice and the attribute of compassion, and
may it endure!'--(this is the meaning of) 'Y. Elohim.'" (*BR*
8.4 T-A 59; 12.15, T-A 112.) (Cf. *Tos. Sotah* 4.1.) See Urbach,
The Sages: 458-60.

πρεσβύτερος γὰρ δίκης ὁ ἔλεος. Cf. *QE* 2.62; *Deus* 108.
In the *Yom Kippur* liturgy we read: "He is merciful, and His
mercy precedes His anger." (From an acrostic poem ascribed to
Yannai, ca. 6th cent.) This statement is based on Exod 34:6,
where we are first told that God is compassionate and only later
that 'he does not remit all punishment.'

77   οἴνου ἀκράτου. Quotation from Ps 74 (75):9. Heb. reads
yayin ḥāmar, "foaming wine." Philo bases his exegesis on the
apparent contradiction in the LXX between ἀκράτου and πλῆρες
κεράσματος, deriving from this the doctrine that qualities or
powers present in God in a pure or "unmixed" state can only be
received or comprehended by us in a "mixed" state.

    ταῖς δυνάμεσι πρὸς μὲν ἑαυτὸν ἀκράτοις χρῆται. For the
notion that God's powers are unmixed, cf. *Op.* 20, 71; *Cher.* 29;
Mut. 184.

78   ἄκρατον μὲν τὴν ἡλίου φλόγα μὴ δύνασθαι θεαθῆναι. Cf.
Op. 71; *Abr.* 76; *Somn.* 1.239; *Fug.* 165; *Spec.* 1.40. The imagery
derives probably from Plato *Rep.* VII 515C ff. and *Laws* 897D.
The same notion is found in *Sib.Or.*, Frag. 1.10-14: "For what
flesh can see visibly the heavenly and true God, the Immortal,
whose abode is the heaven? Nay, not even face to face with the
sun's rays are men able to stand, being mortal, mere veins and
flesh wedded to bones." Cf. *BT Ḥul.* 59b; *Bemid.R.* 14.3; Clem.
Alex. *Protr.* 6.71; Xen. *Mem.* 4.3.14; Ps.-Xenoph. *ap.* Stob. 2
p. 15,5 Wachsmuth. See Festugière, *RHT* 4.13-14.

    ταῖς δυνάμεσι . . . ἀκράτοις . . . κεκραμέναις. Cf.
Proclus, *Elements* 150: "Any processive term in the divine
orders is incapable of receiving all the potencies of its pro-
ducer, as are secondary principles in general of receiving all
the potencies of their priors; the prior principles possess
certain powers which transcend their inferiors and are incomprehensible to subsequent grades of deity."

    ἀμυδρωθεῖσα. See comment. on *Deus* 3.

    πίλημα. First attested in Philo, but obviously a school
definition. Cf. [Arist.] *De Mundo* 394b2; *Placit.* 2.13.7; *SVF*
2.668; Ps.-Justin, *Quaest. et Resp. ad Graecos* 172c (ὁ ἥλιος
πίλημα αἰθεροειδὲς τῇ οὐσίᾳ); *Cher.* 26; *Somn.* 1.22, 145.

79   τὸ σφοδρὸν τῆς ἐν αὐταῖς θερμότητος ἀνεὶς καὶ χαλάσας.
We find a similar idea in *BR* 6.17, T-A: 47: "R. Joshua said
in the name of R. Bon: 'Then the heavens proclaimed His righ-
teousness' (Ps 50:6), in the days to come the heavens will tell
of the kindness which the Holy One, blessed be He, showed to his
world in not placing the luminaries in the first heaven, for had
He done so, no creature could have endured the day's heat." Cf.
16, "'nothing escapes his heat' (Ps 19:7), the sun has a covering;

whence do we know this, 'he placed in them a tent for the sun'
(Ps 19:5), and there is a pool of water before it; when it goes
forth, the Holy One, blessed be He, diminishes its strength by
means of the water, so that it should not go forth and consume
the world."

τῷ ταμιευομένῳ ἐν ταῖς ὄψεσι συγγενεῖ αὐτοῦ καὶ φίλῳ
ὑπαντιάσαν ἀσπάσηται. A clear echo of *Tim.* 45BC: "For they
caused the pure fire within us, which is akin (ἀδελφὸν ὄν) to
that of day, to flow through the eyes . . . so whenever the
stream of vision is surrounded by mid-day light, it flows out
like unto like, and coalescing therewith it forms one kindred
substance along the path of the eye's vision." Philo adopts
here the Platonic theory of vision, which was also that of the
Stoics, cf. *SVF* 2.863-71.

δεξίωσις. First attested in Philo. Cf. *Her.* 40; *Mos.*
1.275. Also Plut. *Lives* 256B, 655B, 708F, etc.

τίς ἂν ἀκραιφνῆ δέξασθαι δύναιτο θνητὸς ὤν. For the
notion that even God's benefits cannot be received by man in
their fulness, cf. *Op.* 23; *Post.* 143, 145; *LA* 3.163; *Mut.* 218.

Ἀλλ' οὐδ' ὁ σύμπας οὐρανός τε καὶ κόσμος. Cf. *Post.*
144.

81   μεσότητας ἔχοντος. The contrast here between μεσότητες
and ἀκρότητες below is interesting, in view of the common Middle
Platonic doctrine (Plut. *Virt. Mor.* 444D ff.; Albinus, *Did.* p.
184,12 ff.) deriving from a remark of Aristotle's in the *EN*
(1107a23), that the virtues are both μεσότητες and ἀκρότητες.
Philo here seems to be playing upon this theme, adapting it to
his own purposes.

82   "ἅπαξ κύριος ἐλάλησε". Ps 61 (62):12, LXX text: ἅπαξ
ἐλάλησεν ὁ θεός. Mss UF of Philo read μίαν ἐλάλησεν ὁ θεός, δύο
ταύτην ἠκούσαμεν. Such "corrections" are quite characteristic
of this family of mss. See Intro. p. 89.

τὸ δὲ δὶς τῷ κεκραμένῳ. For the impurity of the dyad,
cf. *QG* 2.12.

83   μονάδας μὲν οὖν ἀκράτους ὁ θεὸς λαλεῖ. Cf. *Gig.* 52;
Mig. 52 (derived from *Tim.* 67B; cf. *Tim. Locr.* 101A).

γεγωνὸς ἀέρος πλῆξις. This sounds very like a school
definition of speech, though it is not attested elsewhere before
Philo, cf. *LA* 3.183. The definition seems to be known to Plutarch, *De E* 390B, *Def. Or.* 436D, and, though doubtless Stoic,
goes back in substance to *Tim.* 67B. Cf. [Plut.] *Plac.* 4, 16.
γεγωνὸς λόγος (a phrase not found elsewhere except for Plot.
5.1.6.9) is frequently used by Philo as the equivalent of προ-
φορικὸς λόγος. Cf. *Mos.* 2.127; *LA* 3.41; *Det.* 38; *Fug.* 92; etc.
See Rist, *Plotinus*: 100-101.

ἀδιαφορῶν. First attested in Philo. Cf. *Agr.* 27;
Plant. 136.

84   τὸ γὰρ ἀφ' ἡγεμονικοῦ πνεῦμα. For the Stoic theory of
hearing see D.L. 7.158 (*SVF* 2.872): "We hear when the air
between the sonant body and the organ of hearing suffers concussion (πληττόμενον). Cf. *SVF* 2.836.

τὸ γὰρ συνηχοῦν. The γὰρ presumably picks up ἁρμονίως.
The blending of high and low tones is the second way in which
human speech is "dyadic." Cf. *Tim.* 80B: μίαν ἐξ ὀξείας καὶ
βαρείας ξυνεκεράσαντο πάθην.

85   ἀριθμῷ μὲν ἐλάττονα, δυνάμει δὲ πλείονα. It is a basic
principle of Neoplatonism that entities further down the scale
of being are greater in number than their priors, but inferior
in power. Philo seems here to show acquaintance with an earlier
form of this scholastic formula. Cf. Proclus, *Elements* 62:
"Every multiplicity which is nearer to the One has fewer members
than those more remote, but is greater in power"; Plot. 2.9.6.29,
6.7.8. Here, of course, there is no question of a hierarchy of
being. Philo is simply contrasting the one just man with the
many unjust, and saying that his power for good outweighs theirs
for evil. Cf. *Mig.* 120-26, where Abraham is portrayed as single-
handedly saving his environment.

VIII

Deus 86-121

Commentary on Gen 6:8-9: Νῶε δὲ εὖρεν χάριν ἐναντίον
κυρίου τοῦ θεοῦ. αὗται δὲ αἱ γενέσεις Νῶε· Νῶε ἄνθρωπος δίκαιος, τέλειος ὢν ἐν τῇ γενεᾷ αὐτοῦ· τῷ θεῷ εὐηρέστησε Νῶε.

A. *General Comments*

Philo now turns to the next verse in Genesis, "Noah
found grace before the Lord God," the interpretation of which
he has in fact anticipated in the previous section (73 ff.),
where Noah is presented as the paradigm of the ἀγαθοί, who exist
according to the χάρις, or saving grace, of God, as opposed to
the φαῦλοι, who exist according to his θυμός. In 86, however,
Philo turns first to a discussion of the concept of εὕρεσις,
provoked by the word εὗρε in the lemma. He begins with a scholastic distinction, possibly borrowed from some Hellenistic
source,[1] which may have been stimulated by Plato's frequent use
of ἀνευρίσκω in contexts associated with reminiscence (e.g.
Phaedr. 252E, *Meno* 74A, *Soph.* 253E), between εὕρεσις, "discovery,"
and ἀνεύρεσις, "rediscovery." Of the former activity, he then
declares, the Great Vow of the Nazirite, as described in Num 6,
provides an excellent illustration.

His allegorical exegesis of the Nazirite Vow (87-91)
concentrates on two aspects of it, the allowing of the hair to
grow long, and the pollution, and consequent cancellation, of
the Vow, occasioned by sudden death in one's vicinity. (These
are the aspects, we may note, to which he confines himself also
on the other occasions on which he deals with the Vow, *LA* 1.17,
Agr. 175-76, *Fug.* 115.) The Vow is seen as the highest form of
prayer, which consists in recognizing God as the sole author of
all good things, indeed of all existence, not even granting the
status of assistants in production to all the other apparent
causal agents in the world. (For this form of contemplative
prayer, cf. *Fug.* 92; *Gig.* 52; *Plant.* 126; *Mig.* 12; *Spec.* 1.272;
Ebr. 194; Plot. 5.1.6.8-11. See also Rist, *Plotinus* 211-12;
R. T. Wallis, "Nous as Experience," in *The Significance of*

---

[1]Cf. such Stoic neologisms as ἀφορμή (as opp. of ὁρμή),
ἀποπροηγμένον, or εὐπάθεια (as opp. to πάθος). The distinction
between εὕρεσις and ἀνεύρεσις seems not to be made elsewhere in
so many words. [See also on this Supplementary Note 4, p. 71].

Neoplatonism 121-53). The growing of the hair symbolizes the
fostering of the virtues in the mind; the pollution from con-
tiguity to sudden death represents the sudden falls from grace
which may afflict anyone in a state of *prokopē*, and kill the
sprouts of the virtues.

What this leads on to (91-98) is the reflection that
God's grace can make the attainment of virtue and happiness easy,
like the unexpected finding of a treasure. Jacob, the ἀσκητής,
is brought in as an illustration of this, with special reference
to Gen 27:20. This example leads to a contrast between the easy
success of those with natural aptitudes and the fruitless
struggles of those who are "sluggish and slow of soul," the
assumption being that natural aptitude *is* a grace from God.

We may compare with this contrast of these two types
the more elaborate four-way distinction which Philo makes at
Fug. 120-77, where he enters upon a full discussion of Moses'
doctrine on Finding and Seeking (εὕρεσις καὶ ζήτησις). There
are four classes of person: (1) those who neither seek nor
find; (2) those who both seek and find; (3) those who seek but
do not find; (4) those who find without having to seek. It is
these two latter classes that are being distinguished in this
passage. Particularly instructive is a comparison of 93-96 with
Fug. 166-77, where the fourth class is being discussed, since
Philo uses the same texts and examples in both places. First,
at *Fug.* 169, we have Jacob's reply to Isaac in Gen 27:20 (where
it is plain, as it is not here [see note ad loc.], that both are
aspects of the same person, the naturally-gifted individual).
Then, at *Fug.* 175-76, we find the passage of Deut 6:10-11, containing the promises of God to the Israelites, where the exegesis is the same as here, except that at *Fug.* 176 the λάκκοι
and αἱ εὐφυεῖς ψυχαί, who are ready to receive wisdom, while
here they are rather τὰ χωρὶς τῶν πόνων τούτοις πρόχειρα ἆθλα,
the intellectual prizes awaiting such souls.

Philo is not, however, it seems, really concerned to
indulge in heartless mockery of his less gifted associates. It
becomes plain from the next passage (99-103), which is an exegesis of Deut 1:43-44 (in particular the phrase παραβιασάμενοί
τινες ἀνέβησαν εἰς τὸ ὄρος), that the dullards whom he is crit-
icizing are really those who are unregenerate at heart, not
submitting their wills to God, but honoring him in externals
only, and doing violence to their evil inclinations in order to

maintain an appearance of piety. This might seem a reasonably
commendable alternative to *not* doing violence to one's evil
inclinations, but it is not good enough for Philo. He charac-
terizes it as δεισιδαιμονία (103), an interesting further example
of the uses he finds for this concept (cf. note on *Gig.* 16).

        All this, then, has been paving the way for the discus-
sion of what it means for Noah to "find grace" with God. Only
those of pure mind are in a state to "find" and benefit from
the goods that God bestows.

        Continuing his analysis of Gen 6:8, Philo goes on,
first (104-8), to suggest various interpretations of the words
"Noah found grace with the Lord God." (Contrast the far less
sophisticated treatment of the lemma at *QG* 1.96.) That Noah
merely obtained grace seems unreasonable to Philo, since, in his
view, all creatures are recipients of divine grace, but the
explanation that Noah was thought worthy of grace, inasmuch as
he did not "deface with base practices the divinely stamped coin
of his intellect," is not much better, since, strictly speaking,
no one is truly worthy of God's grace. A more likely explanation is that Noah came to the realization that all things are
the grace or gift of God, χάρις being taken in the sense of
"free gift." God's creation of the world is thus a gift of his
goodness (cf. the parallel discussion in *LA* 3.77-78), and elsewhere Philo designates one pole of the Divine Logos as ἀγαθότης or ποιητικὴ δύναμις. Philo proceeds (109-10) to point out
that Noah, according to Gen 6:8, LXX, was pleasing to the Lord
and to God, that is, to the Divine Powers, whereas Moses, and
those of his company, are pleasing to God himself (this conclusion being drawn from a comparison with Exod 33:17: εὕρηκας
χάριν παρ' ἐμοί). Elsewhere in the corpus, Philo makes similar
distinctions between the type of mind that attains to a knowledge of God through his works, and one that achieves a direct
intuition of him (the "sons of heaven" and "the sons of God" of
Gig. 60). In *Abr.* 119-23 we are told that to the mind as yet
uninitiated into the highest mysteries and still unable to apprehend the Existent alone by itself, but only through its actions,
God appears as a triad constituted by himself and his two potencies, the creative and the regent. Elsewhere he speaks of those
who apprehend God through his works as advancing from lower to
higher levels by a sort of heavenly ladder and conjecturing his
existence through plausible inference (εἰκότι λογισμῷ) (*Praem.*

40-46). The latter are liable to take God's image, the Logos,
not as a copy but as the original form of God himself (*Somn.*
1.232, 238, 66, 117, 148; *Mig.* 174; *Conf.* 145-46).

Philo now (111-16) contrasts with Noah and Moses the
mind which loves the body and the passions and is enslaved by
Pleasure, chief cateress of our compound nature, utilizing for
this purpose the casting of Joseph into prison in Gen 39, in a
rather perverse interpretation (Joseph is represented as a
eunuch himself, and the fact that it was the Lord who gave him
favor with the jailer [39:21] is disregarded). Brimming with
all manner of impiety, possessors of the Joseph-mind are in the
true sense of the word prisoners, and are deluded into serving
as the courtiers and deputies of their prison warden, Lord Vice.
However, it is better for them to endure the lot of prisoner,
and through suffering find mercy, than to be prison-keepers, a
seemingly pleasant task, but in reality an unending thraldom.
Philo concludes with an exhortation to the soul to shun evil
and seek to be pleasing to God, though if that be impossible
then at least to his Powers, as did Noah.

Here (117-21) Philo turns to the exegesis of Gen 6:9,
to which he gives a curious interpretation, made possible by
disregarding 6:10, in which Noah's offspring, Shem, Ham and
Japheth, are actually mentioned. For Philo, the "generations
of Noah" consist in his being a man, just, perfect, and well-
pleasing to God, the perfect products of a perfect mind, a sort
of quartet of virtues, presided over by τὸ θεῷ εὐαρεστῆσαι as a
supreme virtue, and the sum of them making up εὐδαιμονία, in the
Stoic manner. The concept of generation then leads him to make
a distinction between the normal sense of γένεσις, something
coming to be (something) out of nothing, and what one might call
the Platonic sense of γένεσις, which consists in the change
from a higher genus to the lower species, which is referred to
by Moses when he says, "But these are the generations of Jacob.
Joseph was seventeen years old, keeping sheep with his brethren,
being still young, with the sons of Bilhah and with the sons of
Zelpah, his father's wives" (Gen 37:2). When Jacob's mind
abandoned the divine heights and sank into the realm of mortal-
ity, then at once Joseph was born, symbol of bodily things. The
treatment of Joseph in this passage is in accord with Philo's
general low estimation of him (cf. *Mig.* 158-59; *Conf.* 72; *Somn.*
2.10-16, etc.). Only in the *De Josepho* is this estimation

reversed (apart from an isolated positive treatment at *LA* 3.237).
No doubt it is Joseph's connection with Egypt (the body) which
drags him down in Philo's estimation (see Colson's Gen. Intro.
to Vol. VI, pp. xii-xiii; note on Joseph, Vol X [by J. W. Earp],
and Goodenough, *The Politics of Philo Judaeus* chap. 3).

B. *Detailed Commentary*

86   συνεπισκεψώμεθα. Characteristic exegetical exhortation,
deriving from Plato (*Crat.* 422C; *Hipp. Maj.* 296B); cf. *Cher.* 91;
Post. 32; *Sacr.* 24.

       οἱ ζητητικοὶ τῶν κυρίων ὀνομάτων. One thinks originally
of such a man as Prodicus, but Philo must be referring to more
recent authorities. This class of person is also alluded to at
Det. 76, as being the experts on the question whether ἀνθρωπότης
is to be termed a γένος, an ἰδέα, or an ἐννόημα (he himself, he
implies, would regard these terms as equivalent). At *Conf.* 5,
we find οἱ ζητητικοὶ τῶν φιλοσόφων being in agreement that the
earth is the central point of the universe. Now Diogenes
Laertius (9.69) gives ζητητικοί as one name for the Sceptics,
but that seems hardly possible here. The term seems rather to
apply to someone of Posidonius' range of interests, covering
both grammar and astronomy. R. Pfeiffer writes: "Aristotle
had apparently drawn up a list of 'difficulties' of interpretation in Homer with their respective 'solutions;' this custom of
ζητήματα προβάλλειν may have prospered at the symposia of intellectual circles . . . Although certain circles of the Alexandrian Museum seem to have adopted this 'method' of ζητήματα,
which amused Ptolemaic kings and Roman emperors, as it had
amused Athenian symposiasts, the great and serious grammarians
disliked it as a more or less frivolous game. It was mainly
continued by the philosophic schools, Peripatetics, Stoics,
Neoplatonists, and by amateurs, until Porphyry arranged his
final collection of Ὁμηρικὰ ζητήματα in the grand style, in
which he very probably still used Aristotle's original work"
(*History of Classical Scholarship* [Oxford 1968] 69-70; 263).
Lieberman has pointed out that some copies of the Hexapla translate *midrash* (in II Chron 13:22) ἐκζήτησις, inquiry, which is
the exact equivalent of the rabbinic use of that word. "Ezra
has set his heart to inquire into the Law of the Lord" (Ezra
7:10). The Hebrew *lidrōš* is correctly translated by LXX:
ζητῆσαι. Didymus the grammarian (2nd half of 1st cent. B.C.E.

and begin. of 1st cent. C.E.) likes to introduce his disquisitions with ζητεῖται, διὰ τί, etc., and the ζητήματα constituted
a notable part of the philologic, the philosophic and the juridic
literature. (See Lieberman, *Hellenism* 48.) Cf. Demetrius (earliest known Greco-Jewish writer; lived during the reign of
Ptolemy IV [221-204 B.C.E.]): ἐπιζητεῖν δέ τινα πῶς οἱ Ἰσραη-
λῖται ὅπλα ἔσχον ἄνοπλοι ἐξελθόντες· (*FPG* 179).

87   εὐχή . . . αἴτησις ἀγαθῶν παρὰ θεοῦ. A Platonic definition, based on *Laws* VII 801A: εὐχαὶ παρὰ θεῶν αἰτήσεις εἰσι, it
being added immediately afterwards that one should be sure that
one is asking for an ἀγαθόν. Cf. *Agr.* 99; *Sacr.* 53.

μηδενὸς ἑτέρου . . . συνεργοῦντος. It seems better to
excise the τῶν before εἰς τὸ δοκεῖν ὠφελεῖν, as τὰ εἰς τὸ δοκεῖν
ὠφελεῖν, meaning, presumably, "those things which are generally
thought to be useful" is very strange Greek.

μεγάλη δὲ εὐχή. This is derived from LXX version of
Num 6:2: ὃς ἐὰν μεγάλως εὔξηται εὐχήν, where μεγάλως (εὔξηται)
is the LXX rendering of *yaplî* (*lindor*), meaning "make an extra-
ordinary, special vow," but interpretable as "great." Cf. *Somn.*
1.252-53, where the special feature of the nazirite vow is
declared to be that one gives to God not only one's offering,
but oneself as well.

καρπότοκος. First attested in Philo, who uses it both
in a literal sense (as here), and metaphorically (e.g. of ἀρετή,
LA 1.49).

μὴ ἰατρικῆς ὡς ὑγείας. Cf. *Spec.* 1.252.

μεταβολὰς . . . καὶ τροπάς. A frequent collocution in
Philo, cf. *LA* 1.8; *Cher.* 88; *Det.* 87; *Ebr.* 91; etc.

89   αἰφνίδιον. At *LA* 1.17 and *Agr.* 175-76, Philo actually
quotes αἰφνίδιον for ἐξάπινα at Num 6:9, though he quotes correctly at *Fug.* 115. ἐξάπινα is a vulgar form, so that we seem
to have here an instance of Philo, when quoting from memory,
unobtrusively "correcting" the LXX idiom.

οἷά τινος τυφῶνος. A variant of the storm-at-sea image
(cf. *Agr.* 174, also dealing with the Nazirite Vow). Here again,
as in *Deus* 27 (see note ad loc.), Philo seems to recognize
the irrational in human nature in a manner which gives the
appearance of being alien to Greek philosophical thought, but

which may in fact exempt the Sage from this liability. The
sudden fall from grace seems to be unmotivated, and can happen
to the best of us, assuming we are still προκόπτοντες. τροπή
is a favorite word of Philo's for this propensity of the human
soul to vacillate, cf. *LA* 2.83; *Det.* 122; *Mut.* 250; etc. For
the concept of sudden changes of purpose, cf. *Somn.* 2.145-49,
and see A. Bonhöffer, *Die Ethik des Stoikers Epiktet* (Stuttgart
1894) 148-49.

90   καὶ ἅπερ ἀπέβαλεν εὑρίσκει. From the context, one
would expect this to be an example of ἀνεύρεσις rather than of
εὕρεσις. Philo must be thinking of the necessity of starting
again from the beginning; and yet the verb ἀναμιμνῄσκεται just
above makes this solution difficult to accept.

τὰς προτέρας τῆς τροπῆς ἡμέρας ἀλόγους. As Colson
points out (ad loc.), the context here (and at *LA* 1.17, where
Philo also deals with the Vow of the Nazirite) requires that he
take προτέρας . . . ἡμέρας as "the former days of the defection," not as "the days before the defection," as the LXX
intended. Also, he toys with the idea that ἀλόγους may somehow
mean παραλόγους, or "repugnant to reason," leaving the decision
as between this interpretation and taking ἀλόγους as "out of
account," as the LXX surely intends, up to the reader.

"οὐ λόγος οὐδ' ἀριθμός". Mosès and Colson quote Theocritus, *Idyll* 14.48: ἄμμες δ' οὔτε λόγω τινος ἄξιοι οὔτ' ἀριθματοί,
but this is only to be regarded as proof that both Theocritus
and Philo are acquainted with the common Greek proverbial expression, arising, it seems, from an oracle delivered by Delphi to
Megara (or to Aegium in Achaea), cf. Plut. *Symp.* V 7, 682F;
Parke and Wormell, *The Delphic Oracle* II p. 1; and Leutsch and
Schneidewin, *Paroemiogr. Graec.* I 19.

91   ὥσπερ γεωπόνον φασί τινες. This is a stock school
example of a chance or accidental (ἀπὸ τύχης, κατὰ συμβεβηκός)
happening, deriving from Arist. *EN* III 3, 1112a27, and *Met.* 30,
1025a14: οἷον εἴ τις ὀρύττων φυτῷ βόθρον εὗρε θησαυρόν. It is
the normal example in later treatments of the topic of fate and
free will, e.g. Ps.-Plut. *De Fato* 572A: οἷον τὸ εὑρεῖν χρυσίον
σκάπτοντα ἵνα φυτεύσῃ, which is verbally closer to Philo.

92   πυθομένου τοῦ πατρὸς αὐτοῦ τῆς ἐπιστήμης. The commentators have been much exercised over the syntax of τῆς ἐπιστήμης.
πυνθάνομαι should not take a genitive of the object of enquiry.
Mosès presumes a περί to have been omitted. Colson would prefer
to take it with πατρός and translate "the father of his knowledge." Colson is surely correct. The comparison with *Somn.*
1.47, where Abraham is described as ὁ πάππος αὐτοῦ τῆς ἐπιστήμης, in the sense of his "intellectual grandfather," seems deci-
sive.

93   οἱ τὰ ὄμματα πεπηρωμένοι. This may be a reference to
the men of Sodom, who are given at *Fug.* 144 as an example of
those who seek without finding. They are τυφλοὶ διάνοιαν, and
are unable to find the door.

      φύσεως εὐμοιρίᾳ. Except for one use in Dionysius of
Halicarnassus (*Ars Rhetorica* 5.3)--if this work is genuine (cf.
George Kennedy, *The Art of Rhetoric in the Roman World* [Prince-
ton, 1972] 634-36)--the noun εὐμοιρία is first found in Philo.
He makes frequent use of the present phrase in discussions of
εὐφυία, e.g. *Post.* 71; *Sobr.* 223; *Congr.* 37; *Mut.* 2. Cf. Ps.-
Plut. *Lib. Ed.* 14C.

      εὐθυβόλῳ καὶ εὐθίκτῳ . . . προσβολῇ. For the collocu-
tion, cf. *Post.* 80. The noun εὐθιξία, found first in Philo, is
identified by him as a component of εὐφυία, along with ἐπιμονή
and μνήμη, at *LA* 1.55; *Cher.* 102; and *Somn.* 2.37, in a way which
suggests some scholastic source.

      τὴν . . . ἀκριβεστάτην . . . κατάληψιν. Note the Stoic
term. In this conceit, objects actually thrust themselves upon
the senses of the natural "finder" and impose κατάληψις upon him.

95   πόλεις μὲν οὖν καὶ οἰκίας. In this distinction of genera
and species of virtues Philo will presumably have in mind some
such distinction as that which Diogenes Laertius attributes to
the Stoics (7.92). Philo on various occasions makes the distinction between εἰδικαί and γενικαί ἀρεταί, e.g., *Ebr.* 138;
Fug. 176, but he never seems to give a list of εἰδικαί ἀρεταί.
On many occasions he speaks of the four generic virtues as εἰδικαί, as opposed to Virtue in General (e.g. *LA* 1.63-65), but that
does not count.

      εἰδικός, as a term opposed to γενικός, is Hellenistic,
being first found in Dionysius Thrax. If we consider certain

passages similar to the present one, such as *Cher.* 7 or *Mut.*
77-80 (where Sarah's change of name is being discussed), we
find εἰδικὴ ἀρετή and εἶδος described as φθαρτόν, seeming to
indicate that εἶδος is understood either as "form immanent in
matter" (necessarily, of an individual body), or simply "individual." This is an interesting complication in the use of the
word.

96   οὐρανίων καὶ ποτίμων δεξαμεναὶ ναμάτων. The association
of the idea of cisterns with that of the sweet water of the
virtues is perhaps provoked by the figurative usage of the
adjective πότιμος which depends on Plato (*Phaedrus* 243D) and
often in Philo (e.g. *LA* 2.32; 3.12; *Post.* 129).

98   ὥσπερ . . . ἐνθαλαττεύουσαι. Storm-at-sea imagery
again. ἐνθαλαττεύω and ὑπόδρομος first attested in Philo, in
Greek prose.

99   "παραβιασάμενοι . . . ἕως Ἑρμᾶ". This translates the
Hebrew *watāzidû*, and seems to mean simply "acting wilfully."
Philo gives full weight to the concept of βία which he discerns
here, as can be observed from his exegesis. Those who try to
force themselves to acquire the arts for which they are not apt
are doomed to failure and disgrace, as also are those who perform moral duties, and divine worship, without sincerity (ἀσυγ-
καταθέτῳ γνώμῃ).

100   πρὸς τοῦ συνειδότος. Philo is the first on record to
use τὸ συνειδός as a term for conscience. He uses it very frequently, e.g. *Deus* 128; *Det.* 23; *Fug.* 159; *Jos.* 47-48; *Spec.*
3.54, often in conjunction with the verb ἐλέγχω. It is hard to
believe that he invented this term, but evidence to the contrary
is lacking. (Cf. article on σύνοιδα in Arndt-Gingrich, Gk-Eng.
Lex. to NT pp. 798-99.) See Intro., p. 207, and A. Pelletier,
"Deux Expressions de la Notion de Conscience," *RÉG* 80 (1967)
363-71.

101   τοὺς τὰς ὀλιγοχρημάτους παρακαταθήκας ἀποδιδόντας.
ὀλιγοχρήματος is found only in Philo, but the example he gives
here goes back at least to Aristotle (*EN* V 8, 1135b3 ff., itself
a variation of Plato's example at *Rep.* 331C-332B; cf. Cic. *Fin.*
3.59). He gives the example again at *Plant.* 103; *Cher.* 14; and

Spec. 4.67. It sounds like a stock school example of an honest act performed for dishonest motives. Cf. also *Decal.* 172: τὸ μὴ ποιεῖσθαι προκάλυμμα πίστιν ἀπιστίας.

κατακεντούμενοι. In metaphorical sense, first attested in Philo, cf. *Deus* 183; *Mut.* 203. Philo likes to use this verb to express feelings of dissatisfaction with oneself, cf. *Decal.* 87: κεντῶν καὶ τιτρώσκων.

ἐπὶ σκηνῆς ἱεροπρεπεστάτην . . . προαίρεσιν. Mangey's reading, ἱεροπρεπεστάτην, agreeing with προαίρεσιν βίου, gives much better sense than ἱεροπρεπεστάτης of mss., adopted by Cohn-Wendland.

102   βωμολοχίαν. Philo uses this term again, at *Spec.* 1.319, to characterize the initiation ceremonies of mystery religions, which he declares to be forbidden to followers of Moses. A certain degree of ritual buffoonery was associated with some mysteries, notably the procession to Eleusis and the rites at the Theban Kabeirion.

ἐπιμορφάζειν. Attested only in Philo, but used by him frequently.

103   ἐπισκιασθέντες διὰ τῶν δεισιδαιμονίας συμβόλων. ἐπισκιάζω in a metaphorical sense is first attested in Philo (more Classical authors seem to have used ἐπισκοτέω). For Philo's concept of δεισιδαιμονία, cf. note on *Gig.* 16.

ἢ †κόλασις μέν ἐστιν ὁσιότητος. Mss. read κόλασις, "chastisement," which seems to make little sense. Benzel reads κώλυσις, which is accepted by Colson. Cohn and Wendland, followed by Moses, read κόλουσις, "curtailing," which is rather more elegant. However, Philo does not use this noun elsewhere, though he uses κολούειν at *Post.* 150.

ὥσπερ οἱ ξενίας ἁλόντες. Details of laws concerning citizenship in Alexandria are not abundant. The best source for the various types of legal status in Alexandria and Egypt is *The Gnomon of the Idiologus* (Select Papyri II 206, Berlin Pap. 1.210). Cf. also the edict of the Prefect Tiberius Julius Alexander (Philo's nephew) in Evelyn-White and Oliver, *The Temple of Hibis in the El Khargeh Oasis*, II. *Greek Inscriptions*, 4. These sources are discussed and translated in A. D. Johnson, *Roman Egypt* (vol. II of the *Economic Survey of Ancient Rome,*

Baltimore 1936, pp. 280 ff. (manumissions), and 711 ff. (*Gnomon
of the Idiologus*). This might be a contemporary reference by
Philo, or an historical one. παρεγγράφω is a technical term for
enrolling oneself illegally as a citizen, cf. Aeschines 2.76;
Lucian, *Bis Accus.* 27. As a leader of the Jewish community,
Philo would be much concerned with claims to citizenship.

τὸ γὰρ βίαιον ὀλιγοχρόνιον. The etymology of βίαιος as
βαιός is very much in the spirit of the *Cratylus* (and of later
Hellenistic etymologizing), but seems to occur nowhere else.

104   στοιχειώδεις ἁπλαῖ φύσεις. Contrast of στοιχεῖα, the
four elements, with συγκρίματα is Stoic in formulation (e.g.
SVF 2.310, 323).

105   νόμισμα. Cf. *LA* 3.95; *Det.* 152: "change, if you can,
the moulding and stamp of the divine coinage"; *Plant.* 18: "Our
great Moses averred it [the reasonable soul] to be a genuine
coinage of that dread spirit and Invisible One, signed and
impressed by the seal of God, the stamp of which is the Eternal
Logos"; *Det.* 86. The metaphor is already found in Plato's
Phaedo 69A: ἀλλ᾽ ἦ ἐκεῖνο μόνον τὸ νόμισμα ὀρθόν . . . φρόνη-
σις. The Cynic slogan παραχαράττειν τὸ νόμισμα was well-known
(cf. DL 6.20, on Diogenes). Cf. F. W. Kohnke, "Das Bild der
echten Münze bei Philon von Alexandreia," *Hermes* 96 (1968) 583-
90.

106   πρῶτον καὶ μέγιστον καὶ τελεώτατον τῶν θείων ἔργων
ἐστὶν οὗτος. A Platonic notion. Cf. *Tim.* 37C; Plot. 2.9.8.16:
"How should one not call it a clear and noble image of the
intelligible gods?" A similar sentiment is expressed in *BR*
12.1: "R. Isaac b. Maryon said, 'Such is the story of heaven
and earth as they were created' (Gen 2:4): their Creator praised
them, who, then, will deprecate them, their Creator lauds them,
who will find fault with them, but they are lovely and praiseworthy."

μήποτ᾽ οὖν ἄμεινον. A characteristic formula for introducing one's preferred solution to an *aporia*, e.g. *LA* 1.90;
2.80; 3.60; etc. Cf. Proclus, *In Tim.* 1.65.9, 153.28, 230.18,
etc. The implication here that the two previous interpretations of χάριν εὗρε are incorrect is more uncompromising than
the exegesis at *LA* 3.77-78.

107   χάριν ὄντα θεοῦ τὰ πάντα. Cf. *LA* 3.78: χάριν ὄντα τοῦ
θεοῦ τὰ σύμπαντα . . . τοῖς γοῦν ζητοῦσι, τίς ἀρχὴ γενέσεως,
ὀρθότατα ἄν τις ἀποκρίνοιτο, ὅτι ἀγαθότης καὶ χάρις τοῦ θεοῦ.
It should be noted that in *BR* 29.2, T-A 269, R. Simon deduces
from the wording in Gen 6:8 that it was Noah who found grace,
not the Holy One, blessed be He, i.e., Noah was not really
worthy in God's eyes, but in comparison with his contemporaries
he nevertheless found grace. Similarly, in *Midrash Mishle* 31,
we read: "'Grace is deceitful and beauty is vain' (Prov 31:30),
Noah's grace was false, for it is said, 'But Noah found favor
with the Lord.'"

        κεχάρισται δὲ ὁ θεὸς αὐτῷ μὲν οὐδέν--οὐδὲ γὰρ δεῖται.
The same idea is clearly expressed in Plot. 6.9.6.40: ἀλλ'
ἔστιν ὑπεράγαθον καὶ αὐτὸ οὐκ ἑαυτῷ τοῖς δὲ ἄλλοις ἀγαθόν;
6.9.6.34: ἀρχὴ δὲ οὐκ ἐνδεὲς τῶν μετ' αὐτό· ἡ δ' ἀπάντων
ἀρχὴ ἀνενδεὲς ἁπάντων.

108   ἀπιδὼν εἰς τὴν ἀΐδιον ἀγαθότητα. Perhaps an adaptation
of the Demiurge's looking to the Paradigm, cf. *Tim.* 28A.

        ἡ τοῦ ὄντος ἀγαθότης. The idea is derived from Plato's
Timaeus 29E: ἀγαθὸς ἦν, ἀγαθῷ δὲ οὐδεὶς περὶ οὐδενὸς οὐδέποτε
ἐγγίγνεται φθόνος. Cf. also *Op.* 21; *LA* 3.78; *Cher.* 127.

        πρεσβυτάτη τῶν * * * χαρίτων οὖσα ἑαυτῇ. Wendland
restores the text as follows: πρεσβυτάτη <θεοῦ δυνάμεων, τῶν>
χαρίτων οὖσα πηγή. Colson and Whittaker, on the other hand,
prefer to read: πρεσβυτάτη τῶν <χαρίτων, πηγή> χαρίτων οὖσα
αὐτή, believing that "the scribe is more likely to have been
misled by the repeated χαρίτων than by the repeated τῶν and that
αὐτή is a less violent change from ἑαυτῇ than πηγή." Perhaps,
in view of the question to which this is the answer, τίς αἰτία
γενέσεως κόσμου; <αἰτιῶν> might be a more suitable supplement.

109   τὸν μὲν Νῶέ φησιν εὐαρεστῆσαι. Here there is no question, we may note, of denying the natural meaning of εὐαρεστῆσαι, that Noah was well pleasing to God.

        δορυφορουμένῳ. This is a favorite word of Philo's to
describe the relationship of God to his powers, or to his angels,
cf. *Abr.* 122; *Spec.* 1.45; *Sac.* 59; *Legat.* 6; *QE* 2.67.

110   δι' ἑαυτοῦ μόνου. Cf. comment. on *Gig.* 45.

τὴν δὲ ἀπεικονισθεῖσαν ἐκ ταύτης δευτέραν καὶ εἰδικω-
τέραν οὖσαν. An analogous contrast between levels of wisdom is
set up by R. Avin's statement in *BR* 44.12 that the Torah is an
incomplete form (*nōbelet*), i.e., only an image, of the supernal
Wisdom. The combination of εἰδικωτέρα with the notion of secondary and image-like is remarkable. It should only mean "more
specific," as above, 95.

111   φιλοσώματος καὶ φιλοπαθὴς νοῦς. Cf. the allegory in *LA*
3.236; *Ebr.* 210 ff.; *Mut.* 173; *Jos.* 61 ff. For the sake of his
allegory, Philo has transferred the characteristics of the
eunuch Potiphar to Joseph. See Gen 39.

     ἀρχιμαγείρῳ. Cf. LXX, Gen 39:1.

     τοῦ συγκρίματος ἡμῶν. Cf. 117 below; *LA* 2.2; 3.191;
Sacr. 49, 105; *Det.* 52: "for if we hold in honor the mind as
father of our complex being, and sense as mother, we ourselves
shall receive good treatment at their hands. Now honor is shown
to the mind when it is cared for by the provision not of things
that give it pleasure but of things that do it good"; ib. 84,
103, 139; *Post.* 58, 68; *Gig.* 62; *Fug.* 164; *Mut.* 184. For σύγκριμα in the sense of the compound of body and soul, cf. *SVF*
1.45.

     ἐξευνουχισθείς. First attested in Philo. Cf. Plut.
Sympos. 692C; *Ebr.* 211-13: "For such a soul [ἐξευνουχισμένης
ψυχῆς] is neither able to drop the truly masculine seeds of
virtue nor yet to receive and foster what is so dropped . . .
None such does Moses permit to enter the congregation of God,
for he says, 'He who has lost the organs of generation shall not
come into the congregation of the Lord' (Deut 23:1). For what
use can he find in listening to holy words, who can beget no
offspring of wisdom . . ." At *LA* 3.237, however, after a disquisition on the eunuch-soul, it is suggested that there is a
favorable meaning for "eunuch," as ἐγκρατὴς τρόπος ψυχῆς.

112   δεσμῶται. Cf. *Ebr.* 101; *LA* 3.42; *Mig.* 9: "Depart,
therefore, out of the earthly matter that encompasses thee:
escape, man, from the foul prison-house (δεσμωτήριον), thy body,
with all thy might and main, and from the pleasures and lusts
that act as its jailers"; *Her.* 85, 109; *Mut.* 173; *Somn.* 1.139.
The exegesis of Joseph in prison enables Philo to draw upon the

Platonic image of this mortal existence as the prison-house of
the soul (e.g. *Phaed.* 114B; *Rep.* VII 517B).

συμφόρημα. First attested in Philo. Cf. *Sacr.* 108;
Somn. 1.220; Plut. *De Prim. Frig.* 955A. The word is practically
synonymous with σύγκριμα.

ἀφροσύνης καὶ ἀκολασίας καὶ δειλίας καὶ ἀδικίας. Cf.
Op. 73.

113   ὁ ἡγεμὼν τοῦ δεσμωτηρίου. It seems rash to speak, as
Mosès does, of "cette figure satanique." It is not necessary
that Philo is involved in anything more than a lively personification here.

114   ὦ ψυχή. For this diatribe-style apostrophe, so beloved
of Philo, cf. *LA* 1.49, 51; 2.91, 106; 3.17.

115   ἀγκιστρευθῆς. First attested in Philo. Used in literal
sense only at *Plant.* 102. Otherwise, *Op.* 166; *Sacr.* 21; *Agr.*
24; etc. Cf. Aristaenet. 1.5.

σπουδαρχίαις. First attested, and only once, in Philo.
Cf. Plut. *Aem.* 38.

λιμοδοξίαις. Found only in Philo, and only here. λιμο-
δοξέω in *Spec.* 2.18; *Flac.* 116. Cf. δοξομανής and δοξομανέω in
Fug. 30 and *Somn.* 2.114.

116   ἐὰν δ' ἄρα ἀδυνατῆς. "The man who is capable of running
swiftly it bids stay not to draw breath but pass forward to the
supreme Divine Logos, who is the fountain of Wisdom, in order
that he may draw from the stream and, released from death, gain
life eternal as his prize. One less swift-footed it directs to
the power to which Moses gives the name God, since by it the
Universe was established and ordered. It urges him to flee for
refuge to the creative power, knowing that to one who has grasped
the fact that the whole world was brought into being a vast good
accrues, even the knowledge of its Maker, which straightway wins
the thing created to love him to whom it owes its being. One
who is less ready it urges to betake himself to the kingly power,
for fear of the sovereign has a force of correction to admonish
the subject, where a father's kindness has none such for the
child. For him who fails to reach the posts just mentioned,

because he thinks them too far distant, another set of goals
have been set up nearer the starting-point--the gracious power,
the power which enjoins duties, and that which forbids offences
. . ." (*Somn.* 1.232, 238, 66, 117, 148; *Mig.* 174; *Conf.* 145-46).
At *Abr.* 124-30 also this theory of different modes of relationship to the Supreme Being is developed at length. It is a distinctive feature of Philo's metaphysics.

οὗ τῶν ἐγγόνων θαυμαστότατον καὶ καινότατον πεποίηται
τὸν κατάλογον. Cf. *Abr.* 31: "a sage has no house or kinsfolk
or country save virtues and virtuous actions; 'for these,' he
says, 'are the generations of Noah.'" Philo chooses, perhaps,
to misunderstand the admittedly curious sentence-structure of
the LXX (following the Hebrew), and takes the γενέσεις of Noah
to be the qualities that are attributed to him in the rest of
the sentence. Shem, Ham and Japheth he omits altogether (as he
does at *QG* 1.97), as unsuitable to his exegesis (Ham, at least,
as is evident from his treatment of him elsewhere, would be
entirely unsuitable, as he represents ἠρεμοῦσα κακία [*Sobr.* 44]).

117   ἵπποι γὰρ ἵππους . . . ὁμοίως δὲ καὶ ἄνθρωποι ἀνθρώπους.
(Cf. Lucret. 1.160 ff.) This is a basic Aristotelian principle,
e.g. *De An.* II 4, 415a25 ff.; *Phys.* II 1, 193b8.

118   τὸ ἄνθρωπον εἶναι, τὸ δίκαιον εἶναι. Cf. *Abr.* 32-33.

119   καὶ ὁδός τίς ἐστιν ἐκ τοῦ μὴ ὄντος εἰς τὸ εἶναι--ταύτῃ
φυτά τε καὶ ζῷα ἐξ ἀνάγκης ἀεὶ χρῆσθαι πέφυκεν. Cf. *Spec.* 2.225:
καὶ τὰ μὴ ὄντα εἰς τὸ εἶναι παρήγαγον; Plato, *Soph.* 265BC. Basic
Aristotelian doctrine, cf. *Phys.* I 7. For the notion of μὴ ὄν
as representing relative non-being, cf. D. Winston, *Philo of
Alexandria* (N.Y., 1981) 7-13.

ὢν νέος. Cf. *BR* 84.7: "Joseph was seventeen years old
and you say he is a lad [New JPS translation renders 'helper']?
rather he performed acts of youth, beautifying his eyes, fixing
his hair, walking mincingly."

νέος ὢν ἔτι, κἂν μήκει χρόνου πόλιος γένηται. For this
widespread literary motif, cf. Wisd 4:8; Men. Frag. 639K; Cic.
Tusc. 1.45; Sen. *Ep.* 93.2; Virg. *Aen.* 9.311; *Cont.* 67; *Abr.* 271;
Fug. 146; *Her.* 290; *Sobr.* 7 ff.; *Plant.* 68; *Legat.* 1, 142. There
is also an ancient Indian parallel. According to Manu (2.150 ff.),

the young Brahmin Kawi instructed his paternal uncles in sacred
learning, addressing them as sons. Angered, they complained to
the gods, who gave the following answer: "The lad addressed you
rightly, for the unknowing is a child . . . not because he is
white-headed is a man old; he who has read the scripture, even
though he be young, him the gods account old." See E. R.
Curtius, *European Literature and the Latin Middle Ages* (New York
1953) 98-101.

Μωυσέως θιασῶται. θιασώτης, with its rather Bacchic
overtones, often has in Philo a derogatory connotation, e.g.
Somn. 2.78: ὅσοι θιασῶται τῆς κενῆς δόξης εἰσίν; *Det.* 45:
Ἠσαῦ τοῦ κακίας θιασώτου (as opposed to τὸν ἀρετῆς ἀσκητὴν
Ἰακώβ), but by no means always, cf. *Cher.* 85; *Sacr.* 7. The
phrase recurs at *Plant.* 39: ὁ τοῦ Μωυσέως δὴ θιασώτης.

οἱ παλλακίδων ὄντες. For Philo, the wives of the patriarchs are their virtues, while their concubines are producers of
illegitimate spiritual offspring, i.e. passions. Cf. *Congr.* 36:
δούλαις καὶ παλλακαῖς συμβιῶναι τέχναις, νόθων δογμάτων οἷα
παίδων ὀρεχθέντα, and *Gig.* 17.

Βαλλᾶς καὶ Ζελφᾶς. Elsewhere, Bilhah is etymologized as
"swallowing" and represents the necessary subsistence of the
natural life (*LA* 1.94-96; 3.146; *Congr.* 29 f.), and Zilpah as
"walking mouth," signifying oratorical power (*Congr.* 24), cf.
Earp's notes s.v. in Loeb Vol. X. Consorting with the sons of
Bilhah and Zilpah, then, is quite natural for a πολιτικός.

IX

Deus 122-139

        Commentary on Gen 6:11: ἐφθάρη ἡ γῆ ἐναντίον τοῦ θεοῦ
καὶ ἐπλήσθη ἀδικίας.
        Textual variants: ἐφθάρη δέ LXX; ἐπλήσθη ἡ γῆ LXX.

A. *General Comments*
        This section, one of the most important in the work,
arises from an *aporia* occasioned by the admittedly rather abrupt

transition from mention of the virtue and the offspring of
Noah to the statement that "the earth was corrupt before God
and filled with injustice." Philo affects, at least, to understand that the appearance of Noah on the scene somehow makes
the earth corrupt and unjust, and naturally wonders how this
can be. For him it is one of those situations where a surface
contradiction constitutes a sure sign that the true meaning lies
beneath. The application of his exegetical method readily
reveals that this is so, and the lemma in fact occasions a pro-
tracted and important discussion of the nature of Conscience
(see further R. T. Wallis' essay in the Introduction).

        The doctrine which Philo derives from this passage is
that the arrival on the scene of an immortal and divine element,
either in the world or in each one of us, causes that element in
us which is "mortal" and ungodly suddenly to appear corrupt and
sinful, whereas it did not seem so before the arrival of something to provide a contrast with it. What is being contrasted
here in fact is what later theology would term "the age of
reason" in the soul with "the age of innocence." If the passage
is considered in this way, it becomes logical that the arrival
of Noah on the earth should, not *cause* it to be corrupt, but
rather reveal its intrinsic corruption.

        To reinforce this point, Philo, as usual, adduces
parallel passages. First he directs our attention to the
so-called Law of Leprosy, in Lev 13:14-15. Here too there is
a paradoxical situation presented, which becomes logical on the
application of his principles. How can it be, first of all,
that leprosy covering the whole of the body is "clean," whereas
that which appears only in patches is "unclean"; and secondly,
how does it come about that the entrance of the priest into the
house of one so afflicted (Lev 14:34-36) makes all in the house
unclean?

        In each case here there is in fact a perfectly good
literal explanation, had Philo been concerned to seek for it
("leprosy over the whole body" is not leprosy at all, but a
relatively harmless skin rash; and in the second passage he
ignores the true purport of the regulation); but he seizes
gladly on what appears a paradox, as being a sign of a higher
level of meaning. In either case, the key element in the interpretation is the fact that there is a point of reference according to which the uncleanness can be judged--in the case of

partial leprosy, the patches of clear skin; in the case of the
visitation of the house, the priest.

Of these two, the priest lends himself more readily to
further allegorizing, and perhaps in the process to some confusion. In 134, the priest is identified with ὁ θεῖος λόγος,
which enters into the soul, and before the entry of which the
soul is not capable of good or evil action, as having no point
of reference. This λόγος, on entry, becomes the ἔλεγχος, the
conscience. It seems thus to have both a transcendent and an
immanent aspect, which is perhaps what Philo wishes it to have.
However, this seems to raise the problem of the relation of the
rational element in the individual soul to the omnipresent Logos
of God. Is it simply an aspect of it in a particular body, or
is it a separate entity? Or should any such distinction be
made? The problem is analogous to, if not the same as, that
with Aristotle's νοῦς πρακτικός of *De An.* III 5.

A third parallel passage is now adduced, the encounter
of the widow woman in Zarephath with the prophet Elijah (I Kings
17:8 ff.), to which is subjoined a reference to the widowhood
of Tamar in her father's house, in Gen 38:11. "Widowhood" is
here interpreted as "widowhood from the passions which corrupt
and maltreat the mind," this being a necessary preliminary (in
the case of Tamar, at least) to receiving θεία γονή (137), in
the shape of the Logos, and being filled with the seeds of
virtue, which result in the production of καλαὶ πράξεις.

The adducing of Tamar here is rather in the nature of a
footnote to the main point which the I Kings passage was brought
in to illustrate. That is that when the Logos enters a suitably
prepared soul, it provokes within it a new consciousness of its
past inadequacies and a firm purpose of amendment. Here the
transcendent aspect is certainly in the ascendent, the force of
conscience being described (138) as ὁ ἑρμηνεὺς τοῦ θεοῦ λόγος
καὶ προφήτης, but we are still talking about the individual
conscience.

B. *Detailed Comments*

122   Ζητήσαι δ' ἄν τις. Common formula for introducing a
problem, or ζήτημα, cf. *LA* 1.33, 48; 2.103; etc., and above,
122. The λύσις follows just below. Cf. note on *Deus* 86.

123   ἐπειδὰν . . . τὸ ἄφθαρτον εἶδος ἀνατείλῃ. The "incorruptible element" in the soul here is Noah, whose appearance
causes the earth (the rest of the soul) to appear corrupt. The
use of ἀνατέλλω suggests that light-imagery which recurs at
various points in the passage, beginning just below with φωτὸς
ἐπιλάμψαντος.

     "ἐὰν ἀνατείλῃ χρὼς ζῶν". It is plain from Philo's para-
phrase below, "ζῶν ἐν ψυχῇ χρῶμα," that he takes χρὼς here as
meaning "color" rather than "flesh," another instance of his
imperfect understanding of LXX language, which is a translation
of bāśar ḥay.

124   προσεπισφίγγων . . . καὶ ὥσπερ ἐναποσημαινόμενος. Both
verbs first found in Philo, and only here.

126   ὀνειδίζων καὶ δυσωπῶν καὶ ἐπιπλήττων. Characteristic
rhetorical triadic construction, cf. Decal. 87, and Intro. p.
141.

128   διὰ συμβόλων τούτων. Cf. Deus 96 and 154 for other
instances in the present work of objects in the text being symbols.

     τὰ μὲν ἀκούσια. This does not refer to "involuntary
acts" in the normal sense, but to acts committed without proper
understanding of their nature. Cf. the Hebrew distinction
between šōḡēḡ and mēzîd, "inadvertent" and "intentional." Cf.
Post. 11, 48; Agr. 178; Ebr. 163; Fug. 65, 76, etc.

     ἐπιμήκιστα. Superlative form only attested in Philo.

129   ζωτικὸν . . . καὶ ὀρθὸν . . . λόγον. The adjective
ζωτικός is generally contrasted with λογικός by Philo, as applying to the irrational soul (e.g. Det. 82, 92; Abr. 140; Mos.
1.100). Here it signifies "giving intellectual life." Philo's
use of the term ὀρθὸς λόγος is too frequent to admit of comprehensive illustration, but at LA 1.46 there is a passage nicely
illustrating the use of it here, interwoven as it is with light-
imagery: καὶ μὴν κατὰ ἀνατολὰς ἐστιν ἡ φυτουργία τοῦ παραδείσου·
οὐ γὰρ δύεται καὶ σβέννυται, ἀλλ᾽ ἀεὶ πέφυκεν ἀνατέλλειν ὁ ὀρθὸς
λόγος, καὶ ὥσπερ, οἶμαι, ἀνατείλας ἥλιος τὸν ζόφον τοῦ ἀέρος

φωτὸς ἐνέπλησεν, οὕτως καὶ ἀρετὴ ἀνατείλασα ἐν ψυχῇ τὴν ἀχλὺν
αὐτῆς ἐναυγάζει καὶ τὸν πολὺν σκότον σκεδάννυσι. Cf. οἱ ἐν
ἀχλύι καὶ σκότῳ βαθεῖ, below, 130.

ὡς κυβερνήτῃ. A generalised reminiscence of the Ship
of Fools simile in *Rep.* VI 488A ff. The reference to τοῖς ναυ-
τιλίας ἀπείροις makes this clear. It is also, of course, a
variant of his favorite storm-at-sea imagery.

διασυνίστησι. First attested in Philo.

130   ἀπροοράτως. Adverb first attested in Philo.

131   "καὶ προστάξει ὁ ἱερεὺς . . . καταμαθεῖν". This presumably is quoted from memory. LXX text: πρὸ τοῦ εἰσελθόντα
ἰδεῖν τὸν ἱερέα τὴν ἀφὴν καὶ οὐ μὴ ἀκάθαρτα γένηται ὅσα ἐὰν ᾖ
ἐν τῇ οἰκίᾳ. There is no significant change in Philo's version,
except that he alters the construction from the strong prohibition οὐ μὴ γένηται to the less emphatic future οὐ γενήσεται.

133   ταῦτα εἰ συνᾴδει τῇ ῥητῇ καὶ προχείρῳ διατάξει. συνᾴδει
has the sense here of "is compatible with." Quite a strong
challenge from Philo to the supporters of literal interpretation.
A good parallel occurs in *Sobr.* 33, a comment on Gen 9:25, where
Canaan, son of Ham, is unexpectedly cursed by Noah because of
his father's action in uncovering Noah's nakedness. "What was
his offence?" says Philo. "Perhaps this question has been considered on their own principles by those who are used to discuss
in details the literal and outward interpretation of the laws.
Let us rather in obedience to right reason (ὀρθὸς λόγος) expound
in full the inward interpretation" (Colson's trans.). Cf.
J. Pépin, "Remarques sur le thème de l'exégèse allégorique chez
Philon," in *Philon d'Alexandrie*, Coll. Nat. du CNRS, Lyons
(Paris 1967) 139 ff.

σκέψονται οἷς ἔθος καὶ φίλον. Wolfson (*Philo* I.131),
plausibly enough, sees here a reference "to the members of the
court of Jewish law (*bêt dîn*) in Alexandria," comparing *Agr.*
157, and *Somn.* 1.102.

134   Συγγνώμη δὲ . . . ἁμαρτάνουσιν. Properly speaking, this
should only refer to those in a state of primal "innocence."
Ignorance after the accession of reason would surely be culpable.
Cf. Plato, *Tim.* 87B, *Rep.* IX 585B; Arist. *EN* 1110b.

135   ὥσπερ φωτός τις αὐγὴ καθαρωτάτη. Continuation of light-
imagery in connection with Logos, cf. note on 129.

        ἐναποκείμενα. ἐναπόκειμαι first attested in Philo.

        ἐπιλήπτους καὶ ὑπαιτίους. ἐπίληπτος in sense of "cul-
pable" first attested in Philo, as is ὑπαίτιος in the sense of
"blameworthy." For this collocution, cf. LA 3.247, De Virt. 206.

        ἀποσκευασθῆναι καὶ ἀποσυληθῆναι. ἀποσκευάζω in sense of
"get rid of" first attested in Philo, as is ἀποσυλάω in sense of
"carry off."

136   τῷ χηρεύειν . . . τῶν παθῶν. Cf. Somn. 2.273: οἱ κε-
χηρευκότες γενέσεως. Like εὐνοῦχος (cf. above 111) χήρα can have
a good or a bad sense (Fug. 114 and Det. 147 being examples of
the latter).

137   κυοφορεῖ καὶ ὠδίνει καλὰς πράξεις. For collocution, cf.
Sacr. 102; Det. 127. A Platonic reminiscence, cf. Theaet. 210B:
ἦ οὖν ἔτι κυοῦμέν τι καὶ ὠδίνομεν, ὦ φίλε, περὶ ἐπιστήμης, ἢ
πάντα ἐκτετόκαμεν; κυοφορέω not certainly attested before LXX,
Eccl 11:5.

        βραβεῖα. For victory imagery, cf. 147 below.

        ""Ἄνθρωπε τοῦ θεοῦ . . .". A paraphrase rather than a
direct quotation of I Kings 17:18: εἰσῆλθες πρός με τοῦ ἀναμνῆσαι τὰς ἀδικίας μου.

138   ὀλυμπίου. Philo likes this adjective, cf. 151, 156
below; Det. 85: τροφὰς ὀλυμπίους καὶ ἀφθάρτους; Plant. 63: οὐκ
ἐπίγειον ἀλλ' ὀλύμπιον κτῆμα. Philo seems to be the first to
use the word in this sense of merely "heavenly."

        διηρεθισμένος τοῖς . . . ἀκατασχέτοις οἴστροις. διερε-
θίζω in sense of "stimulate" first attested in Philo. ἀκατάσχε-
τος is Hellenistic, first attested in Pythagorean "Hipparchus."
This characterization of prophecy as a form of μανία owed much
to Plato's description of it as the first of three forms of
μανία in Phaedrus 244BC. For οἴστροις, cf. Ebr. 147.

        μέγα στενάξασα καὶ μέγα κλαύσασα. Cf. QE 1.15: "For
those who naturally and genuinely repent become bitter toward
their former way of life and are vexed with their wretched life,
weeping, sighing and groaning . . ."; Jos. 87; LA 3.211; Wisd.
Sol. 9:3; Pes. R. 50; ShR 38.4.

139   ἐπιθειασμῷ . . . περιαθρήσει. ἐπιθειασμός, apart from
one use in Thuc. (7.75), first attested in Philo. περιάθρησις
only attested in Philo. A reference here, surely, to Plato's
"etymology" of ἄνθρωπος at *Crat.* 399C as from "ἀναθρῶν ἃ ὅπωπε."

        κύρια ὀνόματα. For use of term κύριον ὄνομα in sense of
"naturally correct name," cf. *LA* 1.75; *Det.* 22, 83; *Mut.* 11-15.

X

Deus 140-183

        Commentary on Gen 6:12: ἦν [δὲ] κατεφθαρμένη, ὅτι
κατέφθειρε[ν] πᾶσα σάρξ τὴν ὁδὸν αὐτοῦ ἐπὶ τῆς γῆς.

A. *General Comments*

        With the elucidation of Gen 6:12, Philo brings his
treatise to a close with an elaborate exposition of one of the
central motifs of his religious philosophy, that of the "Royal
Road." This is his most extended exegesis of the Royal Road,
but he makes use of it also at *Post.* 101; *Gig.* 64; *Mig.* 146-47
(where the connection with Peripatetic ethical theory is made
explicit), and *Spec.* 4.102, 168. The LXX translates *darkô* with
ὁδὸν αὐτοῦ, "his way" (thus apparently making it agree with the
general sense of *kāl bāśār*, "an expression occurring thirteen
times in the narrative of the Flood and denoting sometimes, as
here and v. 13, men alone" [cf., however, *BR* ad loc. which
takes it to include animals], "sometimes animals alone, sometimes both" [Driver]), rather than the grammatically required
αὐτῆς. Philo, being unable to check the Hebrew, interprets this
verse as signifying the destruction of the perfect way of wisdom
which leads to the knowledge of God. The comrades of the flesh
reject this path and seek to corrupt it, since no two things are
so diametrically opposed as knowledge and pleasure of the flesh.
        This leads Philo to think of Num 20:17-20 (145), the
incident of the "Royal Road," which he then proceeds to interpret in detail. When Israel, the people endowed with vision,
wish to journey along that royal road, they find their way

challenged by Edom, "the earthly one," who wishes to prevent
them. They express their determination to proceed. Citing the
well-known story concerning Socrates, who, on beholding a gaily
decked pageant, is said to have asserted: "My friends, observe
how many things there are I do not need" (cf. *Plant*. 65; Cic.
Tusc. 5.91; D.L. 2.25. See also comment. on *Gig*. 34), Philo
points out that whereas Socrates' rejection of external goods
was the act of a lone individual, in Israel we have an entire
and mighty people following this lofty ideal which rejects wealth,
honor, glory, and bodily health and beauty. As proof he quotes
the words of the envoys to the king of all that is good in outward appearance, the earthly Edom, "I will now pass by through
thy land" (148). Philo insists, however, that the rejection of
external goods must be under the guidance of right reason and
not through faint-heartedness, sluggishness, or inexperience of
them, if it is to count as perfect virtue. He is here clearly
following the Stoics who held that to act appropriately is not
in itself either good or bad, in the sense of being morally good
or bad, and had accordingly designated "appropriate actions"
(καθήκοντα) as "intermediate" (μέσα). It is only when the
latter are performed by a wise man that they become "correct"
(or absolutely appropriate) actions (κατορθώματα) (*SVF* 3.498-99;
516-17; cf. *LA* 1.56, 93; 3.210; *Sacr*. 43; *Cher*. 14; *Deus* 100.
See D. Tsekourakis, *Studies in the Terminology of Early Stoic
Ethics* [Wiesbaden 1974] 1-60; A. Bonhöffer, *Die Ethik Epictets*
[Stuttgart 1894, rep. 1968] 193-233). At this point (154),
Philo makes something of the apparent contradiction between
"passing through your land," and "not passing through the fields
and vineyards." These latter he interprets as virtuous sentiments and actions, which one must not pass by, but rather remain
in.

He next turns (155 ff.) to the words, "we will not drink
water of any well of them," and elicits from them the notion that
those upon whom God showers knowledge (cf. *LA* 3.162: "the soul
is fed not with things of earth that decay, but with such words
as God shall have poured like rain"), will not seek for the
scanty springs that lie beneath the earth, i.e., for earthly
goods. Similarly, Israel who claimed that it was God himself
who nourished him (Gen 48:15), would clearly not even cast a
glance upon the waters gathered beneath the earth. He who had
received the undiluted draughts of knowledge that intoxicate the
the soul, sometimes through the Logos (when it is a matter of

ridding the mind of ignorance and error), at other times through
the direct agency of God (when it involves positive knowledge),
would not deign to drink of a well (adducing the exegesis of Gen
48:15 at *LA* 3.177-78, when Philo explains that in both cases it
is actually God who bestows the gifts, but in the case of secondary boons, He allows the Logos to take the credit, whereas
in the case of the principal ones, He takes sole credit).

  We who are convinced that we ought to shun earthly
things, continues Philo (159 ff.), should without delay take to
the king's high road, along which we shall walk unimpeded without flagging or fainting. That the path of wisdom is unwearying
was a common Hellenistic theme. The author of The Wisdom of
Solomon (6:14) assures us that he who anticipates the dawn on
behalf of Wisdom will not grow weary (οὐ κοπιάσει), and the
author of *De Mundo* (319a, 13) writes: "So the soul, by means of
philosophy, taking the mind as its guide, has crossed the fron-
tier, and made the journey [to the heavenly region] out of its
own land by a path that does not tire the traveller (ἀκοπίατόν
τινα ὁδόν) (cf. *Mut.* 254; *Mig.* 145; *Cher.* 41, where Philo
explains that Leah means rejected and weary [κοπιῶσα], because
we all turn away from virtue and think her wearisome). Moreover, in the words "We will not turn aside to the right or to
the left" but advance along the midmost line, Philo finds an
exemplification of the doctrine of the Golden Mean (162-65).
(Cf. *Spec.* 4.102: "Moses opened up a path midway between Spartan austerity and Sybarite luxury." For the doctrine of virtue
as μεσότης, see Arist. *EN* 1106b15, 36; 1107a7; *EE* 1227b8; Plut.
Quomodo quis suos in virt. 84A; *Virt. Moral.* 444CD; Albin. *Did.*
184.13 ff.; Apul. *Plat.* 2.228; Arius Did., in Stob. *Ecl.* 2.39.
11 ff.; 2.137.14-142.13. Cf. *Post.* 101; *Mig.* 146-47.)

  Continuing his analysis of the passage in Numbers, Philo
finds that the words "we will go along the mountain country,"
signify the ideal of wisdom which continuously analyzes and
defines all things in an effort to arrive at their essence, and
is accompanied by a contempt for all that is external or of the
body. Indeed, we may further infer from the words "for if I or
my cattle drink of your water, I shall give you honor" (taking
τιμή in this sense), that if we but touch bodily pleasures with
our finger-tips, we shall provide honor to earthly Edom, who
will then boast that the virtue-lovers, too, have yielded to
pleasure's snares. If this appears to contradict the doctrine
of the mean articulated above, it should be remembered that what

is to be held in utter contempt and not to be given even the
slightest entrée is the enjoyment of bodily goods as pleasures
(ἡδοναί), the latter being πάθη or irrational states, whereas
the rational use of these same bodily things, though they yield
agreeable physical feelings as an ἐπιγέννημα or by-product, is
not to be rejected. (For a detailed analysis of this question
and Philo's ethical theory as a whole, see D. Winston, "Philo's
Ethical Theory," ANRW.)

The phrase "but the matter is nothing" (Num 20:19)
launches Philo on a theme which was well-known in Hellenistic
tradition (172-78). Mortal matters, says Philo, have no real
being or substance. A glance at the fortunes of human empires
reveals their utter instability and changeability. The divine
Logos moves in a circle which constantly redistributes material
goods throughout the world (cf. Jos. 131-36; QG 4.43; Mos. 1.31;
A.P. 9.74; TGF p. 909, no. 372N; Polyb. 38.22.2; 29.21.3-6; 6.9.
10; Plut. Rom. Fort.; Sib. Or. III; Pešer Hab. See Wolfson,
2.420-26; K. von Fritz, The Theory of the Mixed Constitution in
Antiquity [New York 1954] 69-75; G. J. D. Aalders, Die Theorie
der gemischten Verfassung in Altertum [Amsterdam 1968] 123-24;
Goodenough, The Politics of Philo Judaeus [rep. Hildesheim 1967] 76-
78; 86 ff.; E. Langstadt, "Zu Philo's Begriff der Demokratie," Occi-
dent. & Orient. Studies in Honour of M. Gaster [London 1937] 349-
64; Martin Braun, Social and Political Aspects of Philo's Philosophy; F. H. Colson, Philo, LCL, 8.437-39. See also Festugière
RHT 2.523-26, where it is suggested that Philo's source was
Demetrius of Phalerum's Περὶ Τύχης [Fr. 39, Jacoby = Pol. 29.21;
Diod. 31.10]. Cf. E. Bayer, Demetrius Phalereus der Athener
[Tübinger Beiträge 36. Stuttgart-Berlin 1942] 164 ff.)

The treatise concludes (179-83) with an admonition to
make full use of one's inner judge or conscience. Balaam, who
was one of Edom's associates, had failed to do so, disregarding
the monitions of his convicting Angel within, and was thus over-
whelmed by folly and destroyed.

B. Detailed Comments

140   προσηκόντως οὖν. Good example of the way in which Philo
is accustomed to introduce an allegorical or otherwise strained
interpretation of the text, cf. Deus 122.

τὴν ὁδὸν αὐτοῦ. The masculine pronoun referring back to
σάρξ (the Hebrew actually requires αὐτοῦ) is a solecism occasioned

by the Hebrew *bāśār*, "flesh," which is masculine--unless we term
it a "sense construction," taking "flesh" as meaning "mankind."
Philo, not being in a position to appreciate this, must take the
αὐτοῦ as referring not to σάρξ but to God. He rejects as unac-
ceptable the view of one who would see a solecism here. (It is
not necessary that anyone should actually have made such a criticism.) His solution, of course, is that the αὐτοῦ is not reflex-
ive at all, and this leads to his whole exegesis, based as it is
on the adducing of Num 20:17-20. The use of αὐτός without further reference to refer to "himself." "the Master," is somewhat
colloquial (found in the conversation of Menandrian slaves), but
is also a Pythagorean way of referring to Pythagoras, as Philo
himself points out at *QG* 1.99. Roman slaves also referred to
their master as *ipsissimus* (Plaut. *Trin.* 4.2.146) or *ipsimus*
(Petr. 75.11).

141   θηλυκῷ . . . ἀρρενικήν. These terms for feminine and
masculine gender appear to be Hellenistic, not attested before
Dionysius Thrax.

143   ταύτην ἴσθι σοφίαν. The Way itself is Sophia, and its
end is γνῶσις καὶ ἐπιστήμη θεοῦ. Note Philo's favored term
λεωφόρος in this connection, cf. *Post.* 102 (with ἀτραπός); *Deus*
61, 163, 182; etc.
144   τοῦ ὀρατικοῦ γένους. Philo is the first extant writer
to use ὀρατικός to refer to persons, and with the special meaning of "visionary, endowed with insight." In this meaning it
occurs very often, as it is his etymology of Israel (*Her.* 78;
Conf. 91; *Mig.* 18; etc.). The antithesis to this visionary,
"heavenly" class of person is often Egypt, as being earthy and
subject to passions, but here the allegory requires that it be
Edom, which can be suitably etymologized as derived from Hebrew
ʾadāmā, "earth." Edom thus becomes a perfect symbol of the
irrational soul, bound to things of earth. At points in the
exegesis, however, Edom, or its king, seems almost to take on
the characteristics of a Gnostic demiurge (e.g. 166), but this
identification should not, perhaps, be pressed. There is no
place for a being of this sort in Philo's philosophy.

    ἀτριβῆ καὶ ἀπόρευτον. ἀτριβής is Classical, but ἀπόρευ-
τος is first attested in Agatharcides (ap. *Geogr. Gr. Min.* I
p. 11), 2nd cent. B.C.E.

145   "Παρελευσόμεθα . . . δι' ἐμοῦ". This, apart from the
paraphrase ὁ δὲ Ἐδὼμ ἀποκρίνεται φάσκων, for καὶ εἶπεν πρὸς
αὐτὸν Ἐδώμ, is an accurate transcription of the LXX text available to us. There are just a few minor launderings: οὐ δι'
ἀμπελώνων, οὐ πιόμεθα, for οὐδέ . . . οὐδέ; ἐκ is omitted before
λάκκου; and, most significant stylistically, on three occasions
(τὰ ὅριά σου, εἰς συνάντησίν σοι, δώσω τιμήν σοι), Philo trans-
poses a weak personal pronoun to before the noun which governs
it, avoiding the unrhythmical effect of having it at the end of
a clause (though we may note that mss. U and F preserve the LXX
reading--probably, however, corrected from the LXX text).

146   τῶν παλαιῶν τινα λόγος ἔχει. This anecdote about
Socrates, repeated at *Plant*. 65, goes back to the Hellenistic
anecdotal tradition which produces so much of the content of
Diogenes Laertius' compilation. The story is used also by
Cicero in *Tusc*. 5.91 (*Socrates, in pompa cum magna vis auri
argentique ferretur: 'Quam multa non desidero' inquit*), sand-
wiched in between similar edifying stories about Anacharsis,
Xenocrates and Diogenes the Cynic, in a diatribe passage.
Diogenes Laertius gives the story with a vaguer context (2.25):
πολλάκις δ' ἀφορῶν εἰς τὰ πλήθη τῶν πιπρασκομένων ἔλεγε πρὸς
αὐτὸν "πόσων ἐγὼ χρείαν οὐκ ἔχω," but he seems to derive it in
this form from the 1st cent. C.E. gossip-compiler Pamphila of
Epidaurus, whom he has just quoted.

147   τὸν Ὀλυμπιακὸν ἀγῶνα. Imagery of victory in the games,
a favorite of Philo's, cf. 137 above, etc. (See V. C. Pfitzner,
Paul and the Agon Motif [Leiden 1967] 38-48.) We are in the
middle here of a diatribe passage (note the "Du-Stil" τί λέγεις;).

148   τὰ προτέλεια τῆς σοφίας. It is reasonable here, perhaps,
to discern imagery from sacrificial ceremonies in the use of
προτέλεια. The word can be used in later Greek to mean simply
"introduction," but it may never entirely lose its literal meaning of "preliminary sacrifice," and very probably not in Philo.
Elsewhere, he uses it literally at *Congr*. 5 (προτέλεια τῶν γάμων)
and metaphorically at *Abr*. 89.

149   Ὦ . . . ὑποσχέσεως. Typical diatribe-style exclama-
tion; cf. *Conf*. 116, 162; *Mig*. 84; etc.

ὑπερβῆναι παρελθεῖν παραδραμεῖν. Triadic asyndeton, proper to passages of heightened emotion. See Intro. p. 141.

150   τοῦ πλούτου . . . δόξαν δέ . . . ὑγείαν . . . κάλλος . . . ῥώμην. Philo runs through the two lower classes of goods, external and bodily, as things from which the Israel-soul will turn aside. The inspiration behind this passage is distinctly Cynic-Stoic, as one would expect in a diatribe context--the lower goods are not "goods" at all (ὡς μηδὲν αὐτῶν κατατάξαι ἐν τῇ τῶν ἀγαθῶν μερίδι).

ὁ τῆς ψυχῆς οἶκος ἢ τύμβος. A reference to the Orphic tag σῶμα-σῆμα. Philo uses τύμβος in this connection again at *Somn*. 1.139, when contrasting the attitudes with which various classes of soul descend into bodies: αἱ δὲ πολλὴν φλυαρίαν αὐτοῦ καταγνοῦσαι δεσμωτήριον μὲν καὶ τύμβον ἐκάλεσαν τὸ σῶμα.

ἀνανταγώνιστον. In sense of "irresistible" first attested in Philo, cf. Plut. *Phoc*. 14.

151   ὀλυμπίου . . . περίγειον. Cf. note *ad* 138.

γνησίων . . . νόθοις. The γνήσιος-νόθος contrast is much beloved of Philo, cf. *Fug*. 152: τῶν γνησίων ἀγαθῶν τὰ νόθα προτιμήσασα; *Somn*. 2.22. At *Jos*. 258 this contrast is combined in the context of πλοῦτος with the βλέπων-τυφλός contrast, derived from Plato *Laws* 631C (also much beloved of Philo). The γνήσιος-νόθος contrast itself is found in particular at *Rep*. VII 535C-536A.

153   τούτου χάριν. The passage beginning here is an excellent example of the way Philo can squeeze significant doctrine from small details of the text. The addition of διὰ τῆς γῆς σου to παρελευσόμεθα intimates to Philo that one must not turn away from worldly lures simply through faintheartedness or ignorance of them. One must turn away from them in obedience to ὀρθὸς λόγος, which rejects them after having thoroughly surveyed them.

τῶν προβληθέντων . . . δικτύων. For the "nets" cast by Pleasure, cf. *Sacr*. 29; *Post*. 116; *Agr*. 103. Δέλεαρ and δελεάζειν are frequent Philonic locutions in this connection, e.g. below, 168. Also φίλτρα, below, 170.

διακλάσαι. Rare word, attested only in Homer, Iliad 5.216.

154   διὰ δὲ "ἀγρῶν καὶ ἀμπελώνων" οὐκέτι. Philo takes this,
in a perverse sense, to imply that the Israelites will tarry in
the fields and vineyards. These cannot really be those of Edom,
however, who should possess nothing good, but rather "fields and
vineyards" in general, allegorized as the virtues.

        ἤμερα ἐν ψυχῇ φυτά. The image of the virtues as "tame"
or "cultivated" plants in the soul, bringing forth a "cultivated"
fruit, is a common one in Philo (opp. ἄγρια), cf. LA 3.76; Spec.
4.23; Virt. 154. Cf. the distinction between the passions as
"unclean reptiles" and the eupatheiai as "clean" ones, at QG
2.57 (this, however, is a comment on Gen 9:3, which lends itself
to such an exegesis).

        ὠγύγιος εὐήθεια. Cf. Post. 168: ὠγύγιός τις ἠλιθιότης;
Sacr. 78. The adjective is only poetical in Classical Greek,
and not with particularly derogatory reference. This usage may
be just a Philonian elaboration on the use of ἀρχαῖος to mean
"simple-minded," or, more particularly, a variant on the Platonic
διωλύγιος φλυαρία, Theaet. 162A.

        ἐμφορεῖσθαι. Not found in Classical Attic prose (but in
Herod. 1.55).

        ἀκόρεστος. Not found in Classical Attic prose.

155   ἐπινίφει καὶ ἐπομβρεῖ. For collocution, cf. Mig. 121:
ὀμβρεῖ καὶ ἐπινίφει, also referring to God showering down ἀγαθά.
The image of God's blessings as a shower from heaven is a common
one with Philo, connoting normally the unstintingness and spon-
taneity of his beneficence. A good passage occurs at Mig. 31-32:
"The harvest of spontaneous good things is called 'Release'
(ἄφεσις, an allusion to the Sabbatical Year), inasmuch as the
mind is released from the working-out of its own projects, and
is, we may say, emancipated from self-chosen tasks, by reason
of the abundance of the rain and ceaseless shower of blessings
(διὰ τὴν πληθὺν τῶν ὑομένων καὶ ἀδιαστάτως ἐπομβρούντων). And
these are of a most marvellous nature and passing fair. For the
offspring of a soul's own travail are for the most part poor
abortions (ἀμβλωθρίδια, a reference to Theaet. 150B ff.), things
untimely born; but those which God waters with his snows (ὅσα
δ᾽ ἂν ἐπινίφων ὁ θεὸς ἄρδῃ) come to the birth perfect, complete
and peerless" (Colson's trans.).

ἐκ λάκκου. Though λάκκος translates *bĕʾēr*, "well," here, Philo understands it as "cistern" (cf. 156: πότον τεθησαυρισμένον ἐξ ἐπιτεχνήσεως ἀνθρώπων), which it does mean at LXX Deut 6:11, commented on at *Fug.* 175, etc. Philo's word for "well" is φρέαρ.

λιβάδας. In sense of "pools of water" not found before Strabo.

ἀνεπισχέτως. Adj. and adv. first attested in Philo.

νέκταρος καὶ ἀμβροσίας . . . ἀμείνω τροφήν. The comparison of God's grace with the nectar and ambrosia of the Olympians recurs interestingly at *Somn.* 2.249, where the Logos is termed ὁ οἰνοχόος τοῦ θεοῦ καὶ συμποσίαρχος, but himself being the drink that he pours, which is described, among other things, as τὸ γάνωμα and τὸ χαρᾶς, τὸ εὐφροσύνης ἀμβρόσιον. It may be that behind this is an allegorization of Ganymede as the Logos, or an aspect of the Logos (Hermes being, after all, a more obvious representation of it). At *Spec.* 1.303, again, the ἀέναος τῶν καλῶν πηγή from which God rains down (ὤμβρησεν) the virtues is declared to be a drink more immortalizing than nectar. Just below the present passage, at 158, Philo speaks of God dispensing draughts διά τινος ὑπηρετοῦντος τῶν ἀγγέλων, ὃν οἰνοχοεῖν ἠξίωσε. The image of a banquet, in this case organized by Sophia, occurs at Prov 9:5, which Philo may also have in mind, as he seems to in *Prob.* 13.

156   ἐπιτεχνήσεως. Apart from one use in Thucydides (1.71), this noun is first attested in Philo (Ps.-Arist. *De Mundo* 398b10, being of uncertain date). Cf. *Conf.* 185.

ἐξανιμῶντες. Verb only attested here. ἀνιμάω is Classical.

δυσελπιστίας. Found in Arist. *De Ventis* 1251b25; otherwise first in Polybius. Cf. *LA* 3.164; *Jos.* 114; etc.

τὸν ὀλύμπιον θησαυρόν. Cf. n. *ad* 138 above. This use of Deut 28:12 is quite popular with Philo, cf. *LA* 3.104 (where he explicitly identifies the οὐρανός with the Logos), and *Her.* 76, and it provokes a proliferation of imagery connected with the raining of blessings from heaven, such as has been noted above, 155.

157   ἐπήκοοι. ἐπήκοος in passive sense, "hearkened to," is
rare, and attested before Philo only in Plato, *Laws* XI 931B.

        "ὁ θεὸς ὁ τρέφων με ἐκ νεότητος". A reference to the
words of Jacob (Israel) at Gen 48:15 f., quoted more fully at
LA 3.177 and *Fug.* 67.

        ὅσα κατὰ γῆς ὕδατος συστήματα. Here water stored in the
earth is contrasted, as symbolizing earthly goods, with the
heavenly waters poured down by God. Elsewhere, however, as
Colson points out (App. to Loeb Vol. III, p. 489), "the figure
of the well calls up more favourable ideas in Philo," e.g. *Post.*
136 ff.; *Ebr.* 112 ff. But in these passages it is other qualities of the well that attract him, such as its lying deep
beneath the surface, and the purity of the water that it produces, so there is no real contradiction here, especially as
Philo is thinking rather of cisterns here.

158   τὰς ἀκράτους μεθύσματος πόσεις. An evocation of the
sobria ebrietas figure, so beloved of Philo. (Cf. Hans Lewy,
Sobria Ebrietas [Giessen, 1929]) μέθυσμα is otherwise only found
in LXX, so is presumably borrowed thence by Philo.

        διά τινος ὑπηρετοῦντος τῶν ἀγγέλων. This is presumably
called forth by the continuation of Gen 48:15, quoted at *LA*
3.177 and *Fug.* 67, but not here: ὁ ἄγγελος ὁ ῥυόμενός με ἐκ
πάντων τῶν κακῶν; but the mention of οἰνοχοεῖν, as suggested
above (n. *ad* 155), may be drawing on an allegorization of Ganymede.

159   ἀνυπερθέτως. Adj. first attested in Philo; adv. found
in 1st cent. B.C.E. inscr. and in LXX (3 Macc 5:20).

        πειρώμεθα. Exhortation in "Wir-Stil" form, to initiate
a diatribe passage. Cf. Intro., p. 141.

160   ἱκέτισι ψυχαῖς. For the expression, cf. *Det.* 95; *Post.*
31; *Her.* 273.

162   αἱ γὰρ ἐφ' ἑκάτερα ἐκτροπαί. From here to the end of
165 we have an elaborate exposition of the Aristotelian doctrine
of Virtue as a Mean (*EN* II 2 ff.), together with the corresponding excesses and defects, these latter introduced by the essentially musical terms ἐπίτασις and ἄνεσις, which, although

adopted by the Stoics in their ethical theory (*SVF* 3.92, 525),
are derivable from Plato (the actual terms in *Rep*. II 349E, the
general doctrine of virtue as a harmony from *Phaedo* 85C, 92B,
and *Rep*. III and IV). Plutarch, in his essay *On Moral Virtue*,
makes the same connection, declaring that Virtue τὰς ἐκλύσεις
καὶ τὰς ἐπιτάσεις καὶ ὅλως τὸ μᾶλλον καὶ τὸ ἧττον ἐξαιρεῖ τῆς
ὁρμῆς (444F). Following *EN* II 7, Philo refers first to Courage,
with its surrounding vices; then to Prudence, flanked by the
vices of Meanness and Prodigality. After these two, however,
he breaks away from Aristotle's order to complete the tally of
the four cardinal virtues, producing sets of vices corresponding
to Wisdom and Piety (substituting for Justice). Note the use of
δεξιόν and ἀριστερόν, maintaining the imagery of the Road.

ἐκτροπαί. Not a technical term for a deviation from
the mean, but, literally, "a by-path," or "wrong turning."

164   ταῖς μαχομέναις κακίαις. Probably not, as Colson has
it, "the vices that war against us," but rather "the vices that
are in contradiction to each other." Philo frequently uses
μάχομαι in the logical sense, e.g. *Det*. 71; *Post*. 25; *Conf*. 32;
Mig. 152.

165   οὐ θέμις. These uses of θέμις and οὐ θέμις are perhaps
Platonisms for Philo, cf. *Apol*. 21B; *Tim*. 29A, 30A; *Polit*. 269E,
etc. Here the expression seems to mean no more than "it is not
possible," though with a religious coloration.

ἐμπεριπατεῖν. Only previously recorded use of this
word is in LXX, Lev 26:12. Cf. also 2 Cor 6:16 (quoting Lev).

166   πόλεμον ἀκήρυκτον. Possibly a *vox Platonica* here, cf.
Plato *Laws* I 626A. Cf. also *Mut*. 60; *Leg*. 119.

σπείρας οὐκ ἐθέρισε. Metaphor of sowing and planting
popular with Philo, cf. *Conf*. 150: ἀδικίαν μὲν σπείραντες,
ἀσέβειαν δὲ θερίσαντες; *Mut*. 268-69--probably partly stimulated
by Isaac's sowing and reaping in Gen 26:12, but also by Noah's
activity as a planter. Here Edom is imagined as having a harvest of sensual pleasures still growing, which he does not want
the Israelites to ravage, i.e. he does not want to be forcibly
reformed.

ἐπανατάσεων. Cf. above 64.

ὑψηλαῖς καὶ μετεώροις . . . δυνάμεσι. The goods of the
soul, as opposed to the two lower categories of good mentioned
below.

ἐνομιλεῖν. Cf. above, 55.

ὁρικῶς. Adverb found first in Philo, though the adj. is
Aristotelian. In the passage where Aristotle uses it, *Topics*
I 5, 102a9, he has just defined a ὅρος as λόγος ὁ τὸ τί ἦν εἶναι
σημαίνων, making it probable that Philo is acquainted either with
this passage, or at least with a handbook passage based upon it.
Note the etymologizing connection between ὅρος and ὄρος implied
here, made easier by the (presumable) elimination of the rough
breathing. Cf. Intro. p. 171.

πάντων ὅσα ἐκτὸς καὶ περὶ σῶμα. Reference to the
Platonic-Aristotelian categories of external and bodily goods.

χαμαίζηλα. Adj. used metaphorically, as "humble," first
attested in Philo, and by him used thus repeatedly, usually
coupled with ταπεινός, e.g. *LA* 3.19; *Spec.* 3.1.

168   γέρας καὶ τιμήν. γέρας is here simply a synonym for
τιμή, specifying the meaning "honor," which Philo requires of
it here.

φρυαττόμενος γὰρ αὐχήσεις. φρυάττομαι, used properly
of horses whinnying and snorting with exuberance, found first
in Diod. Sic. (4.74) applied to humans (of Niobe's pride).
Philo likes the word, cf. *Cher.* 66: κἂν φρυαττόμενος ὑψαυχένῃ;
etc. Since Aristophanes (*Wasps* 135) has φρυαγμοσέμνακος, an
origin in Comedy may be suspected.

169   οὗ τὸν λεγόμενον ὦνον παρὰ ποιηταῖς. ὦνος is indeed a
characteristically Homeric word, and perhaps that is all that
Philo means here. It is used in the *Iliad* and the *Odyssey*
always as "ransom" for a captive or "price" for someone cap-
tured and sold into slavery. What Edom wants from us is not
money, but τιμή, by which the LXX means "value," "a fair price,"
but which Philo takes to mean "honor." Here is a case where
Philo recognises the natural meaning of the word, but chooses
to dismiss it.

τιμὴν τὸ γέρας . . . παραλαμβάνει. Colson (n. ad loc.)
understands the τό here as meaning "the word 'γέρας'," and

suggests that it would go better with τιμήν, but the τό may
rather be taken as generic.

170   πρός τι τῶν ἡδονῆς φίλτρων. For the phrase cf. *Post.*
135; *Cont.* 69.

         ἐπινεανευόμενος καὶ ἐπιχειρονομῶν. The former verb is
first attested in Philo, the latter only in him. For the collocution cf. *Spec.* 4.215, where those who neglect the sabbatical
year are spoken of as ἐπινεανευόμενοι καὶ ἐπιχειρονομοῦντες.
What exactly Philo means by ἐπιχειρονομεῖν is not quite clear,
but it should imply flamboyant and haughty gestures.

         ὡς σφόδρα ἀναγκαίων καὶ χρησίμων φιλοσοφεῖν. Presumably
a reference to the Epicurean doctrine of "necessary," as opposed
to "unnecessary" pleasures. Cf. *KD* 29 and its scholion; Usener,
Epicurea 456.

171   ἄκριτον φοράν. ἄκριτος is a word which Philo likes, as
an epithet of γνῶμαι (below, 182), ἤθη (*Abr.* 264), τῆς ψυχῆς
ὁρμαί (*Spec.* 2.163), etc. It denotes for him the indistinguish-
able and mindless flux of human existence. Possibly he is influenced by Parmenides' phrase (fr. 6, 7 DK), ἄκριτα φῦλα.

         ἀποδοχήν. A Hellenistic word, first attested in Polybi-
us, in the sense of "approbation." Here contrasted chiastically
with δυσκλεία.

172   τὸ πρᾶγμα . . . οὐδέν ἐστιν. This translates the Hebrew
ên dābār, of which it is rather an expansion. οὐδὲν πρᾶγμα, at
least, is idiomatic Greek for "no matter" (e.g. Plato *Gorg.*
447B). As in the case of τιμή above, Philo presumably knows
that the natural meaning here would be "It is no matter," but
chooses to ignore this in favor of a meaning more promising
allegorically.

         ἐπ᾽ αἰώρας τινος. αἰώρα in a metaphorical sense is not
attested before Metrodorus, the pupil of Epicurus (331-278 B.C.E.).
For Philo, αἰώρα and αἰωρέω are connected with τῦφος, κενὴ δόξα
and εἴδωλα. Cf. *Ebr.* 36: κεναῖς αἰωρουμένων δόξαις; *Somn.* 2.16,
46, 61: διὰ τὸν φρυαττόμενον μεγάλα τῦφον καὶ τὴν ἐπ᾽ αἰώρας
φρορουμένην κενὴν δόξαν. This sentence, with its images of a
swing or litter, walking on air, and deceptive dreams, forms
a fitting prelude to a remarkable diatribe on the inconstancy

of human affairs, featuring the cyclic dance of the Logos
through history.

173.   Μακεδονία . . . διαιρεθεῖσα . . . ἀπεσβέσθη. For the
theory of the succession of Empires, see J. W. Swain, "The Theory
of the Four Monarchies," *Class. Phil.* 35 (1940) 1-21; D. Flusser,
"The Four Empires in the Fourth Sibyl and in the Book of Daniel,"
Israel Oriental Studies, 2 (1972) 148-75.

174   Παρθυηναί. The Parthians reckoned their era from 247
B.C., when they became independent of the Seleucids, and thus
masters of their former lords, the Persians.

175   τί δ᾽ Εὐρώπη . . . ἡ οἰκουμένη; It is noticeable that
Philo studiously avoids mentioning Rome, though the whole tendency of the passage suggests that Rome too will have her day
of reckoning. (Cf., however, *Praem.* 169, where, again, the
Romans are not mentioned by name.) For a somewhat imaginative
portrayal of Philo's views on Rome, see E. Goodenough's monograph, *The Politics of Philo Judaeus* (New Haven 1938). (At
Legat. 16, however, οἰκουμένη does seem to refer to the Roman
Empire, as it often does in the NT [Luke 2:1; Acts 17:6, 24:5],
so it may be a periphrasis rather than a euphemism here.)

       ὥσπερ ναῦς θαλαττεύουσα. Storm-at-sea imagery. For
collocution κλονουμένη καὶ τινασσομένη, cf. *Conf.* 69: σπαράττε-
ται καὶ κλονεῖται καὶ τινάττεται πᾶς ὁ τῶν φαύλων βίος. κλονέω
is an Homeric and generally poetic verb, first attested in prose
in Philo, who liked it (also in Hipp. *Morb.* 4.55, of uncertain
date).

176   χορεύει γὰρ ἐν κύκλῳ λόγος ὁ θεῖος. Philo speaks frequently of the dance of the heavenly bodies (e.g. *Op.* 70; *Cher.*
23), but he never seems elsewhere to speak of the dance of the
Logos. The denial of τύχη is Stoic (*SVF* 2.965-73), but also
Platonic (the ἀνάγκη of the *Timaeus*). For the notion of Time
as a cycle, cf. Arist. *Phys.* IV 14, 223b25 ff.: φασὶ γὰρ κύκλον
εἶναι τὰ ἀνθρώπινα πράγματα. The relative ὅν here refers to
λόγος rather than to κύκλῳ, but to the λόγος *in its circuit*.
On τύχη cf. Bion of Borysthenes F16 Kindstrand; Demades, ap.
Diod. 16.87.2. For detailed discussion, see PW 7A:2 (1948),
s.v. *Tyche*, cols. 1643 ff.; K. J. Dover, *Greek Popular Morality*

(Oxford, 1974) 138-44; M. P. Nilson, *Geschichte der griechischen
Religion* (Munich, 1961) 2.200-18; C. Schneider, *Kulturgeschichte
des Hellenismus* (Munich, 1969) 2.830 ff. See also G. W. Trompf,
The Idea of Historical Recurrence in Western Thought (Berkeley,
Los Angeles, London, 1979) 167-70.

  τὴν ἀρίστην πολιτειῶν . . . δημοκρατίαν. Cf. *Abr.* 242;
Spec. 4.237; *Virt.* 180. Whence Philo derives this concept of
"democracy" is a mystery. It is also unexpected to find him
terming it the best of constitutions. Neither Plato nor Aristotle would rank it thus, Plato ranking highest the rule of one
man, or of a small body of sages, democracy being the second-
worst arrangement, leading to tyranny; while Aristotle ranked
highest a balanced constitution which he termed simply *"politeia"*
(*Pol.* III 7, 1279a38). It is in fact this latter which Philo is
here commending and terming δημοκρατία. The Logos in this cosmic democracy apportions to each race and nation its due. What
Philo thought of what would be vulgarly termed "democracy" he
makes plain in such a passage as *Agr.* 45-46, where he terms it
ὀχλοκρατία, describing it as φαυλοτάτη τῶν κακοπολιτειῶν, and a
παράκομμα τῆς ἀρίστης δημοκρατίας. He contrasts democracy and
ochlocracy again at *Conf.* 108, where he identifies the distinctive mark of democracy as being that it honors ἰσότης, which
must be taken as denoting "geometrical equality," giving to each
his due. Cf. Plato *Menexenus* 238C. See especially C. G. Starr,
"The Perfect Democracy of the Roman Empire," *American Historical
Review* 58:1 (1952) 1-16. Cf. Aelius Aristides, *To Rome* 60: "But
a common democracy of the earth has been set up under one man,
the best, as ruler and orderer; and all come together as in a
common market place, each to receive what is worthy of him."
Starr points out that hints of the concept that the Roman Empire
is the perfect democracy may be found in the first century, in
such phrases as Philo's remark that Augustus was "the distribu-
tor to every man of what was suited to him" (*Legat.* 147), and
its roots may well go back into the Hellenistic period, even
though we cannot detect them.

177   σκιά τις ἢ αὔρα . . . παρατρέχουσα. Cf. Wisdom of Solomon 5:9: παρῆλθεν ἐκεῖνα πάντα ὡς σκιὰ καὶ ὡς ἀγγελία παρατρέχουσα.

      ἀμπωτίζοντα. Verb attested only in Philo, cf. *Spec.*
2.143. The image of the ebb and flow of the sea in connection
with human affairs is so basic to Philo as hardly to require illustration. Cf. n. *ad* 26 above, and the report of Theophrastus'

remarks on the question of the ἀναχώρησις of the sea in *Aet*.
120 ff.

μετὰ συρμοῦ καὶ πατάγου. For συρμός see note ad *Gig*. 13.
For the collocution, cf. *Abr*. 160.

λιμνάζει. This verb used transitively, meaning simply
"flood," or "make a lake of," is not attested before Philo.
ἠπειρόω, likewise, is not attested before Ps.-Arist. *De Mundo*
(400a28), probably more or less contemporary with Philo. The
whole description here is more proper to one of the periodic
shifts in the land-surface of the Mediterranean area than to
simple tidal action.

178   πιότητος ἀρχαίας. πιότης in metaphorical sense of "prosperity" first attested in Philo. Cf. *Post*. 120-23, an exegesis
of the name Noeman (Gen 4:22), which Philo etymologizes as "fat-
ness"; *Mig*. 101, etc.

179   πεπηγότι ὅρῳ καὶ λόγῳ. It becomes clear just below that
this thoroughly Aristotelian emphasis on definition as a means
to wisdom is provoked by what must seem to us a far-fetched pun
on ὄρος (in παρὰ τὸ ὄρος πορευσόμεθα) and ὅρος. But if Philo
pays no attention to the rough breathing, which he would not at
this era have pronounced, the connection becomes a little less
preposterous, an ὅρος being, after all, a kind of ὄρος (of a
valley or plain), which, in Greece at least, would often be the
boundary of a state.

180   ταῖς ὑψηλαῖς καὶ ὀρικαῖς . . . ὁδοῖς. This indicates
that Philo takes παρὰ τὸ ὄρος to mean along the crest of the
mountain, rather than along its foot.

μετακλῖναι καὶ μεταναστῆναι. μετακλίνω in sense of
"move" (intrans.) first attested in Philo. μετανίστασθαι is
used frequently by Philo in connection with Abraham's (the προ-
κόπτων's) turning from Chaldaea (earthly things) (*Mig*. passim,
e.g. 20: ἀπὸ τῶν αἰσθητῶν ἐπὶ τὰ νοητὰ μετανίστασθαι).

Ὁ μὲν οὖν γήινος Ἐδώμ. A comment on the final part of
the lemma, ὃ δὲ εἶπεν· οὐ διελεύσῃ δι᾽ ἐμοῦ.

ὁμοζήλων. First attested in Philo. Cf. *Cher*. 40; *Prob*.
85.

ἔμπαλιν. Wendland's reasonable emendation for meaningless ἐν πᾶσι of mss.

181   γῆς θρέμμα . . . οὐκ οὐρανοῦ βλάστημα. Reminiscent of
the contrast between the sons of earth and the sons of heaven,
elaborated in the three-way division towards the end of the *De
Gigantibus* (60 ff.).   Balaam is etymologized at *Cher*. 32 as
"foolish people," μάταιος λαός (Hebr. *bal* + ᶜ*am*), the ass to
whom he speaks being his ἄλογος προαίρεσις.   He is a most suitable ὁμόζηλος for Edom (cf. also *Conf*. 159; *Mig*. 113; *Det*. 71).
βλάστημα in a metaphorical sense is poetical, first attested in
prose in Philo, used here for *variatio*.   Cf. *Mig*. 140; *Congr*.
57; *Prov*. 2.109.

τὸ τῆς ψυχῆς μεμυκὸς ὄμμα.   A Platonic expression, *Rep*.
VII 533D and *Phaedr*. 251 but also an allusion to part of the
verse Num 22:31 not quoted by Philo, "ἀπεκάλυψε δὲ ὁ θεὸς τοὺς
ὀφθαλμοὺς Βαλααμ καὶ ὁρᾷ τὸν ἄγγελον κυρίου ἀνθεστηκότα ἐν τῇ
ὁδῷ."

ἐπικλυσθεὶς κατεπόθη.   At *Conf*. 66 Balaam is said to
live in Mesopotamia, signifying that "his understanding is sub-
merged in the inmost depths of a river, unable to swim its way
upward and lift its head above the surface."   The influence of
the *Phaedrus* myth (248A) is conspicuous here, with suggestions
also of Odysseus battling the waves off Phaeacia.

182   οὐ δυσθεράπευτα . . . ἀνίατα. This would be the case
with those in the heavenly ride of the *Phaedrus* myth who have
not managed at any stage to raise their heads above the rim of
the heavens and catch a glimpse of eternal truths.   Note the
Stoic term ἀρρωστήματα, cf. above, 65.

ἐπιστάντος ἐλέγχου.   The figure of Conscience returns
here in the final passage of the treatise, appearing now very
much like a guardian angel (especially if we could take λόγος
θεῖος as meaning not *the* divine Logos, but *a* divine *logos*),
although it is still internal to the human soul (ὁ ἔνδον δικαστής, below, 183).   Philo here makes one of his relatively
infrequent references to Scripture outside the Pentateuch, to
Psalm 90:11-12, a passage made use of later in the NT with
reference to Jesus:

ὅτι τοῖς ἀγγέλοις αὐτοῦ ἐντελεῖται περὶ σοῦ
τοῦ διαφυλάξαι σε ἐν πάσαις ταῖς ὁδοῖς σου·

ἐπὶ χειρῶν ἀροῦσίν σε
μήποτε προσκόψῃς πρὸς λίθον τὸν πόδα σου.

ἐπὶ νουθεσίᾳ καὶ σωφρονισμῷ καὶ τῇ τοῦ παντὸς ἐπανορθώ-
σει βίου. A nice rhetorical triad. For the collocution of the
first two terms, cf. *Mut*. 135: ἡ νουθεσία, ὁ σωφρονισμός, ἡ
παιδεία; *Virt*. 75. For the last phrase, cf. *Mos*. 2.36. Interesting parallel in 2 Timothy 3:16. σωφρονισμός also in 2 Tim
1:7.

183   "φθορὰν τὴν μετὰ τῶν τραυματιῶν". This passage of Num
(31:8) is used again in the same connection, referring to Balaam,
at *Mut*. 203. Presumably the unsportsmanlike behavior of the
Israelites in killing the wounded of Midian was an incentive to
allegorization of this passage.

δυσκαθάρτοις. In sense of "hard to purify" first
attested in prose in Philo.

τὸν ἔνδον δικαστήν. Cf. above 128 and *Op*. 128: τὸν τοῦ
συνειδότος ἔλεγχον, ὃς ἐνιδρυμένος τῇ ψυχῇ καθάπερ δικαστὴς ἐπιπλήττων οὐ δυσωπεῖται.

ἀναδικάζοιεν. Only occurrence in Philo. The verb is
proper to Attic legal terminology (Isaeus *fr*. 145). Here it
seems to mean "challenge," "appeal against."

ABBREVIATIONS

ANRW

Aufstieg und Niedergang der römischen Welt, Philosophie und Wissenschaften, ed. W. Haase. vol. II.21. Religion. Berlin, 1982

Bemid. R.

Bemidbar Rabbah

Ber.

Berakot

BR

Bereshit Rabbah, ed. J. Theodor, with additional corrections by C. Albeck. 3 vols. Jerusalem, 1965

BT

Babylonian Talmud

CNRS

Centre National de la Recherche Scientifique

ETL

Ephemerides Theologica Lovanienses

FGH

Die Fragmente der griechischen Historiker, ed. F. Jacoby. Berlin and Leiden, 1923 ff.

FPG

Fragmenta Pseudepigraphorum Quae Supersunt Graeca, ed. A. M. Denis. Leiden, 1970

Ḥul.

Ḥulin

LAB

Liber Antiquitatum Biblicarum

M.Q.

Moed Qatan

PAL

Philon d'Alexandrie. Lyon 1966: Colloque. Centre National de la Recherche Scientifique. Paris, 1967.

PW

A. Pauly and G. Wissowa, Real-Enzyklopädie der classischen Altertumswissenschaften. 1892 ff.

R.

Rabbah

REG

Revue des études grecques

R.H.

Rosh HaShanah

RIL

Rendiconti dell'Instituto Lombardo, Classe de Lettere, Scienze morali e storiche

RSR

Recherches de Science Religieuse

ShR

Shemoth Rabbah

SP

Studia Philonica

Tos.

Tosefta, ed. M. S. Zuckermandel. Rep. Jerusalem, 1963

359

TDNT   *Theological Dictionary of the New Testament*, eds.
            G. Kittel and G. Friedrich. Trans. and ed. G. W.
            Bromiley. 10 vols. Grand Rapids, 1964-76.

ABBREVIATIONS OF PHILO'S TREATISES

Abr.   *De Abrahamo*

Aet.   *De Aeternitate Mundi*

Agr.   *De Agricultura*

Anim.   *De Animalibus*

Cher.   *De Cherubim*

Conf.   *De Confusione Linguarum*

Congr.   *De Congressu Eruditionis Gratia*

Cont.   *De Vita Contemplativa*

Decal.   *De Decalogo*

Det.   *Quod Deterius Potiori Insidiari Soleat*

Deus   *Quod Deus Sit Immutabilis*

Ebr.   *De Ebrietate*

Flac.   *In Flaccum*

Fug.   *De Fuga et Inventione*

Gig.   *De Gigantibus*

Her.   *Quis Rerum Divinarum Heres Sit*

Hypoth.   *Hypothetica*

Jos.   *De Josepho*

LA   *Legum Allegoriarum*

Legat.   *Legatio ad Gaium*

Mig.   *De Migratione Abrahami*

Mos.   *De Vita Mosis*

Mut.   *De Mutatione Nominum*

Op.   *De Opificio Mundi*

Plant.   *De Plantatione*

Post.   *De Posteritate Caini*

Praem.	*De Praemiis et Poenis*
Prob.	*Quod Omnis Probus Liber Sit*
Prov.	*De Providentia*
QE	*Quaestiones et Solutiones in Exodum*
QG	*Quaestiones et Solutiones in Genesim*
Sacr.	*De Sacrificiis Abelis et Caini*
Sobr.	*De Sobrietate*
Somn.	*De Somniis*
Spec.	*De Specialibus Legibus*
Virt.	*De Virtutibus*

REFERENCE WORKS

The following books are cited by short title or by the author's name alone:

Baer, R. A. *Philo's Use of the Categories Male and Female.*
　　Leiden, 1970.

Bréhier, E. *Les Idées philosophiques et religieuses de Philon
　　d'Alexandrie.* 3rd ed. Paris, 1950.

Dillon, J. *The Middle Platonists.* London, 1977.

Dodds, E. R. *Pagan and Christian in an Age of Anxiety.* Cam-
　　bridge, 1965.

————. *Proclus, The Elements of Theology.* Oxford, 1963.

Festugière, A. J. *La Révélation d'Hermès Trismégiste.* 4 vols.
　　Paris, 1949-63.

Freudenthal, J. *Hellenistische Studien.* Breslau, 1875.

Goodenough, E. R. *The Politics of Philo Judaeus.* New Haven,
　　1938.

Gutman, Y. *The Beginnings of Jewish-Hellenistic Literature.*
　　2 vols. Jerusalem, 1958-63. (Hebrew)

Hengel, M. *Judaism and Hellenism.* 2 vols. Philadelphia, 1974.

Lewy, H. *Sobria Ebrietas.* Giessen, 1929.

Lieberman, S. *Hellenism in Jewish Palestine.* N.Y., 1950.

Lilla, S. R. C. *Clement of Alexandria.* Oxford, 1971.

Nikiprowetzky, V. *Le Commentaire de l'écriture chez Philon
　　d'Alexandrie.* Leiden, 1977.

Rist, J. M. *Stoic Philosophy.* Cambridge, 1969.

————. *Plotinus, The Road to Reality.* Cambridge, 1967.

Völker, W. *Fortschritt und Vollendung bei Philo von Alexandrien.*
　　Leipzig, 1938.

Wacholder, B. Z. *Eupolemus, A Study of Judaeo-Greek Literature.*
　　Cincinnati, N.Y., L.A., Jerusalem, 1974.

Wolfson, H. A. *Philo, Foundations of Religious Philosophy in Judaism, Christianity, and Islam.* 2 vols. Cambridge, Mass. 1948.

Zeller, E. *The Stoics, Epicureans and Sceptics,* trans. by O. J. Reichel. rep. of 1879 ed., N.Y., 1962.

SELECTED BIBLIOGRAPHY

1. *Editions, Commentaries, and Translations*
(in chronological sequence)

Turnebus, A. *Philonis Iudaei in libros Mosis, de mundi opificio, historicos, de legibus. Eiusdem libri singulares.* Paris, 1552.

Mangey, T. *Philonis Judaei opera quae reperiri potuerunt omnia. Textum cum Mss contulit, quamplurima etiam è Codd. Vaticano, Mediceo et Bodleiano, scriptoribus item vetustis, necnon catenis graecis, ineditis, adjecit, interpretationemque emendavit, universa notis et observationibus illustravit.* London, 1742.

Aucher, J. B. *Philonis Judaei Paralipomena Armena translata.* Venice, 1826.

Harris, J. R. *Fragments of Philo Judaeus: Newly edited.* Cambridge, 1886.

Cumont, F. *Philonis de aeternitate mundi. Edidit et prolegomenis instruxit.* Berlin, 1891.

Conybeare, F. C. *Philo About The Contemplative Life.* Oxford, 1895.

Bréhier, E. *Philon: Commentaire allégorique des saintes lois après l'oeuvre des six jours:* texte grec, traduction française, introduction et index. Paris, 1909.

Cohn-Wendland *Philonis opera quae supersunt.* vol. I-VI, rec. L. Cohn, P. Wendland, S. Reiter. Berlin, 1896-1930. Editio major.

Colson-Whitaker *Philo with an English translation,* by F. H. Colson (and G. H. Whitaker for vols. I-V). I-X. London-Cambridge (Mass.), 1929-1962.

Marcus, R. *Philo Supplement. I-II. Questions and Answers on Genesis and Exodus,* translated by R. Marcus. London-Cambridge (Mass.), 1953.

Geoltrain, P. *Le traité de la vie contemplative de Philon d'Alexandrie, Semitica X.* Paris, 1960.

Cohn, L. *Die Werke Philos von Alexandria in deutscher Übersetzung.* Band I-VII hsgeg. von L. Cohn, fortgeführt von I. Heinemann, M. Adler, H. Lewy, J. Cohn, W. Theiler, Breslau, 1909-1964.

Smallwood, E. Mary. *Philonis Alexandrini Legatio Ad Gaium.*
    Leiden, 1961.

Arnaldez, R., Pouilloux, J., Mondésert, C. *Les oeuvres de Philon
    d'Alexandrie* publiées sous le patronage de l'Université
    de Lyon. Paris, 1961.

Mayer, G. *Index Philoneus.* Berlin--New York, 1974.

Alexander, P. J. "A Neglected Palimpsest of Philo Judaeus:
    Preliminary Remarks editorum in usum," pp. 1-14 in
    Studia Codicologica [Festschrift for Marcel Richard].
    Ed. Kurt Treu. TU 124. Berlin, 1977.

                    2. *Philo's Exegesis*

Amir, Y. "The Allegory of Philo Compared with Homeric Allegory,"
    Esh 6 (1970) 35-45 (Hebrew).

Belkin, S. *Philo and the Oral Law.* Cambridge, Mass. 1940.

_____. "The Symbolic Midrash in Philo compared with
    Rabbinic Midrash," in *H. A. Wolfson Jubilee Vol.*
    Hebrew sect. 33-68. Jerusalem, 1965.

_____. "The Midrash *Quaestiones et Solutiones in Genesim et
    in Exodum* of Philo Alexandrinus and its Relation to the
    Palestinian Midrash," *Horeb* 14 (1960) 1-74. (Hebrew).

_____. "The Midrashim of Philo Alexandrinus in the Light of
    the Palestinian Midrashim," *Sura* 4 (1964) 1-68 (Hebrew).

_____. "Philo and the Midrashic Tradition in Palestine,"
    Horeb 13 (1958) 1-60 (Hebrew).

_____. "The Interpretations of Names in Philo," *Horeb* 12
    (1956) 3-61 (Hebrew).

Borgen, P. and Skarsten, R. "*Quaestiones et Solutiones*: Some
    Observations on the Form of Philo's Exegesis," *SP* 4
    (1976-77) 1-15.

Boyancé, P. "Echo des exégèses de la mythologie grecque chez
    Philo," in: *PAL* 169-86.

_____. "Etudes philoniennes," *REG* 76 (1963) 64-110.

Cazeaux, J. "Aspects de l'exégèse philonienne," *RSR* 47 (1973)
    262-69.

_____. "Interpréter Philon d'Alexandrie," *REG* 84 (1972)
    345-52.

Christiansen, I. *Die Technik der allegorischen Auslegungs-
    wissenschaft bei Philon von Alexandria* (BBH 7). Tübin-
    gen, 1969.

Coppens, J. "Philon et l'exégèse targumique," *ETL* 24 (1948)
    430-31.

Culpepper, R. A. "Philo's School" in his: *The Johannine School* (Missoula, 1979) 197-214.

Daniélou, J. "Die Entmythologisierung in der alexandrinischen Schule." In: *Kerygma und Mythos* 6, 1, 38-43 (Theologische Forschung 30). Hamburg, 1963.

Delcuve, G. *L'exégèse de Philon étudiée dans le Commentaire Allégorique*, mémoire dactylographié présenté à l'Ecole Pratique des Hautes Etudes, section des sciences Religieuses. Paris, 1945.

Dillon, J. "Ganymede as the Logos: Traces of a Forgotten Allegorization in Philo," *SP* 6 (1979-80) 37-40.

Frankel, Z. *Über den Einfluss der palästinischen Exegese auf die alexandrinische Hermeneutik*. Leipzig, 1851.

_____. *Über palästinische und alexandrinische Schriftforschung*. Breslau, 1854.

Hamerton-Kelly, R. G. "Sources and Traditions in Philo Judaeus," *SP* 1 (1972) 3-26.

_____. "Some Techniques of Composition in Philo's Allegorical Commentary with Special Reference to *De Agricultura* --A Study in the Hellenistic Midrash." In: *Jews, Greeks and Christians*, 45-56. Ed. R. Hammerton-Kelly and R. Scroggs. Leiden, 1976.

Hanson, A. T. "Philo's Etymologies," *JTS* N.S. 18 (1967) 128-39.

Hay, D. M. "Philo's References to other Allegorists," *SP* 6 (1979-80) 41-75.

Hecht, R. D. "Patterns of Exegesis in Philo's Interpretation of Leviticus," *SP* 6 (1979-80) 77-155.

Heinemann, I. *Altjüdische Allegoristik*. Breslau, 1936.

_____. *Philons griechische und jüdische Bildung*. Breslau, 1932. rep. Hildesheim, 1962.

_____. "Die Allegoristik der hellenistischen Juden ausser Philo," *Mnemosyne* 4/5 (1952) 130-38.

Heinisch, P. *Der Einfluss Philos auf die älteste christliche Exegese* (Alttestamentliche Abhandlungen I/2). Münster, 1908.

Kahn, J. G. "Did Philo Know Hebrew? The Evidence of the Etymologies," *Tarbiz* 34 (1965) (Hebrew).

Lauterbach, J. Z. "Ancient Jewish Allegorists in Talmud and Midrash," *JQR* 1 (1910-11) 291-333; 503-31.

Lewis, J. P. *A Study of the Interpretation of Noah and the Flood in Jewish and Christian Literature*. Leiden, 1978, 42-74.

Lucchesi, E. *L'Usage de Philon dans l'Oeuvre Exégétique De Saint Ambroise*. Leiden, 1977.

Mack, B. L. "Exegetical Traditions in Alexandrian Judaism: A Program for the Analysis of the Philonic Corpus," *SP* 3 (1974-75) 71-112.

_____. "Weisheit und Allegorie bei Philo von Alexandrien," *SP* 5 (1978) 57-105.

Mantel, A. D. "Did Philo Know Hebrew?" *Tarbiz* 32 (1962-63) 98-99 (Hebrew).

Nikiprowetzky, V. "ΣΤΕΙΡΑ, ΣΤΕΡΡΑ, ΠΟΛΛΗ et l'Exégèse de 1 Sam. 2,5 chez Philon d'Alexandrie," *Sileno* 3.2-4 (1977) 149-85.

Otte, K. *Das Sprachverständnis bei Philo von Alexandrien*. Tübingen, 1968.

Pépin, J. *Mythe et Allégorie*. Paris, 1976.

_____. "Remarques sur la théorie de l'exégèse allégorique chez Philon," in: *PAL* 131-67.

Ritter, B. *Philo und die Halacha*. Leipzig, 1879.

Rokeah, D. "A New Onomasticon From Oxyrhyncus and Philo's Etymologies," *JST* 19 (1968) 70-82.

Royse, J. R. "The Original Structure of Philo's Questions," *SP* 4 (1976-77) 41-78.

Sandmel, S. *Philo's Place in Judaism*. Cincinnati, 1956.

_____. "Philo's Environment and Philo's Exegesis," *Journal of Bible and Religion* 22 (1954) 248-53.

Shroyer, M. J. "Alexandrian Jewish Literalists," *JBL* 55 (1936) 261-84.

Siegfried, C. *Philo von Alexandreia als Ausleger des Alten Testaments*. Jena, 1875. rep. Amsterdam, 1970.

Sowers, S. G. *The Hermeneutics of Philo and Hebrews*. Zurich, 1965.

Stein, M. (Edmund). *Die allegorische Exegese des Philos aus Alexandreia* (BZAW 51). Giessen, 1912.

_____. *Alttestamentliche Bibelkritik in der späthellenistischen Literatur*. In: *Collectanea Theologica* 16, 38-83. Societas Theologorum Polonorum, 1935. rep. Lwow, 1935.

_____. "The Hellenistic Midrash." In his: *The Relationship between Jewish, Greek and Roman Cultures*, 93-105. Ed. J. Rosenthal. Tel-Aviv, 1970. (Hebrew).

_____. *Philo und der Midrash* (Beihefter zur ZAW 57). Giessen, 1931.

Treitel, L. "Agadah bei Philo" In his: *Philonische Studien*,
     85-113. Ed. M. Braun. Breslau, 1915.

Walter, N. *Der Thoraausleger Aristobulos* (TU 86) Berlin, 1964.

3. *Philo's Bible*

Barthélemy, R. P. D. "Est-ce Hoshaya Rabba qui censura le
     Commentaire allégorique?" in: *PAL* 45-78.

Colson, F. H. "Philo's Quotations from the O.T.," *JTS* 41 (1940)
     237-51.

Conybeare, F. C. "Upon Philo's Text of the LXX," *Expos.* IV.4
     (1891) 456-66.

Howard, G. E. "The 'Aberrant' Text of Philo's Quotations
     Reconsidered," *HUCA* 44 (1973) 197-209.

Jellicoe, S. "Aristeas, Philo, and the Septuagint Vorlage,"
     JTS N.S. 12 (1961) 261-71.

Kahle, P. *The Cairo Geniza*. London, 1947.

Katz, P. "Notes on the Septuagint," *JTS* 46 (1946) 33-33.

_____. *Philo's Bible*. Cambridge, 1950.

Knox, W. L. "A Note on Philo's Use of the OT," *JTS* 41 (1940)
     30-34.

Marcus, R. "A textual-exegetical note on Philo's Bible," *JBL*
     69 (1950) 363-65.

Pick, B. "Philo's Canon of the O.T. and his Mode of Quoting the
     Alexandrian Version," *JBL* 4 (1884) 126-43.

Ryle, H. E. *Philo and Holy Scripture*. N.Y., 1895.

Schroeder, A. *De Philonis Alexandri Vetere Testamento*.
     Greifswald, 1907.

Walters (Katz), P. *The Text of the Septuagint; its Corruptions
     and their Emendation*, ed. D. W. Gooding. London, 1973.

Wendland, P. "Zu Philo's Schrift *de Posteritate Caini*. Nebst
     Bemerkungen zur Rekonstrucktion der LXX," *Philologus*
     57 (1898) 248-88.

4. *Style and Diction*

Adler, M. *Studien zu Philon von Alexandreia*. Breslau, 1929.

Alexandre, M. "La culture profane chez Philon," in: *PAL* 105-29.

Barnes, E. J. "Petronius, Philo, and Stoic Rhetoric," *Latomus*
     32 (1973) 787-98.

Billings, T. H. *The Platonism of Philo Judaeus*. Chicago, 1919.

Bultmann, R. *Der Stil der Paulinischen Predigt und die kynisch-stoische Diatribe* (= Forschungen zur Religion und Literatur des Alten und Neuen Testaments 13) Göttingen, 1910.

Conley, R. "'General Education' in Philo of Alexandria," *Center for Hellenistic and Modern Culture: Colloquy* 15 (1975).

Fischel, H. *Rabbinic Literature and Greco-Roman Philosophy*. Leiden, 1973.

Hersman, A. B. *Studies in Greek Allegorical Interpretation*. Chicago, 1906.

Kustas, G. "The Diatribe in Ancient Rhetorical Theory," *Center for Hermeneutical Studies in Hellenistic and Modern Culture: Colloquy* 22 (1976).

Laporte, J. "Philo in the Tradition of Wisdom," in *Aspects of Wisdom in Judaism and Early Christianity*, ed. R. Wilken, Notre Dame, 1975.

Michel, A. "Quelques aspects de la Rhétorique chez Philon," in: *PAL* 81-103.

Pouilloux, J. "Philon d'Alexandrie: recherches et points de vue nouveaux," *Revue de l'histoire des Religions* 161 (1962) 135-37.

Priessnig, A. "Die literarische Form der Patriarchenbiographien des Philon von Alexandrien," *Monatsschrift für die Geschichte und Wissenschaft des Judentums* 37 (1929) 143-155.

Sandmel, S. *Philo of Alexandria: An Introduction*. Oxford, 1979.

Smith, R. W. *The Art of Rhetoric in Alexandria*. The Hague, 1974.

Thyen, H. *Der Stil der jüdische-hellenistischen Homilie* (= Forschungen zur Religion und Literatur des Alten und Neuen Testaments 65). Göttingen, 1955.

Trisoglio, E. F. "Apostrofi, parenesi e preghiere in Filone d'Alessandria," *Rivista Lasalliana* 31 (1964) 357-410; 32 (1965) 39-79. reprinted Torino, 1964.

von Arnim, H. *Quellenstudien zu Philo von Alexandria* (Philologische Untersuchungen XI). Berlin, 1888.

Wendland, P. *Philo und die kynisch-stoische Diatribe* (Beiträge zur Geschichte der griechische Philosophie und Religion). Berlin, 1895.

5. *Freedom and Determinism*

Carson, D. A. "Divine Sovereignty and Human Responsibility in Philo," *Nov. Test.* 23 (1981) 148-64.

Harl, M.   "Adam et les deux arbres du Paradis chez Philon
        d'Alexandrie. Pour une histoire de la doctrine du
        libre-arbitre," *RSR* 50 (1962) 321-88.

Levi, A.   "Il problema dell'errore in Filone d'Alexxandria,"
        Rivista critica di storia della Filosofia 5 (1950)
        281-94.

Segalla, G.   "Il problema della volontà libera in Filone
        Alexandrino," *Studia Patavina* 12 (1965) 3-31.

Winston, D.   *The Wisdom of Solomon.* N.Y., 1979, 46-58.

Wolfson, H. A.   *Philo* 1.424-62.

6. *Daemonology*

Babut, D.   *Plutarque et le Stoicisme.* Paris, 1969, 388-440.

Boeft, J. den   *Calcidius on Demons* (Phil.Ant. 33) Leiden, 1977.

Boyancé, P.   "Les deux démons personnels dans l'Antiquité
        grecque et latine," *Rev. de Philol.* 61 (1935) 189-202.

Brenk, F. E.   "In the Light of the Moon: Demonology in the
        Early Imperial Period," *ANRW* II.16.3. Berlin, 1979.

Detienne, M.   *La Notion de daimon dans le pythagorisme ancien.*
        (Biblioth. Fac. Philos. et Lettres Liège, 165.) Paris,
        1963.

Nikiprowetzky, V.   "Sur Une Lecture Démonologique de Philon
        d'Alexandrie, De Gigantibus, 6-18," in: *Hommage à
        Georges Vajda Études d'histoire et de pensée juives,*
        ed. G. Nahon et C. Touati (Louvain, 1980) 43-71.

PW, Suppl. III. 1928. s.v. *Daimon.*

RAC IX, fasc. 68-69. Stuttgart, 1975, cols. 546 ff. s.v.
        Geister (Dämonen).

Smith, J. Z.   "Towards Interpreting Demonic Powers in Hellenis-
        tic and Roman Antiquity," *ANRW* II 16.1 425-39 (and
        bibliography cited there).

Soury, G.   *La Démonologie de Plutarque.* Paris, 1942.

7. *Conscience*

Bréhier, E.   *Les idées philosophiques et religieuses de Philon
        d'Alexandrie,* 3rd ed. Paris, 1950, 295-310.

Chadwick, H.   Art. *Gewissen,* in *RAC.*

Davies, W. D.   Art. Conscience, in *IDB,* A-D (1962) 671-76.

Dupont, J.   "Syneidesis aux origines de la notion chrétienne de
        conscience morale," *Stud. Hellenistica* 5 (1948) 119-53.

Krüger, G. "Die Herkunft des philosophischen Selbstbewusst-
      seins," *Logos* 22 (1933) 225-72.

Marietta, D. E. "Conscience in Greek Stoicism," *Numen* 17 (1970)
      176-87.

Maurer, C. Art. σύνοιδα, συνείδησις in: *TDNT* 7 (1971) 898-919.

Milgrom, J. "On the Origins of Philo's Doctrine of Conscience,"
      SP 3 (1974-75) 41-45.

Nikiprowetzky, V. "La doctrine de l'elenchos chez Philon, ses
      résonances philosophiques et sa portée religieuse," in:
      PAL 255-73.

Osborne, H. "Synesis and Syneidesis," *Classical Review* 45 (1931)
      8-10.

Sevenster, J. N. *Paul and Seneca*. Leiden, 1961, 84-102.

Schwyzer, H. R. "Bewusst und unbewusst bei Plotin," in: *Les
      Sources de Plotin*. Fondation Hardt. Entretiens Tome V
      Vandoeuvres-Genève, 1960.

Zucker, F. *Syneidesis-Conscientia*. Jenaer akademische Reden.
      Heft 6, Jena, 1928.

8. *The Nature of God*

Beckaert, A. *Dieu et la connaissance de Dieu dans la philosophie
      de Philon d'Alexandrie*. Thesis, typewritten, Paris,
      1943.

Boyancé, P. "Le dieu très haut chez Philon," in: *Mélanges
      d'histoire des religions offerts à Henri-Charles Puech*.
      Paris, 1974, 139-49.

Braun, H. *Wie man über Gott nicht denken soll, dargelegt an
      Gedankengängen Philos von Alexandria*. Tübingen, 1971.

Dillon, J. "The Transcendence of God in Philo," *Colloquy 16*.
      Center for Hermeneutical Studies. Berkeley, 1975.

Kuhr, F. *Die Gottesprädikationen bei Philo von Alexandrien*.
      Diss., Marburg, 1944.

Neumark, H. Die Verwendung griechischen und jüdischer Motive
      in den Gedanken Philons über die Stellung Gottes zu
      seinen Freunden. Diss., Würzburg, 1937.

Pohlenz, M. *Vom Zorne Gottes*. Göttingen, 1909.

Whittaker, J. *God Time Being*. Oslo, 1971.

Wolfson, H. A. "The Philonic God of Revelation and his Latter-
      Day Deniers," in his: *Religious Philosophy*. Cambridge,
      1961, 1-26.

INDEXES

383

IV. PSEUDEPIGRAPHA

V. RABBINIC LITERATURE

VI. PLATONIC PASSAGES

VII.   Stoicorum Veterum Fragmenta,
ed. H. von Arnim. 4 vols.

VIII. PHILONIC PASSAGES